DAY TRADING AND STOCK MARKET INVESTING FOR BEGINNERS

This Book Includes:

Build Your Passive Income for Real Financial Freedom with Forex, Swing, Options, Tips and Tricks, Tools, Strategies and Psychology

WARREN DOUGLAS

DAY TRADING FOR BEGINNERS

Table of Contents

STOCK MARKET INVESTING FOR BEGINNERS

Table of Contents

DAY TRADING FOR BEGINNERS

The Simplified Guide to Make Money Online for a Living: Options, Day, Swing, Forex, Stock Trading Tips and Tricks, Tools & Tactics. Includes Powerful Psychology Strategies.

WARREN DOUGLAS

PART ONE

Introduction

Forex trading is an avenue that is making people earn a more significant income. There are many platforms where you can put that little penny in the trading and amerce that profit. However, it needs you to be that wise speculator who knows who reads the indicator promptly and knows the point to make that trading. Remember that forex trading is all about the trading of currencies. Therefore, you have to be knowledgeable about how the different currencies perform. The following are the basics where a beginner should know.

You should first be interested in knowing how the currencies behave in the market. That is where one ought to recognize the values of different currencies. The major currencies traded across the globe shows significant value in the market. Some of these currencies include the Us Dollar, Sterling Pound, Swiss Franc, Japanese Yen and the Euro. That is not to say that other currencies are not traded but this one has the commanding value in the forex exchange. Therefore, it requires the broker and the trader to be updated on the value of the stated monies. This is because in some instances the currencies may deteriorate and increase their worth significantly. Another thing to contemplate is how the paired currencies behave with each other. For example, in the forex chart you may see the Us Dollar \combine with the Euro or any other pair.

Another thing you ought to know is the type of indicators available and how one can make trading. These indicators follow specific movement criteria. First and foremost, before knowing that indicator thinks of the scales used in the chart. The chart represents a graphical diagram with both the independent and the depend scales. The independent scales are normally plotted on the horizontal axis and the dependent scale on the vertical axis. Therefore, you have to know the different variables in trading. Some of these variables are the price movement, the volume, and many others. Check on these charts ad test the movement of these variables appropriately.

Concerning the indicators, you should be aware of how these indicators behave. They are of different types and are influenced by the variables you use. For a beginner it is essential to have that knowledge of how they behave is crucial. You have to know the different types of these indicators so that you can follow their trend. Think of the indicators like the Moving Average Convergence and Divergence. This indicator measures the two exponential moving averages. There is the Bollinger band indicator that measures the standard deviation of those currencies. Some terms like the volatility market you also need to know them. Remember that the volatility of the currency is its behavior to have either a sharp increase or decrease in the market. That is where you can either gain a sizable profit or loss.

That is not to forget the relative strength index which is beneficial for ascertaining the overbought and the oversold. These indicators are very many in particular, but when you have their information is nothing that should stop you from earning. Even the types of charts like the candlesticks. Line charts and bar charts should be at your fingertips. There are different charts for every level of your trading. For example, in your case as the beginner, you can use the thence stick or the basic charts.

Another thing is the trend analysis. You should analyze the direction in which the indicator flows whenever you make a trade. That should help you in analyzing the peak times and recession periods of a paired currency. You also can anticipate the next performance of the paired currency if you are experienced in reading the behaviors of the indicators. You still use this information to know the right point of the market entry and the exits of the point. Those brokers who analyze the trend accordingly and are in a position of obtaining a sizeable return.

After knowing the basic you do not just start trading when you have the minimal qualities required in this business. You will realize how you will get frustrated when you stake a lot of cash then the trading fails. At other junctures you need to apply essential speculation tactics. That is the knowledge of probability and analyzing the statistics for you to stand a chance in trading. Some of these qualities are.

Be that guy who is good in decision making. Remember that the facility needs intelligence and critical thinking. You may find yourself succeeding a lot in a particular segment of trading. However not to realize that it may be a trap where even after making sublime returns you will eventually gain a hefty loss. Some other times you need not consider only short-term profit but fight for long-term returns. You may identify a promising venture but where whose returns are realized in a long term basis. However, if you are that person who needs quick money you will not be patient on that venture but look for short term profits. Moreover, those who take time in making a decision realize a pattern trend and make the right move.

Be that risk-taker who does not fear to make a loss. If all people were risk-averse, then there would no forex trading. Hey, remember that this business is like a gamble. I am sure that many people do not like hearing this term, but whenever you are dealing with uncertainties you are gambling. No matter what you do you have to sacrifice that penny expecting two possibilities which are either a win or a loss? Even other renowned investors cite that 'you have to stake big to win big'. Therefore, be a risk-taker who stakes big and hopes for massive earnings of returns. Even if you fail seldom, do not give up but eventually you will win.

Persistence is another quality required for you beginners in the forex trading. When you are persistent you normally are tolerant. You never give up hope even after failing many times. Why your needs are learning from your mistakes. Do not repeat the same strategy that you did which failed you. Be that person who sees the failure as a lesson to improve their ways of staking. Adopt a trial and error strategy which will eventually give you a winning edge. You do not expect to keep winning all the time, you will undoubtedly lose in some instances. You will realize you will keep developing tactics of trading with this trial and error strategy. You will too familiarize yourself with the trend analysis.

Timing is also operational in the business. You have to flexible enough to identify a profitable opportunity. The way the currencies behave is like a pendulum that goes in every direction. You can use a stopwatch and identify the specific time the trading signals a return and risks or an entry point or an exit point. Those seconds or minutes you waste may be the advent of your failure. Do a demo trade in which you do not have to input some cash? Look at the behavior of the currency and how they react in any substantial change. You may identify the correct timing when you need to stake. Therefore, you will have that confidence to stake your money in trading.

Intelligent speculation is required for this job. This trading requires you to be wise in reading the trends. Statistics and probability of knowledge are also needed. Those brokers are reputable in making the wise traders are the one who clearly predicts the next behavior of the trading. Their experience in reading the scales and indicators further enhances effective trading. Intelligence speculation is a skill that is learned by various strategies. One of those strategies is the trial and error method where you will consequently have that experience of trend analysis. Knowledge of the different currencies, charts and indicators gives you that winning margin. Lastly, you can consult specialists to train you about the analyzing of the currency trading.

Adequate preparation is needed in this exercise. How best can you be in a particular exercise if you are not that fully prepared? You must be that person who is willing to set your record straight. Efficient preparation starts with the person who keeps the trading records and is able to analyze the performance of the currencies using them. Always appreciate the usage of the demo account in which you practice the trading. In this, you are not fearful of losing your cash. Once you are used to frequent rehearsals you are comfortable with making the trading.

CHAPTER 1:

What Is Forex Trading?

Forex is short for foreign exchange and is basically an exchange of currencies. For example, when you are traveling from one country to another, you will need to exchange your home currency for the other country's currency. If you live in the United States and are traveling to Europe, you will need to exchange the American dollar for euros.

Forex is one of the biggest trading markets. One reason is that every country has a currency. The other reason is that most people understand foreign exchange and how it works. Furthermore, everyone participates in forex in some way, whether this is at an individual or business level. The market is open 24 hours a day from Monday morning to Friday evening.

What do we trade in the Forex Market?

The answer is simple – MONEY. Yes, the forex market is all about money in different currencies. For beginners' trading in forex can be confusing because one is not buying anything physical, which is why many tend to be skeptic about forex trading. You can consider buying forex as when you buy a share in a country. It is similar to buying a company's stock in the market. The rate of a particular currency represents a direct reflection of the thinking of the market about its present and future health of the currencies economy.

Remember, the Japanese yen example I made at the beginning. Let us assume you decide to buy the yen, what it means is that you are investing in the Japanese economy by buying a share of the country. In order words, you are "banking" on the Japanese economy that it will do well. You are buying this yen with the intention of selling it in the market in order to gain profit.

Generally, the exchange rate of a particular currency against other currencies represents the economic conditions of the economy.

Principles of Forex Trading

Learn the Market's Trends

It is essential for one to be able to predict the changing nature of the foreign exchange market in order to be successful in Forex Trading.

Accordingly, a person should understand the general direction of the marketplace. Trends can be uptrend, downtrend, or sideways trend. Identifying a pattern can profit a person in that he or she will be able to trade with the trend.

Uptrends are trends that move upwards, indicating an appreciation in currency value. Downtrends move downwards as an indication of depreciation in currency value. Sideways trends show that the currencies are neither appreciating nor depreciating.

Stay Focused and Control Your Emotions

Forex Trading is a challenging marketplace that can cause a person to lose confidence and to give up in the toughest of times. That is understandable given that traders put in their hard-earned money.

As a result, when a person experiences loss, he or she can lose focus when negative emotions become overwhelming. Some of the negative emotions a person may experience include panic, frustration, depression, and desperation.

It is, therefore, essential for one to become aware of the negative emotions that result from Forex Trading so that he or she may minimize the emotional effects of loss and remain focused.

Learn Risk Mitigation Tactics

In order to achieve the profits that a person anticipates, the person needs to minimize the likelihood of financial loss.

Since the forex market keeps on changing, the risks, therefore, keep on changing. The most crucial risk management rule is that a person should not risk more than he or she can afford to lose. Traders who are willing to invest more than they make, become very susceptible to Forex Trading risks.

Consequently, a person can mitigate potential losses by placing stop-loss orders, exchanging more than one currency pair, using software programs for help, and limiting the use of financial leverage.

Establish Personal Forex Trading Limits

A person should know when to stop Forex Trading. One can stop Forex Trading when he or she has an unproductive trading plan, or when he or she is continually experiencing losses.

An ineffective Forex Trading plan may not bring trade to an end, but it will not function as well as a trader may expect. In that case, the trader can consider stopping the trade, constantly changing markets, and the decreasing volatility within a particular foreign trading tool may also cause a trader to take a break from Forex Trading.

In addition, when a person is not in a good physical or emotional state, he or she may want to think about taking a break to deal with personal issues.

Use Technology to Your Benefit

Being up-to-date with existing technological developments can be gratifying in Forex Trading.

Given that forex markets utilize the online forum, high-speed internet connections can increase Forex Trading performance significantly. In order to make the most of Forex Trading, a person must take it as a full-time occupation, and he or she must embrace new technologies. Similarly, receiving forex market current information with smartphones makes it possible for forex traders to track trades anywhere.

Forex Trading is an aggressive enterprise that needs a trader to have an equally competitive edge. Therefore, a forex trader needs to maximize his or her business's potential by taking full advantage of the available technology.

Make Use of a Forex Trading Plan

A Forex Trading plan comprises of rules and guidelines that stipulate a forex trader's entry, exit, and money management principles.

A trading plan provides the opportunity for a forex trader to try out a Forex Trading idea before the trader risks real money. In so doing, a trader can access historical information that helps to know whether a Forex Trading plan is feasible and what outcomes he or she can expect.

When a forex trader comes up with a Forex Trading plan that shows potentially favorable outcomes, he or she can use the trading plan in real Forex Trading situations. The idea is for the forex trader to adhere to the trading plan.

Buying or selling currencies outside of the Forex Trading plans, even if a trader makes a profit, is poor trading, which can end any expectation the plan may have had.

Forex Trading Basics

While the concept of forex trading is easy, executing your trades in the market is difficult. This doesn't mean you won't become successful. What it means is that you will need to educate yourself and work hard. The first step anyone should take is to learn as much as possible about forex trading.

Understanding Pairs

The main difference between the stock market and the forex market is that, in forex, you are essentially trading pairs of currency (that is you buy one currency and sell another), while in the stock market, you buy shares of a company. This is not an option when you are forex trading. Whether you are trading, selling, or buying, you have to use pairs. For example, the Japanese yen is often paired against the Canadian dollar and the Euro against the American dollar.

What's a Pip?

A pip is a 1% movement in the currency value. A pip is a basic unit that is used when talking about currency quotes. It is the last number of the quote, so when you are following the movement of two currencies, you observe from the last two digits so that you can say that a currency moved by the number of pips that differentiates the second. The value of the pip is determined by the size of the trade. You make a decision to buy or sell a currency pair depending on your estimation, which is when you make the market order.

Entry Order

When you use an entry order, you enter your currency pair trade at a specific price. If the price of the currency never reaches the specific price, then your trade is not enforced. If the price is reached, then your trade is completed regardless of your presence at the time.

Stop-Loss Order

A stop-loss order is the price at which you want your dealer to exit the trade when the trade moves against your interests. A stop-loss order prevents losses.

1. Limit

A limit is the price at which you want the dealer to exit the trade when it's moving in your favor. Knowing when to exit the trade even when things are looking up is useful because you can hardly predict when a currency will start to drop.

2. Margin

When you are buying or selling at a good margin, that means that you control a large amount of currency for an initial investment that is way smaller in comparison. For example, a 100-by-1 margin means that you invest $1,000 for a trade of $100,000. Buying and selling on a margin is safe and appealing because the only amount you risk to lose is the amount you invested, but you have the opportunity to profit a greater amount.

Leveraging Ratios

You are betting at leveraging ratios. A $1,000 bet on 1,000 value of the currency is considered 1:1 leverage.

Trading platforms allow you to follow and market currency in a way that creates a profit. When you're successful in trading one currency so that its value increases against the currency you used to buy it, you can make a profit. You are speculating whether the currency will rise or drop. Your chances of profiting essentially increase with the success of your predictions.

With forex, you trade using leverage, which means that you only need to invest a portion of your positions. By using stop-losses, you can prevent losing your investment.

When it comes to currency rates, many factors have an influence. Interest rates, unemployment numbers, political events, and many more affect the country's currency value.

Currencies may rise and fall in different values for different reasons, one of them being large companies exchanging currencies for the purpose of international trading. The time and circulation of market information is also a significant factor. False and accurate information circulating the market can influence banks to swiftly market currencies, which additionally affects the changes in currency values.

3. Diversification

You want to ensure you have diversity within your portfolio to tackle risk. In fact, because the forex market is open 24 hours a day during the weekdays, the market holds more diversity. Therefore, don't just focus on the popular currencies, such as the American dollar and the Canadian dollar. You may also trade other pairs such as American dollar/British pound (USD/GBP) or American dollar/Japanese Yen (USD/JPY).

CHAPTER 2:

Technical Terms to Know

As with most specialized areas, the Forex market comes with its own terminology that can be utterly undecipherable to the uninitiated. Before we discuss how to trade in Forex, let's get you acquainted with those words and phrases to help you navigate the information more easily.

Ask Price: This is the price that a seller is willing to accept for a trade on the market.

Spread: This is the difference between the bid and ask price and is where the broker makes their money. The more volatility in the market, the wider the spread is likely to be.

Exchange Rate: A familiar term for vacationers, this refers to the value of one currency in terms of another. For instance, how many Euros you would get for one Australian dollar.

Currency Pairs: The Forex market does not deal with individual currencies, but with pairs of them. For example, the U.S. dollar combined with the Canadian dollar. Some are much more widely traded than others.

Cross Currency: A trade in which neither of the given currency is the $ U.S. dollar.

Cross Rate: A currency exchange rate between two stipulated currencies in which neither of them is the known official currency of the specific state in which that rate is given. For instance, if an American publication quoted an exchange rate for the Canadian dollar and Japanese yen.

G7 and G20: These seven countries – the United States, Italy, Japan, France, Germany, Canada and the United Kingdom – are the countries with the most major economic developments and represent over two thirds of the world's wealth. Their currencies are stable, creating currency pairings that have high volume and volatility. The G20 includes these countries but also others including China, India, Argentina, Australia, South Africa, South Korea, Mexico, Saudi Arabia, Turkey, Brazil and the European Union. These together make up four fifths of the world's trade and 85 percent of the gross domestic product on the planet. These currencies are the ones you will focus on as a trader.

Restricted Currencies: Some governments do not allow trading or speculation with their currencies. This can be because there is a limited availability, concern about the effect of speculation or a desire to control foreign investment.

Pip: This refers to the smallest possible increment by which a currency can move in price. Some currencies are quoted to four or five decimal places, so a pip refers to 0.0001 or 0.00001 of that pound, franc or Euro. Others are quoted only to two decimal places, so a pip is 0.01.

Volume: In Forex trading, this refers to the number of units being traded at one time. One currency may only have five or ten transactions taking place on it over the course of a day, while another may have thousands upon thousands. The former therefore has a low volume of trade, while the latter has a high volume.

Volatility: This refers simply to how much change there is in the trading price of a currency over time. The more that price changes, the more volatile that currency is said to be.

Margin: If you don't have enough money to invest in a trade, you can get a secured loan from your broker to increase your capital. This is known as using margin. Doing so involves a great deal of risk as, if the trade is not successful, you will find yourself in significant debt.

Margin call: This term refers to your broker requiring you to settle your account, usually when a trade reaches a certain level of risk.

Advantages of forex trading

- High liquidity

Forex trading has very high cash. Getting in and out of the trade is relatively easy. You will not need to pay a massive premium on it

Low barriers to entry

Anyone can open a forex trading account. You don't need to be a high net worth individual to have a forex trading account.

- Better risk management

Compared to other business, forex trading has better risk management. You are in a position to manage your risk. Let us say you have a small capital of about $500 if you are thinking of just risking one percent of your money, and you can play Nano lots. You have no transaction cost, all you need is to pay the spreads; this allows you to even risk five dollars on trade. Thus, helping you manage your risk better.

- Trade anytime you want

Forex trading is open 24/5 so you can trade anytime that you wish to from Monday to Friday. So, the market is accessible when you wake up or when you are sleeping. The choice is yours throughout the day and night to choose the best time to trade. All you need is to know whether you are a long term or short-term trader. This you can test by what is called a "pillow test" if you can put a position and go to bed at night and have a good night's sleep, then you are trading on the proper side. However, if you can put your pillow in position and you can't lie on it because you have to be on the screen watching the trader all the time, you will realize that you are trading too much or you are risking too much. Either your trade heights are too large, or your stop loses are too far, and you know that loses is something you don't want to take; however with this, you are prone to making high loses. If you can put on a trade and be comfortable or walk away from the computer, you are trading the right style.

- Simple underlying concept

Forex trading is based on simple underlying concepts. This trade is just comparing the relative values to currencies. When you are trading forex, you are using a pair of currencies. An example is the EUR/USD. You will just think about which one of the two currencies will gain strength and buy and sell based on that. All you will need is to study the strength of any of the paired currency and make sure that you sell the currencies to make a profit or before it pulls back. This is just straight forward as compared to other things like agriculture.

- Tradable the same as stock or futures using technical analysis

Technical analysis is the trick when it comes to forex trading. Yes, you can use fundamental analysis as well but technical widely used by many people in the world because of its simplicity. You will only wait for the price indicators to direct you on when to enter the market and when it is time to put a stop. Something that other businesses won't do. These patterns are built by fractal geometry, and you only need your mind to make that simple move of entering and stopping once you are done with the analysis. However, to get the best, you also need to know if you are a fundamental or a technical trader. Ask yourself if you love looking at charts, different indicators. Most traders will find that they work on the technical side, that is they will be looking more into the charts and various indicators as compared to the number that will be working with fundamentals. Whichever one you choose is all upon your personality; however, you need to work with that one that seems to be the best.

- Superior leverage

With forex trading, you will be able to control a large number of assets with a relatively small commitment of capital. As a trader, you need to make leverage your friend. Leverage is like fire. You need to learn how to make fire, and at the same time, you also need to learn how to use it wisely so that you do not burn yourself. Fire will warm the cave and cook your meet and also keep your predator's way. However, the light will also destroy all your possessions. Leverage is like fire; all you need is to use it on balance. Thus, you need to employ some severe money management tips.

To make the best in your trading, make sure that you avoid the mistakes that have been mentioned above. Again, invest more and more in yourself. Make learning a habit to improve your trade to the next level.

CHAPTER 3:

Financial Freedom with Forex

Financial freedom. These are two words with an important presence throughout our lives. For many it means economic independence, it is to start living from their own income to maintain the lifestyle they have achieved.

Financial freedom is a concept that is increasingly being addressed these days. People want to achieve financial freedom and are looking for ways to do so.

Financial freedom is totally attainable. To achieve this, it is important to put in place a comprehensive strategy to reach it. It requires adjustments beyond savings and self-reliance. Key knowledge can be acquired to achieve this goal.

Financial freedom is living in abundance, in every sense, including monetary abundance. The reason for this is that income exceeds expenditure and there are sufficient means to lead an economically sustainable life.

Achieving financial freedom goes beyond what money can buy. It's looking at your bank account and feeling the peace of mind that you are assured of a lifestyle for many years to come.

Seeking financial freedom is something positive, it is something that moves us every day to surpass ourselves as human beings, it is a reflection of the potential we have within us to achieve and feel well.

Motivation factors

Financial freedom is beyond our ability to stop working at any time. For many this goal is fine, and for others it is the choice to work in those areas or activities that they are passionate about.

It is to move from living to work and generate income, to living with the enjoyment of work. Financial freedom allows you to decide where you want to be, when you want to be, and how much time you want to spend on personal and social activities.

It's living in a time where passive income works for you. It's a feeling of greater financial security.

To be free financially is to be in a better position to ensure quality of life over time.

To be financially free is to have additional assets, savings, investments, and income. This allows you to live a lifestyle that suits you.

Financial freedom also allows for early retirement. It is an attractive option for those who wish to seek that way of life. It's a reachable thing.

A motivating factor for financial freedom is peace of mind. When passive income exceeds recurring expenses, there is greater economic flexibility.

Having financial freedom increases the possibility of making the desired experiences a reality, and with this comes the satisfaction and excitement of living the life desired by each person.

Benefits of financial freedom

Working on what we are passionate about

Having a financial cushion or peace of mind fund, gives us the opportunity to choose the projects to undertake. You get to be selective in your finances and more aware of the really exciting jobs. Work becomes a motivation.

More professional success

Having financial freedom allows us to take another step towards professional success. Proactivity is developed in the personal, in the work and in many aspects of life.

We work from the vocation of service to contribute to others, to add value to humanity, we live from the passion and gifts of each one. Ideas flow better and more often.

Living where you want

Achieving financial freedom can produce a significant change in the environment. If the opportunity arises to work and live in another country, you can take on this experience because you already have an economic safety net.

Throwing yourself into dreams

To undertake, to take a sabbatical year, to plan a personal time, to elevate the spirituality, to look for another professional sector.

All this is allowed by financial freedom, it is to do what is really important to us and it is something you can achieve, you have the potential to achieve it.

A golden retirement

Financial freedom means having a life where financial resources are guaranteed to maintain the desired lifestyle, until retirement.

You can build the retirement of your dreams by taking daily steps forward, this can be achieved by keeping the focus on achieving this freedom.

Take a vacation whenever you want

Financial freedom allows for disconnection from work at any time, in any form. A sabbatical? It's possible. You can easily choose the destination you want to visit. It's enjoying exciting experiences.

Contributing to the future of the children

Children can also be part of this financial freedom. It opens up more alternatives for their future. Access to higher levels of education is more affordable.

In addition, they live with a financial model that they can copy from you and even improve upon. You can give them one of the best gifts they can have: learning to live with financial freedom from a young age.

How do you determine the number required to maintain the desired lifestyle?

A key step, which is important to start, working on your quest for financial freedom, is to know the numbers you need to live comfortably.

Everyone has different tastes according to their lifestyles and the environment around them. Therefore, there is no standard for defining financial freedom.

Each person must determine the amount of money he or she wants to have available each month to cover recurring expenses, as well as those activities that generate personal satisfaction, such as going out with friends, going to the movies, traveling, among other hobbies.

Besides that, other variables must be considered: one of them is to have clarity and to think about the personal objectives in the short, medium and long term. We must set specific goals that we want to achieve so that we can determine the amount of resources we will use to achieve them.

Revenue and expenditure must be assessed at each of these time points. Hence the recommendation to think about the amount of money required to live properly today and in the future.

You don't need to be precise; you can start by writing down all your income and expenses on a daily basis for a month or two to get a clearer picture of the movements in your personal finances. This is a big step towards financial freedom.

CHAPTER 4:

Forex Trading Tips and Tricks

I'm here to share some ideas, tips, tactics, and insights into purchasing, selling, selling, and saving effectively in Forex online. FOREX or Foreign Exchange is also the world's largest and most competitive trading market, and FOREX traders are actively active. Many people agree that FOREX is the best home company any person can try. More and more FOREX markets use modern computer systems and Internet access every day.

It means that the foreign exchange is not delivered to someone that owns an exchange directly, and FOREX also buys and sells foreign exchange from day traders that same day.

In comparison to inventories and futures, Forex is made by commodity producers, including major banks and big brokers worldwide, who collectively sell in 24 hours–five days. The Forex market is "open" and the largest financial network in the world (one-day daily sales of trillions of dollars).

Forex trade means exchanging currency pairs such as the Eurodollar / USD mix, where a holder of this mix simply buys the Eurodollar and then sells the short US dollar.

This is the deal: like any other market, many "traders" lose when Forex is traded. So their loss is primarily attributed to the lack of effective negotiating practices, sound financial so risk control concepts, and the lack of discipline. For most situations, the mindset and commitment to the market may be incorrect. Others may not even grasp the market cycle, which plays a critical role in any trader's life, as it clearly says: "Your buddy is the cycle."

Some have even been fooled by deceptive individuals or dubious traders who pledge outwardly instantaneous riches and secret policies.

There is a lot of uncertainty and disinformation, and Forex still has a little 'wild west,' but I am here to discuss various techniques and methods used by active forex traders worldwide. Unfortunately, this knowledge is only available to a few Forex traders.

Forex Trading is all about discipline, commitment, and stamina. Using the correct Forex trading technique to make use of your resources may be excessive. Hundreds and thousands of forex trading approaches can be listed online. A number of metrics and variations are applicable to all Forex trading policies. Such metrics and studies measure assistance, resistance, and pattern in the Forex market only.

You can find more valuable than in other business courses or seminars that you have to pay for. I do not, however, believe in sugarcoating or giving you false expectations of success. Enough swindlers still exist. I want to tell you the truth, whether you like it or not, so that you can determine in an informed fashion whether the forex markets work.

The Forex markets have nothing mystical, since all economies are fundamentally guided by human nature–fear and greed, supply and demand. Every market has its own particular features, but you can succeed greatly in Forex when you understand how the fundamental drivers of human emotions work as 95 per cent of the emotions are regulated by the market. Some traders think trading is a "go rich easy" in rising forex markets.

Forex trade has many benefits over other forms of financial instruments such as bonds, futures, commodities, etc. It does not say, however, that Forex trading faces no risks. There are natural risks related to Forex trading. Therefore, anyone must consider all terms and conditions relevant to foreign exchange thoroughly. There are various online outlets and offline outlets that include tips on Forex trading. Such ideas are basically SECRETS.

As I said, trade in foreign currencies is regarded as one of the lucrative and attractive investment opportunities, as anyone can easily do from home, offices and elsewhere. In order for the Forex trader to succeed, nobody is required to make advertisements, advertising etc. online. The only requirement for forex trading is that an individual has to open a computer device with safe and registered brokers and quick internet access.

Now, you have to be careful if you open a Forex account with any trader because some may be fraud. Both future and forex operations in the United States are carried out by the Commodity Futures Trading Board (CFTC). In foreign exchange markets only the CFTC approved entity, which is also a member of the NFA and controlled by the CFTC, may be dealt with by individuals. Make sure the broker or bank is listed by the relevant regulatory authorities in that area for non-US brokers / banks.

You can open the Forex account for $300 (mini) to $2000 (standard). After the account is opened, a person must know how the forex market works, the demo business, and go live trading after a while. In fact, there are several codes to be observed.

A person can also use all secrets when trading with a prototype to see how the secrets work. This must be said without a doubt that by dealing with Forex if anyone can implement all the secrets correctly, he or she will comfortably earn decent money.

All successful traders have forex trading techniques to make competitive companies. These Forex trading approaches are typically based on a plan for seeking successful trades. So the approach is based on a certain kind of market research. Efficient traders need to consider and also forecast market fluctuations.

There are two basic approaches to the analysis of Forex market movements. These are technical research and simple research. However, it is much more likely that technical modeling would be used by traders. However, it is important to consider all forms of research in order to determine which form will fit well for the Forex trading strategies.

There is a misunderstanding in the forex industry, as there are many types in traders and ads, which make the business impossible for others, and then I'm going to show you the securities of forex trading.

What is priced on the Forex market? The answer is money. Exchange of forexes is where the currency of one country is traded with another. Forex exchanges are almost always replaced by pairs, with most currency pairs being exchanged with the United States Dollar (USD). We are referred to as the Majors. Euro Dollar (USD), GBP / US$, Japanese Yen (USD / JPY) and Swiß Franc (USD / CHF) are the common currency pairs. The most significant commodity currency pairs that have been exchanged are the Canadian Dollar (USD / CAD) and the Australian AUD / USD, exchanged over the global network of banks, multinational companies, importers and exporting companies, brokers and monetary traders on the telephone and online, because of the fact that there is no centralized market in Forex. But if you really want Forex big, I would highly advise you as a "beginner." Pay attention to one or two large currency pairs. Find them very well to make sure you understand their period of uncertainty.

To order to facilitate the exchange of Forex more, you can confine the trading to the most competitive and frequently traded pairs EUR / USD and GBP / USD. It reduces the time requirements for selling, without giving a decent chance.

Traditionally, money exchange has always been a' just qualified' market, and is primarily available to banks and major companies, but now electronic forex trading companies can provide small traders such as yours and I online thanks to the rise of our new e-economics. Almost anyone with a computer and internet access will now exchange currencies, just like the country's largest banks.

Kill Those Bad Habits in Your Forex Trading

The Forex market is full of opportunities for professional traders. There is a possibility that anyone who can read, work hard, and show patience and self-restraint will do financially very well. It is important to learn Forex that the trader has input from experienced traders. Use this article to find tips on Forex trading.

Once money comes in, people seem to be gullible. This will over trust them in their future decisions. Fear is another intangible factor which can affect decision-making and lead to poorer trade decisions. Remember that you need to control your emotions and use the skills you are trained for.

Most successful Forex traders would recommend that you hold some sort of report. Full a diary in which successes and defeats are highlighted. Holding a diary will allow you to watch how you are doing in the future.

Don't expect anyone else to watch your company but yourself. You do better than anyone other than you and your trading plan. The software cannot be completely commercialized. If you want to be effective, you really need a human touch to grow forex trading.

Do not purchase an insecure, unmodifiable Forex download. You must strive to improve the program. Your software can be better adapted to the specific approach. Test that the app is customizable before you buy it.

Do you want to do any Forex trading? Before you continue this journey, you need to grasp how the business functions in depth. Know the value of currencies and how currency markets change. You look at foreign currencies traded on this market. If you have the expertise, you are likely to pick currencies that increase your value.

Don't believe that you're going to come and change the whole Forex cycle. Experts in forex trading need a lot of time and energy to learn and practice because it's very, very difficult. You have an unbelievable opportunity to find a trading method that works better than those tried and true approaches. Were you working and finding a good approach?

You should be very cautious when using Forex robots since they sometimes hurt buyers. Buyers never profit, just the people who market this commodity. It's better to know yourself where you want your money to go.

Few things like perseverance will help Forex investors. Every trader has bad luck at some point. Perhaps the distinction between a successful trader and an incompetent trader is that good traders actually do not give up. If things feel terribly bleak and you forget how a good trade feels, carry going and finally win.

Forex trading information is available online everywhere at any time. You are best prepared for the event if you learn the ropes certainly. It can be very helpful to join a forum in which other participants and experts in forex trading can speak.

How do you consider selling Forex over other options? The Forex market is open all day, meaning that you can trade at any time. A little can go a long way when you invest in Forex. Those two benefits mean that Forex is open to virtually all and at any time.

Forex trade, or foreign currency trading strategy, is planned to make money through foreign currency trading. Most individuals do it to raise money on their hands, or just for a full-time career. Before you start buying and trading, you'll want to know exactly what you do.

Using what you want and what you plan to pick an account and the correct functionality. You have limits, and you are realistic. You're not going to master the company immediately. In general, it is easier for most forms of accounts to have lower leverage. First of all, a realistic account should be used because there is no chance of losing it. Know everything you can about Forex markets.

CHAPTER 5:

Forex Trading Strategies and Tactics

There are many different ways that people run their businesses ranging from traditional means to more sophisticated means.

The most important aspect in every successful business however, and more especially in Forex trading, is the selection of the most assorted strategies to be applied in different conditions.

Those who have followed entirely one system of trade have found out that it won't offer solutions to the ever-changing technology and complexity of the market demands for Forex trade.

It is important for every single trader to have the knowledge and skills of challenging the market circumstances of which is not very easy. It demands a deep knowledge and revelation of the economics.

In this topic we are going to provide you with the necessary but simple strategies that if applied can lead to a successful Forex business. Recall: these strategies are friendly for the novice traders who would wish to step up their knowledge and skills.

There are various ways in which these trading strategies can be classified. We will consider the basic classifications.

Analysis-Based Trading Strategies

Technical Analysis

As the name suggests, 'analysis', this method focuses primarily on the evaluation of the market trends through charts as a means of predicting the to-be price trends of the market.

In this method, an evaluation of assets is done basing on statistics and past analysis of market actions like the then volumes and the past prices.

Technical analysis is not done with a primary objective of weighing the underlying value of assets; instead, charts with other measuring tools are used to define the patterns that are helpful in future forecast in market actions.

It is believed that the market's future performance is easily determined by the past trends in its performance.

Trend Trading

In technical analysis, a trend is a very critical aspect. The tools used in this type of analysis, have a common motive which is simply to determine trends of the market. Therefore, to trend is to move; in this context it means the way the market is moving.

As we know, fore market is a wavy and zigzag motion that represents the successive trails that define clearly troughs and peaks which are sometimes called lows and highs'?

Depending on the available trends of the lows and highs, it is possible for a trader to define the nature of the market type.

Other than the popular notion of the highs and lows, there is yet another format of the trends in Forex trading called: uptrend/downtrend and sideways trend.

Support and Resistance

It is quite imperative to know the meaning of the horizontal level before defining the support and resistance strategy. This is the level in the price signifying market support of resistance. In technical analysis, resistance and support refer to the lows or highs in prices in that order.

Support in this case refers to an area on a chart that shows that the interest in buying is stronger than the selling force.

This is revealed through successive troughs. On the other hand, resistance level, as represented on the chart refers to an area where the buying force is outweighed by the selling concern.

Range Trading

It is also referred to as channel trading. This signifies the absence market direction that may be associated with a lack of trends. It is used to identify the movement in the prices of currencies within the channels of which it is tasked to establish the range in the movements.

It can be achieved by linking sets of lows and highs to the horizontal-trend line. This is to say that the trader is tasked to establish the resistance and support levels with the area in the midst which we refer to as trading-range.

Technical Indicators

When we talk of the technical indicators in reference to Forex trade, we simply refer to the calculations that are inclined to the volume and the price of a given security.

When used, they are meant to corroborate quality and trend in the chart patterns as well enable traders to identify sell and buy signals altogether. These indicators in technical analysis can create sell and buy signals via divergence as well as crossovers.

Whenever the prices go across the moving-average, crossovers are seen however, divergence occurs only if the indicator and the price trends both move in different and opposite directions implying that there is a weakening in the price-trend.

Forex Charts

In Technical analysis, we refer to a chart as a representation of the shifts in prices within a given time frame graphically. It reveals the movement in the security price over a period of time.

Different charts can be applied in search of diversified information and the skills and knowledge of the researcher. There are several types of charts available such as: point, candlestick, line-chart as well as bar charts.

Forex volume

Forex volume indicates the total lots by number, traded in a certain time interval. The higher the volume, the higher the level of pressure; this is as indicated by chart specialists.

They can easily define the downward or the upward shifts in volume by observing the volume bars on the lower side of the charts. When a price movement is accompanied with a high volume, it becomes more valuable than if it is accompanied by low volumes.

Multiple Time-Frame Analysis

Lot price must be tracked over a period (turnover) and in a unique time frame. This is so because a lot price will tend to go through a series or time frames.

Trading-Style Based Strategies

This is yet another technique which offers a different way of classifying the trading styles. Through trading styles, trading strategies can be created which could include but not limited to buy-and-hold strategy, portfolio trading, trading algorithm, order and carry trades,

It is entirely dependent on your level of understanding, power and your weaknesses that determines the strategies that you will apply. Everyone needs a trading strategy which best suits his desires according to his ability to apply it.

There is no single ever trading style that one must apply whenever he wants to trade because, what suits one person may not suit you and your needs.

Day Trading

This is the act holding a position as well as disposing it off the very same day. This implies that, this type of person does not hold as security for more than a day. There are several strategies that are applied in day trading: fading, momentum, scalping as well as pivot trading.

You have the right if only you have the ability of conducting more than one type of trade in a single day as long as you do not hold a position for more than one day. This means than before the closure of the market, you must have liquidated all your open positions.

There is a challenge in this day trading in that, if you cling on a position for so long, the chances of losing it go high. Based on whatever style you are using, the targets in the price may vary.

Scalping Strategy

This is characterized by short and quick operations and is applied mainly to achieve vast returns on small price variations. Scalpers are able to initiate over 200 trades per day with an intention of making good profits on small shifts in price levels.

Fading strategy

Fading in this case refers to a trade that is initiated against trends. When the trend shifts upwards, faders do sell hoping that there will be a price drop-down; similarly, they may buy as the prices go up.

They buy when the price is escalating and sell when the prices are coming down a notion called fading. It is very contrary to other trends and also to nature of business.

The trade is usually against the usual trends with reasons such as: the buyers at hand may be risking, the currency lots are usually over purchased as well as the earlier may be set for profits.

Daily-Pivot Trading

Currencies are very volatile and as such, traders may wish to capitalize on that to make profits. This is exactly the case with pivot strategy.

A turning point same as the pivot point is a very critical yet unique pointer obtained through the computation of the statistical average of the low, high as well as closing-prices of currency-pairs.

The secret to this strategy lies in the aspect of purchasing currencies at their lowest prices and selling them of at their best prices in the course of the day.

Mathematically it could be represented as follows: [pivot point= (close + low + high)/3]

Momentum Strategy

This is characterized by defining the strongest position that will end up trading highest. In this case, the trader may drop the currency with signs of dropping in price and go for that currency that has positive signs of going up through the day.

A momentum trader has got several indicators which help him detect the trends in the currency lots before he makes his decisions called momentum-oscillators. Such a trader will tend to invest deeply to news feeds which he entirely depends on for price predetermination and decision making.

Buy & Hold Strategy

In this case, a position is bought and held for quite long before being sold so that the prices escalate even if it takes long. Whoever does this has no business with the short term price changes as well as indications. However, this type of strategy best suits the stock traders.

In this case, technical analysis becomes invalid because the trader here is a passive investor who has no rush in determining the market trends of the stocks and currency lots.

Order-Types Trading Strategies

Trading on order will help the trader to join or move out of a position at the very right time by use of various orders which include but not limited to market, pending limit, stop-loss, and stop as well as other orders

At this particular moment, most advanced platforms are fitted with different kinds of orders for trading that are not the common buy/sell buttons. Every order type signifies a certain strategy. You must have the knowledge of how and perhaps when to handle orders before you can use them effectively.

The following are trader orders that can be applied by traders.

- Market order- is put to enable the trader to buy/sell at the ripe price.
- Pending order-enable traders to buy/sell at set prices.
- Limit order-guides the trader to buy/sell assets at specific price levels.
- Stop-loss order-is placed to lower a trade risk.

Algorithmic Based Strategy

This is as well referred to as 'automated' Forex trade. There is software designed to help in predetermination of times for purchasing and selling of the securities. This software operates on signals drawn from the technical analysis.

To trade with this type of strategy, you need to issue instructions over the kind of signals that you would wish to search for and its subsequent interpretation. This is an example of a high trading platform which comes with other supportive platforms for trading.

However, Net-TradeX is a platform for trading whereby other than its normal functionalities, presents automated-trading through its advisors.

CHAPTER 6:

How to Use Different Tools?

This is a term used to help a person decide the kind of property they should use to earn and make a living. According to bankruptcy law, the exemption for tools of the trade is usually determined by the state in the state exemption statutes. The exemption can also be determined by federal law in the federal bankruptcy exemptions. The period of time in which a person lived in a state before filing could also be a determinant of the exemption. Lawyers assist their clients in understanding which properties are exempt and the exemptions apply.

Anything a person can prove they use as a tool for trade is marked as a separate exemption from assets they own. This means that a person can be allowed an exemption for households separately from assets they use to make a living. One person may provide their vehicle as a property they own while another may produce their vehicle as a taxi which earns him his daily bread.

Having the right tools for trading will guarantee success for anyone starting. An experienced trader may not really be concerned about the tools they use but for beginners, the tools count.

Examples of Tools Used for Trade.

- Light speed financial broker – here a broker or a group of brokers breaks into different groups of specialization. The specialization is determined by the services they offer and the financial instrument used. The options for these brokers are Forex, stocks, long term investing and scalping brokers. Light speed brokers are very convenient for day time traders because of their direct accessibility and fast executions.

- Trade ideas stock scanning software – after establishing a good broker, the next step is finding the stock to trade with. The ability to determine stocks before they make a big move is what determines a more profitable trader. Trade ideas software helps in stock scanning for volume spikes, HOD movers to establish the gainers and the losers and things like that. This is the best software there is that scans the market and finds the winning stocks.

- signal charting – the third step is getting high-quality charts. The broker you chose makes come his standard charts. Those will work for you for some time until you decide to use ones that allow you to draw and write formulas. Signal allows one to run charts on 8 monitors without time delay. This is advantageous to people who like observing several stocks at once. it also allows installation of custom scripts. Custom scripts can be used as custom indicators for reversals and drawing support and resistance lines.

- Breaking news provider- After, you look at the catalyst to determine why stocks are moving higher. Reasons for the stocks could be moving up in consideration to the market, or a strong sector while other times it may be a unique catalyst like earnings. Breaking news provide the headlines for when the stocks are spiking.

- TAS market profile – this software is best in helping make trade decisions. It has several tools in it. Among them is a TAS scanner which allows one to observe stocks moving at different timings with different levels of buying and selling.

Having the right tool may not guarantee success in the trading world but it will give the right directions that will help make trading easier. The right tool will also provide an advantage for a trader over other traders who do not have the tools.

Indicators of Trade

This is a measure or gauge of trade that allows analyzing of prices and provides trade signals. Indicators provide trade signals that alert a trader when it is time to trade. Day trading indicators are not to be used as the only plan. They should be used along with a well laid out though to make it a useful trading tool. No matter the kind of trade one is involved in, having many trading indicators may bring inconsistency with trading decisions due to the complexities involved. Keeping it simple could simply be the trick to making clear and less stressful trading decisions.

Trading indicators should not, therefore, be taken as the only method relied on trading. However, using indicators alongside other trading variables may come in handy. Getting rid of the many indicators helps traders have a simplistic approach to the market.

Role of Technical Indicators

- Get the direction trend
- Determine the momentum or lack of momentum in the market
- Determine if and if not, the market is growing
- Get the volume to determine how popular a market is with traders

Getting the same type of indicators that on the chart that give the same information is where the issue is. This is because you may give conflicting information or get more information than you may be stressful. The main shortcoming of most indicators is that since they are gotten from price, they delay the price. There are rules that one can use to determine useful indicators for day trading, swing trading, and position trading. This include among others:

Choosing one trend indicator such as moving average and one momentum trading indicator is the simplest rule.

Knowing well the perimeters you want to investigate before you decide on the trading indicators which you will use on your charts. Then know well the indicator you chose in terms of how it works, calculations it does and the effects it will bring for your trading decisions.

Indicators work only depending on how they are incorporated into the trading plan. Some indicators like MACD and CCI are best at calculating information. Others like alligator indicator are fast at showing a market that is trending and ranging. Other indicators will show directions and act as entry and exit signals of trade. The usage of a basic indicator along with a well laid out trading plan by back, forward and demo can you put you ahead of trade with many complicated indicators. Netpicks offers systems that test trade plans, prove trading systems and trading indicators.

Threat of Optimization

There is a hindrance or barriers for when one is searching for trading indicators that work for one's style and trading plan. Most systems sell standard indicators that are fine-tuned to show successful results from the past. This is a disadvantage since it does not take into account the market changes. Using the standard settings for all indicators help avoid over-optimization trap which helps a trader not to focus on today's market progress and miss on the future.

Best Technical Trading Indicators

For day trading, a trader should test several indicators individually then later as a combination. One may end up with say 3-5 good ones that are evergreen and decide to switch off depending on the market at that particular day or the asset trading.

Regardless of the type of trade, day, Forex or futures the idea is to keep it simple with the indicators. Use one indicator per category to avoid repeating the same thing and distraction.

Combining Indicators

Combining pairs of indicators on the price chart helps to identify points to initiate trade. A good example is a combination of RSI and moving average convergence which combined suggest and reinforce a trading signal. When choosing sets it's important to find one indicator considered a leading indicator and another that is a lagging indicator.

Leading indicators show signals before the forms for entering trade has been made. Lagging indicators on the other hand show signals after the formation have happened. Therefore, lagging indicators can confirm leading indicators and help a trader from trading on wrong signals.

Choosing a combination of pairs that include indicators of different types instead of the same type is highly advisable. It does not make sense to observe a combination of the same type of indicators because they will still give the same information.

Multiple Indicators

Using multiple indicators boosts trading signals and may increase the chances of telling out false signals.

Refining Indicators

It is important for a trader to take notes and record the performance of the indicators they are using. Knowing the weaknesses of an indicator to determine if it gives a lot of false signals, if sometimes it fails to signal or if it signals too late or too early is essential. Knowing these things about the indicator will help determine what the indicator is best suited for. You may find that the indicator is suited for Forex instead of stocks while you thought it was just ineffective. This might help you decide if you want to trade the indicator for another or to just simply change how it's calculated. Doing this refining, will help an indicator work best for you, and also for you to find the best indicator for different types of trading.

CHAPTER 7:

What Is Divided Investing?

The idea of dividend investing is considered one of the best ways for investors to collect steady and consistent returns. There are several people who invest in these dividend stocks to take advantage of that dependability before utilizing some of those incoming funds to invest back into more shares of stocks. It is kind of like playing with some house money after winning a few rounds of blackjack at the casino. The main difference is that if you make smart investing decisions, you'll have a better chance at yielding some gains than beating the dealer. Because there are many dividend-paying stocks that represent different organizations that are considered a safer bet for investments. The prices might increase over time, which leads to bigger gains for shareholders. Additionally, those companies will raise dividend payments over time, such as providing a 3 % dividend after one year at about 2.5 %. At the same time, those are never set in stone.

But a company that builds a profile and gives its shareholders dependable, increasing dividends will do everything possible to continue pleasing their investors. There are companies that will pay consistently increasing dividends; they are usually considered financially healthy, generating a dependable return on investment on the different dividends. Stable companies usually feature any falling stock prices to make it less alarming for the shareholders in the general market. Because of this, they can be considered less of a risk than the companies that do not pay those dividends and, in turn, see more sharp ups and downs in the price. With a lower risk for the investors of these dividend stocks, they can be a more attractive option for a variety of investors, such as the young bucks who are hoping to get more income over the long haul and for those who are looking to build up their retirement fund. Even those already in retirement use the money from dividend investing in providing a regular income while they are not working. Another reason that these dividend stocks have built confidence among dividend investors is the correlation between the share prices and the yield of gains from the dividends. When one rises, the other follows. There is also the consideration for the power of compounding your investments, which is taking the generated earnings and putting them back into the stocks that will continue to build more and more.

In other words, the money you have generated from your earnings will generate additional earnings, and the generated earnings will continue to multiply as the investor continues to reinvest in the long run. This process can hypothetically turn one penny into a very large sum of money after about a month. If you take that one penny and continue to double your account every day for 30 days, you could see your money grow from a few cents to a few dollars. Ten dollars becomes $20, which becomes $40, then $80, $160, $320, $640, up to thousands and, eventually, millions. Sure, there are a lot of things that have to happen, and it requires a little luck. But in theory, it can happen, even if it is a bit unrealistic. This is not to say that any investor can expect to see their money grow when they begin to utilize dividend investing. But it shows that money can, and likely will, grow in a process that Albert Einstein once called the eighth wonder of the world. Many who enter the world of dividend investing will see the eventual rise of their rate of return as they continue to reinvest the money that comes in their returns on investment. Let us say that you have 100 shares of a stock that sells at $50 per share. This is an investment of about $5,000. In that first year, the company offers a 2.5 %dividend that provides an income of $125. If the investor continues to see dividend growths of 5 % each year, that $5,000 initial investment will be valued at more than $11,200 after about 20 years. This is with the assumption that there will be no change in the stock price, and there is the reinvestment mentioned earlier.

Now let us have that same company pay a quarterly dividend rather than one that pays annually. That $5,000 investment will grow to a little more than $11,650 in two decades for a gain of about 133 %. Because of the process of compounding, a $50,000 investment can become a $116,500 sum after that same period of time during which there are reinvestments into the dividend folder.

The Pros of Dividend Investing

Regenerating Cash Flow

There are moments when a company will declare that they offer a special dividend, which on paper, does not necessarily bring a benefit to the investor. In this case, a company usually gives the money back since they feel there is no use for it, thinking you could probably get a better return in another way. That could be a sign that the company does not have any new products, or they are in the middle of a saturated marketplace with a minimal chance for growth. If a company is prepared to grow, they retain the earnings so that they can be reinvested back into the company's expected expansion, but companies with minimal growth potential usually give the money back to their shareholders.

Dividends are best when a company has products and services that can help generate a cash flow that comes in a dependable fashion. Investors want to see the company they have shares in replenishing a dollar cut to its stock price for every dollar paid in dividends. The goal is to bring as much surplus money from one fiscal quarter to the next. This regenerative flow of money usually comes from companies that have minor debt and a little more experience as a business.

The Benefit of Trade-Off

Every investor should keep the potential trade-off in mind whenever they decide to invest in dividend stocks.

While you are receiving that consistent and steady flow of income, there is generally a lost opportunity in the growth of the stock, and a market that becomes hot can easily do better than the percentage gains an investor receives from their dividend investments. But even if the stock market has that sort of turnaround—a change of pace from what it has been in the past decade—an allocation that brings gains of 20 % or more, which can come with dividend stocks, can go a long way in increasing the performance of an investor's stock portfolio. By doing so, it also gives an investor a little bit of extra money that can be reinvested at times when there is a pullback from the market. This allows the investor a chance to gather up any other stocks that have grown at a discounted cost to purchase.

Security with Dividends

Despite the chances that a dividend can be trimmed or suspended, investors have to be certain that the company from which they have bought stocks will continue to pay them for the long-term. But the good news is that there is a long list of safe, dependable options to choose from. One of the easiest ways to start is to look into mature large caps like the choices found within Russell 1000 Index. Those 1,000 companies usually offer yields that range from 1 to 5 %, sometimes even more. There is even stronger dividend security found among what are affectionately called "Dividend Aristocrats." These are companies that have been consistent in how they pay their shareholders and have increased regularly for at least 100 fiscal quarters, which equals about 25 years.

That type of longevity is what attracts the investors the most and makes dividend investing a very popular choice.

Now, there are some pitfalls since everything in the world is not sunshine and lollipops. Sometimes, you have to take the good with the bad.

Tax Benefits

The folks at the Internal Revenue Service are known for always looking for another income to tax, which also includes any money made from those that come from the dividends. There are even dividends that are taxed as much as three times in a majority of jurisdictions. The first comes from about a federal withholding tax at about 20 % of the dividend's earnings, which comes out as soon as there is a payment made to your account. After this, 80 % of that amount is considered your income and is taxed twice for federal and state income taxes. So maybe, there is not that much left of that initial dividend payment you were thinking about. On paper, this looks to be a negative circumstance that might make you question whether or not you should invest in dividends, especially when you consider that the money lost is coming from the stock. For every dollar paid in dividends, the stock value falls a correlative dollar while allowing a collection of only 50 cents. So how do you counter that?

Consider Yield Spikes

This can be a scary possibility when you think you have found a great booming company before it, all of a sudden, burns out and drops before you have a chance to sell, potentially losing a larger gain. Either you could learn how to monitor and have the ability to sell as soon as you see any inkling of a decline, or you could focus more on investing within those more established companies that offer a more consistent payout and have almost no yield spikes.

An investor might become a victim of the yield spike if they have conducted a search for the different stocks in the marketplace, sorted what they found based on the highest yield of a specific time frame, and then picked the top three or four payers, doing so with the highest of expectations. Oftentimes, an investor may find yields that show an increase of 20 %, 30 %, and even up to 50 %. But recent performance may show a stock price drop, and that the most recent dividend payment was made between a few weeks and a month ago. This combination means that the yield percentage reached a high that it probably will not be sustainable for the long-term road. The drop in the stock price is usually a sign that the next dividend payment is going to see a big decrease as well, and that is if it is not suspended, like many companies in this predicament have done in a way to give itself time to sort things out. It is something to look out for when looking at the market.

CHAPTER 8:

Divided Investing Tools

In any business, the tools are really crucial to how the business operate. In forex trading, this is as well as a similar situation. The new traders or the experienced traders need the tools to master their trade and also make the right decisions to reach their goals.

Nowadays the trading tools can be with fee or without fee. Many platforms offer free trading tools for traders to use in the basic level. Some platforms offer the subscription. Traders become the members and pay the services monthly or yearly.

Economic calendar

The economic calendar is helping the traders get the fresh and updated news such as what happens in the future of the market, important related to trading economic data, new policies from the central bank, the elections and monetary policies updated around the world and much more. These are really important for trading especially forex market.

You can get the economic calendar from brokers or financial websites. It will provide the big picture about the economy such as the events that impact the economy in what level, unemployment rate, expecting the market conditions. Traders will have to keep close eyes on these things because trading currencies will be effective.

The level of impact in each event will be effective the economy. The currency pair will get effective as well. The market volatility of forex trade will be either low or medium or high depends on the events.

Pip calculator

Pip is the measure unit, and it is the most popular and smallest measure unit in forex trading especially between the currency pair. The pip calculate is convenient to use. Many traders use this forex trading tool to easy in exchange the pair currency. The users just have to enter the detail of their position, the amount of the currency, size of trade, currency pair and also the leverage.

Time zone converter

Forex market has 3 biggest markets around the world. One market closes, then another market opens. That is why some traders can trade 24 hours. Besides that, the market also overlaps with each other so the traders can also trade 2 markets at the same time.

With the right strategies, traders can get double profit. Time zone converter helps traders know exactly which market is opening in exactly what time. The experienced traders often trade around 3 or 4 morning Eastern time because they can trade in London market which is the biggest market for forex. It also overlaps with the Asia forex market.

Volatility calculator

Traders should focus and always keep eyes on the market volatility. It can help you have the good view about which is a good currency pairs to choose for trading. You do not want the currency pairs with limited scope of volatility because it will not the best trade.

Volatility calculator will give the general the history exchange of these currency pairs and give you the overall of how much volatility the pairs will be. You will decide if you want to trade on those pairs or not.

The history exchange can help the user pick what is the time frame that they want to focus on week, month, quarter or even years. The more market volatility is the better chance for traders to make the profit.

The traders can see the time frame with the currency pairs yield the most return, and they can start to trade on that time frame when it comes. It is working both ways that high return will also be high risk included. The traders can manage to diversify the trading to protect the money by risk management strategies.

Currency correlation

Forex trading is all about currency pairs. Traders is sure to not ignore the correlation between the currency pairs. The easy way to signal the currency pairs correlation is mark them positive or negative correlation.

The correlations range from -1.0 to 0.0 to +1.0. These are easy to understand: -1.0 is the perfect negative or inverse that often marked with color red color, 0.0 is no correlation, +1.0 is the perfect positive that often marked with blue.

The correlations between of currency pairs are calculating based on the history data between them. One of the popular currency correlation tool that many traders are known of is Mataf. Besides, You can also search and will see a lot of online websites offering this tool for free.

Trading platform

Many trading platforms are available nowadays. The most used platform by experienced trader is MetaTrader 4. The feature of this platform is one of the best and comprehensive in the market. MetaTrader 4 has strong analysis functions. The chart is really clear and easy to understand. Traders can put in currency pairs directly to the chart to comparing the up and down of the market.

MetaTrader 4 has a lot of advantages. Many traders use it, so if you run into the problems, you can easily to find the right answer quickly. MetaTrader 4 can operate and link with other software. Users can run automated trading with this platform smoothly.

MetaTrader 4 is not only used for forex trade but also used for different types of trading such as stocks, bonds, gold and much more. Traders can download MetaTrader 4 on its online website. They can try, test their data. This platform is really for the serious traders.

CHAPTER 9:

Divided Investing Strategies and Tactics

A dividend is a cash payment that a company makes to investors out of its profits. Not all companies pay dividends. So, if you are seeking to become an income investor, you should pay strict attention to make sure that the stock that you are buying actually pays dividends.

Dividends are quoted with stocks as a dollar amount and yield. The dollar amount that is quoted is given as the dollars paid per share on an annual basis. However, most stocks actually pay dividends out quarterly, so to estimate how much you would receive each quarter take the forward dividend and divide that by four. The forward dividend is actually the expected dividend payment for the upcoming 12 months.

Dividends, Yield, and Payout Ratio

Dividend stocks also have an associated yield. This is the dividend payment divided by the current share price. This will help you compare one investment to another. For example, you might want to compare a stock with a $50 share price and $2 dividend payment to one with a $200 share price and a $15 dividend payment. The first one has a 4% yield, while the second one has a 7.5% yield. The yield also helps you compare the value of the dividend investment and its income generating potential to other investments that pay interest, either by comparing yields or interest rate to the stock dividend yield. However, with other types of investments, it's also important to consider that stock prices also grow with time (at least in many cases…). The appreciating stock price is probably going to mean that all other things being equal, the company will probably increase it is dividend payment with time in order to keep yields relatively constant, so that they can attract investors. This adds extra power to dividend investing as opposed to simply sinking your money in something and living off the interest – the yield will stay the same with dividend stocks but the dividend payment per share may be growing as the share price appreciates in value. So, something that paid

$4 per share when you invested in it originally could pay $6 a share now, for example.

In addition to the dividend payment and yield, you will want to check the payout ratio. This is the ratio of the dividend payments made by a company to total earnings. If it is less than 100%, then the company is in a healthy place when it comes to paying dividends, since this means it's not struggling to meet dividend payments, and there is room to give without having to cut dividends. If the value is 100% or higher, that means that the company is probably in some level of financial difficulty. The nature of that difficulty is something that would have to be investigated in each case, but it could mean that the company won't be able to keep up with dividend payments in the future. The payments could either be cut or even eliminated entirely.

You can also do research in order to find dividend stocks that pay increasing dividends consistently. Stocks and their dividends can be looked up on various online sites to check this information, you are going to want to look at the number of years in a row that the stock paid increasing dividend payments. An increasing dividend payment probably means that the company is steadily increasing its profits, but that also tells you that they are able to increase the dividends to at least keep up with inflation, something that will guarantee that the dividend can be used to generate an inflation-beating income for you as the years go by.

Compound Interest

Most of us at least vaguely remember the lectures on compound interest in our algebra classes, and those who studied business and finance probably have a solid grip on the concept. For those that need a refresher, compound interest is basically a description of the way that your investments gain in value by reinvesting earned interest in order to grow your investments even further, that is by "compounding" them. Dividend stocks can be used in the same way by reinvesting your dividends, until you are in a situation where you either have to or want to begin using the dividends in order to get income payments. Until that time, you can reinvest dividend payments into the purchase of additional shares of stock, and so effectively grown your "principal" by which you are earning your yields. Over time, this can be a very powerful force, allowing you to grow your investments rapidly.

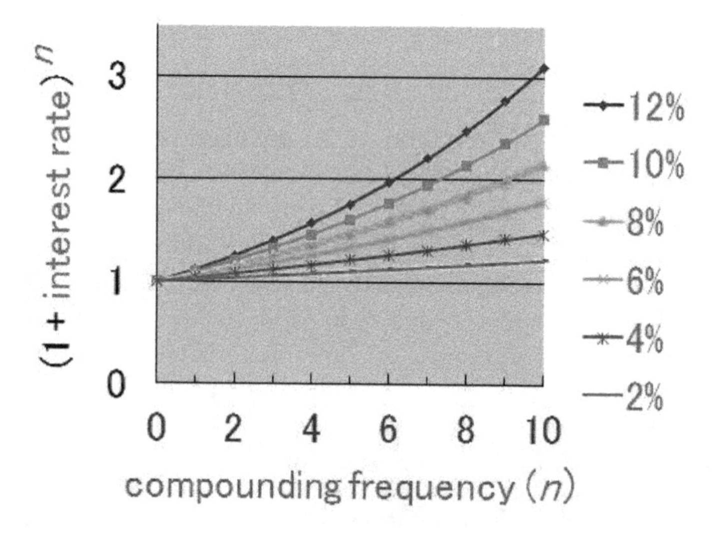

Graph showing the value of compound interest with different growth rates, by Karzov.

Some dividend stocks and brokerages offer plans called DRIPS, which are dividend reinvestment plans. These types of plans allow you to elect to have your dividend payments reinvested into new share purchases. By setting this process up to function automatically, this will help you grow your investment fast while avoiding the temptation to take cash out, which would hurt your long-term prospects.

DRIPS can also be used to help you grow and IRA or other retirement account. This can be very helpful because, using an IRA as an example, you are limited in the amount you can add to the account from the outside as cash contributions to buy more stocks. By using DRIPS inside the account, you can accumulate additional cash in the account without violating the contribution limits, and then these can be used in order to buy more shares of stock. You can continue this process until you get to a point where you are able to start taking out the dividend payments as income. DRIPS can be used at any time; you don't have to have stocks in an IRA in order to use them. You can setup DRIPS in any investment account, or alternatively if you are disciplined enough, you can manage it manually and use cash dividend payments in order to buy more shares of stock to help grow your portfolio faster.

How much is needed to invest?

One downside of investing using the income investing strategy is that in order to obtain a decent income from your dividend stocks, you are going to need to invest in purchasing a large number of shares. If we imagine, for example, that a given stock pays $4 a share, and we have 10,000 shares of stock, this will give us an annual income of $40,000 a year. But what will that cost us? If the stock is $120 a share, you would have to lock up $1.2 million in order to earn that $40,000 income.

Therefore, we see that dividend investing is primarily going to be a wealth plan that people can begin implementing while they are relatively young, so that they will have the time required to buy enough shares of stock to provide a meaningful annual income. Combined with other investments and social security payments, that $40,000 can definitely help you maintain a comfortable middle-class lifestyle.

Of course, this is just one example, by investing in different stocks that pay higher levels of dividend payments, you can come up with scenarios where you won't have to buy as many shares to get there. But in any case, you are not going to be able to get into this situation where you are going to get a comfortable level of dividend payments without doing a large amount of investing. If you are an older investor who hopes to get into dividends and you don't have other shares of stock or investments that you could sell in order to buy dividend stocks, you are going to have to be very aggressive about buying dividend paying stocks in the coming years. The fact is no matter what you invest in, you are going to need a significant number of shares in order to generate an income from it.

Don't Just Pay Attention to Yield

When investing in a dividend stock, you should treat your investment as you would any other. That means you should not carelessly invest just based on the yield that is being offered. Many stocks that are not good investments will try and attract investors by paying a high yield. That can seem tempting, because on paper it could provide you a way to accumulate enough shares to earn a good income without having to spend as much money. That is, many dividend stocks that have high yields have low share prices.

Of course, those don't necessarily represent stable companies or those that have a good future ahead of them, and so you might not be making the best decision by putting your money into these companies. You can find some stocks that are penny stocks or near so that pay very high yields. The naïve investor might think this is an opportunity, so they could load up on a large number of shares and then enjoy the dividend income without having to come up with a million dollars to invest. Unfortunately, as we noted when introducing the concept of penny stocks, dividend stocks that have low share prices probably do for a reason. That is red flag that this is a company that investors are avoiding, and that is why the share price is so low. You could invest in it and enjoy a few quarters of good dividend income, only to find that your investment – and the dividend payment – gets wiped out later.

So, in addition to the yield, you want to note the actual dividend payment and the share price. If things look OK then, you will want to do fundamental analysis on the company in order to determine whether or not it's a good investment overall. Only then, should you consider investing.

Earning Dividends from ETFs

Many exchange traded funds offer the opportunity for income investing. Some invest in bonds, and so provide the opportunity to earn a "dividend" from a stock (the ETF) which has actually invested in other kinds of assets, such as U.S. Treasuries or junk bonds. This will provide you with a way to diversify your investments while also earning dividend payments.

Many exchange traded funds also offer dividend payments while investing in a large, diverse, array of stocks. The yields or absolute dividend payments as far as dollar amount per share may not be as attractive; however as an investor you should appreciate the diversity that these types of investments can offer.

Dates to Be Aware Of

When investing in dividend paying stocks, you need to know the ex-Dividend date. This date is used by the company to determine who is entitled to receive a dividend payment. If you don't own the shares on or before the ex-dividend date, you are not going to be able to receive the dividend payment for that quarter. The company will also announce a "date of record" that closely follows the ex-dividend payment when those who are going to receive dividends are officially recorded by the company. They will also announce the date that the dividend payment is actually sent out. Dividends are typically paid on a quarterly basis.

CHAPTER 10:

Think Like An Expert

Never proceed without knowing the mood of the market: While using a personalized trading plan is always the right choice, having one doesn't change the fact that it is extremely important to consider the mood of the market before moving forward with the day's trades. First and foremost, it is important to keep in mind that the collective will of all of the traders who are currently participating in the market is just as much as a force as anything that is more concrete, including market news. In fact, even if companies release good news to various outlets and the news are not quite as good as everyone was anticipating it to be then related prices can still decrease.

To get a good idea of what the current mood of the market is like, you are going to want to know the average daily numbers that are common for your market and be on the lookout for them to start dropping sharply. While a day or two of major fluctuation can be completely normal, anything longer than that is a sure sign that something is up. Additionally, you will always want to be aware of what the major players in your market are up to.

Never get started without a clear plan for entry and exit: While finding your first set of entry/exit points can be difficult without experience to guide you, it is extremely important that you have them locked down prior to starting trading, even if the stakes are relatively low. Unless you are extremely lucky, starting without a clear idea of the playing field is going to do little but lose your money. If you aren't sure about what limits you should set, start with a generalized pair of points and work to fine tune it from there.

More important than setting entry and exit points, however, is using them, even when there is still the appearance of money on the table. One of the biggest hurdles that new options traders need to get over is the idea that you need to wring every last cent out of each and every successful trade. The fact of the matter is that, as long as you have a profitable trading plan, and then there will always be more profitable trades in the future which mean that instead of worrying about a small extra profit you should be more concerned with protecting the profit that the trade has already netted you. While you may occasionally make some extra profit ignoring this advice, odds are you will lose far more than you gain as profits peak unexpectedly and begin dropping again before you can effectively pull the trigger. If you are still having a hard time with this concept, consider this: options trading are a marathon, not a sprint, slow and steady will always wins the race.

Never double down: When they are caught up in the heat of the moment, many new options traders will find themselves in a scenario where the best way to recoup a serious loss is to double down on the underlying stock in question at its newest, significantly lowered, price in an effort to make a profit under the assumption that things are going to turn around and then continue to do so to the point that everything is completely profitable once again. While it can be difficult to let an underlying stock that was once extremely profitable go, doubling down is rarely if ever going to be the correct decision.

If you find yourself in a spot where you don't know if the trade you are about to make is actually going to be a good choice, all you need to do is ask yourself if you would make the same one if you were going into the situation blind, the answer should tell you all you need to know.

If you find yourself in a moment where doubling down seems like the right choice, you are going to need to have the strength to talk yourself back down off of that investing ledge and to cut your losses as thoroughly as possible given the current situation. The sooner you cut your losses and move on from the trade that ended poorly, the sooner you can start putting energy and investments into a trade that still has the potential to make you a profit.

Never take anything personally: It is human nature to build stories around, and therefore form relationships with, all manner of inanimate objects including individual stocks or currency pairs. This is why it is perfectly natural to feel a closer connection to particular trades, and possibly even consider throwing out your plan when one of them takes an unexpected dive. Thinking about and acting on are two very different things, however, which is why being aware of these tendencies are so important to avoid them at all costs.

This scenario happens just as frequently with trades moving in positive directions as it does negative, but the results are always going to be the same. Specifically, it can be extremely tempting to hang on to a given trade much longer than you might otherwise decide to simply because it is on a hot streak that shows no sign of stopping. In these instances, the better choice of action is to instead sell off half of your shares and then set a new target based on the updated information to ensure you are in a position to have your cake and eat it too.

Not taking your choice of broker seriously: With so many things to consider, it is easy to understand why many new option traders simply settle on the first broker that they find and go about their business from there. The fact of the matter is, however, that the broker you choose is going to be a huge part of your overall trading experience which means that the importance of choosing the right one should not be discounted if you are hoping for the best experience possible. This means that the first thing that you are going to want to do is to dig past the friendly exterior of their website and get to the meat and potatoes of what it is they truly offer. Remember, creating an eye-catching website is easy, filling it will legitimate information when you have ill intent is much more difficult.

First things first, this means looking into their history of customer service as a way of not only ensuring that they treat their customers in the right way, but also of checking to see that quality of service is where it needs to be as well. Remember, when you make a trade every second count which means that if you need to contact your broker for help with a trade you need to know that you are going to be speaking with a person who can solve your problem as quickly as possible. The best way to ensure the customer service is up to snuff is to give them a call and see how long it takes for them to get back to you. If you wait more than a single business day, take your business elsewhere as if they are this disinterested in a new client, consider what the service is going to be like when they already have you right where they want you.

With that out the way, the next thing you will need to consider is the fees that the broker is going to charge in exchange for their services. There is very little regulation when it comes to these fees which means it is definitely going to pay to shop around. In addition to fees, it is important to consider any account minimums that are required as well as any fees having to do with withdrawing funds from the account.

Find a Mentor: When you are looking to go from causal trader to someone who trades successfully on the regular, there is only so much you can learn by yourself before you need a truly objective eye to ensure you are proceeding appropriately. This person can either be someone you know in real life, or it can take the form of one or more people online. The point is you need to find another person or two who you can bounce ideas off of and whose experience you can benefit from. Options trading don't need to be a solitary activity; take advantage of any community you can find.

Knowledge is the key: Without some type of information which you can use to assess your trades, you are basically playing at the roulette table. Even poker players show up to the table with a game plan. They can adapt to the circumstances and learn to read other players. That way, they can tell the contenders from the pretenders. Options trading are no different. If you are unable to use the information that is out there to your advantage, then what you will end up with is a series of guesses which may or may not play out.

Based purely on the law of averages you have a 50/50 chance of making money. That may not seem like bad odds, but a string of poor decisions will leave you in the poor house in no time.

So, it is crucial that you become familiar with the various analytics and tools out there which you can use to your advantage. Bear in mind that everyone is going to be looking at the same information. However, it is up to you to find out what can, or might, happen before everyone else does. This implies really learning and studying the numbers so that you can detect patterns and see where trends are headed, or where trends may reverse. The perfect antidote to that is vision and foresight. Practice building scenarios. Try to imagine what could happen are trends continuing. Or, what would happen if trends reversed? What needs to happen in order for those trends to continue or reverse?

When you ask yourself such tough questions, your knowledge and understanding begin to expand. Your mind will suddenly be able to process greater amounts of information while you generate your own contingency plans based on the multiple what ifs. That may seem like a great deal of information to handle, but at the end of the day, any time spent in improving your trading acumen is certainly worth the effort.

CHAPTER 11:

Master the Market with Confidence

The education we received instills fear in our hearts to step outside the box and take a chance on change. Fear of risk paralyzes us and returns us to the structured template which we incorrectly perceive as secure. The way to break free from the chains of fear is to recognize our ability to overcome obstacles, or in other words, boost our own self-confidence.

Self-confidence

On the way to success in stock trading, as with life and business, we must cope with obstacles. Most people avoid that, since they believe from the outset that their chances of success are poor. Lack of belief in oneself indicates a poor level of self-confidence and deficient self-esteem. People who are born with a strong sense of self-confidence are very few and far between. The rest of us need to learn methods for improving our self-confidence.

Self-esteem is built while we are young. Initially, we develop insights such as "I'm good at..." or "I have a problem with..." At this point, we switch our brains onto autopilot and adopt positive or negative programs as though they are decrees from heaven. One random unsuccessful coping episode can create the feeling of failure that causes us to quietly accept that the situation is due to our own negative traits. The feelings we experience during failure are, in fact, the way we choose to translate reality. We may translate failure into disappointment, depression, lack of appetite, oversleeping. But we can choose differently: we can translate failure into challenge, the urge to improve, to feel adrenalin flowing strongly. Only you can choose how to translate your reality. What differentiates between the behavior of an outstanding athlete and a failed one? Their perception of reality. Being confident of winning lets the outstanding athlete translate reality positively. The way sports champions translate their reality is identical to the way successful stock traders translate theirs. When Thomas Edison was asked if he felt he had failed after 700 attempts at developing the ideal electric light bulb, he answered that he had discovered 700 ways that do not work.

If you were not born with Edison's self-confidence, don't throw up your hands helplessly. Self-confidence can be improved through diverse techniques known as "internal communication."

Boosting Self-esteem through Internal Communication

Internal communication includes those 1000 words that pass through our minds each minute. When we think, we use our own unique vocabulary, telling ourselves what is allowed and what is not, who we are and what we think about our abilities and limitations. The key to self-confidence depends on the words we choose. To improve self-esteem and self-confidence, we need to examine our vocabulary of words and phrases, and if necessary to change our internal dictionary.

We need to peel away all words that do not offer a positive contribution, such as "perhaps," "I'll try," "I can't," and more. Do these strengthen or weaken you? Change them to "I can" and "I will succeed." Talk about yourself to yourself in the first person: I'm successful, I'm a money-making machine, I'm a magnet for other people, I'm sure of myself, I'm happy, I'm pleased. The more we use constructive phraseology, the better our perception of self becomes. Believe in yourself and your abilities, since the views of others are negligible. As long as you maintain your self-confidence and belief in yourself, you will succeed and your financial success will improve in direct correlation to your self-esteem. Good internal communication improves your quality of life, your self-confidence, and no less valuable, your external communication.

External Communication

This is the way you express yourself, the words you say, your body language, your facial expressions. External communication is power. It is your power to impact others and the way they perceive you. Everything you wish to achieve, everything you lack, you can reach through those very same people. First, you need to find them and connect to them. If you mingle with people who have money, sooner or later something of it will cling to you too. If you mingle only with the people you grew up with, you won't get far. During the most challenging financial timeframe of my life (see what I mean? I swap "difficult" for "challenging") when I had not a penny to my name, I joined an exclusive golf club. That was my way of mingling with the haves rather than the have-nots.

Despite my dreadful financial state, how did I manage suitable external communication with millionaires as an equal among equals? When you come from a lower economic class, it's not so easy to communicate naturally with someone who is leagues above you. Try imagining how you'd behave if invited to lunch, one-on-one, with Donald Trump. Would your external communication be natural? Now try to imagine the lines of communication between Trump and Warren Buffet. Would they be more natural? Of course, they would.

How does one millionaire approach another? Does he look him straight in the eye when speaking, or look down? My way of structuring good external communication was to structure constructive internal communication. I constantly repeated to myself, "I'm a millionaire. A check for one million dollars is on its way to my account, but hasn't been deposited yet." Once I convinced myself I was a millionaire and that the check was merely delayed in the mail, being a millionaire was a given. With that problem behind me, my external communication altered. The expensive membership fees quickly paid off and were dwarfed by the scope of deals in millions of dollars I closed on the golf course.

External communication puts amazing power into the hands of those who know how to use it. Look how far external communication led people like Barack Obama, or at the other extreme entirely, Mussolini and Hitler. Strong external communication is the outcome of correctly applying internal communication, which is the source of power in individuals who succeed.

Aspiring to Be Powerful

The aspiration for power has impacted human history more than all the forces of nature put together. For those doing the controlling, their power is positive; for those being controlled, that power is generally negative. It makes no difference how you feel about power. You need to accept the fact that in the world we live in, the powerful control and the powerless are controlled. So what is it that you prefer: to set your own agenda, or live your life according to an agenda set by someone else? Simply put: are you the sheep or the wolf?

Power itself can be controlled. Power does not necessarily mean controlling the fate of other people. We can accumulate great power, but use it only to the degree where we have absolute control over our own fates. Power does not have to carry negative connotations, but can be used positively by assisting others. I tend to lecture free of charge to high school students, college students, and soldiers. The demand for my knowledge gives me a great feeling of being powerful in a different way.

The significance of power altered as civilization developed. In prehistoric human history, the powerful individual was the physically strongest. Over time, as the world developed into an economic organization, the focus of power shifted to those with capital. The wealthiest was the most powerful. At some point, an interesting shift became apparent when the socially-accepted norm determined that power would be passed down by inheritance from the nobleman to his son. If you were not born into nobility, your chances of succeeding, influencing, and accumulating power and assets were zero. The only way that might happen was if you were close to the nobleman in some way. These dark times, in which nobility was richly remunerated and the commoner found no positive incentive, typified the Middle Ages, a time in which the world almost stopped progressing. The Industrial Revolution, when the holders of capital and therefore power were those who owned machines, put an end to the power of nobility.

In our own times, power once again changed hands, moving from those who held capital and assets to those who also held knowledge. Up until some decades ago, it would have been impossible to compete with heavily-invested companies such as General Motors or IBM. To compete with a giant like IBM, a dreamy capital in the billions of dollars would have been needed. All this was true until a "geek" in jeans named Bill Gates overthrew IBM from the top by the use of initiative and knowledge. So too for Apple, Facebook, Google and tens of other companies that now control our lives, but were established not by holders of capital but by holders of knowledge. The beauty of our current times is that the chances of success are open to every single person, even if you have no physical power, capital, or title of nobility. Knowledge is power. Knowledge is the key to success. And knowledge can be bought.

Knowledge and Action

Knowledge moves the world. Until the end of the nineteenth century, if you had neither capital nor title, you could never break out from the class into which you were born. In those times, knowledge was for the privileged few, and banks funded the upper classes rather than those with knowledge. Our world is completely different: we live in an era where knowledge is readily accessible, and capital seeks good ideas even if the person presenting them is a youngster with a ponytail who never even finished college. Billionaires like Bill Gates and Steve Jobs were not born into the nobility--they were simply born into the right time. And they didn't have a college degree.

Knowledge and ideas are available to anyone seeking them. If knowledge is available to all, how is it that there are not more people who are successful, happy, driving Ferraris and living in Beverly Hills villas? Because knowledge in itself is not enough. Knowledge is the potential for power, but to realize it, actions are needed. Success begins with knowledge and ends in actions.

Knowledge in stock trading is also available to anyone seeking it, so why isn't everyone rich? Because operating in the stock market also requires integrating knowledge with action. The world is full of people with broad knowledge but who are inactive. What is unique about the successful individuals is that they, unlike the bulk of the public, take action. Their success, their power to control their own futures, derives from accrued knowledge and cumulative actions.

If you want to succeed, use another people's knowledge and emulate the successful. You don't even need to come up with an original idea. Did Steve Jobs invent Apple's graphic interface, the mouse or the iPad? No. He took existing ideas and upgraded them to such a state of perfection that he created an entirely new market. He fine-tuned solutions and took action. Nor did Bill Gates invent the DOS system which turned him into such a wealthy individual. He bought it from an inventor who did not realize its inherent potential.

CHAPTER 12:

The Best Mindset

With a correct attitude towards forex trading, you can be sure to achieve your goals. Here are a few suggestions that can help you develop the correct attitude and mindset for forex trading and trading in general.

Be Patient

This is a virtue when it comes to forex trading as it helps one cover everything at the right time and with the right state of mind. Patience can get you out of trouble as sometimes you might be forced to enter into a market hastily without understanding how it works. For beginners, patience is the key aspect as you get to understand the pros and cons of forex trading. Patience also keeps you away from reacting out of a bad day in business and even making wrong choices and decisions that can cause big losses. As the adage goes, Patience pays, so take your time off a hectic day and trust the process.

Be Objective

In forex trading, one is required to be objective and not trade with emotions. As stated earlier, a forex trader should keep the eyes on the final product, that is, his financial goals. Being subjective or acting on emotions is disastrous for any business and learning to act by the book is key to a successful forex trading career. This means that you should not also listen to people who claim to be Pros in the game and trust your trading patterns instead of sheepishly following the crowd. This doesn't however mean that you should not trade on mass thinking but if you do, always keep in mind that the masses are not always right.

Be Disciplined

This ought to be a major aspect in every business and as earlier pointed out, discipline keeps one out of overreacting for a loss or a win. This cuts across happy and sad moments in business as both sides can affect the outcome if not subjected to some discipline. Being able to control yourself, to not overtrade or under trade and take just enough risks is a skill that can be learned by following procedures and sticking to the game-plan. Remember, you should never, ever, stake half your capital, risk all your profits or worse, trade with money you don't have or money you can't afford to lose.

Be Realistic

Just like any other business, one should be real and expect a particular profit according to the capital traded-in. Always remember that forex trading is not like Lotto or betting where one can win a jackpot of a million dollars by stalking just a little money. It takes time to build up your skills, your knowledge and your confidence and secure good profits with forex trading. Therefore, one should expect the right amount of returns on investment and what comes with it. By not giving up, being disciplined and patient, and doing your research, you might end up achieving your goals and reaching top-level in the forex world. This mentality also helps one to limit the number and types of transactions or operations on a daily or weekly basis and to stay in the game even after losing a small percentage of the initial investment. This is a business opportunity just like any other.

With all said and done, there are rules to abide by in order to reach your potential and most importantly realize your potential in terms of profit. Below are 12 rules that can help you achieve your goals in forex Trading.

1 Trust the Process

Forex trading is a business and needs time and effort to grow and consolidate which means that there is more than just waiting for profits. Profit oriented businesses can end badly if the thresholds one has set are not met and the overall approach is not thoroughly planned. Any business is not only buying and selling as it involves huddles and logistics to make the whole institution work and doable. Some profit oriented forex traders tend to give up easily if they don't meet their target after a few operations or a short period of time. However, one can set a timeline and work towards meeting the set target without having to achieve a specific point which might turn to be the opposite.

To achieve your goals, some points are process-oriented and help in reaching the high note in forex trading and are outlined.

2 Outline Daily Activities

Day to day activities can only be achieved when put down on paper for a specific task in forex trading. Having in mind the right thing to do on a specific day is good as it helps avoiding distractions and other things that may get in the way on a business day. This means that the more you know what you are doing on a busy day, you will not waste time doing other things that do not help achieve your goal and the needs you want to build your forex trading skills.

3 Analyze The Market

As pointed out earlier, trading with emotions is bad for business as it does not go by the plans and strategy but with the reaction of business gone wrong or even a big win. Being greedy is so bad in forex trading and it is advisable to analyze the market first before trying out forex trading and giving a shot on the most promising patterns. When you play by the rules, you train the mind to follow the right procedures and even helps in becoming more discipline in forex trading. Training the mind helps in a vulnerable situation which will make you hold on when there is a crisis.

4 Be Defensive

This is another important rule to follow in forex trading for it is the core purpose of joining the business and what will keep you survive storms that will come your way in one way or the other. This simply means that you should not trade everything including your capital, defend your initial capital and aim at making profits. When you make a target and do not meet it, then at least you tried, but trading profusely just to meet the target with limited time is not good at all as it is an offensive approach. You should always protect your capital as it is the only thing keeping you in the business and one mistake can send you to factory reset, i.e; going back to the drawing board wondering when the rain started beating you.

5 Have A Trading Plan

Just like any other venture, Forex trading needs a business plan that has been tested to be working and giving impressive results. The plan involves things that you need to do from A-Z, this may include the rules of engagement, trading pattern, market analysis, and other key aspects that make the business run well. After making the trading plan, you can test it virtually to see if it will go well with the market and if it is good, then give it a green light and start the forex trading. But make sure that you outline the plan as it is the backbone of the whole venture.

6 Know That Trading Is A Business

Forex trading is like a business and should be treated as such for one to get the best out of it by giving the attention it deserves. Other researches have talked about not comparing trading with job opportunities or hobby to be done on leisure time. This means that one should not expect a salary and works on getting profits and give attention and not only focusing on it when you are free. With this, a forex trader will learn to prioritize forex trading just like any other business.

7 Outline Risk

Make sure that you point out the risk you intend to get yourself into and do not give it too much until you are out of business. Do not risk an amount that you cannot afford, risking is only for the amount you are capable of and not anywhere near initial capital. Remember as said earlier, if you lose capital that means that you are out of business and you will not want that to happen to you. Only risk an amount that you know if they go then you will not struggle with bringing back the business into living.

8 Use Technology

The modern era of inventions and innovations can be a plus in forex trading as it helps improve the outcome of a venture. Technology has played a big role in forex trading, thanks to innovators who come with new things every day to enhance the world in bringing people closer. With technology, one can trade anywhere in the world monitor charts using a computer or even mobile phones. This means that one can travel all over the world as well as working at the same time. This has been evident for bloggers and travel entrepreneurs who blog for a living and promote products online while they travel. This can be the same for forex traders and it helps in even having a good time and relaxing the mind while working.

9 Have A Stop Loss

This is somehow similar to outlining risk but specifies the amount that one should be willing to lose in particular trading. In Forex trading, you should only lose what you afford and it is very important to outline the amount or percentage that one should only lose in trading. This also acts as a disciplined mode as it helps in controlling the mind and emotions not to surpass the limited amount of possible risk.

10 Focus On The Bigger Picture

What is the purpose of starting forex trading? Can you make the business to be aligned in that direction? Are you getting some profits and losing sometimes? then you are on the right track heading to greatness in forex trading. Business is not about just making profits but making impacts on a personal level and getting more skills. So what is your bigger picture? To have gained at least 10 per cent in the financial year 2020-2021? Having this in mind, then you can be sure of aiming in the right way as compared to only focusing on maximizing profits.

11 Keep Learning Markets

Forex trading is an ongoing process even after mastering markets and getting out of an amateur venture. One does not stop learning at anything and things keep changing in the forex world this is important to keep an open mind in everything to do with business. Some of the skilled forex traders can fall prey of crowd psychology and some markets are unpredictable making forex trading a learning experience every time one is trading.

12 Be A Progressive Trader

Every forex trader wants to earn profit as it is the main reason for venturing in forex trading in the first place, but are you only profit-oriented the first day in the market or you are moving forward? Learning also can be a huge progress as it helps one avoid making similar mistakes and open ways for more profit in the future.

CHAPTER 13:

Manage Risk and Save Money

Talks about how to save money when Forex Trading, more accurately help you understand how to manage your money when Forex Trading. Many people don't realize that but understanding how to budget your money is very important, especially when you're Forex Trading.

When to say no?

One of the main questions people have is when to say no, and the truth is you need to say no when you feel like you have been losing money for a couple of days. Now we won't get very technical on the exact number and the exact date when you need to cut the trade. However, it is more about the mindset that will help you to save money when Forex Trading and have the right mindset went to say no when not to say no. The first thing you need to understand one Forex Trading would be that you need to say no whenever you start to lose money. If you want to practice forex trading safely, then you need to make sure that you will be saying no as soon as you see the money drop. Another time you need to say no would be when you feel like your trend is falling. For example, if you are gradually losing your trade then doesn't wait on it and in fact get out of the trade as soon as possible.

Save your money.

Before we start saving any money, we need to realize saving money requires you to set goals. We will show you how to set goals accordingly and in a fashionable manner which will help you save the most amount of money in the long run. The truth is that your same goals can help you achieve your financial dreams, whether it be buying a new house or paying off your debt. The sooner you start to build better wealth, more likely chances you will have to live a better financially free life. There is no way oh, you will achieve your goals without a set goal in your mind, so it is essential that you set financial goals in order to achieve them sooner than later. The first step with setting goals would be to set them as attainable as possible.

If we told you, that you have one year to become an Olympic athlete and you have never worked out in your life before would you be able to do it? Probably not. It is important that you set the tangible goals; this will help you stay on track and keep you motivated when the tough gets going. If you set a goal which is not attainable realistically, then the chances of you giving up will be very high. Which is why you need to set goals with your attainable for you, and to do that you need to analyze your financial reporting income? Sit down, and find out how much you make monthly yearly. And then based on your income, you need to realize how much you need to save in order to achieve a certain goal in a certain time frame. Having a time frame is pretty important; as it will help you push further to achieve that goal of Financial Freedom.

For instance, if you tell yourself that you need to save $30,000 as compared to saving $30,000 and 24 months, this will give you more of an advantage to achieve that goal sooner than later, and if you keep it reasonable, you should have no problem achieving these goals. Once you sit down and find out what your income is and what your goal is financially speaking, then you can slowly start setting time frames to achieving a certain goal. If your goal is to pay off $1,000 credit card, then you can set a goal I'll be saving 250 every month until you have reached your thousand-dollar mark within 4 months, you will be able to pay off your credit card.

Now you see how the time frame can help you save more money before you start any saving goals sit down and find out what you need to save on and how much time you will be giving yourself to save that certain amount of money. Once you have a solid budget, and where you want to save your money to achieve certain financial goals it would be now time to set specific categories for your saving goals. You need to prioritize your savings, and find out where you need to put money and where you shouldn't so much. Simply prioritize the amount you need to save and how long you need to achieve certain saving goals for, and where you can cut back on saving and not affect your life so drastically.

For example, if you really need to buy that house in 24 months and you need $30,000 down, but you already have $4,000 saved for emergency funds then you need not put extra money towards your emergency funds and put more money towards your house. Simply categorize your savings, and prioritize them accordingly. Once you start prioritizing your savings, you will be in a much better hand to save more money and to achieve your financial goals. Once that is done, it would be now time to cut down on certain spending which are not important to you. if you decide to live a minimalist lifestyle as we talked about before, this step won't be as important to you since he will be doing that already.

But if you aren't following a minimalistic lifestyle, then pay attention as it can help you save a lot more money. If you feel like, you're spending way too much money on your groceries and you can slowly cut back on it then do so. Wherever you feel like you can cut money back on, and put it towards your savings then do that. You don't need a lot of money to be spent, so find out where you're spending way too much money on and then slowly start to cut back on it until you are the reach your certain number of dollars every month. Once you have your emergency funds at a decent level, you can now decide to hire a financial advisor. As we mentioned, a financial advisor can be of great use as they will help you save more money overall.

Not only the financial advisor will help you save more money, but it will show you where I can invest your savings to make even more wealth. Which is a good thing, if you want to be a financially free person. Don't be scared to ask financial advisors' question, if you fear but your financial advisor is in the best then get a new one, many financial advisors are really good at their job. One of the best things financial advisors do is that they help

CHAPTER 14:

Set Your Budget

If you have just started in Forex trading, you must have been wondering whether you need to have a huge amount of money in order to start trading. So, is it possible for you to trade the Forex market with little money?

The fact is that you can trade with little money, but your profits will be limited. With a few tips though, you can successfully trade the markets without having to put down thousands of dollars on the line.

Educate Yourself

Before you can place your money on the line, you need to be educated about what to do before you jump in. Make sure you understand the basics of trading the Forex market and know whether your limited funds will give you profit.

Understand the risk management processes as well as other concepts before you put any money on the line. If you have put some money on the line, then you should withdraw part of it and put it in a course. It will give you concepts that you can use to turn your money regardless of how much you have.

Learning resources also introduce you to analysis techniques that give you an idea of what trade to place and when to do it.

Start Small

As a new trader, it is prudent that you start off with a small amount compared to putting all your money into the trade. Remember that you can't have the success you desire trading dollars when you cannot trade for pennies. To do this, you need to find the right broker that gives you a low limit trading account.

Patience is Key

Forex trading is all about having patience. When you start small, you might see it be frustrating and slow, but it keeps you disciplined. Make sure that you start small and grow your account step by step.

Profitable Forex investing takes time and patience. All those traders that you see making money on the market were novices on their first day, some were even worse than you. However, most of them started small and grew step by step to become the pro traders that they are right now.

Do It Regularly

As you refine the craft, make sure you make trading your habit. To do this, start investing regularly as you learn the ropes. Add funds to your account several times a week and you will see the account grow. The good thing is that you won't lose too much in any trade compared to putting up a lot of your money for trading.

How to Earn With Forex

There Are A Few Steps To Make Money With Forex. Let Us Look At What You Can Do.

Grow Your Skills

When you have the right skill, you will make money with forex trading. The forex market is dynamic, and you have to keep up with the changes. As you trade, you get more and more knowledgeable about the things that happen in forex trading. Take time to learn new techniques and engage with other traders to understand what they do to be successful.

The best way to learn about Forex trading is to make sure you look at the various reasons the market is moving in a specific direction. For instance, you might look at the analysis methods that are used by top traders and why they use them. You also need to understand what triggers make the prices to move in a given direction as opposed to another.

Learn to Perform Analysis

The analysis is all about using charts and other visual tools to come up with a decision. Forex trading gives you two major types of tools to use – fundamental and technical analysis. Fundamental analysis focuses on events that will change the performance of a currency pair. On the other hand, technical analysis involves looking at price action and its effect on the market – including the trends, momentum, and reversal patterns.

Just know that you have a chance to make more profit when you perform the right analysis before placing a trade.

Work with the Right Broker

A Forex broker makes it possible for you to execute transactions. This is just one of the major functions – a broker handles various other tasks that are vital to trading.

Before you can choose a broker, make sure that you understand what they offer in terms of features that are left by traders. If you come across fraud alerts or issues with the withdrawing of funds, then look for another broker.

So, making money on Forex is all about buying a currency pair at a low price, and then selling it off at a higher price to make profits. The profit, which represents your income, is the difference between the price you buy the price of buying and selling the currency pair. You pay the broker a commission from the trade called the spread.

If you believe that you don't have the capacity to place trades with your money, then you can use a feature given by the broker called the leverage. This is money that you follow from the broker to make your deposit higher.

Remember that the higher the deposit the more the risk.

Advantages of Trading Forex

When you get into forex trading, you enjoy various benefits that come with the trades that you place.

Low Commission

The commission is the money that the broker makes on each trade that you place. Usually, when you trade in a different place, the broker takes a percentage of the money that you deposit to the account.

However, many brokers don't attach any fees on the trade, meaning that you can enjoy high-profit margins when you trade Forex.

Trading Flexibility

Forex gives you a lot of flexibility for both traders and investors. You don't have a limit to the amount you place on trade each day, which allows both smalltime traders as well as seasoned investors to make money.

Additionally, you don't have too many rules and regulations when it comes to Forex trading. This means you have the flexibility to work 24 hours without any disruption.

The flexible working hours make it possible for those people working day jobs to have some time to trade as well.

You have Complete Control over Your Trades

One of the top advantages of trading Forex is that you have total control when you place a trade. You don't have to run a trade that you are not comfortable with.

It is all upon you to decide when and how to place a trade without any obligation. You also decide the level of risk that you can take in every trade.

Demo Accounts Ideal for Practicing

As a rookie in the business, you need all the guidance and information to make it in the market. For you, a demo account is all you need to achieve the skills necessary to give you the push you need.

The demo account is a simulation of the way the live trading system works, and it gives you the practice you need.

When you use the demo account, you don't face any risk and it gives you an idea of whether the market is ideal for you or not. You also get to test, improve, and organize the new skills that might be beneficial when you start live trading.

Total Transparency in the Information You Get

The Forex exchange is a huge market and it operates 24 hours across different countries in various time zones. However big the market is, you get all the information you need to place trades. You will get information about the current forecast as well as the rates.

The information is real-time meaning that you get the information when it is displayed. This information is ideal for analysis so that you make deductions to the trend of the market.

Low Cost of Investment

Compared to other investments in the markets, Forex trading comes with a low cost of investment. The low cost of investment is due to the direct involvement by dealers which results in covering of risks; this means it doesn't need so much brokerage.

High Leverage

Compared to other forms of investments, Forex gives you the highest level of leverage than other investing markets. Even though you place a smaller amount of capital into the business, you have the capacity to win or lose big in the deals.

Wide Currency Pairs

When you enter the Forex market, you can trade in many currency pairs to your own advantage. With so many options to pick from, you get to enter a spot trade or opt for future agreement contracts.

You can choose the pair according to the budget or the type of risk that the pair comes with.

High Liquidity

The Forex market has the biggest number of players compared to other markets.

This leads to high liquidity that brings to the fore big players that fill large orders of the trade. It eliminates the manipulation of price, thus this promotes efficient pricing models.

High Volatility

In Forex, you can easily switch from one currency to another if you find it more profitable.

Remember that there is a high risk associated with investing capital in such a market, but with volatility, you end up with higher profit especially when you switch to a different currency that promises a good return.

This, in turn, gives you a higher advantage and increases profit.

Works for 24 Hours Each Day

The trading program operates 24 hours each day in a week which means you will always have a chance to trade no matter the situation. You can get from your day job and then handle any trades that you want during the evening.

You can take up Forex trading as a day job and you can work within the normal hours or your own preferred time. The good news is that you can still access the various tools and information that helps you to run the trades.

High Confidence Levels

When you make a profit, you get stimulated to run more trades. This creates a lot of goodwill. You can also get into the trade more thus make more money than ever.

CHAPTER 15:

Start Investing Step By Step

Trading Forex can be a very interesting hobby for other people in the current world. This form of a thrilling kind of hobby can be a great source of generating revenue. To lighten up people's light, over five trillion US dollars are traded in a day. To formally understand the trade, the process is divided into three namely learning basics terminologies in Forex, opening of an online Forex brokerage account and starting the trade.

Learning Basic Terminologies in Forex

Understanding basic Forex terminology

The first two terminologies an individual is supposed to understand are the base currency and quote currency. During the Forex trade, two currencies are always traded. The currency that is being got rid is referred to as the base currency. The other currency being bought is known as the quote currency. For a person to buy the quote currency, he or she will be guided by the foreign exchange rates. The foreign exchange rates help a person to know how much he or she will have to spend.

There are two positions in the process of trading currencies. A person can choose to take a long term or short-term position. A long-term position involves a person buying the base currency and in turn selling the quote currency. On the other hand, buying the base currency and selling the base currency is referred to a trader taking a short-term position. The trader always has a price which he or she can willingly buy the base currency in exchange to get quote currency. This price is always known as a bid fee.

Bid prices can change during the process of broking currencies. This leads to the rise of an asking price. It is the price an individual is able to sell the base currency in return to gain the quote currency. Bid price mostly is the best price available in the market a person can buy the other currency. The difference between the asked price and the bid price is known as a spread.

Reading the Forex quote

There are two numbers an individual will observe in the Forex quote. The numbers present include the bid price and the asking price. The bid price is always situated on the left side while the asking price is always situated on the right side.

Descending on what currency a person wants to buy and sell

This process starts with a person predicting an economy. An individual can take a common economy like the United States of America economy. An individual can believe of the US economy declining. This situation is bad for the American dollar since it will depreciate in terms of value. Therefore, the situation will lead to a person offloading the dollar in exchange for the other forms of currency which strong economies.

The individual can look at a country trading position to know which currency to buy and sell. The better country to look at is that with a high amount of goods that are inconsistent demand. There are high possibilities for such a country to have high numbers of exports and thus make more money from international and local trade. The phenomenon will be a strong boost to a country and in turn, boosting the currency. The information favoring such a country gives a trader the best currency to invest in.

The decision over which currency to buy and sell can be determined by the political temperatures of a country. The most crucial times are during the elections in a country. The currency is approximated to rise if a person winning the election has an agenda aligning to favorable fiscal policies. The currency can be favorable to buy if the regulations on economic growth are loosened. The action likely leads to an increase in the value of a country's currency.

Economic reports of a country can also help a person in making the decision on which currency to buy and sell. An individual can choose to focus on a country's Gross Domestic Income or a country's Per Capita Income. Other information that can be critical includes the employment rate and inflation rate. This critical information will provide a trader with accurate information about the value of the currency to buy and sell.

Learning how to calculate profits

The process involves a person's ability to be able to measure the value change in two currencies. Pip measures the difference between the two traded currencies. One pip is usually equated to 0.0001change in value. A good example can be drawn from an exchange of the Euro to the American dollar. If the trade of EUR/USD shifts from 2.646 to 2.647, the value of the currency is said to have increased by ten pips. The next step involves an individual multiply the pips numbers his or her account with the current exchange rates. The value got will help an individual know if he has made a gain or a decrease in his account.

Opening of Online Forex Brokerage Account

Researching of different brokerages

There are several factors an individual is supposed to consider while choosing his or her brokerage. These factors to be kept in consideration include:

Going out for the experience

This should be the main consideration when choosing a brokerage individual or a company. The person or company is decided on is supposed to have a minimum experience of ten years in the market. The experience will be able to help a person to know the company is on track. Experience also indicates the company or an individual is good at taking care of his or her clients.

One is supposed to ensure that the brokerage is regulated. The regulation of brokerages is mostly done by the chief oversight body. It is very pleasing if a broker chose on has a total submission to the government. The situation gives an individual reassurance on broker transparency and honesty. There are several oversight bodies across the globe and they include;

United Kingdom; Financial Conduct Authority

Switzerland; Swiss Federal Banking Institution.

Australia; Australian Securities and Investment Commission.

The types of available products by the broker are also another factor for an individual to consider. There are some factors that help an individual to know if the brokerage has a wide business reach and a large client base. One of the determining factors these occurrences is also trading securities and commodities.

Visiting the website of a broker is not supposed to be left out. This website is supposed to have a good professional look. The links provided on the website are supposed to be functional also. If there are any doubts on the website, an individual is supposed to steer clear from the broker.

Checking on the transactional cost of each trade is also advantageous to a person interested to be successful in Forex trade. An individual is supposed to check how much the bank will charge him or her to wire funds into his or her Forex account.

An individual is supposed to be able to focus on the essentials. These essentials include focusing on good clientele support and transactions that are easy and transparent. An individual is supposed to be attracted to a broker who has a good reputation.

Requesting information about opening an account

There are two forms of account an individual can open to be able to trade in the Forex market. An individual chose to open a personal account or he or she can choose to open a managed account. Having a personal account will help an individual to manage his or her account. On the other hand, having a managed account tasks the broker with the ability to execute the trade on behalf of the individual.

Filling out the correct paperwork

There are several ways the appropriate paperwork can be filled. An individual can choose to order the paperwork by mail services. The other method will entail downloading the papers from the internet in the form of a PDF file. The next step will involve an individual checking the transaction charges by the bank for transferring funds to an individual's brokerage account. This fee is important because it affects the profit calculation in the Forex trade.

Activation of the account

The most common occurrence entails the broker sending the activation link to an individual's email. The link sent always contains guidelines that help an individual to start.

Starting Trading

Analysis of the market

Market analysis is always the first step while starting to trade in the Forex market. There are several ways an individual can use to analyze the market. They include:

Technical analysis; technical analysis entails the use of chats or historical data. These forms will help a Forex trader to be able to predict the movement of currency basing his thought on the recent events. These data can be obtained from several sources. The main form sources include from the brokerage or the MetaTrader which is a common platform for those in the Forex trade.

Fundamental analysis; this form of analysis involves taking a keen look at the key areas in a country's economy. The information got from these fundamental areas form a key to a person trading choice.

Sentimental analysis; this form of market analysis is highly subjective. An individual using this form of market analysis will try to get a good analysis of the market mood. This will enable an individual to know if the market is bullish. It is very difficult to put a finger on the sentiment of the market. However, an individual can be able to make very good guesses that influence his or her trade.

Determining an individual's margin

This is highly dependable on the broker's strategy in place. An individual can make investments of small amounts of money and still be able to make huge trades in the Forex market. An example can be used of an individual with a desire to trade one hundred units at one percent margin. This will make the broker put one thousand American dollars in an individual's account to act as security. If an individual makes the gains, it will add in his or her account to its value. On the other hand, loses will deduct from the individual's account from its value. Such occurrences have made individuals invest 2% of the funds in a specific pair currency.

Placing of an individual order

An individual at this point can place orders of various kinds. These orders include:

Market order; this order includes an individual using the market order to instruct his or her broker to buy or sell at the present market rates.

Limit orders; this point entails an individual instructing his or her broker to trade at a precise price. An individual can sell the currency when it lowers to a certain price or he or she can buy when it gains up to a certain price.

Stop orders; this order involves two of the options. An individual can decide to buy currency above the present value in the market.

CHAPTER 16:

Building Your Portfolio

Stage 1: Determining Your Appropriate Asset Allocation

Discovering your financial situation and goals is the primary assignment in building a portfolio. Significant things to consider are age and how much time you need to develop your investments, just as the measure of funding to invest and future payment needs. An unmarried, 22-year-old college graduate simply starting their profession needs an alternate investment system than a 55-year-old married individual hoping to help pay for a child's education degree and retire in the next decade.

A subsequent factor to consider is your character and risk tolerance. Is it accurate to say that you will danger the potential loss of some cash for the chance of more prominent returns? Everybody might want to harvest exceptional yields a seemingly endless amount of time after a year, however, if you can't rest around evening time when your investments take a short drop, odds are the significant yields from those sorts of benefits are not worth the stress.

Explaining your present circumstance, your future requirements for capital, and your risk resilience will decide how your investments ought to be assigned among various resource classes. The chance of greater returns comes to the expense of greater risk of losses (a guideline known as the risk/bring tradeoff back). You would prefer not to wipe out the risk to such an extent to improve it for your circumstance and way of life. For instance, the youngster who won't need to rely upon their investments for money can bear to face greater challenges in the mission for exceptional yields. Then again, the individual approaching retirement needs to concentrate on ensuring their advantages and attracting pay from these benefits an assessment effective way.

Conservative vs. Aggressive Investors

For the most part, the more risk you can hold up under, the more aggressive your portfolio will be, committing a bigger segment to values and less to bonds and other fixed-salary securities. Alternately, the less risk you can expect, the more traditionalist your portfolio will be. Here are two models, one for conservative investors and one for the modestly aggressive investor.

Conservative Portfolio

The principal objective of a moderate portfolio is to ensure its value. The designation appeared above would yield current pay from the bonds, and would likewise give some drawn-out capital development potential from the interest in great values.

Stage 2: Achieving the Portfolio

When you've decided on the right asset allocation, you have to divide your capital between the suitable asset classes. On an essential level, this isn't troublesome: equities are equities, and bonds will be bonds.

In any case, you can additionally break down the different asset classes into subclasses, which likewise have various risks and potential returns. For instance, an investor may isolate the portfolio's value parcel between various modern sectors and organizations of various market capitalizations, and among household and foreign stocks. The bonds part may be assigned between those that are short-term and long term, government debt versus corporate debt, etc.

There are a few different ways you can approach picking the assets and securities to satisfy your asset designation procedure (make sure to dissect the quality and capability of every benefit you invest into):

Stock Picking – Choose stocks that fulfill the degree of risk you need to convey in the equity segment of your portfolio; segment, market top, and stock sort are components to consider. Dissect the organizations utilizing stock screeners to waitlist potential picks, at that point complete more inside and out examination on every potential buyer to decide its chances and risks going ahead. This is the most work-concentrated methods for adding securities to your portfolio, and expects you to consistently screen value changes in your property and remain current on organization and industry news.

Bonds Picking – When picking bonds, there are a few elements to consider including the coupon, development, the bonds type, and the credit rating, just as the general financing cost condition.

Mutual Funds – Mutual funds are accessible for a wide scope of benefit classes and permit you to hold stocks and bonds that are expertly looked into and picked by finance supervisors. Finance supervisors charge an expense for their administrations, which will bring down your profits. Account funds present another decision; they will in general have lower expenses since they mirror an established index and are along these lines inactively managed.

Trade Traded Brokers (ETFs) – If you lean toward not investing with mutual funds, ETFs can be a practical other option. ETFs are shared supports that trade like stocks. They're like mutual funds in that they speak to an enormous bushel of stocks, generally assembled by part, capitalization, nation, and such. In any case, they contrast in that they're not effectively managed however rather track a picked account or another basket of stocks. Since they're inactively overseen, ETFs offer cost reserve brokers over mutual funds while giving expansion. ETFs additionally spread a wide scope of advantage classes and can help balance your portfolio.

Stage 3: Reassessing Portfolio Weightings

When you have a built-up portfolio, you have to analyze and rebalance it occasionally, because adjustments in price developments may make your underlying weightings change. To survey your portfolio's real resource assignment, quantitatively classify the investments and decide their qualities' extent to the entirety.

The other factors that are probably going to change after some time are your current money related circumstance, future needs, and risk resilience. If these things change, you may need to alter your portfolio likewise. If your risk resilience has dropped, you may need to decrease the quantity of values held. Or then again maybe you're currently prepared to take on more serious risk and your advantage designation necessitates that a little extent of your benefits be held in progressively unpredictable little top stocks.

To rebalance, find out which of your positions are overweighted and underweighted. For instance, say you are holding 30% of your present assets in little top values, while your advantage assignment recommends you should just have 15% of your benefits in that class. Rebalancing includes deciding the amount of this position you have to lessen and dispense to different classes.

Stage 4: Rebalancing Strategically

When you have found out which securities you have to reduce and by how much, choose which underweighted securities you will purchase with the returns from selling the overweighed securities.

While rebalancing and straightening out your portfolio, pause for a minute to consider the duty ramifications of selling assets at this specific time.

Maybe your interest in development stocks has acknowledged firmly over the last year, yet if you somehow managed to sell the entirety of your value positions to rebalance your portfolio, you may bring about greater capital gain taxes. For this situation, it may be increasingly valuable to just not invest any new assets to that advantage class later on while proceeding to add to other resource classes. This will diminish your development stocks' weighting in your portfolio after some time without bringing about capital additions taxes.

Simultaneously, consistently think about the viewpoint of your securities. If you presume that that equivalent over-weighted development stocks are unfavorably prepared to fall, you might need to sell regardless of the expense suggestions. Investigator feelings and research reports can be valuable instruments to help check the viewpoint for your property. Also, charge loss selling is a technique you can apply to diminish charge suggestions.

CHAPTER 17:

Hard Work, Focus and Dedication

Following are a list of things required for becoming a successful Forex trader

Trading plan: A forex trader should have a trading plan that should be prepared well in advance. The trading plan should list out his entry and exit conditions as well as his money management rules. This is of utmost importance and he should religiously follow his trading plan to the tee. In order to become a successful forex trader, he should never deviate from the trading plan.

Discipline: This is one of the most important qualities needed to be a successful forex trader. A trader should be disciplined and methodical in the way he goes about with forex trading. He should not only meticulously plan his trading, but should also be disciplined enough to follow it.

Ability to do analysis: A forex trader should have the ability to analyze the technical charts and other financial data in order to become a successful forex trader. He should invest in himself and learn how to use the financial tools that would help in becoming a better trader. Trading is a very competitive job and one needs to be always one step ahead of others in order to be successful.

Emotional stability: It is very important to keep emotions and trading separate. In order to be successful, the trader should be able to trade like a machine and not let emotions affect his trades. He shouldn't let losses affect him nor should he get overly excited about the winning trades.

Hard work: Nothing beats hard work for becoming a successful forex trader. The trader should be prepared to put in a lot of hours and research the forex market thoroughly before each trading day. Most successful forex traders have a pre-trading session wherein they analyze the global markets, check charts, read various financial newspapers, note down key economic events of the day etc. before they start their trades.

Good knowledge of charting and analysis tools: In order to be a successful forex trader, it is very important to have good knowledge on the usage of charting and other analytic software. The usage of this trading software's raises the odds of success considerably, so it is important to have a good understanding of them.

Constant Learning: Trading field requires constant learning. The trader should be prepared to learn throughout his trading career. Something that might work now might not work after 5 years. So it's very important to constantly adapt and keep learning in order to be a step ahead of others. A good trader should be on the constant look out of learning new things that might help him with his trading be it the usage of a trading software or a new way of analysis.

Mastering fear: It is very important to master fear in order to be a successful forex trader. The trader should be prepared to take losses now and again and should understand that it's a part and parcel of the game. The inability to book losses and holding on to a losing position can result in more losses. The trader should also be ready to take a trade when a good opportunity arises and should not allow fear to hold him back.

Thinking on your own: It is very important to think on your own and make trading decisions and to not just blindly follow the crowd. As the saying goes, "buy into the fear and sell into the greed!" Now, this does not mean to always do the opposite to what others do. It just means that the trader should have an open mind and should have the ability to think on his own and make decisions accordingly.

Awareness of the global events: Forex markets are affected by the major international events that occur. The key economic events happening globally as the forex markets are traded globally and affected by these economic events. A few examples of the key economic events are Federal Bank interest rate decision, ECB rate decision, GDP data of key economies, job data of key economies, inflation data of key economies etc.

Never blame the market: The market might behave irrationally but the trader should be responsible for reading the market cues and making trading decisions. Instead of playing the blame game he should learn from each mistake and learn from it. The trader should understand the risks associated with trading and have a proper money management rule in place.

Trading journal: It is important to maintain a trading journal and make an entry of all the trades he makes. The reasons for taking that particular trade should also be noted down. This would help in analyzing the trades later and help in avoiding the mistakes made. This would also help in identifying the good trades made and look for similar patterns later on.

Choosing the right broker: It is important to choose the right broker. Some of the factors that should be considered while selecting a broker should be a) low brokerage b) fast and reliable trading terminal c) ease of trading and good research and charting software's that the broker provides.

Money management rules: This is perhaps the most important among all things that are mentioned till now. A money management rule is basically the rules that define the maximum loss a trader can afford to take per trade or at a point of time. Most forex traders never risk more than 2- 5 % per trade. They also never risk more than 10-20 % at a particular point across all trades. It is very important to follow these rules; else you run the risk of wiping out your entire trading account in a matter of days, if not hours! It is always better to limit your losses and live to fight another day!

CHAPTER 18:

How to Understand and Analyzed Charts

The charts used in Forex are similar in a superficial sense to the charts that you may have seen on the stock markets. Typically, Forex traders are going to be using candlestick charts. In fact, this is almost a universal practice. So, the first thing that a beginning Forex trader needs to learn, beyond the basic fundamentals, is how to read and understand Forex charts.

Remember What the Chart Is Charting

This sounds like a crazy statement, but you have to remember that the currency pair A/B means that if the value shown in the chart increases, this favors the currency A. What this means is that the value of currency A is increasing relative to the value of currency B. You can also look at it in the sense that if the graph on the chart is increasing, the value of currency B is decreasing.

So, if you buy the currency pair A/B, and the increasing graph or upward trend is a trend that is working in your favor.

Now consider a downward trend. When the trend is going downward, you are losing money if you had bought the currency pair A/B, because this means that the value of currency A is decreasing relative to currency B.

Where some new traders get confused is when you sell the currency pair A/B. In this case, the meanings on the chart are reversed, because if you sell the currency pair A/B, this means that you are betting on the currency B. So, when the chart is un an upward trend, if you had sold the currency pair you are losing money. This is easy to understand. For the sake of simplicity, let's say that you had sold the currency pair for $1. To exit the position, you have to buy back the currency pair. But if it increases in price to $2, then you would lose $1 buying it back. The values given here are for illustration only, but it nicely illustrates the general concept.

Now consider the opposite situation. That is, we are still talking about selling the currency pair A/B, but this time we see a downward trend on the chart. This means that the price of the currency pair is decreasing. We can, of course, frame this result in many ways. One of the ways that we can do so is to say that the currency B is increasing in value, with respect to currency A. Now let's say that once again we sold the currency pair A/B for $1. Now we imagine that is has decreased in price to $0.50. Then we can buy it back, and we make a $0.50 profit.

Of course, these prices are not realistic for a Forex trade, but it clearly shows the concept of how this actually works. If you understand the concept explained here, and you've understood how to read the change in pips from the chart and how to convert that into dollars moved based on your position size, then you are well on your way to becoming a Forex trader who at least understands what is going on.

What is a candlestick

The next thing to come across is the use of candlesticks, which you always see on Forex charts. A candlestick is a graphical way to represent price action. By price action, we simply mean how high did the price go, how low did it drop, and what the opening and closing prices were. The candlestick charts also give a visual representation that we can eyeball, in order to see at a glance whether the price went up or down for a given time period.

So, what each candlestick represents is a "trading session." The trading session can be one of many different lengths of time. Different traders are going to choose different lengths of time used for the trading sessions shown on the chart, depending on what their needs are. Some traders are interested in very short time frames, so they may use one-minute trading sessions. Others are going to use 5- or 15-minute trading sessions. You can also use 4-hour trading sessions or even one-day trading sessions. It's up to you to decide what time interval to use, and this is going to be decided in part by your trading style.

Before we show the basics of a candlestick, you need to understand how and why these are used. The basic idea that is behind the candlestick is to have a visual way to look at the chart and determine whether or not there is going to be a price reversal. Price reversals and trends are the bread and butter of this business. The first thing you are going to want to look for when you are trading currencies is if there is a trend one way or the other.

If there is a strong upward trend and there are signals that the trend is going to continue, then this is a currency pair that you want to buys. Conversely, if there is a downward trend, this could be a currency pair that you want to sells. This little fact that we have described is one important way that Forex trading differs from stock market trading, at least for most people. Granted, there are many people who trade options or who short stock, and they will make more complicated market plays. But you see with Forex that it automatically offers you ways to make money, no matter which way the market is moving. It's always in pairs, and you don't have to be wedded to one single currency.

That means that you don't have to be focused only on the dollar and hoping that it's going to always rise with respect to the Euro. As a Forex trader, you really should not care which direction the currency is moving. You can earn profits either way. The only time you care about which direction it's moving is after you've entered a position. Then and only then is the time that you need to be concerned about this issue.

Trend reversals are really the important thing to look for. If the market has been in a downward trend for some time, and you have been sitting on the sidelines, you are going to be looking for a trend reversal. It's never a good idea to get involved in a trade when it's too late. If you have been following the currency pair A/B and the currency pair has been in a long-time downtrend, even if you like the currency B, you are probably better off waiting for a reversal, and buying the currency pair, rather than joining the trend late in the game. So, in this example, when the candlesticks gave you the signal that the trend was reversing, you would buy the currency pair. The trend reversal signal would indicate that the downward trend has come to an end, and now is the time to get in a position in order to take advantage of the coming upward trend.

Structure of a Candlestick

The candlestick has three parts. The first part is the rectangular area that is found in the center of the candlestick. This is called the body. The body of the candlestick tells you the opening and closing prices of the trading session. However, there are two types of candlesticks. Traditionally they are black and white, but I am going to skip over that because who uses black and white charts anymore. I can assure you that almost nobody does.

The background of most charts these days is either black or white. We are going to take the latter possibility, first because most Forex traders actually use black background charts. But you can use white backgrounds and some traders too.

There are two types of candlesticks. A candlestick can indicate that the price dropped for the trading period, in which case it is called a "bearish" candlestick. Or the candlestick can indicate that the price increased over the trading period, in which case it's a bullish candlestick.

On a chart with a white background, a bearish candlestick is red in color. A bullish candlestick will be green in color. On a black chart, the bearish candlesticks are usually solid white, and the bullish candlesticks are the green outline.

That is all pretty basic to understand. Now let us use a basic fact to explain the price action described or illustrated by a candlestick. If there is a bearish trading session, that means that the opening price was higher than the closing price. As a result, the top of the candlestick body – which is a higher pricing point – represents the opening price for the trading session. In contrast, the bottom of the candlestick, which is the lower price on the chart, represents the closing price for the trading session.

A bullish candlestick works in the opposite way. A bullish candlestick indicates that the price went up during the trading session. So, the top of the candlestick is the closing price for the trading session. The bottom of the candlestick is going to be the opening price for the trading session.

A candlestick has lines that come out of the top and bottom of the body. These lines are called shadows or wicks. They have the same meaning whether or not the candlestick is bullish, or whether it's bearish. The wick or shadow coming out of the top of the candlestick body tells you the high price of the trading session. The bottom wick tells you the low price of the trading session. The basics of candlestick setup are shown below.

CHAPTER 19:

Technical Analysis

What Is Technical Analysis?

Let's begin by understanding what technical analysis means. In financial markets, technical analysis refers to the study of the patterns of prices of particular assets. Basically, there exist many ways with which technicians use to identify patterns in the market. However, the following are the common ways;

Technical analysis chart patterns

This analysis involves the use of technical drawing tools like Fibonacci levels, horizontal and trend lines for the identification of classical chart patterns. The patterns identified can include consolidation patterns and symmetrical triangle formations etc. These patterns are important in giving clarity on the strengths and weaknesses of buyers and sellers in the market.

Technical analysis of candle patterns

This method involves the use of technical analysis charts like candle charts where the price levels (such as high, low, open, close) of a given timeframe with the goal of identifying the characteristics of buyers and sellers within a given time period.

Technical analysis indicators

This analysis method involves the use of price action indicators to provide a detailed understanding of the market condition. For instance, indicators will provide signals when the market is overbought or oversold. Some indicators will provide signals when there is rising or falling momentum.

Forex Technical Analysis

The Forex market is very liquid. This means that it attracts all types of traders ranging from one-minute traders to daily traders. Forex technical analysis supports all these different types of traders involved in the market. All the different types of technical analysis, including chart patterns, candle patterns, and indicator is used in Forex technical analysis. As a beginner, we prefer that you download MetaTrader 4. MetaTrader 4 best fits the needs of a beginner because it supports multiple languages, has advanced charting capabilities, trading is automated, it can be fully customized, and you are able to change trading preferences based on your needs, for example, you can customize it to technical analysis, or provide you with trading news.

Does Technical Analysis Work?

In most cases, as humans, we tend to have limited time and focus; thus, when analyzing these factors, we are likely to make errors in the cause and effect. However, with technical analysis, a more reliable way that comes with the short-cut is provided to analysts.

Technical analysis is also referred to as chart analysis. With chart analysis, traders are able to analyze historical price movements.

The Basics of Technical Analysis

As a trader, here are some of the basics about technical analysis that you should have in hand.

· Price action discounts everything

The technical analysis derives its logical framework from Dow Theory. According to Dow Theory, the price of an asset accurately reflects all the relevant information about the asset. This means that any factor that impacts on supply and demand by default will end up on the chart. When it comes for the case of researching or the events outside price action, Dow Theory renders them useless because these are things that cannot be quantified thus may give unreliable data.

· Price moves in trends

As observed, most technicians are always seen to favor trends, including the nature of the market. This is another reflection of Dow Theory. Basically, markets can move in an uptrend (bullish market). In such a case, it means that the market will continuously create higher highs as well as higher lows and the big picture which is the price, will be seen to be jumping up and down but mostly within an upward corridor. A bearish market has similar market behaviors as it is characterized by a downtrend of lower lows as well as lower highs.

There is also a ranging market which is a horizontal trend. However, this is a trend that is not desirable to trend-based traders. This is due to the fact that traders are not able to know what will happen next, particularly when faced with ranging periods. In a ranging market, the bulls and the bears somehow have equal powers; thus, there is no side strong enough to dominate the other for a long period of time. It is also important to note that Forex statistical analysis does not give major concerns on why things happen. This means that Forex statistical analysis will not look into why certain trends occur. Therefore, as a technical reader, it is important that you be able to understand this. Most technicians do not know how to quantify answers because they often feel that trends are empirically proven facts.

The Pros of Technical Analysis

· Traders using forex technical analysis only need to have a few basic tools. In most cases, these tools are usually free.

· Traders using forex technical analysis are sometimes offered with high probability directional views as well as the entry and exit points from the market.

· With the advancement in technology today, traders are able to choose technical analysis tools and indicators they wish to use in helping them identify the available trading setups.

Disadvantages of Technical Analysis

· Technical analysis is widespread and widely used. Therefore, Forex technical analysis can sometimes trigger abrupt market movements, particularly when many traders come up with the same conclusions.

· There are complex markets that technical analysis fails to cover some aspects, thus calls for the combination of technical analysis and fundamental analysis.

CHAPTER 20:

Fundamental Analysis

When you are trading in stocks, the area is very limited. You only have the task of looking into the financial reports of the company and ascertain the financial health of the company. Believe me when I say this that even on that, most people fail. Although the data is comparatively smaller to look at most people, fail to see a clear picture of the state of the company.

When it comes to understanding the fundamentals of a currency or the economy on a macro level, the task gets bigger and more tedious.

Does that mean you can ignore fundamental analysis?

Some traders believe that if they are going to buy a currency with a short-term outlook, then they do not need to go for the fundamentals of a currency. However, this is a point where I think they are not being completely honest.

Although fundamental analysis is a tool mostly used by long-term investors like big importers exporters, professional traders, and hedge fund managers, it is something that you must understand.

Fundamental analysis of the forex is one area that gives you a clear insight into the health of currency in respect of the currency you are thinking of trading it with. It is important to understand that fundamental analysis helps you in understanding the way a currency is going to behave in respect of another currency. Therefore, you are just not trying to know if one currency would go up but also whether it would go up against the currency you are trading it with because this is where your money is.

A Peek into the Intrinsic Value of the Currency

This is a very important aspect of fundamental analysis. This study helps you understand the intrinsic value of a currency. On the surface, an economy can be looking perfect, but there can be many things that may change the outlook of the economy in the long-run, and this is you can lose money.

It doesn't matter that you are putting your money in that currency only for a short period as the market shifts are hard to predict, and they can start showing effect anytime.

There are 3 main goals of fundamental analysis in forex:

Long Term Goals: For this, developing a clear understanding of the economic, social, and political factors is very important. An economically, socially, and politically stable country will have a better chance of keeping the value of its currency stable. Wars and natural calamities can also affect the value of a currency. The forces that drive the market like central bank announcements and the government policies also affect the value of a currency in the long term, and that's why it is very important to keep this data into mind.

Short-Term Goals: The emotions of the market also play a very important role in determining the value of a currency. If sentiments like fear and greed are driving the market, then the reasons behind them need to be understood. Things that lead to herd behavior in traders also need to be understood. Ignoring these factors can lead to losses. Many people who highly favor technical analysis are only interested in price action. They feel that markets already factor in all these things. However, the job of a trader is not to rely heavily on others as it is the money of the trader on the line and not of others.

Price Movement Prediction: It is correct that for traders, the only important thing is the movement of the price of a currency in their favor. However, this can't be a wild guess. On a broader scale, the price of a currency moves as per the demand and supply factors in relation to the counter currency. If, as a trader, you are not able to see it clearly and just rely on the price movement shown on the charts, you can be up for unpleasant surprises.

Therefore, fundamental is definitely a study of the intrinsic value of a currency, and it is done with a long-term view, but it can't be completely discounted by traders. As a trader, you must have a clear understanding of the currencies you are dealing with. You must know the demand and supply factor in relation to the counter currency, and that would affect the price movement eventually. The sustainability of an economy is a very important factor that must be kept in mind. No matter how small is, the time frame for which you might invest in the currency but ignoring these critical points can be dangerous.

Fundamental analysis helps you in building confidence about a currency. If you have knowledge about the fundamentals of a currency, you will be able to manage your risk in a much better way

Fundamental Analysis Helps in:

· Correct Analysis of the Economic Indicators: This is a very important thing when you are going to invest your money into a highly volatile market. The forex market can start moving very aggressively at times. If you have a fundamental understanding of the economy, you are far less likely to get very concerned.

· Better Outlook about An Economy: Through fundamental analysis, you are able to develop a better outlook about an economy, and it certainly helps your decision-making skills. This comes very handily when you are under emotionally pressurizing situations that are common in the forex market. If your fundamental analysis is weak, you will solely rely on the advice of others, which can be even more harmful.

· Comparative Analysis: This is one of the most important aspects of fundamental analysis and can help your trading decisions. Although fundamental analysis is mostly about the health of the economy and tells very little about the way the currency is going to move on an intraday trade, this fact cannot be discounted that it also gives you a clear picture of the general trend of the currency. You are going to trade two currencies, and the most important thing that would concern you is the way they are going to move against one another. Demand and supply factors play a very crucial role in it. By doing a thorough fundamental analysis, you will be able to identify these factors clearly, and they will help you greatly.

You Can't Use Fundamental Analysis for:

Determining the Entry and Exit Points: This is a thing that must be very clear in your mind. The fundamental analysis gives you a clear idea of whether you should take a position in a currency or not. For a long-term investor, this is a crucial science. For a short-term investor, this is a good knowledge point, and it helps in building confidence. However, it can't be used to determine the entry and exit points. The price at which you can enter into a trade and the price at which you must book your trade are a few things that are beyond the purview of fundamental analysis.

Important Indicators to Consider for Making Fundamental Analysis of the Currency of a Country.

Non-Farm Payrolls: These indicate very important trends in the economy. This data can reflect the rate of economic growth and inflation. An expanding non-farm payroll is obviously great for an economy.

Interest Rate Changes: Interest rates are declared by the central banks from time to time, and they are very important as higher interest rates would obviously attract more investors. The currency valuation may go up, and there will be a higher demand for that currency. Lowering interest rates would have the opposite impact.

Inflation Rate: Higher inflation means that the currency in a country is losing its power, and people are being forced to pay more for buying the same number of things. It affects the value of currency negatively.

Retail Sales Data: This data is also indicative of the health of the economy. The analysts get an insight into the revenue earnings of the businesses in the country and liquidity.

Housing Data: This data reflects a positive or negative trend in the country. If the housing data is positive, it shows that the economy is moving up steadily, and hence the opportunities to invest in forex are good.

Trade Balance Data: This data is indicative of the foreign exchange reserves maintained by a country. This data has a direct impact on the demand and supply factor.

GDP: This is indicative of the overall growth of an economy. The better the GDP, the more positive it would be the long-term outlook about that economy.

Business and Consumer Confidence: This again shows the general outlook of the market about an economy. It can have an inflationary effect. Declining business and consumer confidence would show a slowdown in the economy while increasing business and consumer confidence shows positive growth.

CHAPTER 21:

The Most Common Mistakes to Avoid

Mistakes to Avoid in Forex Trading

Skipping the Trading Plan

Trading without a plan is in effect gambling with your investment and is likely to wipe you out. Plans are essential for success in any business venture and forex trading is no exception to this rule. To become a successful currency trader, you need to have a clear vision, meaning that you should have a good idea of possible market moves, strategies that you will use and the trades you plan to execute.

Overtrading

Overtrading is a common mistake that both novices and seasoned traders make in the forex market. It is usually a result of emotions such as greed where you are trying to reach a specific target and thus end up making more trades than you should. Revenge is also a common factor for over trading where a trader is trying to recover from losses by trading more and more, the net of this is that you end up making even more losses and may eventually wipe out even your trading capital.

To mitigate the effects of over trading, it is important to plan ahead on the number, duration, and frequency of trades that you will make over a certain period of time. This will act as your guide and help you in avoiding the emotional influence that can cause you to trade more than you should.

Over Leveraging

The power of leverage works in two ways, this means it increases your potential losses in much the same way it magnifies your potential profits. Leverage also exposes you to heavier losses because when you over leverage you are in effect playing with more money so in case of a loss you will lose more. Further, leverage is a constant liability to the forex trader because the leverage amount must be paid whether you make profits or loss on your trade. It is also important to remember the leverage attracts interest and in the long term, this cost will accrue.

Determining the correct level of leverage will be instrumental to your trading success. To keep your leverage within acceptable limits and minimize your risk exposure, simply consider the following;

- Use stops to limit exposure.
- Keep trades small.
- Limit capital per trade.

Poor Risk Management

Risk and rewards are natural components in the forex market. Poor risk management leads to losing money in forex trading and it can even mean losing even your trading capital. Making money should be secondary in terms of goals, your primary focus should be holding on to your trading capital because without capital you will essentially be out of business.

Risk management is an essential part of the strategy of any trader who wants to succeed in forex trading. Some basic tips for effective risk management include

- Investing only what you can afford to lose
- Knowing your limits
- Setting a Risk Reward Ratio
- Limiting your risk per trade
- Choosing your leverage wisely
- Keep your risk consistent

Setting the Wrong Goals

Doing things, the right way might net you fewer profits but will be more sustainable in the long term. If you set making money as your only goal, especially at the early stages of your forex trading venture, chasing the money may soon become the very reason for failure. Chasing money will more often than not cause you to break the rules of your trading plan in an attempt to make more money faster.

Breaking these rules may once in a while you net you some profits but in the long run, it almost always leads to an empty trading account balance. Instead of focusing only on how much money you need to make within a certain period, focus instead on your strategies and processes. By improving your trading skills and strategies consistently you will inadvertently end up making money using good trading practices. Like most endeavors, in forex trading, the process is ultimately more important than the results in the long term.

Ignoring the Psychological Aspect of Trading

Psychology plays a big role in terms of avoiding making mistakes in trading forex. Emotions are a normal and ever-present factor in the human experience and pretending that negative or positive emotions will not influence your trading decisions and patterns are simply self-delusion. Understanding market psychology and yourself is a good starting point in recognizing and overcoming this mistake.

We have already looked at how overconfidence, fear, anxiety, and greed can impact your trading. It is therefore important to develop and adhere to a trading plan so that you avoid making emotional decisions when trading the market.

Giving up

Most traders who approach the forex market as a means of making a quick fortune eventually give up when they realize that success will not come overnight. It may be cliché but good things really do come to those who wait. Provided that you risk only what you can afford to lose, patience, persistence, and determination to succeed will eventually pay off and make your forex trading investment worthwhile.

It is unrealistic to expect that you will become a trading expert overnight so if you quit or give up at the first challenge you face you will be likely to be throwing away a potentially lucrative investment opportunity. It is prudent to await the growth of your skills and methodologies; this will come with the more experience and exposure that you will gain with time in the forex market.

CHAPTER 22:

Practical Aspects of Trading

Now that you know the basics of forex, it's time to learn about the practical aspects of trading. The first step is to open an account with a forex brokerage. These brokerages will essentially act as your intermediary with the markets, taking your orders and buying or selling currency on your behalf. You interface with your broker through a trading platform, which is a piece of software that lets you open and close, as well as manage, your market positions. It also comes with technical analysis tools such as charting software as well as providing you with important information like real-time currency quotes as well as an economic calendar that tracks political and economic events that can affect the markets. Trading platforms can be downloaded and installed on your computer or be web-based, allowing you to trade on any computer with an Internet connection.

What are the things you have to look for when choosing a forex broker?

How much leverage do they extend?

One of the things you may have noticed when looking at currency quotes is that price movements are typically very small. In order to make any kind of profit, you need to trade large amounts of currency. The standard lot size traded is 100,000 units, although smaller lot sizes are available such as micro lots that are only 1,000 units. Unless you have a lot of trading capital at your disposal you will not be able to trade a lot this big. Fortunately, brokers are willing to loan their traders money so they can trade using larger amounts of capital.

Thus, if a broker provides you with leverage of 50:1, you can trade $50 for every $1 in your trading account. This enables you to make larger trades and increase your potential profits; of course, the opposite is also true and you can potentially lose more money. Look for a broker that offers the largest amount of leverage since this will give you flexibility as to how much you can actually use.

How much is the initial deposit required?

Due to the highly competitive nature of the industry, these days many brokers allow you to open an account with a minimal first deposit. The type of account you open can also determine the size of the deposit; thus, you should also look at the different accounts offered and what their respective benefits are.

What are their policies for withdrawal and deposit?

To ensure that you have no difficulties dealing with your trading account, you should look at how your account can be funded and how you withdraw money from it. Typically, brokers provide a variety of options for how to make deposits and withdrawals, including using credit and debit cards, PayPal as well as other payment solutions such as Skrills or even through bank transfers. Remember that not all these options are available in your particular home country.

What investment options do they offer?

In order to ensure that you have the widest range of choices, you should look for brokers that offer the greatest number of currency pairs. They should offer not only the major pairs but also many of the minor pairs (those not crossed with the US dollar) as well. Of course, if you want to diversify your trading activities, you should look for a broker that also offers other investment assets such as commodities and precious metals.

How is their customer service?

To ensure that any issues you have with the broker will be speedily resolved, you should look for one that has reliable customer service that is open 24-hours a day. Ideally, you should be able to communicate with service representatives directly through live chat, but there should also be a variety of other ways you can reach them, including toll-free numbers and e-mail.

What trading platform do they offer?

The majority of brokers usually offer MetaTrader 4 or 5 as their trading platform, since this has become the industry standard as the most-used platform. Other brokers, however, may offer their own proprietary platform as an option. In addition, you might want to consider looking for a broker that offers both downloadable and web-based versions of their platform, as well as offering mobile versions that you can access from devices such as your smartphone or tablet.

Do they offer demo accounts?

Demo accounts allow you to make paper trades that don't use real money. Thus, you can practice using the platform to see if you feel comfortable with it. You can also use the demo account to test your trading system as well as sharpen your trading skills, before you start trading with a live money account. Brokers may offer demo accounts on an unlimited basis or only allow you to use them for a limited time.

How is the broker regulated?

Since forex brokers are not subject to regulatory oversight from government agencies such as the Securities and Exchange Commission, it is very important that you use those that have voluntarily signed up to be regulated by a reputable organization. Forex brokers that accept US traders should be members of the National Futures Association and registered as a Retail Foreign Exchange Dealer with the US Commodity Futures Trading Commission.

Outside the US, recognized regulatory agencies include the Cyprus Securities and Exchange Commission, the UK Financial Services Authority and the Financial Conduct Authority and the Australian Securities and Investment Commission.

What incentives do they offer for new members?

In order to convince traders to sign up with them, brokers usually offer a wide variety of bonuses and incentives. For example, brokers commonly offer a welcome bonus that matches the amount of your initial deposit up to a certain amount or offer you a certain amount of "free money" that you can immediately use to start making trades. However, you should understand that you are generally not allowed to withdraw the bonus and can only withdraw any profits you make from it, usually after meeting requirements such as trading the bonus a certain number of times.

In addition, brokers may offer rewards and incentives to encourage members to continue trading with them, such as bonuses for every additional deposit you make to your trading account as well as membership in a loyalty club that gives you points for every trade or deposit you make.

What fees do they charge?

Although brokers do not generally charge commissions and make their money from the spreads (difference between the bid and ask price) every time you trade, these can still substantially differ among different brokers. So you might want to look at the size of the spread. Even if the difference is only a few pips, this can still add up to a substantial amount over time and can affect your profits over time.

Opening an Account

Once you've selected a broker, you can open an account with them. To do so you will have to fill up an application form and provide some basic personal information as well as financial information such as your net worth and annual income. The broker will process your application and activate your account. You may also be required to fax or e-mail a copy of a valid ID such as a passport before the account is approved.

If the broker offers multiple account types, you will have to make an initial deposit depending on the type you want to sign up for. These accounts have different benefit levels based on the size of the initial deposit, so you can choose the one that best meets your needs. Regardless, you can only start trading once your trading account is funded.

These bonuses are usually in the form of a certain amount that you cannot withdraw but can only use to make trades. The profits you earn can be withdrawn, but only after certain conditions are met, i.e. the amount of the bonus has to be traded a certain number of times.

Before your account is active, make sure that you read any risk disclosures that are provided so you'll better understand the risks of trading. And of course, you should always read the fine print, i.e. terms and conditions.

Types of Market Orders

Once you have signed up with a broker, you can start making trades using the trading platform. This will let you familiarize yourself with how to use the trading platform to make trades.

There are two basic types of orders that you can make through the platform – market orders and limit orders. Market orders are those you make to buy or sell a currency at the best available price. But you are also provided with a variety of options that let you control when the order will be executed based on your strategy. For instance, if you want to enter the market when a particular price is reached, you can set a "Market Range" order that executes when the currency price falls within the range you set; otherwise the order is cancelled.

You can also set market orders that are "Time-in-Force" meaning that they execute at a certain time frame and when other conditions are met. For instance, the Immediate or Cancel (IOC) order ensures that as much of your order is filled as possible at the best market price. If the entire order cannot be filled, the remaining order is cancelled. Fill or Kill (FOK), on the other hand, only executes if the entire order can be filled at the best price available; if not, the order is cancelled.

You can also combine two market orders based on price levels through the One Cancels the Other (OCO). In an OCO order, you set two price levels, either of which can trigger the market order; when one is triggered, the other is automatically cancelled. For example, you want to trade the EUR/USD, which is currently at 1.1120. You want to buy at 1.1190 or open a selling position at 1.1090 to sell the currency short. If the 1.1190 price level is reached, a position will automatically be opened and you will buy the currency, which will cancel the sell order. If the 1.1090 price level is reached first, then the opposite happens.

Limit orders, on the other hand, are intended to protect you against losses or lock in your profits. The major types of limit orders are stop-loss and take-profit. When these orders are executed, your position is automatically closed and you exit the market.

To illustrate, let's say you are trading the EUR/USD currency pair long (buy) and it is currently at 1.2340. In order to protect you against excessive loss, you set a stop-loss order at 1.2300. Thus, if your trade goes against you, the stop-loss order automatically closes the trade when it hits 1.2300 in order to prevent your losses from becoming too high.

A variation of the stop-loss is the trailing stop. This means that you are essentially placing two stop-loss orders. When the first stop-loss level is hit, the second one automatically goes into effect. If the price of the currency pair hits this second level, it closes your position and you exit.

CHAPTER 23:

Forex Theories and Models

There are several theories and models behind the foreign exchange market. While you don't have to master them all, it is still ideal to understand the general ideas behind the research.

The primary economic theories found in the forex market are more about the parity settings. Basically, parity refers to the economic justification of the price at which the currency pairs must be traded according to important factors such as interest rates and inflation. According to these economic theories, if the parity setting cannot sustain, there is an arbitrage opportunity for market players.

But arbitrage opportunities, like in other markets are often immediately discovered and discarded before even providing the individual investor the chance for capitalization. Other forex market theories are based on economic factors such as capital flows, trade, and how the country is running its monetary operations.

Asset Market Model

In the Asset Market Model, you have to look into the flow of money into a country from foreign sources for buying assets such as bonds, stocks, and other financial assets.

If you see that the country is experiencing large surge of foreign investments, the price of its currency will rise as the domestic currency has to be purchased by these foreign investments. This model also considers the capital account of the balance in comparison to the present account.

This model is popular among forex investors as the capital accounts of countries are beginning to significantly surpass the current account as foreign money flow increases.

Balance of Payments Theory

There are two divisions in a country's balance of payments - the capital account and the current account. These two measures the outflows and inflows of goods and capital of a country.

In the balance of payments theory, you have to look at the present account that deals with tangible goods trade so you can get a general direction of the exchange rate.

One indicator that a country's exchange rate is not in balance is if it runs a large current account deficit and surplus. In order to adjust to this condition, the exchange rate should be adjusted gradually.

Look if the country is running more deficit (higher imports vs exports) as the currency is more likely to depreciate. Meanwhile, a surplus (higher export versus import) will lead to the appreciation of the country's currency.

You can determine the balance of payments of a country by using the formula below:

BCA + BKA + BRA =

BCA refers to the present account balance

BKA refers to the capital account balance

BRA refers to the reserves account balance

Economic Data

Economic theories could affect the movement of the currencies in the long-run. When it comes to daily or weekly transactions, forex players focus more on economic data.

Countries are often regarded as the largest companies in the world and that holding currency is basically getting a share of that country. Economic data like the current Gross Domestic Product (GDP) are usually regarded to be similar to the latest earnings data of a company.

In a similar manner that current events and financial news could influence the stock price of a company, news involving a country could also have a significant effect on the movement of the currency of that country.

Significant changes in the political condition, GDP, consumer confidence, unemployment rate, inflation, and interest rates could result in substantial losses or gains depending on the nature of the news and the present situation of the country.

The volume of economic news that you might need to monitor every day from around the world could be overwhelming. However, as you go along the forex market, it will become a lot clearer which news could have the largest influence. Below are several economic factors that are basically regarded to have the biggest influence in the foreign exchange market.

Retail Sales

The data on retail sales measures the volume of sales that retailers have gained during the period. This basically reflects spending in the country. The data does not cover all stores, but only monitors a basket of stores of different types to gain an idea on how people are spending.

This data will provide you a general ideal of the country's economic stability. In general, strong spending indicates a strong economy. In the United States, the retail sales data is released by the Department of Commerce once a year.

Employment Data

Another economic indicator that you should take a look when you are into forex is the employment data or the number of people who are currently employed in the country.

In the United States, this data is called non-farm payrolls and published by the Bureau of Labor Statistics every first Friday of the month. In most instances, strong increase in employment shows that a country is experiencing a strong economy, while the opposite means otherwise.

If a particular country is going through significant problems in the economy, strong employment data could affect the currency price, because it is an indicator that the economy is recovering.

Meanwhile, high employment could result to inflation, so this indicator might affect the currency price. To put it simply, the movement of currency and economic data will usually depend on the circumstances that are prevailing if the data is released.

Gross Domestic Product (GDP)

The GDP of a country is used as a measurement of all the completed goods and services that a country has produced during a specific period of time. Calculating the GDP is divided into four divisions: total net exports, business spending, government spending, and private consumption.

Economists regard GDP as the best measurement of the economic health of a country with GDP increases indicating economic growth. As you already know, a healthy economy entices more foreign investments.

This will usually lead to increases in the currency value, as the money moves into the country. In the United States, this information is published by the Bureau of Economic Analysis.

Durable Goods

Durable goods refer to those who can last longer than three years such as automobiles, gadgets, and home appliances. The data for durable goods is used to measure the volume of manufactured goods that are produced and shipped for a particular period of time.

This data will provide you a general idea of the amount of individual expenditure on these goods on top of the information on the health of a specific sector. In the United States, this data is published by the Department of Commerce.

Capital and Trade Flows

Transactions between countries build large cash flows, which could have a significant effect on the currency value. Remember, a country that is importing more than its exports may experience depreciation on its currency because of its need to bid its own money to buy the exporting nation's currency. Moreover, higher investments in a country could lead to significant increases in the currency value.

The data on trade flow takes a closer look at the difference between the exports and imports of a country. There is a trade deficit if the imports are higher than exports.

In the United States, the Department of Commerce publishes the trade flow data every month. This shows the volume of goods and services that the country has imported and exported during the last month.

Meanwhile, the data on capital flow focuses on the fine distinction in the currency volume that is surging through exports or investments to currency that is being offered for foreign imports or investments.

In general, there will be a surplus of capital flow if a country is enjoying a high volume of foreign investments where foreign investors are buying domestic assets like real estate and stocks.

The combined total of the trade and capital flow of a country is known as balance of payments data. This is divided into three categories: financial account, the capital account, and current account.

The financial account focuses on the cash flow between countries mainly for investments. The capital account focuses on the exchange of cash between countries for the purpose of buying capital assets. The current account focuses on the flow of goods and services between countries.

Macroeconomic and Geopolitical Events

The most extreme fluctuations in the foreign exchange market is often influenced by geopolitical and macroeconomic events such as financial crises, changes in the monetary policy, elections, and wars. These can all change or reshape the economic condition of the country, which includes its market fundamentals.

For instance, an election gridlock in a country could place a large strain on the economy of a country and may affect the volatility in the region and thus affecting the currency value. In forex trading, it is important that you are updated on these geopolitical and macroeconomic events.

Interest Rate Parity (IRP)

IRP is quite similar to PPP, because it suggests that there should be no arbitrage opportunities if the two assets in two countries have the same interest rates and the risks for each country is also virtually the same.

The law of one price is also the basis of IRP, because purchasing one asset in one country must also yield the same return as the same asset in another country. Otherwise, the exchange rates will have to be adjusted to bridge the difference.

Below is the formula for getting the IRP:

$$(i_1 - i_2) = \left(\frac{F - S}{S}\right)(1 - i_2)$$

F - Refers to the exchange rate in the forwards market

S - Refers to the exchange rate in the spot market

I1 - refers to the interest rate in country 1

I2 - refers to the exchange rate in country 2

In terms of interest rates, the most concentration by market participants is placed more on the bank rate changes of the country's central bank. This is used for monetary adjustment and establishment of the monetary policy of the country.

In the United States, the bank rate is determined by the Federal Open Market Committee (FOMC). This rate is used by commercial banks for lending and borrowing to the US Treasury.

The FOMC convenes eight times every year to discuss the current economic factors and decide whether to lower, raise, or not change the bank rate. Forex market participants should take note of the outcome of these meetings to guide you in forex trading.

Monetary Model

This forex model concentrates on the monetary policy of a country to help in figuring out the exchange rate.

The monetary policy of a country primarily deals with the supply of money in the country, which is determined by the amount of money printed by the treasury as well as the interest rate set by the central bank.

Countries that adopt a monetary policy, which quickly grows its supply will likely experience inflationary pressure because of the increased circulation. This may lead to currency devaluation.

CHAPTER 24:

Using Dividend Stock Screener

It's not easy to pick a dividend stock to invest in, which is why screeners are accessible to you with various parameters such that you can identify the particular form of stock you want to invest in. This is important to keep in mind that securities in which you invest will help you meet your financial objectives, revenue targets, and life goals. Using a portfolio screener, you will locate the dividend shares that suit your needs. Most blogs and brokerages sell you, dividend screeners, with their requirements. The stock or volume ratio, gross margin, PEG levels, dividend yields, and market capitalization will be checked at the dividend securities.

There are also dividend stock screeners that allow users to look at dividend growth in recent years. Using these choices, you can conveniently and rapidly draw up a shortlist of the businesses that match your needs. If the category of stocks is established, you can invest in the screener and have a forum for all the listed firms. There you have to analyze closely the underlying considerations such as whether short-term or long-term influences influence the stock. Looking at the dividend past, you can even have a clear idea of how the distribution is handled. There you need to find businesses that consistently raise their payouts, especially if you have a frequent growth in dividends.

Income stocks give investors a minimum cash flow source that provides reliable and large income returns. The dividend yield is also regarded as the dividend price ratio on every company's shares, whereby the dividend payments are taxable distributions, or the dividend price per equity is calculated by a business split up by the market value. Dividends based securities were found to be most valuable when used as a reliable source of profits. The dividend stock screener to select from should be able to list all companies which set up dividend shares in which to invest. This screener will also be easy to use and quickly browse across different stocks.

Since all of these screeners exist, it is interesting to look at any of the various screening places from past screener users. Often ensure that the criteria are well-sorted to render finding the correct screener simple.

Top Dividend Stocks to Buy Now

2 Most buyers around the world are searching for the right securities to purchase in these difficult financial times to acquire. This is especially relevant for recent purchases in the summer of 2011 with the imminent debt crisis in Europe. It seems like another major financial crash is a slim possibility if Greece and Italy don't get back on track. Nonetheless, for certain factors, this period is distinct from 2008, and the US banks are definitely much more capitalized today. We do not expect a potential slowdown or financial crisis and think the recent downturn in the economy would be a perfect opportunity to allocate high-income stocks to your investment portfolio.

Many people do not realize how good interest in stable dividend stocks can be, which offer big returns year after year. For starters, between 1970 and 2005, dividend paid stocks produced an average annual return of more than 10 percent. This is six percent higher than unpaid inventories registered in the same era. What essential is another six percent over 25 years annualized? You'd have produced enough to be a millionaire instead of $200,000 with an original expenditure of $50,000. Therefore, investing in any of our suggested dividend stock picks could deliver high dividends as well as double-digit development for the next five or six years. This could produce an annualized return of more than 20 percent.

Our opinion is that investors must have quality stocks that regularly pay cash dividends, particularly when there are current market volatility and a long recovery period. This is also a safe financial policy in prosperous and bad times. Over the last decade, everybody seems to have overlooked about dividends securities, but dividends remain the most significant way to earn money over securities in the long term.

While evaluating good dividend securities, we consider utilizing some significant main parameters. The first is that the business has a ratio of profits (PE) < 14. The traditional average demand is 15, and the current PE rate is 17. The PE level would then be willing to revert to the normal or recent average, and still get the demand upside down. The second goal is to demonstrate consistent progress over time with high annual incomes. The third is a major bonus because last year, the business has a tradition of consistently raising the dividend. There are a variety of other conditions for businesses that are valued at < 2.0 (historical average 1.94) and have a Product Revenue Ratio < 1.0 (historical average 0.86). A few other parameters are also helpful.

We concentrated on discovering a diversified collection of 10 really large dividend shares that are ideal for every retirement portfolio. Such businesses are inherently stable, and for years to come can have strong sales and steady growth.

10 Top Income Stocks to be Buy with Interest, Steady Development, and Reliable Dividends:

1) BBL - BHP Billiton (PE < 11)

2) BMS - Bemis Co Inc (PE < 12)

3) COP - Conoco Phillips (PE < 8)

4) DD - E.I. du Pont de Nemours and Co. (PE < 10)

5) EMR - Emerson Electric Co (PE < 12)

6) MT - Arcelor Mittal (PE < 6)

7) NSC - Norfolk Southern Corp (PE < 11)

8) PEG - Public Service Ent Group (PE < 13)

9) UL - Unilever (PE < 13)

10) UTX - United Technologies Corp (PE < 12)

Their estimated worth is the upside of at least 20 percent in 1 year. Research these firms and their finances to know how to locate these kinds of assets independently.

In the end, an investor would do well both today and in the future, by investing in a top dividend stock. Continue to read some of our reports on strong stocks to be bought in Brazil, China, and elsewhere.

Monthly Dividend Stocks

Monthly dividend securities are investments that every month of the year pay a dividend. If you're still an investor in dividends (or income), you realize that most dividend payout stocks payback of their shareholders every three months or every three months, and that such monthly dividend stocks are likely to be fresh to you. (There are also taxable dividend-paying inventories).

As a key feature of monthly dividend stocks, they are typically owned by businesses, trust firms, REITs, restricted partnerships or closed-end trusts in an income-generating fund and trading as individual stocks on daily stock markets (i.e., you may use the online discount broker to purchase them and sell them). It varies from other quarterly dividend paid stocks, which typically (but not always) are specific firms, monthly dividend stocks.

Since several monthly dividends generate profits from various outlets, they have relied on the diversification of revenue streams which can render their monthly cash dividend payments less volatile than individual business dividends-General Electric (GE), a big blue-chip corporation, will serve as a perfect illustration of the danger and in February 2009 it reduced its dividend of 68 percent. This is a very clear example of a business which is deemed one of the most financially stable in the country, which is commonly owned, tracked by multiple experts, which then cut its dividend, even when one year before it was reduced, most people assumed it should hold its cash payout to investors annually.

When you are an investment buyer in a monthly portfolio, make sure you do some analysis on what securities, bonds, or other properties that are generating income potentially generate for your chosen stock. When your stocks are concentrated in one sector, such as oil producers, and oil prices are reduced in that situation, your dividend payout (and the price of your monthly dividend stock) may decline in accordance with the oil price.

There is one form of monthly dividend store that deserves a special cautionary note for investors who are finding regular dividends in their portfolios. Although such inventories have a regular dividend profit tax, the rules of Canada have updated and will be applicable in 2011. In practice, the rules on such transactions have been modified such that they are regulated in Canada as normal companies (now not charging tax) starting in 2011. Such additional income taxes would lower the profits on these assets as part of the money provided by taxpayers as an annual allowance of dividends must also be charged to the Federal government for these new taxes. Please be mindful that 15 percent of these cash dividend distributions to US citizens are actually excluded by the Canadian government as a non-resident withholding tax, although US citizens may still qualify for a partial refund.

As you can see, monthly dividend inventories may be part of people who want dividend accumulation and a constant stream of profits, but as always, before buying into these inventories, you have to do your research.

Buying Dividend Stocks for Monthly Income

Investing in securities may be especially advantageous for citizens that intend to retire. You have to remember that making money from stocks so much relies on the sort of stocks you have invested in. Many inventories have distributions, although the distinction is the dividend payout size. There are stocks that pay dividends per quarter or year. The safest securities are those that offer dividends weekly. It is simple for you to schedule your retirement with the monthly dividends. You ought to grasp what dividends are and how they function before you venture into the practice of purchasing dividends.

CHAPTER 25:

Currency Futures and Cryptocurrencies

What Are Currency Futures?

Futures markets and easy access to the currency speculation they provide have been around for decades. So, I chose to put a little more emphasis on the relatively new and somewhat unknown world of FOREX. However, it is essential that traders fully understand the opportunities available to them in future currency markets. As you will see from this text, I am trying to be a champion of monetary speculation through centralized and regulated futures as opposed to ready-to-use products (FOREX).

Although the futures market is the most mature market, many novice traders are unaware of the possibility of speculating on currencies through futures. Even worse, they are not aware of the benefits of doing so. This is likely because futures markets have been overshadowed by the widespread and aggressive marketing techniques used by foreign exchange dealers to acquire new customers and gain a speculative market share from futures brokers. Nevertheless, currency futures are traded in abundance on the CME Group's Globex Futures trading platform and may offer a more liquid trading environment than most credits.

Like foreign exchange contracts, futures contracts are electronic contracts that create or receive the underlying asset at a particular future date. In other words, the seller of a future contract agrees to deliver the declared goods on a predetermined delivery date; the buyer of a futures contract agrees to receive the goods declared on the stipulated delivery date. The only variable in a futures transaction is the price at which it is made - and buyers and sellers in the market determine it. Traders often underestimate the big difference between traded shares versus leveraged futures trades and FOREX environments. When an equity trader buys part of a particular business, he buys an asset. As the owner of these shares, he is entitled to any future cash flow generated by the share, such as dividends and capital gains (assuming the stock is sold at a profit). Traders and futures do not trade or sell an asset; instead, they negotiate a liability that is derived from the underlying asset's value; thus, they are known as derivatives.

Unlike foreign exchange contracts, currency futures are delivered only four times a year, according to the quarterly cycle. As you may recall, currency traders technically deliveries to positions that have been occupied for more than two days but are forced to flip them daily to avoid making or receiving deliveries. Forex traders, on the other hand, only have to worry about rolling positions in March, June, September, and December. Scrolling is simply deleting a contract that expires and entering the next available contract month. For example, a trader bought a futures contract on the yen in December with the delivery of the underlying asset that was approaching, would sell a yen in December to exit the position and buy a yen in March to restore a long position. Again, this process is called rollover and must be run manually by the merchant. This is different from FOREX, where the broker automatically launches the customer's positions.

Contract expiration

Now, you know that futures contracts are expiring agreements between buyers and sellers of these contracts to trade the underlying currency. You also know that most speculators have little interest in participating in the delivery process. However, it is a bit more complicated to avoid the delivery obligations inherent in the conclusion of a future contract than to spend the day before your official salary.

The expiry of the contract is the day and time when a given month of maturity of a future foreign exchange contract is no longer negotiated, and the final settlement price is determined. That's when the delivery process begins. Except for a few obscure contracts, CME-listed currency futures are delivered four times a year on the third Wednesday of March, June, September, and December. If there is no holiday or other holidays, the last trading day for the CME coins is the Monday before the expiry date. As a result, traders should be outside their positions well before they expire. Traders who are not interested in creating or receiving the underlying currency should leave their positions on the last Friday, but preferably before.

The WEC publishes an official renewal date in which traders are advised to move from the due month to the month following the contract. The suggested date for doing this is exactly one week before the last trading day and probably does not prevent hitting the flock. You would not want to hold open positions until the last trading day because the market will likely have declined to this point. This will not only result in wider gaps between supply and demand but may also result in irrational volatility.

As a reminder, foreign exchange renewals occur daily, while renewals of futures contracts occur only four times a year. However, one of the advantages of FX trading is that your broker will automatically roll over your positions without you lifting a finger. A futures broker will not give you the same courtesy, but if you negotiate with a legitimate broker, you will do everything possible to inform you of the expiration of the contract and prevent the delivery process from occurring. While this may be among the most common fears among futures traders, accidental possession of positions during delivery is rare. If you make the mistake of triggering delivery, do not panic! It is repairable, but it can cost you a few hundred dollars to give up your obligation. This is something you would like to avoid.

Unlike currency transfers, which involve the inconvenience and potential cost of interest rate differentials, term traders should not be overburdened with credit and interest rates. The commission and the natural spread between the bid and ask minimal prices (usually a tick) are only the cost of a futures contract.

Futures markets have high standards

Without the standardization of contracts, buyers and sellers would be forced to negotiate the details of each transaction. As you can imagine, this would significantly slow down speculation and eliminate liquidity and market efficiency.

Despite significant differences in the size of contracts between futures and foreign exchange contracts, trading in both arenas uses standard contracts that can be easily purchased or sold in any order. In currency futures, there are three standard contract sizes. For example, futures traders have the opportunity to negotiate a full contract that varies in size (except for the yen and the pound sterling) from 100,000 to 125,000 units. A mini-contract is measured at half of the standard, and E-micro futures represent one-tenth of the size of the original futures contract.

How can a futures market guarantee every trade?

Once again, FOREX trades are subject to counterparty risk. If the person or entity that assumes the other part of your foreign exchange transaction is unable to fulfill your obligation, you can not be compensated by specific speculation especially if you trade through a trading desk where your brokerage acts as a market maker. As you can imagine, it is not always able to fulfill its financial obligations. This is especially true if you can accumulate significant profits, as this can result in huge losses for the counterparty. Such events are rare in frequency, but I think we can all agree that once, it's too much! It is not because it was not a common problem in the past that this will not happen in the future - and it is difficult to justify taking unnecessary risks in negotiations. It is hard enough to make money in the markets based on controllable factors, not to mention the fate of your trading account for the finances of others. REFCO, the well-known US-based FOREX broker that collapsed in 2005, turns balances into customer accounts in cents after the bankruptcy courts split the remains.

One of the most interesting features of futures is the foreign exchange guarantee. Each transaction canceled by a futures exchange is guaranteed; unfortunately, such a guarantee does not mean that you will earn money. Instead, it is the guarantee that, if you speculate correctly, you will be compensated for the deserved amount based on the price of entries and exits. Most traders believe that this will always be the case, regardless of the markets they trade and the broker they use, but this is not the case. FOREX traders do not have the same luxury of knowing that market integrity is always protected by applicable rules and regulations.

Although the NFA recently limited the leverage offered by currency brokers, they were free to provide clients with significant leverage. As wonderful as some traders thought it was, that's exactly why currency brokers could never guarantee business; excessive leverage is more risk to the counterparty and the trader. Futures markets stipulate and impose margin requirements for each foreign exchange contract at a rate generally greater than that of similar foreign exchange contracts. This allows them the risk management needed to provide operators with a performance guarantee.

Margin is a necessary nemesis; without ensuring that speculators have sufficient funds in hand to cover potential losses, stock exchanges and futures brokers run the risk that speculators move away from their trading losses to let them hold the purse. Even with the margin required on the deposit, it is possible for traders to lose more than the funds in their trading account (yes, this is possible with leveraged speculation, and this happens). If this happens, it creates a negative balance on the customer's account, called the balance owing, and gives rise to a chargeable customer of his brokerage firm. As a result, the role of the broker has been entrusted to the lender and not to the entity bringing together buyers and sellers. To strengthen the ability of futures markets to secure transactions, it is customary to keep the broker-dealer responsible for covering the client's obligations with the exchange until he can reconstitute the entire account. ... Where appropriate.

Term exchanges act as a bank, giving traders access to products of substantial value in exchange for a "payment" or a minimum margin. Fortunately, the rules that are actively enforced concerning the appropriate margin and the fact that futures exchanges hold brokerages accountable for their clients' debit balances contribute to market liquidity and stability attempts - a feature that real estate, cannot always portray.

On the contrary, while foreign exchange traders seem less exposed to the risk of counterparty default in the current environment, thanks to NFA's new margin rules which limit leverage to 50 to 1, these gap trading platforms seem to make currency futures much more advantageous. More attractive for FX

Now that we have made it clear that FOREX traders are subject to counterparty risk and that futures traders are not, let's look at the process that allows futures exchanges to guarantee transactions executed with a little more detail. As you know, to establish a position in the US futures market, an operator must have a specific amount of margin on the deposit. If the trader's positions change unfavorably to trigger a margin call, an adjustment, settlement, or deposit of funds is then required to continue the speculative game.

CHAPTER 26:

Basic Economic concepts, every Trader Should Know

Expansion – Recession

As the pace of business activity fluctuates, World Economies have always undergo their business cycle's changes. It is a currency trader's job for that matter, to recognize where in the cycle, each Economy around the World is, and to anticipate changes in the economic climate before it is apparent to the masses.

Economic Cycles are broken down into two main categories: expansion and recession. Expansions are corresponding with a strong and growing economy while recessions are defined by a decline in economic activities, which eventually results in suppressed growth.

These economic cycles create "risk-on," and "risk-off" market environments based on which investors allocate their money. To know where the Money flows, or correct to say in what currencies Money is flowing into, has great importance to us as Fx traders. There are certain currencies to be traded in each Market environment.

Expansion:

An economic expansion is a period of economic growth as measured by an increase in GDP as well as a jump in the level of economic activity. When a country's Gross Domestic Product goes up over a specific period of time, it is viewed as, having an economic expansion. An Economic growth takes place either as a natural process or through government interference - stimulation.

Generally, this is how it happens:

To create Demand or to add Money into a financial system, the Fed purchases Treasury bonds in the open market. By doing so, it swaps bonds for cash that investors put in banks. In turn, the financial institutions are more willing to lend out this excess of Money. Low-interest rates, accessibility of loans gives small companies and big corporations an opportunity to increase their business activities. For instance, acquire factories, purchase manufacturing plants and equipment, and hire more employees, so they can produce more goods and services.

To create supply, the Fed can change its Reserve requirements or lower Interest rates, thus taking Money out of the System. Interest rate manipulation is among several tools the Federal Reserve uses in managing the Economic cycles.

Key features of an Expansionary cycle:

- Higher disposable incomes
- Rising employment
- Increased consumer spending
- Household demand rises
- Business production increases
- Rising sales
- Better Wages

Summary:

Consumer + Business, and Gov. Demand rises

Recession:

A Recession is a considerable decline in economic activity commonly defined as a drop in GDP for a couple or more back-to-back quarters. As a result of the Recession, the following areas of the Economy are negatively affected: stock market, housing market, labor market and the list goes on. In this type of environment, cash supply starts to diminish as businesses and customers restrict funding and spending. The lower spending usually results in higher unemployment.

Companies may still show earnings as they sell off inventory, but eventually deteriorating economic climate catches up with them.

Clearly, the Recession is not good, however; it is not as extreme as Depression. Generally, it is considered that if recession lasts long enough, then it might be classified as a Depression.

Key features of a Recession cycle:

- Businesses cut their production
- Workers work less
- Lower disposable incomes
- Companies eventually Fire
- Higher unemployment rates

Summary:

Consumer+ Business and Gov. Demand declines.

Inflation – Deflation.

Inflation:

Whenever the overall price of products and services rises, it is claimed that Inflation is rising as well. Inflation measures by how much the normal rate of prices on goods and services increases over time period. Rise in inflation is frequently triggered by the oversupply of money, in other words, when we have too much Money chasing fewer goods. Central Banks attempt to avoid an extreme increase in inflation, because as the cost of goods and services rises, so does the value and the purchasing power of the currency fall. That means Consumers and Businesses are able to purchase less since the rise. The Inflation rate constantly changes based on circumstances; however In the United States, the Fed makes an effort to keep a certain level of inflation, which is usually 1-2%. Commonly Inflation is assessed by the economic indicators such as Producer Price Index and Consumer Price Index.

Deflation:

Logically, deflation is the opposite of Inflation it happens when prices of goods and services are falling. When we have a reduction in the supply of money or credit, we have cause for the decline in prices, leading to a possible deflation. Simply put, deflation is when too little

Money is chasing too many goods. It is also important to mention that deflation is affected by spending or to be exact, the lack of Government, Private sector and Investment spending. At times, deflationary forces can hit the Labor sector fairly hard by increasing unemployment level as the overall demand in the Economy decreases. On the other hand, deflation makes more affordable to struggling consumers items such as food, fuel, and housing.

GDP - Measuring the Economy

Gross Domestic Product (GDP) is the overall value of the products and services a country generates in an entire year. Federal Reserve or the Fed utilizes the GDP as their gauge of the Economy. To be more exact, the Fed evaluates the growth of the GDP each quarter and uses as a benchmark of Economic growth. The Fed also uses the growth rate to choose either to apply an expansionary monetary policy to fight off recession or contractionary policy to control Inflation. Gross Domestic Products is also used as a way of measuring the size of a country's Economy.

The key word here is the "growth rate," which is the percentage increase in the economy's output from quarter to quarter. It evaluates how fast the economy is growing. Now, why is this so important? GDP growth rate is the most relevant indicator of economic health. When the economy is expanding, meaning - jobs, business activity, government spending, personal income increase, it reflects in positive GDP growth rate. Investors compare country growth rates to discover the best venture opportunities. In addition, Investors evaluate the growth rate to determine if the economy is transitioning from one state to another so they can readjust their capital allocation.

Bottom line:

GDP represents the Economy, the four components of GDP to be precise. GDP formula as follows C+I+G+NE where:

C= Consumer consumption - the biggest, percentage-wise, and by far the most crucial component which includes Retail Sales.

I= Investment – business investment: construction, manufacturing and inventory levels.

G= Government spending.

NE= Net exports - this depends if the country is Importer or Exporter.

Balance of Payments

The Balance of Payments presents the total of trade balance, foreign trade activities, and balance between import-export. Simply put, balance of payments is the track-record of a country's transactions with the rest of the World. The Balance of Payments is considered to be positive when incoming payments exceed outgoing to other countries and economies. The excess is a positive factor for growth and strength of the domestic currency. There are two parts to the Balance of Payments, Current Account, and Financial Account.

The Current account measures a country's trade in capital as well as import- exports of goods and services. Basically, it is a country's net income, trade balance, and direct payments. Current account is in balance when businesses, government, and consumers have sufficient income and savings to fund business growth, infrastructure spending and purchases in the country. The objective for most countries is to bring more earnings by exporting more goods and services than it imports. When this happens, it creates a surplus in trade balance. Deficit occurs in the opposite, when a country exports fewer goods and services than it imports and also, this is important; it takes less capital from foreign investors than it sends out.

The Financial account measures International ownership of assets. To be exact, the financial account evaluates the change in international ownership of assets. It allows you to find out if the amount of assets held increased or decreased. It must not be mixed up with the current account's income, like dividends and interests, which are earned on these assets. The assets include securities, such as bonds and stocks as well as commodities. The owners can range from individuals up to central banks and the governments.

The financial account further divides into two categories. The domestic ownership of foreign assets and the foreign ownership of domestic assets. When domestic ownership increases, it adds to a country's financial account. In case if the foreign ownership rises, then it subtracts from the financial account.

The importance of financial accounts is due to the fact that it is a large component of balance of payments, and it can offset a trade deficit when it has a significant enough excess.

Trade & Capital Flows in relation to FX Market.

Trading services and goods between countries constitutes Trade flows. There are countries that are net exporters, for instance, Japan, China and net importers like the USA and the Great Britain. Naturally, exporters trade more to international clients than they import from international producers. Understand this, when worldwide clients must buy exporter country's products and services, they must transact in that country's currency; they need to exchange their money for the other. This process creates demand for that country's currency as cash flow is being injected regularly. Good example of this was the Japanese currency in late 2003, when despite the economic weakness, it's value appreciated because of very strong exports. For the countries that are net importers, as they import more from international producers, the currency depreciation would be the case. In order to purchase international goods importer have to sell its domestic currency and buy a foreign one. Please note that a country might be a net importer in one area, but be a net exporter in others.

Example:

The UK imports mostly finished manufactured goods but export basic materials, food, beverages, financial services and business services.

Bottom line: trade in goods and services are the largest component of the above-mentioned Current Account. For that reason, a trade deficit is usually enough to create a current account deficit which occurs when a country imports more goods and services than it exports.

Capital flows distinguish money sent from overseas investors as they allocate their capital in foreign Markets. A country might have either a positive or negative capital flow. A positive capital flow means that investments from foreign sources exceed that country's cash outflows into other economies. More money comes in instead of leaving. Investors have to change their money for the currency of the country they invest into. As more money comes in, it creates demand for that country's currency. More demand means more value. The opposite is true for the negative capital flow. When a country has a negative capital flow, it causes to lose value of their currency. As demand for the currency decreases so does the value. Countries that experience economic growth, especially growth in financial market; offering high-interest rates on their financial assets, tend to attract a majority of foreign investors. As the foreign investments flow into the country, demand for the currency increases as well as the valuation.

CHAPTER 27:

Forex Trading Questions

Fundamental versus Technical Analysis

Should you use technical or fundamental analysis? Well, it is up to you to decide. But don't focus on entirely one. If a trader uses technical analysis but forgets to consider fundamental analysis, then that is not the best trader. Fundamental analysis impacts the forex market, especially major news. Many traders close all open trades before the release of any important news.

The Naked Trade and Price Action

You should give a try to one. Most indicators are computed based on the change in price. You will find traders who don't know how to read data from a chart. So, the most important thing is to disregard all indicators, moving averages, and other chart indicators. Focus on the naked chart. That way, you'll see the price movements and make your decision. Naked trading will help you to learn more about price action. You will see first signals from price action and later from price indicators.

What is the level of risk in forex trading?

Like any other type of investment, there is a risk in forex trading. Since the currency market is volatile, it can experience sharp changes in prices. That is why you are advised to conduct thorough research, and if possible, consult a financial advisor before making any move.

It is also good to note that there are scammers out there who pretend that they are certified brokers. As a result, you should carry out due diligence on any broker that you want to work with. New traders should verify that a broker is registered with certified bodies.

How can you trade a currency that you don't have?

You may want to trade a currency that you don't have. Don't worry; there are a few ways to do so. There are contracts that you can get into to invest currencies that you don't have. For example, it is possible to trade the euro without owning it by selling or buying options that include the currency. Besides that, if you purchase spot contracts or forward contracts that include your currency of choice, it may provide you with the right exposure.

Stay Away From Magic Trading Systems

The internet has many things about forex trading. For example, there are ads created that promise efficient automatic trading systems. Don't be deceived by these ads. Magic trading systems may just cost you to lose your money.

Main Forex Currency Pairs

Brokers have many different currency pairs. But the major four currency pairs used by traders include:

- USD/JPY
- USD/CHF
- GBP/USD
- EUR/USD

Which is the best Pair to trade?

If you are new, start with the major currency pairs because they have the lowest spreads. The EUR/USD is one of the best trading currency pairs.

How many pairs should you trade?

For new traders, you can start with one pair. Monitoring two or more pairs is hard. When you decide to trade with more than two, you will struggle to follow the price movements. To be safe, pick one pair, and stick with it.

Each pair has its properties. If you switch between currency pairs, you'll realize that.

How much money is enough to start forex trading?

Many new traders who want to start forex trading ask the following question. Remember. There are forex brokers who can allow you to open a forex account with as little as $100. But is that sufficient? Yes, but only when a broker has nano or micro lots. Also, if you want to make some good money trading forex, $100 is not enough.

You can't earn big if you're starting capital is $100. That amount is right only if you want to learn how to trade in forex. You can use this money to make a few mistakes, try out new things, and gain experience with forex trading. But don't risk your $100 if you aren't ready to lose it. A new rule with forex trading is to trade with money that you can afford to lose.

Nowadays, there are a lot of ads that promise one to make millions of money trading forex. If you want to be a millionaire, first, you must be ready to dedicate your time into forex trading. Next, you should have enough capital to help you make profits. So, how much is enough? That depends on the size of your pocket and how much you are ready to start to chuck in. A thousand dollars is not that bad. You can make some profit with $1000. But if you are serious enough, and you want to make huge profits, $10,000 is a good starting capital.

As you can see, capital is also the key to how much you can make in forex trading. So, always aim to start with a high capital.

How can I compete with big banks?

When trading, big banks hire experts who may have more knowledge and experience. As a result, you can gain a lot by doing your best to be ready. When you determine currency pairs, some traders apply fundamental analysis, which requires an individual to evaluate economic fundamentals in different nations. When you apply this technique, you can look at GDP, unemployment in two countries, inflation, and exchange rate. Also, you should use technical analysis, which requires interpreting charts to gain a better sense of the market sentiment on a particular currency pair. For instance, if you decide to take a long position on GBP/USD, you may need to work with some technical indicators to determine the currency pair's market history.

Traders can use both fundamental and technical analysis before carrying out any transaction. That way, they could increase their chances of successfully competing with banks.

Which time frame is the best?

New traders will want to know how long they should wait before they make profits. Well, that depends on your trading strategy.

Just know that if you set a low time frame in your trade positions, you won't have that time to analyze your decision. Once the price hits a given level, you'll start to see strong counter moves. If you want a swing trade, you must set high time frames such as 1 hour. Besides that, you should not focus on a single time frame alone. Consider higher time frames to give you time to monitor everything. Lower time frames may make you think like there is a downtrend, but higher time frames show that the main trend is going up.

How much can I make in a day

Many traders want to know how much they can make trading forex. Some think that they can be multi-millionaires in just a month. Others believe that forex is a platform for one to get rich quickly. Here is the truth. The psychology of forex trading is that brokers want more clients to register and trade. That is why you'll find compelling online ads that want you to join forex trading and make a lot of money. The truth is that many traders are losing money in forex trading. So don't join forex with that belief that you are going to be rich in just a week or even months. You have to be patient and be ready to learn the forex market. Additionally, if you look for stats about forex trading or follow favorite forex traders, you will come to learn that Forex is not easy as many people think.

In short, there is no fixed amount of money one can make trading on Forex. You can either make zero or even lose all your capital. It all depends on how smart you are going to be in the way you trade. There are days when traders make no profit because they are waiting for the best time to open their trades. Each trader has his way of trading. When a trader feels like the market isn't favorable, they close all their trades and watch the market for the right time to arrive.

CHAPTER 28:

Choosing the Broker

When choosing a broker for stock trading, all you need to do is look at their commission structure, and you're good to go. Simply choose the one that offers the lowest commissions, and once that's done, you're all set. With forex brokers, it isn't just the commissions you need to look at.

The slightly different regulatory framework governing forex brokers means that they can offer you more products to trade, but it also means that the line between fiduciary duty and self-gain becomes blurred a bit. Thankfully, things in the US aren't as 'wild west' as they are internationally, with brokers setting up in tax havens and disappearing overnight.

The main thing you need to look at is the honesty of the broker. That's really all it comes down to. There are a few ways of evaluating this, so let's take a look at them.

A/B Booking

Stock market brokers cannot and will not ever take positions against their clients. This used to be a common practice with stockbrokers back in the day, and the firms who did this were called bucket shops. The reason for this was that the firm would place all of its customers' orders in a 'bucket' so to speak and then move the market against all of them, thereby earning their customers' capital.

Bucket shops still exist in the forex world. In addition to this, even the honest brokers will not bother to be too friendly in the way they deal with you. For example, when the overnight swap rate is negative, you can bet that the broker will pass it along to you in full. When it is positive, it will magically be lesser, and they will find reasons to siphon some of it off due to new costs springing up. There's not much you can do about this, and you just need to bear it.

Either way, back to bucket shops. The way to spot a bucket shop is to identify whether they practice what is called 'B booking.' Every bucket shop has two order books. The A book is reserved for traders who know what they're doing or customers who don't know what they're doing but whose business is important, nonetheless. The broker cannot make money from such people and thus passes their orders along to their liquidity provider, which is a big bank, and onto the dealer network. Thus, the A book receives true market prices but pays slightly higher commissions on their trades.

Then there's the B book. This is reserved for those who have no clue what they're doing or have low capital levels in their account, usually under $10,000.

When it comes to the B book, the counterparty to your trades is the broker themselves. Why does the broker do this? Well, for one it isn't illegal to trade against your customer in forex. Given the higher leverage and the presence of CFDs, it is even justifiable to a certain extent since the broker needs to manage their risk.

The other reason is that the opportunity to make money is too good to pass up. As I mentioned earlier, over 90% of trader's wipeout in their first year. As far as the broker is concerned, the majority of people who sign up for an account will be gone in a year, so they might as well try to make as much money from them as possible. Given that such people don't know what they're doing, the easiest way to make money is to simply fade whatever they do.

The B book usually pays zero commissions, and this feature acts as a self-selecting attribute in many ways. Only traders who don't know anything about trading will think this is a good thing. The reality is that the B book orders cost the trader more since they'll be paying a larger spread than usual, and the prices they receive on trades are not actual market prices but are prices from the broker.

When you first sign up for an account, unless the broker makes it explicit, you will be placed in the B book. The way out of this is to make it clear that you know what you're doing by trading well and managing risk well. Once they find out that they cannot make money from you, you will be nudged towards the A book.

The best way of avoiding all of this nonsense is to, of course, not open an account with an A/B booker in the first place.

STP and ECNs

As an alternative to the A/B bookers, we have straight-through processing (STP) brokers and electronic communication network brokers (ECN). STP brokers are also referred to as direct market access (DMA) brokers. Let's tackle them first.

STP/DMA brokers rose initially as a marketing rebrand of A/B bookers. Therefore, there is a subset of brokers who are STP but still follow the A/B booking pattern. STP implies that all of your orders will go straight through to the liquidity provider and this will not be rerouted onto the broker's own books in order to trade against you. However, STP doesn't guarantee this as it is close to impossible to determine where the orders are going. Also, it isn't illegal in FX to do this.

However, a large number of STP brokers do push orders directly to the liquidity provider and thus offer fast execution at lower commission rates. Their dealing desks are usually automated and are only concerned with matching incoming orders with the offers from their liquidity provider. A single STP can have multiple liquidity providers, although the common practice is to have up to two since liquidity connections cost quite a lot of money.

The downside is that as a trader, you will receive the prices that are available to a small part of the FX market. Remember, no one has a full view of the market, but it is possible to look at prices existing in a majority of it by connecting to multiple liquidity providers (LPs). Thus, restricting yourself to a single LP doesn't guarantee that you'll receive the best price.

This is a problem for traders who trade huge amounts of volumes, and these traders prefer ECNs. An ECN is the same as an STP except that they have access to a far larger pool of LPs. Thus, the commissions you pay are higher, but the prices you receive will almost always be better than what you get with STPs.

As a trader just starting out, you're best off sticking with an STP instead of an ECN. You might receive slightly worse prices, but if you don't know what to do with a good price, there's not much point to receiving one in the first place.

Other Considerations

If I was addressing international traders, this would be a large part, but in the US, you need not worry about liquidity or jurisdictional concerns too much. Brokers in the US are regulated very well, and thus, you can be assured that your capital is safe. You will need to consider the costs of trading, though.

Costs are simply the commissions. Most brokers will quote you what is called a round trip price, which is the total commission for buying and selling a standard lot. You can expect to pay from $5-$9 for this. You may also see brokers offering no commission accounts. As explained before, stay away from these.

There are a lot of gimmicks that brokers use to lure people in. A common advertising trope that has been increasing recently is the promise to make your losses whole again. There isn't a single serious trader in the world who would expect a broker to compensate them for their losses, so safe to say, steer clear of such companies.

A lot of beginners complain about the fact that the prices they receive from some brokers are not good enough or that cheating of some sort happens. Here's the thing: If the broker is regulated by a respected authority, as all brokers in the states are, there is literally no upside for them to try and steal the $2,000 capital lying in your account. A lot of broker mentions this sort of thing, and a lot of them tend to be the results of mistakes committed on the trader's part.

Remember that your broker doesn't owe it to you to make the market simple or to provide you tips on how to trade them. They're there to execute your trades. Asking your broker for trading advice is like asking the salesman at Nike for fitness advice. Don't be the chump that does this. Do your homework and understand the risks involved.

Another key consideration for you is to look at the types of instruments the broker offers for trading. Having a wide variety of products is one thing, but if you don't know how to trade them, there's not much use in them being offered. So, let's look at how you need to go about trading and expanding your expertise.

CHAPTER 29:

Benefits of Forex Trading

The World's Largest Financial Market

I've already mentioned the size of the forex market in comparison to the whole world's stock markets. I say 'comparison' for lack of a better word. The truth is that there is no comparison. What benefits does a large size give you as a trader, though? Well, for starters, you are almost always assured of liquidity.

Liquidity is extremely important when it comes to trading because if there isn't a market for you to operate in, there isn't much you can do. Think of it this way: You head over to a market where vegetables are bought and sold and carry carrots with you. You've bought these carrots on the cheap and are sure that whatever price you receive will result in a profit for you since your costs are so negligible.

Upon reaching the market, though, you find that no one wants carrots. You have tons of the stuff with you, and now you're stuck with merchandise that no one wants to buy. The only other person operating in carrots knows the condition of the market and knows the price you paid for them as well, thanks to word getting around the small carrot market. The end results? You're left with the choice of hanging onto your stock or selling it to this person at prices lower than what you paid, thereby taking a loss.

This is an example of an illiquid market where one side has extreme dominance over another. It makes it far easier for a player to establish a monopoly on it and dominate the market. A fully liquid market has a large supply of buyers and sellers and thus, you need not choose between such hopeless options as above.

It stands to reason, then, that the larger the market is, the more players it will have in it and the lesser the chance of a single person dominating. A large market also opens up other opportunities in that a greater number of products will be traded in it. Thus, if one product isn't working out for you, you can safely switch to another and aim to make a profit there.

Aside from its size, another massive advantage forex trader have is that the market never closes, except on the weekends.

The Financial Market That Never Sleeps

If New York City is the city that never sleeps, then the forex market is the market that doesn't sleep. This is in contrast to the stock market which is usually open for eight hours per day and then shuts down. After-hours trading exists, but this is a fraction of what takes place during the market session. The closure of the stock market brings many risks with it, most notably gaps.

I've already defined what a gap is. When the market closes for a long time, there is a far greater chance of the next day's price not opening at the closing price. This is because opinions change overnight and new developments come to light. The longer you switch 'off' a market, the greater the chance of an overnight price gap.

With forex, this doesn't happen. The market is continuous, and thus the only gaps occur when Sydney/Auckland opens on Monday morning (local time). While the market is open all day, you should not make the mistake of thinking that volumes are constant along with liquidity and spreads. These keep changing throughout the day and depending on the session, liquidity changes for a pair.

The forex market has roughly four sessions each, with each session indicating when a major financial center is online. The first to open is Auckland, but the forex day is considered open at 7 AM Sydney local time. Next, Tokyo opens at 9 AM local time followed by London at 8 AM and then New York at 8 AM local time. Table one provides the open and close times, converted for time zones.

Session Name	EST Time
Sydney 7 AM-4 PM local	5 PM- 2 AM

Tokyo 9 AM-6 PM local	8 PM-5 AM
London 8 AM-5 PM local	3 AM-12 PM
New York 8 AM-5 PM local	8 AM-5 PM

Table 1: Forex Session Times

This time zone hopping will take some getting used to, but once you have traded for a few weeks, you'll know which center is open and which is closed. I would like to draw your attention to two facts. First, as you can see, Sydney opens almost as soon as New York closes. Next, you will see that the sessions overlap with one another, with Sydney and Tokyo having the greatest overlap.

Tokyo and London overlap for two hours, and London and New York overlap for four hours. These four hours are the most heavily traded portions of the day. You have the two biggest financial centers in the world slugging it out at the same time. The London and Tokyo overlap also sees significant volume increases, not least because London is the last European financial center to come online.

During that overlap, you have all of continental Europe and all the financial centers of Asia online, including Hong Kong and Singapore. Post the New York close, volumes dip drastically since you have just Oceania online. The Aussie and kiwi pairs see good volume, but the rest of the forex world is asleep. San Francisco is online for a while, but it really isn't comparable to New York in terms of volume.

Knowing the way, the forex calendar works is crucial to your success. The times you choose to trade will determine the pairs you wish to trade. In addition, it will also determine the style of trading you choose. For example, if you live in the Midwest, you're an hour behind New York. Usually, people need to be at work by 9 AM.

So, if you were to wake up early at say 6 AM, you can analyze the market and enter positions between 7-8 AM. You probably cannot day trade, but swing trading is a great option for you if you use the four-hour charts. You leave for work and return at 5 PM. New York has closed but you can assess how your trading day went from 6-7 PM and enter more positions between 7-9 PM when Tokyo is online. You go to bed and wake up the next day at 6 AM and repeat the process all over again.

When trading like this, it makes sense for you to trade the Aussie, kiwi, and yen pairs. Trading European crosses is not going to do much for you since you'll be operating during times when these just aren't active. Of course, the EURUSD will be active, but it doesn't make sense to trade the euro outside of Eurozone hours, does it?

You can see the flexibility that forex trading offers you. The stock markets are operational exactly when you're at work and thus, don't leave you much time for trading. This problem is solved for you with forex. The best times and pairs to trade depends entirely on your situation. Liquidity during market hours is never an issue unless you're trading exotics, and you're always going to get good prices.

It is really is the best of all worlds.

Considerations

When choosing times to trade, make sure to include adequate rest into it. The last thing you want is to be trading exhausted or half asleep. A lot of beginners think they need to remain glued to the screen throughout the day and keep adjusting their positions. Well, you need to do nothing of the sort.

Always take the time to relax and practice your skills before opening your terminal and analyzing the market. Just remember that you are not obliged to trade all the time. Real money is made not during trading hours but outside of them.

This is when you need to study your trades and make sure you're sticking to your odds and letting the math work for you. It is also when you will be taking stock of your mental state and making improvements to your strategies. Other considerations include the inherent volatility of some instruments.

Some instruments will just not suit your trading style, and no matter how hard you try, your profitability in them will be low. Switch instruments and keep trialing new ones. There are a large number of pairs out there, and liquidity is not an issue, so you will find ones that suit your style.

Speculation on Rising and Falling Prices

While all markets enable you to profit from both rising and falling prices, the dynamics of how this plays out in forex is a bit different. Before I get into that, let's talk about short selling. Short selling, or shorting, is when you sell an instrument before buying it. You're still buying low and selling high if you make money, but the order in which you do it is reversed.

Shorting requires your broker to borrow the instrument you're selling since you don't own it yourself. The maintenance margin for such transactions will be a bit higher because you will need to account for the borrowing interest. To close the position, you simply buy the instrument back. While all of this sounds complicated, the number-crunching takes place behind the scenes, and there's nothing special for you to do.

In stock markets, thanks to the truncated market sessions, bearish trends, where prices decrease, tend to be shorter and sharper than bullish trends, where prices increase. Often, stock market bearish trends will experience bigger gaps on open before suddenly ending and reversing upwards. This is because of the fact that retail traders, the smallest traders of the bunch, tend to not take part in bear trends.

In the forex market, bear trends tend to last longer even if they don't last as long as bull trends. While retail participation here is again lower, the fact that the market doesn't close gives you more time and opportunity to enter the trend and profit. There's no way to enter in a gap since there are no buyers or sellers there. Thanks to the absence of gaps in the FX market, you will receive better prices.

Another crucial aspect of the market is its decentralized nature, which is far more significant these days thanks to technological advances.

Conclusion

Many people are turning to trade in order to generate their income, invest in their future, or simply give themselves extra cash for the month. Whatever your reason is for getting into trading, you learned four different types of trading strategies. First, you learned positions trading, which allows you to hold your position for months to a year. Second, you learned about swing trading, which focuses on the position you hold for a few days to a couple of weeks. Third, you were given some information on day trading, which focuses on buying and selling all your trades in one day and finally learned about scalping trading, which is often called the minute strategy as you hold a position only for a few seconds to a minute or two.

Now you not only understand these four strategies better, but you also understand the basics of forex trading. You also understand the basic risks involved, have the know-how needed to achieve the winning mindset, know how to search for a trusted broker, and how to get a start and gain a profit.

To become a successful trader, you need to continue your education, studying in more detail the type of strategy you want to focus on. This means you have to read more books, research online, join at least one online community and begin talking to a mentor or to more experienced traders who are willing to help and guide you. Even though the market is competitive, people still want to help one another and make sure they have the best possible experience.

Above all, some of the most important steps to remember are the following: do your research, set your daily schedule, have patience, have the right mindset, and be self-disciplined. Also make sure you are paying attention to what the charts show you. You will want to note the candlestick charts, so you can understand if the price in moving in an upward or downward trend. You will also want to look at the trend charts, which will give you a variety of colored lines to explain how well the currencies are performing and if they would be a good fit for you. Taking into consideration all these different factors, you will become a successful trader no matter what strategy you decide to use. One of the biggest parts of becoming successful is believing you can be successful.

Through all the information you have read, you will be able to apply your favorite forex trading strategy. Through practice, you will be able to master your preferred strategy which will allow you to gain bigger profits. It doesn't matter which strategy you decide to use. What matters is that you are confident in your abilities and remain consistent with your strategy.

There are many websites online that offer you the possibility to try out Forex trading by using the trading platform in DEMO mode BEFORE you even start trading with real money, and such websites will have to become an integral part of your study as you explore this field of trade.

PART TWO

Introduction

One of the biggest hurdles new traders have to overcome is acquiring the mindset of a successful trader. This is even more prevalent in the cryptocurrency market because its sheer volatility allows the potential for large losses in addition to large gains. These losses can be discouraging for even seasoned pros, but the important thing to remember is that losses will happen (professionals estimate a 55:45 win/loss ratio for even the best traders), and how to deal with them when they do.

Acquiring a successful mindset is the single most important skill a trader must possess. More so than any technical tool. We must remember that we as humans have our own natural biases, and even delusions and these will hamper our trading ability. So the following is a list of important mindset and trading psychology factors that you must be aware of if you're going to become a successful trader.

Why is paper trading useless?

For years now, common trading advice has been that you should paper trade (trade with fake money) to get the hang of reading charts and learning when to buy and sell. However, I think this advice is limited at best, and even potentially harmful.

You need to make mistakes by risking real money so you can learn from these mistakes. Your brain and emotions simply don't react the same way if you know; deep down, that any losses you make are just on paper. To put it simply. *You need to lose money to truly find out if trading is for you.*

However, it's up to you how you react to these losses. Are you freaking out and trying to recoup them as soon as possible? Are you up until 4 A.M. trying to get back some of the day's lost cash? If the answer is yes, then trading probably isn't for you. However, if you can accept that everyone has bad days, by learning to analyze your mistakes and decipher where exactly you went wrong, you may well wind up as a successful trader in the long run.

Paralysis by Analysis

So, now that you've spent your time reading and studying charts, it's time to go to your preferred trading website and deposit money into your account. So you do so, and begin looking at charts, and you are waiting… and waiting. But you just can't seem to pull the trigger. This happens to a lot of new traders, especially those who are naturally risk averse. You want everything to go perfectly and you want to start out on a good note. However, this is trading that you need to make mistakes in order to get better.

This is also why you need proper money management in trading, because say you lose on 8 out of your first 10 trades (not uncommon by any means), you'll need to have properly managed your bankroll in order to be able to fight another day.

Knowing when not to trade

One of the more important qualities of a good trader is restraint. In other words, being able to understand that there are days where you don't need to make a trade. Maybe there are no obvious patterns appearing, maybe it's just a slow day in the market. Either way, you need to learn to take days off. This is good for preventing trader's burnout, especially in the 24-7 cryptocurrency market.

Accepting That the Market Is Always Right

One of our great cognitive biases as human beings believes we are better than we are at certain things. For example, are you an above average driver? I bet 90% of people will answer yes, but statistically, only 50% of people can be above average at anything, that includes trading as well.

What I'm getting at, is we often make excuses for our bad trades, such as the old classic "the market is wrong" excuse. The market will move in ways you don't expect, and if anyone had found out a way to truly predict market direction, they would be a retired trillionaire by now. Your technical analysis will not influence the market; it will only help you make better decisions.

Accepting that you are wrong

Following on from the above point. The market isn't wrong, you are. You need to be able to accept that you will be wrong on many trades, even multiple trades in a row. Remember; judge yourself by your results, and not on any perceived "clever moves" you may have made. You will always have losers, but you need to be able to take a step back and accept this in order to move forward.

Taking intermediate profits

If your profits are only on paper, you haven't made squat. You need to convert some of your gains back to cash from time to time. Taking profits helps you mitigate your need to win even more money. If you don't, this decision leads to greed taking over, which inevitably leads to losing money in the long run. If you enter a trade at $70, with a plan to exit at $80 because you see resistance there, then exits at $80. Don't let the coin go to $80 and then revise your plan and hope it goes to $100. There is no greater force that turns winning trades into losers than that of greed.

Survivorship Bias

Winners speak up, and losers stay quiet. If you spend any time in the trading community, you'll be constantly surrounded by stories from traders who turned $300 in $50,000 in just a few weeks. Or a 19 year old kid from Russia who made $200 million in under a year. Of course success stories exist, but there doesn't mean there aren't as many, and in the case of trading, even more, silent parties who lost money trading cryptocurrency. So the lesson here is to only measure yourself against yourself. If you're making continuous profits, then you're doing something right.

Recency bias

You're only as good as your last trade is something that many traders suffer from, especially if they have a run of losers. This leads to negative mental energy and a loss of confidence in oneself. What you need to learn to do is not focus on these losses, but look at the bigger picture. Instead of focusing on your next trade, focus on your next 100 trades. By focusing on the next 100 trades, you remain committed to your trading fundamentals as opposed to chasing short term results and dopamine hits.

CHAPTER 1:

Why You Need A New Stream Of Income?

Throughout the years, numerous people have thought about whether they can bring in money day exchanging. You are likely one of those people yourself. Have you at any point simply kicked back and considered how pleasant it makes your living day trading? You could bring in money while in your pajamas. You would be on your schedule without explaining to any chief. You could have the opportunity to do the things you need to manage without going through two hours a day trapped in traffic. Does this sound engage you? Provided that this is true, you should do everything possible to find out how to bring in money day exchanging.

As a matter of first importance, what is day exchanging? Does it imply that you need to make a considerable number of dollars every day? Do you need to win each trade? Not! Numerous day traders don't make a trade every day. The object of the game isn't to have the most movement. It's to get the most cash-flow! Like this, you shouldn't take trades each day only for taking trades presently if you can think of a methodology that permits you to bring in money every day exchanging, at that point, good luck with that. Be that as it may, for some people, this is unimaginable.

Do you need to win every trade to bring in money day exchanging? If you did, nobody on the planet would be a day trader. Everybody misses deals now and again. There is nothing of the sort as an ideal exchanging framework. The market isn't 100% predictable. You're going to encounter losses. In any case, the fact of the matter is that you have to manage those losses and limit them. On the off chance that you limit the damages to a little rate and let your gains develop, you will outpace the competition.

This can be done through sound money management. You never need to wager a lot on a single trade. Never put the entirety of your money on one business. This is merely requesting inconvenience. You ought to presumably just invest 1-2% of your bankroll on each trade. Like this, when you lose, it won't hurt so terrible. If you can reliably win, you will, in any case, be earning substantial sums of money. At the point when you get your account built up, you'll be bringing in great wealth.

When you get the money management segment of day exchanging down, you have to discover a framework that can net you powerful outcomes. This implies you have to locate a winning structure as quickly as time permits. Things being what they are, there is presently a great framework that is low maintenance called Day Trading Robot. This Trading Robot is a computer program that really can foresee practical stock examples. At the point when it finds a decent arrangement on a stock, it reveals to you when to buy it. You make the purchase and win the trade. It truly is that basic.

Pros and cons

Day trading is a lucrative engagement. However, that does not mean that it is way simple than any other actual job. And yes, you get to be your own boss. You get to do it your way, on your time, with your strategies for a living. It is amazing. We do not get so lucky in this life though; drawbacks have to appear too. Below, let us venture on the different pros and cons that come with day trading.

Benefits:

- *Own boss*

Getting to work the way you desire has always been the best thing ever. Your plan, your moves, your strategies. This is so good. Imagine going for a wanting vacation without first passing through the Human Resource department with some great explanation so that your reason can be valid enough. Moreover, getting to work for you already gives you the full energy to make things really alive. You have enough spirit to learn and bring out the best in you. Do yourself a huge favor and be your own boss.

- *Comfort.*

A peaceful working environment enhances the quality of the end product, or rather, the aftermath turns out to be so successful. A peaceful environment creates a much-concentrated workspace, day traders get to strictly master the actual day trading activities and learn more every day. This will in the end accomplish their big plans as indicated by the large chunks of profits that would be made.

- *Risk management.*

Exposure to day to day cases of day trading will definitely make you a better risk-taker. Day trading is made up of so many risks that act as day to day lessons. The trader gets to master the good moves and discard mistakes so as to become a successful day trader.

- *Technologically advantaged.*

Day trading exposes you to the internet as you try to get access to various sources. The internet is technology, so full of technology. You are exposed to new sites and different technological techniques. This builds you because technology is the present and the future.

Drawbacks:

- *A solitary lifestyle.*

Day trading is a peace of mind activity implying that physical noise should not be part of it. This creates a lonely kind of environment since the trader is mostly by himself or herself trying to master the possible good moves. You are really going to enjoy day trading if the best company is normally just your company.

- *Inconsistent salary.*

Your smart trading work will be reflected by the salary you obtain every single trading day. When you decide to take a day off, no gains are promised. At one particular point, you may gain like $3000 and the next day you experience $2000 loss, no consistent salary is promised, your smart moves are the ones that will get you a Lamborghini.

CHAPTER 2:

Thinking with a Positive Attitude

Before you proceed with learning the technical elements for how you can successfully day trade with options, I want to pause for a moment to provide you with some crucial mindset tips for making your trades successful. When it comes to trading, your mindset can either be the weapon you use to win or the weapon you point against yourself in a battle of self-sabotage.

People who are not in the right frame of mind when trading has a tendency to let fear and frustration rule their judgment, which can lead to them making poor trade moves that ultimately result in losses. If you want to hedge yourself against risk, you need to hedge yourself against your emotions too and learn how to trade logically, rationally, and objectively.

Although there are many different mindset strategies you can use to help you improve your trade skills and make better quality trades, the following five are the most important for beginners. Please take these tips seriously, as they can make or break you in the stock market and you always want everything working in favor of your success.

Beginners are especially at risk of making emotional trades based on the fact that there is a large amount of excitement and uncertainty swirling around when you are new to trading. If you get caught in this emotional state, however, your earliest experiences making trades may not be positive and could even put you off of the idea of trading altogether, solely because your mind was not in the right place.

Stay Committed, Be Persistent

You must be committed to your trades and stay persistent in your desire to win if you are going to be successful with trading any form of stocks.

Without commitment and persistence, you are going to find yourself struggling, as you will be unwilling to stay focused on what it takes to succeed.

Those who are not committed and persistent fall behind on their research and conduct low-quality tech analysis readings which can result in low-quality trades that lead to excessive losses. In the options market specifically, you might also find profitable options expiring before you act on them because you have not remained consistent in your approach to your trades.

A great way for you to stay committed and persistent in your trades is through setting a goal for yourself which will clearly outline the reason why you have begun trading in the first place.

When you have a goal, you know what you are set to achieve and you have a strong reason for why you need to stay committed and persistent so that you can reach that goal.

I strongly encourage you to outline a goal for yourself before you get started so that you can leverage your goal to help you stay committed and focused throughout your trades.

Some great examples of goals include:

- Pay off debt and accumulate a nest egg for yourself/your family
- Set aside funds for your children to go to college
- Afford to travel and enjoy the world
- Replace your salary with profits from trades so you can quit your day job
- Buy a house or investment property with your profits

Pick a goal that is relevant to what you want for yourself and your life so that you are motivated by it, as this is an important step in making your goal worth going for.

Be Aware of Your Emotions

Self-awareness, particularly around your emotions, is a strong asset for you to have when it comes to trading. When you are trading, you need to be aware of your emotions surrounding your trades so that you can avoid letting fear, frustration, anger, or uncertainty rule your trades. People who trade fearfully or with frustration tend to make decisions that are not founded in logic, which can result in massive and unnecessary losses incurred. As a result, they may grow even more fearful or frustrated with trading because they are not seeing the results they desire, which makes it even more challenging for them to make successful trades going forward.

Rather than starting that cycle, it is better to become aware of your emotions and practice staying aware of them during every trade you make.

The way that I manage my emotions and stress during trades comes in the form of a quick and simple self-check which I make periodically throughout the trading process. Generally, whenever I conduct tech analysis, choose my position, execute a trade, and complete a trade, I engage in an emotional check to see how I am doing. If I discover that I am feeling fearful or uncertain, or even frustrated, I manage my emotions first. Then, once I am feeling more balanced, I make my trade decision. This way, I can guarantee that every decision I make is founded in logic and reasoning, not fear and frustration.

Always Make Decisions Founded in Logic

It can be surprisingly easy to engage in trades based off of how your emotions are feeling, or even based off on what you hear out in the world around the topic of trades. You might find yourself noticing that whenever you hear about the market in the news or in trade circles that you spend time in that you feel persuaded to change your mind based off on what you are hearing from other people.

While it is important to take their information into consideration and use it to help you educate yourself, it is important that you never make a decision based off on what someone else has told you, or based off on your emotions. Instead, always conduct your own research to validate this information to ensure that you are making your decisions based off on logic and reasoning.

In today's society, it can be easy to get swept away by what other people are telling you. When I was brand new to trading, I tended to doubt myself and trust others' judgment anytime I was engaged in groups where people who had more experience than me were trading. I assumed that because they had been trading longer, they had greater experience, and therefore, what they said must ultimately be true, which lead to me making some trade moves that I did not validate with my own research.

Most of those fell through with losses, which made me realize the importance of this. Make sure that you hedge yourself against this risk by always validating everything with thorough research and tech analysis to ensure that you are always making the best decisions possible.

Stay Humble

Regardless of how and where you trade, the stock market is a place where you need to stay humble. Just like fear and uncertainty can push you to make poor trade deals, being overconfident can also lead to you making poor trade deals. People who are overconfident in the market tend to lose respect for how volatile the market can be and forget that just like you can profit plenty, you can also lose plenty. This can lead to terrible decisions and cocky trading, which may ultimately lead to potentially devastating losses in your trade deals.

Staying humble is not just to protect your pride, it is also to protect your trade deals to ensure that you are always hedging yourself against possible risks and losses.

You must always thoroughly conduct every step of tech analysis and trade research before getting involved, even if you have been on a winning streak. Do not roll the dice or gamble with your trades or assume that you know exactly how to win every single time just because you have won a few trades in a row or earned yourself massive profits. Stay humble, or the market will humble you.

Be Open to Learning

The final mindset note I will leave you with is that you need to be open to learning. As you get involved with trading, you will find a strategy that works for you and that you will want to stick with that strategy because it is familiar and comfortable. That is great, and everyone should be on the lookout for finding a way that works for them. After all, this is a strong way to ensure that you feel confident in the decisions that you are making so that you can make strong deals.

With that being said, you should always be open to learning and evolving your strategy so that you can do even better over time.

Continually learning is not just about improving your strategy either, but it is also about staying up with general trader trends. Trader trends are different from market trends in that we are not discussing what direction the market is moving in, but rather the strategies that traders are using to trade on the market itself.

Keeping up with these trends ensures that you are always trading similarly to how other successful traders are trading, which improves your chances of generating success with your trades.

CHAPTER 3:

Psychology and Mindset

Day Trading, like any other form of investment, is subject to influence from human emotion and psychological impact. Whenever money or capital is in play, people tend to take matters rather personally because of the inevitable consequence of the hope that comes along with the promise of significant returns. People will strive to make money while at the same time, avoid circumstances that may cause them to lose their capital. It is from this zero-sum mentality that the influence of psychology or emotions may creep into a sensible mindset. Such control takes over every aspect of the Day Trading instincts that you learned over time.

Your knowledge goes out of the window when a situation that triggers your psychological response arises. A high degree of counter productivity thus ensues. It, eventually, leads to the dismissal of logical decisions in favor of hunches as well as the need to chase after fleeting profits and cover your past losses. For you to manage your Day Trading expertise through challenging scenarios, you need to look out for emotions that alter your reasoning capability adversely. Try to improve and nurture a productive mindset, while at the same time, avoid promoting a mental culture that justifies negativity falsely. The following few behaviors and traits are central to your particular mindset whenever you decide to participate in Day Trading:

Do Not Rationalize Your Trading Errors

This mindset t is one of the leading obstacles to the progress and eventual success of your Day Trading endeavors. You are often prone to justify any trading mistakes that you make to the detriment of moving forward. For instance, you get an entry into a particularly promising trade deal later than necessary in spite of your much earlier knowledge of its potential for profitability. However, you decide to justify this misstep by convincing yourself of your preference for trading late over missing the same deal entirely.

The downside to such delays is often a faulty sense of size estimation in taking your trading position. Hence, the resulting increased exposure to financial risk you become disadvantaged by. Beware of your procrastination when it comes to productive openings that are currently available in Day Trading. If you possess this tendency, consider getting rid of it as soon as possible before it costs you a lot more capital in the long run. In case you are not prone to the frequent postponement of your responsibilities to a later date, be alert for the development of this mentality with the trading company that you keep. You can quickly become influenced by the kind of traders from whom you seek advice on more complex trading strategies. When present, stockbrokers affect your trading ethos, as well.

Poor trading etiquette from these external sources will rub off on you and vice versa. Try to keep the company of well-known responsible trading partners and stockbrokers when the need arises. Another rationalization scenario involves a run of profitable results. Based on a series of trade deals that made you successive returns, you begin to convince your brain of your seemingly high intelligence. This false belief in your skills may lead you to overestimate your trading expertise. Before long, you may start engaging in Day Trading on a hunch rather than apply logic to your decisions. You stop referring to your trusted trading plan and jump into many trading opportunities haphazardly. After a while, these instances of carelessness and trading arrogance will catch up with you because they always inevitably do. Your chances of plunging into a financial disaster go up.

With your eventual financial ruin come the cases of psychological meltdown leading to a negative feedback loop. A wrong decision from your misplaced sense of conceitedness will invariably lead to high-risk exposure. As a result, you suffer significant losses eventually, and consequently, your emotional health suffers, causing you to spiral into a state of depression. This loop is often self-propagating, meaning that it feeds onto itself. Bad decisions lead to adverse outcomes and a fragile mindset, which, in turn, is prone to make more bad decisions, and the loop goes on and on. Keep in mind that in Day Trading, such a feedback loop is often disastrous. All these adverse effects arise from your initial false sense of justification for a wrong deed.

Beware of Your Trading Decisions

This advice is so apparent that it sounds redundant when mentioned. However, decisions are typically the product of your reasoning and judgment at a particular moment. When it comes to decisions on Day Trading, psychological influence is often a determining factor in the process. Keeping your wits about you is very crucial, especially when everything seems to be out of control. You need to realize that every trade has its ups and downs and how you deal with the challenging times is often more consequential. Try to maintain a logical mindset when making Day Trading choices from a variety of bad options. When it seems that an imminent financial downturn is inevitable, the extent of your loss becomes essential. In this case, you will need to make a sensible decision on the degree of losing margins that you can tolerate adequately.

At this point, you are probably in a state of so many overwhelming emotions that your foggy mental faculties become clouded. An expected human response is to run away from danger, naturally, but in certain situations, fleeing may not be an option. A reflex in a trading scenario often leads to an impulsive decision. Such a choice is, in turn, typically not well thought or deliberative. You should confront your unfavorable circumstances head-on and attempt to fix the situation, however hopeless. This sense of perseverance is usually the essence of most trading excursions, especially when the times become financially rough. Going through the loss of some capital and other Day Trading challenges is often a painful experience that can lead to illogical decisions.

Always remember to uphold vigilance and adhere strictly to the guidelines in your trading plan when confronted with obstacles during your trades. The trading plan usually has instructions on how to handle these seemingly desperate situations. In addition, the prior preparation of any trading guide is generally free of emotional or psychological influence; hence, you can rely on it to maintain neutrality. Also, beware of making trading resolutions when going through a phase with a foul mood. Such conclusions are bound to lead you into a financial catastrophe, especially if you are not careful. Learn to put off the verdict to a time when you can resume logical thinking. When you make any rash decision, it can only result in your further exposure to even more risk.

Keep Your Emotions in Check

Learn to stick to a Day Trading system and method that you trust. Such a strategy may be one that has a history of always making significant returns. Once you master and fully grasp how to apply a specific approach to your trading deals, try to fine-tune it to your preference based on your ultimate objectives. Afterward, stick to this tried, practiced, and tested system in all your searches for valid trade deals. On some days, the stock market may be slow with a low volume of trade. The volatility in such a case is often negligible. However, due to an unchecked emotional influence, you develop a sense of greed or lust for profits.

The desire for benefits on a slow day is common. It leads to the urge to trade on anything to make a small profit. In this situation, you will move from Day Trading into gambling. Trading requires a logical mindset on your part with a lack of psychological attachment whatsoever. Gambling is a consequence of emotional and mental factors running amok in your Day Trading system. If a particular trading style worked on multiple times in the past, teach your brain to consider it. Your trusted trading system will indicate a lack of valid trade opportunities on a specific slow market day. In this case, curb your emotions, desires, and urges to chase a quick profit; however strong they seem.

You should never allow yourself to resort to gambling under any circumstances. Gambling is detrimental to healthy and responsible Day Trading behavior. The risk exposure exponentially rises when you grow accustomed to the desire for profits. If a given day of trading is unfavorable, you should not take part in invalid and unworthy deals. In addition, you should only trade on verifiable opportunities. At certain times, you may experience a series of successive returns in a relatively short period. Learn to know when to stop and how to curb your lust for wanting more returns. Trust your system to trade only on valid deals; however, multiple opportunities are available. An emotion that goes unmonitored in such situations is the greed for more profit.

You convince yourself psychologically that the various deals could be a sign of your lucky day. This mentality in a false belief is wrong, and you need to be aware of it. Your psychology can play deceitful tricks on your logical mind leading to high-risk trading deals. You must realize that in Day Trading, it is almost impossible to get more returns out of a system than what the stock market offers. Emotional corruption also comes into play in a scenario where you bite off more than you can chew.

The greed for substantial amounts of returns may cause you to take high-risk trading positions for a chance at quick profits. However, you must remember that profits and losses are both possible outcomes from a Day Trading session. Therefore, you need to learn to trade in amounts that you can afford to lose. After all, Day Trading involves taking a chance based on a speculative position. You should practice trading in small amounts of money within the confines of low-risk deals. In this case, a potential loss may not be as damaging as the earlier high-risk trading position driven by greed. Eliminate the role of emotions in Day Trading and learn to accept the uncertainty of an unknown future outcome.

Be Patient When Trading

Patience is a crucial trait to have when you take part in Day Trading due to the upswings and downward trends in stock prices. It can become challenging to identify the right entry or exit point for a particular trading opportunity, given the fluctuating nature of a volatile market. However, when you master the art of being patient and studying the trade intently, you can come up with a winning strategy. Having a planned approach is essential, and you should prepare one before engaging in any Day Trading. Often, most seasoned traders include trading strategies for different market conditions in their trading plans. Hence, when making your trading plan, consider incorporating a trading strategy within it.

If unsure of how to proceed, you can always seek the assistance of qualified stockbrokers. They have the experience of encountering various Day Trading scenarios in the real world. If trustworthy, they could provide you with invaluable insights on coming up with a proper strategy. Now it is up to you to stick to the plan in every session in which you participate.

CHAPTER 4:

How your Quantum Brain Can Work For You?

All over the world, stock markets open in the morning. Those day traders who think they can start trading while munching on their breakfast, with no preparation, are among those who make losses. All businesses open in the morning. No successful businessman just gets up, yawns and starts his business activities. Successful professionals arrive in their office with a clear idea of how they will tackle the work and related challenges. Likewise, to succeed in day trading, one must prepare beforehand. These preparations include many aspects; such as mental, physical, emotional, and financial.

Professional traders have clear advice for day traders; never trade if you are tired or stressed; never trade if you are feeling highly emotional, and trade with clear money management concepts. Day trading is a sophisticated business activity, where people try to earn money by using their intelligence. Therefore, physical or emotional stress can cause harm to your trading business. You will not be able to make rational decisions if you are tired or feeling stressed.

Before you start the day's trading, you should be physically, mentally and emotionally alert. A good night's sleep is necessary for traders to tackle the roller coaster ride of stock markets. Here are a few steps that will help you prepare for day trading with a cool temperament and calm mind.

Before going to sleep, keep your trading plan ready. Check the stock chart, make notes on the chart what big patterns the price created. Note down the important support and resistance levels. Then mentally go over this chart and imagine how you will trade in the next session, in different trend conditions.

Do not spend too much time watching the news about stock markets or anything else. Watching the news may create doubts in your mind about stock trends and influence your decision-making power for the next session. If possible, do some breathing exercises or meditation before going to sleep, which will sharpen your focusing power and reduce stress.

Also, prepare your money-plans for the next trading session. How much will you invest? What will be your loss tolerance level? And, what will be your profit booking point? During the trading hours, these decisions have to be made in a split second, and if you are already prepared, you will not hesitate to make the right decision. These will also help you set your goals for intraday trading. Just stick to your goals and you will not face any decision-making problems during the trading hours.

The final stage of your preparation will be an hour before the markets open in the morning. This is the time when you check the news reports about the business and financial world, and the economic calendar. By doing so, you will know what events could influence that day's trading pattern in the stock market. You can also check how the world markets are trading in that session. Sometimes all markets trade in one direction, which will be beneficial to know before your local stock markets open.

Planning for Trading

In day trading, financial instruments are bought and sold within the same session. Sometimes more than once through the same day. To be successful in this endeavor, traders need to know where the price might make important moves. Technical charts are very helpful tools in deciphering this price moment. Anybody involved in stock trading relies heavily on stock charts, which is why successful traders always create their trading plans before making any trading decisions.

When you create a trading plan, you are creating an 'assistant' to help you during the trading hours. This assistant will have all the information you will need for day trading; such as trade entry, trade exit, profit booking, stop loss and major price moments. Nobody goes looking for a treasure trove without any map. Likewise; no trader worth his or her salt will trade without a trading plan. Let us look at how a trading plan is created:

A trading plan is based on research, takes time, but saves a lot of effort and precious money during the trading hours. It is one of the most essential tools required for success in day trading. Every day trader has heard this saying 'fail to plan, and plan to fail'. Professional traders don't tire of emphasizing the importance of a trading plan. If you take their advice and prepare a trading plan before the markets open, you are halfway through to successful trading.

A trading plan is prepared before markets open and so, it is open to revisions and changes after markets start to trade and price changes. Every trader has a different trading style and based on that his trading plan could differ from others. But every trading plan must have a few essential details. These are:

1. Major support and resistance levels: One must mark the major support and resistance levels on the trading chart because these will symbolize the trade entry and exit points. These levels should be visible on charts to help in decision making during the chaotic trading hours.

2. Trade entry rules: Your trading plan should include when and why you will enter a trade. This could be a detailed explanation like 'if the price goes above X level, then buy'. Or it could be just a green arrow pointing to that price level.

3. Trade exit rules: Like the trade entry point, mark a trade exit or profit booking points on your trading plan. You must follow these rules meticulously, otherwise, these will become useless, if you plan and do not follow them.

4. Money management rules: Some traders like to note down on their trading plan, how much money they will invest in the next session. They keep checking their profits and losses through the session, and if the day's loss reaches its threshold; they stop trading. This is a good example of money discipline while trading because, in the excitement of trading, one can lose sight of what is happening with the investment capital.

These are the most basic rules to include in the trading plan. As you gain experience and get a hold of trading patterns in stock markets, you can expand your trading plans and include more trading rules in it. But always remember, these rules must be followed. A trading plan is based on research about markets, so every rule is important. Breaking any rule will be like going against the market, which is always harmful to any trader.

CHAPTER 5:

What to Expect

The first thing you need to know as a trader is that you will run volumes of trades and experience a lot of risks. Trading the markets is one of the riskiest investment techniques, and many people go for day trading because they have the potential for higher gains over a short period. If you have a small account, day trading gives you the chance to grow small accounts in such a short timeframe.

Risk comes about because you have to execute hundreds of trades in such a short time. You also have the capacity to place any trade you want, for as low as $500 or as high as $25,000 in a single trade. The trades are also at high speed, which means the market can swing any way – up or down. The direction of the market determines whether you make a loss or a profit.

Day trading gives you two realms of strategies to go with – high risk trading strategies or Lowe risk strategies. The goal of a successful trader is to maximize profit while lowering risks. Every time you place a trade, you need to evaluate the risk of the trade and then weight it against the potential reward. Often times this is made worse by our emotional reaction to various price directions. For instance, since you experienced a loss recently, the next logical step would be to take a higher risk on the next trade so that you can compensate on the loss. Experienced traders have a heightened level of awareness that they use to recognize a loss and reward and will make sure they take the right decision. However, you have to learn the skill over time.

You can develop a sense of decision making by keeping a journal as you trade.

Different Types of Risk

When talking about risk, you need to consider the different types in order for you to understand what we are saying. As a day trader, your primary role is to know the distance between the entry and the stop. Stop loss needs to be based on a resistance area on the chart or recent support.

Majority of your losses need to happen when a trade hits the stop price. This means you won't make any profit on whatever you are trading.

The second type of risk id the volatility of the market. As day traders, volatility is a friend to all of us, but it is also risky because markets that are extremely volatile tend to result in higher losses than what you actually planned for. Since there is a sense of inherent risk in trading, you need to try and avoid placing a trade when the volatility cannot be predicted, for instance when there is breaking news.

The other type of risk is exposure risk. Exposure results when you multiply the price of shares by the number of held shares. As an investor, you increase this risk when you hold on positions for a very long time. To mitigate this risk, you need to hold onto shares for a short time.

If you are holding onto large positions for a long time you stand to experience stock halts. Halts can take hours or days, though they are rare. The most common halts are those waiting for the release of news or volatility halts. Anytime a stock halts, it can lead to a different price. The biggest risk is that the stock might reopen at a very different price, which might be lower than the current price of the stock. You can take steps to reduce the effect of the halts by understanding what leads to the halts in the first place.

CHAPTER 6:

Trading Is a Work, Not a Hobby

Trading is a field that is exciting and also diverse. Deciding what kind of trader you would like to be is an important question. You should largely settle on it before you start trading, because mastering your "trade" is going to be something that will have a large influence on your profits. You are less likely to be successful if you are indecisive and playing around with different things without becoming a master of any of them. The focus is much better. Remember that when trading your hard earned money is on the line. So even if you keep your day job, this is not a game or a hobby, it is a real business. I am sure you would not try starting and running a business on an ad hoc basis, or trying to launch a restaurant, hardware store, and home cleaning business at the same time. In the same way, you should decide whether you want to be a day trader, a swing trader, a position trader, or an options trader. Then go from there, and master whatever you choose. Trying to focus on too many alternatives means spreading yourself thin; and it is likely to lead to losses, or at best sketchy and minimal profits.

Some basic considerations, with the idea in mind of matching your own personality with each trading style/type.

Day Trading

Day trading is definitely a trading style for action-oriented individuals who can focus 100% of their attention. You are also going to need to be at your computer 2-4 hours per day during day time trading hours, so it is a full-time commitment and not something you are likely going to be pursuing as a hobby. Day trading uses the tools of technical analysis extensively. You will spend hours each day doing research on stocks to trade. You will also spend a great deal of time researching and observing, in order to decide the best point where you should enter your positions. Once you have entered a position, you are going to have to stay glued to your computer. Because of the way day traders stick to highly volatile stocks, they need to earn profits within a single trading day, you are going to have to keep a close eye on what is going on. Your exit point is going to have to be precise. It is a high stress style of trading that is a high risk, with the possibility of losing thousands of dollars in a couple of hours. If you are risk averse when it comes to money, being a day trader is probably not your cup of tea.

To be a day trader, you also need to have a lot of capital on hand. That means $25,000 in your account in the United States. Don't risk the $25,000 if you can't afford to lose it.

Swing Trading

If you are not quite cut out for day trading but like the idea of profiting off price movements and doing some technical analysis, swing trading is probably more your style. A swing trader holds positions for days or weeks. That makes it lower pressure, although the pressure can get high if you cannot wind down a position profitably. While you will be using technical analysis, it is not going to be to the same level of "live or die" in the moment. Swing trading is a much more relaxed lifestyle. You can do it on a part-time basis, and you can trade large caps and index funds which are generally avoided by day traders. Swing trading represents a good middle ground, and it is a good alternative for those who do not want the high pressure, or who would like to trade on a part-time basis. Swing trading does not have capital requirements.

Position Trading

Position trading is really just swing trading on a longer time frame. Position traders do not trade very frequently, and they are looking for long term price swings or even price appreciation. The time frames are from months to even 1-2 years. Unlike long-term investors, position traders are not looking to hold positions for the long haul. Position trading can fit naturally into a swing trading business. Alternatively, it is something that can be used in conjunction with traditional buy and hold investing for the long-term. More fundamental analysis is needed when doing position trading, but otherwise there is no specialized knowledge used, and therefore it would be similar to swing trading, just over a longer time scale.

Options Trading

The beauty of options trading is that a trader can get started for a few hundred dollars. If you are disciplined, that is, you can avoid trading on a large scale until you know what you are doing from some experience, you can build up profits slowly over time. When you have losses, they are going to be limited to a couple of hundred dollars or less. Keep in mind that options trading requires lots of specialized knowledge. So while you could in theory do it in conjunction with other types of trading, it is not recommended. Instead, if options trading appeals to you, then you should devote all of your attention to it. That is, other than any long-term investing in stocks that you have on the side. We do not advise trying to swing trade and options trade at the same time. Become a master of the one that appeals to you more and ride it to maximize profits.

Minimizing Risk

No matter what trading style or method you decide to adopt, mitigating risk is an important part of any trading business. Mitigating risk means that you never risk more than you can afford to lose. It also means that you have defined points where you take profits and exit trades. Let us look at each of these in turn.

The standard recommendation is that you can risk 1-2% of your account on a trade. That means if you can afford to lose $500 on a single trade, then if you are willing to lose $1 a share, you can buy 100 shares of stock. In order to get the amount you can afford to lose from a single trade, you simply calculate 1-2% of the total value of the cash in your account. Certainly you should not put your life savings on the line trading stocks. It is quite possible that over time you will find them evaporating into nothing. You can decide as a percentage what you are able to risk. You can stick to 1-2% or if you are comfortable going higher, that is your business. However, you should probably not go above 3% as a beginning trader. Whatever rule you choose, you should stick by. It is important to stick by the rules and not "adjust" them when you find yourself in a desperate situation.

Begin by taking the amount in your account and multiplying it by the percentage you can afford to lose. Let us say we have an $8,000 account, and we are willing to risk 2%. That means the gross amount we can risk on a single trade is $240.

When we enter a trade, we use this to determine how many shares we are going to buy. The next step is to determine how much we are willing to lose on a single trade. If the stock is highly volatile, you may not want to exit the position at the drop of a pin. The stock might drop down and rally, so we would not want to miss that. So the amount you are willing to lose per share on a given trade is something that is going to be situational. On one trade, you might only risk $0.50, while on another you might be willing to risk $2 per share. Some traders will decide to standardize and risk the same amount of all trades. The amount you can risk (that is the percentage of your account) is divided by the amount you are willing to risk per share. So if we can risk $240, and we are willing to risk $0.50 per share, we can buy $240/$0.50 = 480 shares.

The amount you are willing to risk per share is not something to keep in mind. It is something you are going to immediately enforce after buying the stock. This will be done by submitting a good until canceled limit order after you buy the stock – in order to sell it. If a stock is trading at $50 a share when you purchase it, then if you have determined your loss per share that you are comfortable with is $1 per share, then you will enter a limit order to sell with a $49 per share limit price. So it will not be executed unless the stock price drops to $49 or lower per share.

With a limit order in place (called a stop loss order in this context), you do not have to sit in front of your computer all hours of the day hoping to prevent a catastrophic loss. You have defined how much you are willing to lose. So you should be able to relax knowing how things are setup, and take it as fate if the situation arises where the shares are sold at a loss. In that case you can take note of what happened and hopefully learn from your mistakes to do better next time.

We can also enforce discipline by using the same method to take profit orders. In this case, you canceled the order you bought, and set the price to the one you are willing to accept. So this is another limit order submitted with your broker soon after you have purchased the stock.

If you do nothing but implement these rules, you are well on your way to becoming a successful trader.

CHAPTER 7:

The Fear of Losing Money

We are afraid of losing money because we are conditioned to believe that losing money means we are failures. And I can tell you it surely feels like it. Nonetheless, losing money is inevitable. Even the advanced traders have lost money, and probably more than they made. It is just that no one really talks about it.

Not every position you take will result in profits. The markets simply do not work in anyone's favor all the time and, especially in the beginning, you'll likely find yourself to be on the trade's wrong side, and you'll blow one or two accounts.

The most important part is to stand up strong, try again and improve your trading skills.

Some people trade on demo accounts for ages due to their fears of trading live, make a mistake and losing money. But losing money is part of this business, and it teaches you valuable lessons. The bottom line is that you will never learn how to become a better trader by trading on a demo account.

Fear of increasing the value of investments or learning new trading strategies.

So, how do you go about changing your outlook and the trading view from a failure filter to a success filter? Well firstly, let's define what a success filter is. As you develop an outlook for success, you will strengthen a belief that you will succeed, noticing the good trades as they are setting up and mentally deleting the bad trades from your awareness (just like in the red car bias). You make sure you are on the chart when the correct trades are forming, and you are able to easily catch trades. The number of your winning trades' tallies with the backtested results of the system. You easily avoid bad trades; they recede below your observation as you are focusing on trades that are likely to succeed.

So, what is a practical way to turn a failure filter into a success filter? This goes back to how "process thinking" redefines success and failure. I am also going to bring in something that you may regard as a bit woo-woo... affirmations! To change your belief about your trading failure, I suggest you combine process thinking (about skills & strategies) with success affirmations. This is very different from "results thinking" because it assumes you have the power to control your trading results. Process thinking assumes you have the power to control your trading actions, and combined with affirmations, replace and refresh the failure belief with more powerful success beliefs.

While you redefine failure and success in trading, let's observe how trading success is not an end goal.

People think about trading success as if it is a destination rather than a journey. There is no point in time that you can say I am guaranteed to be a trading success because that can change the next day if your behaviors change or the market changes.

Trading is an ongoing journey of increasing excellence; the only thing you can say for sure is that you are becoming an increasingly better trader. How do you become an increasingly better trader? If you learn from each mistake, make adjustments to your trading routines, your trading system will increase your performance.

There are no gold medals for trading success. The only gold medal you can win is the increased size of a trading account, and there is no definitive point where you say I have reached perfection. Rather, you might always be striving for perfection while knowing you will never get there.

So how can this redefine success and failure in trading? If it means that you learn from a mistake and adjust your trading to become a better trader, then you have succeeded in your quest to achieve trading perfection. Thus, the goal is to learn from your mistakes to increase performance. Every mistake you make is looked at with the viewpoint of. Here is an opportunity to improve your performance, not fail.

Trader's dependency: addicted to trading

There are crypto traders who decide to trade all day long without taking a break. All their life revolves around crypto trading. Thus, they are always present in the market. This is a dangerous step in over-relying on trades. As it happens, in cases when the market crumbles, these traders become affected the most since they have invested a great deal of their time and resources.

You need to be very careful. Do not get greedy and rush to trade, but instead take your time to learn. The markets will be there with more good opportunities in the months and years ahead.

Lack of self-discipline or inability to consistently follow plans

Discipline is a very important part of trading. Maybe discipline is even the most crucial aspect of trading. However, it gets rarely mentioned. And to be fair, many traders are guilty of lacking the discipline for various reasons, and I am one of them. I admit it. It is indeed very difficult to bring the required discipline to the table, as it is very hard to stick to one system or method, especially when it is not performing successfully. When one thinks it is the method that is not working on their behalf, s/he starts to tweak, change it and "jump around." The truth is there is no perfect system that is working 100% of the time. Every trading method has periods in which it performs below average and generates losses. It takes time to develop a method that fits one's trading style and develop the discipline to stick with it, even when the trades become difficult. And if it does work, one becomes greedy and wants to make even more. And that's where it goes wrong again.

Self-discipline is the mental technique to redirect our focus on the positive elements to create success when our goal is encumbered by some other components in our mental environment. Such a technique is created by us, not inherently available within our mindset. A term known as "mechanical trading" is, basically, the function of changing beliefs, or more correctly, changing energy from one belief (the wrong belief) to another. If there is anything in your mental system that contradicts the principle, "I am a consistently successful trader," then you have to employ the self-discipline technique to reinforce this principle is a dominant part of your identity. Once you obtain the true principle you desire, you no longer need self-discipline because the process of being consistent is just a natural function of your identity at that time. Trading is not a function of struggles, conflicts or contradiction; inversely, it is mostly effortless and fun once you operate from a set of proper beliefs.

CHAPTER 8:

Hard Work, Focus and Determination to Achieve your Goals

Hard work in day trading is different from what you might originally assume. A trader should not work 100 hours a week like investment bankers or corporate lawyers or other highly paid professionals do because, for us day traders, there are no end of the year bonuses. More than anything else, day trading is perhaps most similar to being a professional athlete because it is judged by one's daily performance. Having said that, day traders should work hard, consistently and productively, each and every day. Watching your trading screens intently and gathering important market information is how we define hard work in day trading. You must ask the following questions constantly and at a rapid pace for several hours every day:

- Who is in control of the price: the buyers or the sellers?
- What technical levels are most important?
- Is this stock stronger or weaker than the market?
- Where is most of the volume being traded? At the VWAP? Or the first five minutes? Or near moving averages?
- How much volume at a price causes the stock to move up or down?
- What is the bid-ask spread? Is it tradeable?
- How quickly does the stock move? Is it being traded smoothly or is it choppy, jumping up and down with every trade?
- Is the stock trading in a particular pattern on a 5-minute chart? How is the stock being traded on a 1-minute chart?

These are some of the questions that I ask myself and then answer before trading a stock. All of this information should be gathered before you make any trade. This is what we mean by hard work. As you can see, day trading is an intense intellectual pursuit that requires hard work.

It is essential to develop the routine of showing up every day to trade, whether it is in your real account or in a simulator. Searching for support and resistance levels each day, including before the market opens, will benefit your trading in the long run. Turning off the PC early after a few bad trades is a strategy that should be reserved for the rare occasions when it is absolutely essential to give your brain a break. Usually, spending some time in a simulator after some losses will clear your mind sufficiently. Novice traders using a simulator should keep on trading and practicing until the Close. After all, trading in the simulator is not nearly as stressful as real trading with real money. Using a simulator with no commission and no P&L is still no excuse for overtrading. At all times the focus must be on sound strategies with excellent risk/reward opportunities.

I am often asked, "In your first months of trading, did you ever feel like you couldn't do it?" The answer is "Yes, and often!" I still, at least once a month, get really frustrated after a few bad losses and consider quitting day trading. Frequently in my trading career I have wanted to quit, and at times I have actually believed the myth that day trading is impossible. But I did not quit. I really wanted to be a successful trader and to have the lifestyle and the freedom that comes with it. So I paid the price for my mistakes, focused on my education, and eventually survived the very difficult learning curve of trading.

CHAPTER 9:

How to Take Decision

When we become stressed during any life experience, our emotions have a tendency to hijack the experience and prevent us from being able to make logical rational decisions. Naturally, this would not be productive to you making the best decisions with your trades which means that this needs to be avoided at all costs.

Fostering the right mindset allows you to remain objective and logical in every trade decision that you make so that you are always making decisions that lead to your profits, rather than mistakes that lead to your losses.

It does take time to learn how to foster this particular mindset, especially with the amount of stress that you might face with trading. Ideally, however, if you practice at it every single day you will find that it becomes a lot easier for you to see your trades objectively. As a result, you will find that your trades become more productive and your passive income stream grows exponentially.

While there are many things that you can do to help you manage your mindset and your emotions and keep yourself primed for the psychology of trading, there are five significant steps that you can take today to get started. Enforcing these mindset strategies right away can help you start your trades with the best mindset possible so that you can experience larger levels of success right from the very beginning.

Never Take Anything Personally

In life, it can be challenging to separate yourself from your experiences, especially when high emotions such as stress and overwhelm come into play. Early on, you might feel like every trade you make reflects you personally and like any bad trade, you make means that you are a bad trader or that you are incapable of earning an income through trading.

This type of response is fairly natural, but it is also unhelpful when it comes to learning how to trade to earn a profit.

Experiencing losses and trade deals gone wrong is a natural part of trading, and virtually everyone experiences it. While senior traders are not as likely to experience as many losses as new traders, they do still experience losses that cut into their bottom line. This is natural, especially when you are trading on something as volatile as the stock market. With day trading, in particular, you never know exactly how that day is going to go, nor do you know whether or not sudden shifts in news and rumors could completely change the direction of the stock. As such, you are certainly exposed to risks that can be completely beyond your control. While you can protect yourself against them as much as possible, there is no real way to completely avoid risks and so they are always a possibility.

The alternative of feeling like a bad trader when you experience a loss is feeling like a great trader when you experience a win. It is common amongst new traders who are on a winning streak to develop a sense of indestructibility that suggests that maybe they are incapable of experiencing losses because they somehow have the system beat.

This arrogance can lead to new traders exposing themselves to massive risks and losses because they stop taking their trades as seriously and reduce the amount of research and risk management they conduct before every trade. As a result, they may experience a massive setback due to this arrogance.

In either scenario, creating a personal attachment to what your trades "mean" about who you are as a person is not healthy. Both can lead to self-doubt or arrogance which has the capacity to destroy your trade deals and reduce your effectiveness as a trader.

Instead, you need to go into every single trade deal knowing that your level of results in the trades is not reflective of you as a person. You are neither good nor bad for participating in trades that earn profits or losses. You are just a trader, trading. Keeping your personal attachment out of the trades will help you stay objective and continually practice logic and rational reasoning in every single trade you make.

Maintain a Healthy Respect for the Market

This particular mindset strategy is incredibly important, and it can be one of the most challenging ones to maintain. As a trader, you can easily become complacent by losing focus, becoming arrogant about a winning streak, or becoming doubtful from a losing streak. If you are not careful, you will quickly find your respect for the market shifting away from healthy respect and it could drastically impact your trade deals.

You must always remember that the market is volatile, that it is not guaranteed, and that anything can happen at any given time. No matter how much research you do, and no matter how much effort you put into guaranteeing your success, you are never guaranteed anything on the stock market. No amount of preparation can completely prevent you against losses, no matter what. Although options are certainly less risky than other trade styles and can help you create predictable loss amounts, you still do not want to be exposing yourself to these risks.

The single best way that you can protect yourself mentally and practically from being exposed to threats in the market is through maintaining a healthy respect for it. In exercising this healthy respect, you should always seek to educate yourself as much as possible around a trade deal you are going to make and execute that trade deal with confidence.

You should also seek to continually educate yourself on the market so that you can improve your confidence and respect in the market. Never allow yourself to grow complacent or ignorant of how powerful the market can be, as this can lead to you exposing yourself to unnecessary risks and incurring massive losses.

Maintain a healthy respect for the power of the market, always.

Improve Your Emotional Intelligence

It is helpful to learn how to improve your emotional intelligence overall when it comes to trading. Emotional intelligence will help you not only manage your stress but also manage all of the emotions that contribute to stress, such as fear, anger, frustration, worry, regret, disappointment, sadness, and uncertainty.

Improving your emotional intelligence as a trader will have a huge impact on your ability to decrease your emotional involvement in trades and trade with an objective approach in every single deal.

Aside from supporting you with the emotions, you have gained directly from the market, emotional intelligence will also help you manage emotions that you experience from elsewhere in your life.

This means that you will have a significantly lower chance of bringing outside troubles into your trading mindset, which will drastically reduce the amount of stress you bring with you into trades. This way, if you have anything bugging you in your day to day life, such as in your relationships or career, you will be less likely to allow those things to influence your trade deals.

Managing your emotions all around will have a significant impact on helping you trade more rationally, intentionally, and effectively. Ensure that you are practicing emotional intelligence in all areas of your life and continually improving your emotional intelligence each day so that you are minimizing the risk that your emotions may pose on your trade deals.

Keep Up with Stress Management

As I have already mentioned, stress can play a huge role in your ability to make strong trade deals. If you are attempting to trade with an incredibly stressed out and overwhelmed mind, you are going to find yourself making poor decisions that may ultimately cost you a significant amount in the end.

One example that proves the impact of emotions on traders lies in a phenomenon that happens every single time the market hits a recession. When a recession strikes, many traders develop an intense fear at the rapidly dropping prices of various stocks and jump out of their trade deals as fast as they can, regardless of how much they are losing.

Their fear of experiencing a complete loss leaves them reacting instead of responding to the situation at hand. As a result, many people inevitably lose out on massive amounts of income and some even find themselves amidst devastating losses.

Alternatively, those who respond to the situation quickly recognize that a recession is in the works and, based on the history of what tends to happen during recessions, they maintain their positions. In fact, they often leverage their positions and invest in the plummeting stocks once they begin to hit all-time lows because they know that historically every single time the stock market drops it always corrects itself eventually.

These individuals end up coming out of recessions far wealthier than they went into them because they leveraged what was happening in the market, rather than acting impulsively based on their stress levels.

Of course, the market is not always in a recession and so you might not see these massive, across-the-board plummets while you trade, but the same general rule of thumb still applies. If you allow yourself to become excessively stressed and act emotionally when your chosen stocks begin to move out of favor, you are likely going to make big mistakes out of your emotional judgments.

If instead, you were to slow down and follow the plan you had already set in place, you would continue to see increases in the value of your stock, or at the very least you could minimize the number of losses that you experience.

Understand that when we talk about stress management, we are not talking about eliminating stress entirely. Even the most senior traders in the industry will tell you that they continue to experience massive amounts of stress around the stock market on a consistent basis.

The difference is, they do not let their stress alter or rule their decision-making skills. Instead, they let their stress exist in the background, yet they continue to expertly behave according to the plans they have already designed at the beginning of every trade deal they have ever entered. As a result, they maximize their profits and their stress and emotions no longer pose such a massive threat to their bottom line.

Always Stay Hungry for Knowledge

Trading is not a one and done skill that can be learned and then executed the same way over and over again without ever requiring further education on what you are doing. If you want to be a great trader and earn massive profits, you need to stay hungry for knowledge so that you can continually improve your trading skills over time.

The best way to create your own method for doing all of this is to keep practicing and applying new strategies that you learn about as you go and seeing how they fit for you. When you find ones, you like and that work for you, continue using them and refining them so that they work even better over time.

CHAPTER 10:

Feeling and Action

We want to teach you about your emotions and how you can affect your trade performance. Containing your emotions and being disciplined walk hand in hand in maintaining successful trade. Having emotions is natural as a human, but these emotions, if not properly managed, can send your trade on a downhill path directs to failure, but that is not our desire. That is why we have carried out extensive research on how to positively deal with this. Our findings have been summarized to several guidelines on how you can have these emotions in line and how to use them to your advantage.

How to Control Your Emotions as a Trader

It is completely necessary that as a trader, you should be at full capacity to control your emotions. Letting these weaknesses go out of hand will be fatal for your trade. It can easily ruin all the hard-earned profits in a night. An example is when you have experienced several losses in your trade; you end up over-leveraging, destroying your account with a single trade.

A well-equipped trader should know that trade is a game, and as a game, there are chances that you will lose one time and win the other nothing is static. You need to stay detached from the results of every trade and have an open mind. Having an emotional attachment on every trade will just inhibit growth as a trader as you will be in constant fear of repeating the same mistakes if you had losses and if you had profits you might end up sticking onto that one trade idea not taking note of the different trends in the market. Expect anything prepares for everything.

You need to focus when involving yourself in day trade. Focus on your goal; focus on your objectives. You need to know what to do to have your trade-in control. If you want to achieve all those goals and objectives, what can you actually do to have your emotions in control and work on not spoil your trade? These can be easily achieved if you just follow these simple guidelines:

One, you need to take a break; however, small it is and just walk it out or just listening to music. Knowing the rush nature of the day trade, you need a break lest you will be trapped in uncontrollable emotions. To have a break from the constant high tempo at which you are trading, you need to off yourself from your trade for a while. Doing this will help clear your mind and is also a reminder that you are the one in control. You control the trade, and the market doesn't push you to trade. You can also opt for meditating on your break as it will also prove to be very beneficial for you. Meditation will enable you to drain away any stressful thought, all the negative energy, and allow positive inner peace to dwell.

Check on volatility. When are the prices in the market volatile? You will work best when the prices are in this state. Working in a congested market will lead to frustrations, and we don't want that, do we? You first get frustrated; then you are angry after that you are fully stressed, then pretty soon your will waves of emotions clouding your judgment.

You need to have a break on trading after three losing or winning trades follow-ups. After three wins, why will we advise you to stop, you are the super trader after all. Well, this is exactly why we are telling you to take a short break. How you view yourself. This self-pride will pretty much be the downfall of you and your trades, as you will end up overtrading and over leveraging. This can drastically pull you down. What if you have three follow up losses? The losses will put you down, and you have diminishing thoughts on yourself, making you feel like a loser making you. This overflow of emotions can easily affect your confidence as a trader and your judgment as you go by the trade.

Another guideline is that you should not be so focused on your last profits or losses while in trade. If something is bound to make you emotional, in your trade, it is your profit and loss records. Many traders take this as a scale of your self-worth and value. This is the wrong perception to be having in mind when venturing into a trade.

Lastly, you need to ask yourself this vital question, do I fear? Traders are normal human beings, and as beings, they are prone to the feeling of fear, to be afraid, and to get scared. This is an intense emotion and so destructive, is it? If the answer is yes, that you do fear, you need to go back what rules are placed in trade, go through your strategies, and the plans you set. Ensure you have confidence that you have made the right choice, then finally reduce the size of your trade to a size more appropriate, which you can easily handle.

These guidelines are few but have a lot of weight, follow these steps, and watch how you will rise. But always have it in mind that mastery of your emotions is important, but it does not give you a trading edge. This comes about with your trading methods.

Having to conquer and control our emotions is key, but you also need to work on your disciple. Having a trade disciple can tame those emotions. Despite it being hard to master, we have simplified it for you as we have your best interest at heart. As a trader, you need to have established a routine for the premarket, and you should have productive training habits. You also need to have it in mind that trading disciple is practiced at all times.

Lack of discipline during trade will lead to making mistakes common in trade such as rushing into things without taking time to reflect on their outcomes might end up executing the trade prematurely, and you will also risk violating the management rules, you will get caught up in the act of over-trading and revenge trading. All this will have a final result, loss of money, and emotional trauma.

There are guidelines on how to be disciplined in your trade:

One, you need to lay down a trading plan. Take time and plan before you start your session. Analyze what instruments are in your possession, have trade scenarios that are specific to your trade, and take note of all ideas that will be advantageous to the trade. This prevents you from entering the trade prematurely and without knowledge of trade mistakes. You will also line your trade and the strategies you had planned out for it.

Secondly, you need to mind the trade routines. You always need to follow your trade routine. Set a trading routine consisting of your analysis of the premarket, the hours that major markets trade, and the days end hours. Have a usual check of the economic trade calendar for any report and analyze the trade prizes. You should work on never breaking your routine. Let it be fixed and static.

You are required to have a journal on your trade. What did you not do right, and how you could have done it better? What new techniques will better work this time around? Your former trades should be taken in as a learning experience and as a lift to the higher economic ground. They should not be used to put you down, but they are meant to elevate you even higher.

Often you should strive to become a winner in this corporate world. Ensure you work for your trade to be highest in the ladder. You need to secure and protect your profits.

You also need to follow trade methods that have been proven. These methods are not to be changed. If you try a methodology that is not proven and doesn't seem to work in some session of trade, don't just wake up in the morning and come up with another one. Find a proven method of trade that productively works for you and strictly go by it.

In addition, you are not required to chase markets. Patiently wait as it sets up. The market is equivalent to a shadow as following it will lead you nowhere as you can never reach for it. But if you are still, it will settle on you. Understand that this is a process; each step pushes you closer to achieving your goals and objectives.do not make any haste. Decisions Research on ways you can increase your profits and reduce your losses.

Mastery of these guidelines will see you through in becoming a disciplined trader and working on your emotions. These emotions are not all bad can actually be used to give out positive results.

How can we manage our emotions to good suite us and our trade? This is known as Emotional Intelligence (EI). How do we improve our emotional quotient to work for us in this trade? You first need to be aware of your qualities, your strengths and your weaknesses have them in control. First, we need to be aware of the components of emotional intelligence, which are distinct in nature, namely, social skills, self-awareness, self-regulation, empathy, and intrinsic motivation.

Having control of EI will improve your trade satisfaction and improved performances those under you will benefit from your knowledge. It is also good when encountering failures. Having on self-awareness of how your emotions work will help you control them and think of how you can possibly restructure your behavior. This would be difficult for traders who constantly have control of these situations. The most often have high self-esteem, and it will take them a long time to accept that this time around, they have lost control. They will end up giving negative feedback in their response.

You should not wait for an emotional crisis to emerge for you to alienate your feelings. In fact, you should not even eliminate them, doing so will make you emotionally unintelligent, you just need to be ready for the game changers and how to possibly react on them.

As a trader, you need to understand that emotions can either be constructive and destructive forms of energy. Traders experience emotion, and a lack of emotion can prove to be fatal as it can kill the desire to act. While if you are unable to control your emotional reaction on excessive pain, you can easily blind how you think rationally and easily crowd your judgment. You just need to stabilize your emotions. Follow all the tips and guidelines as stated to get the best out of your trade. We need you to count profits.

CHAPTER 11:

Stop Negative Emotion

So, in order to achieve consistently profitable results, you need to acknowledge that emotions are unavoidable. They're biological. They're embedded in your brain and will take over your psychology whenever your default mental programming begins to perceive potential danger in any shape or form.

This is why many inexperienced traders get angry, frustrated and fearsome when they lose. Successful traders on the other hand manage their emotions and immediately look to learn from their mistakes. They don't view them negatively.

They accept that risk and loss are part of the game. If they lose because of a psychological or methodical mistake then they immediately look to correct it. If they lose because they end up on the wrong side of probability then they accept it. Their emotional intelligence is very different to that of an inexperienced trader.

Traders with a properly trained mind have learned to confine themselves to the present moment. They understand that the only control they have is in the here and now. They cannot change the past and they cannot control the future. All they can control is the execution of their performance.

This is where the knowledgeable and rational left brain combines with the emotional right brain to form a formidable trading mindset.

The next time you look at the balance of your trading account remember that it's not a reflection of how well you understand trading. Your trading account balance is an indicator of your level of emotional intelligence. So what is an emotion and what are its fundamental elements?

To put it in simple terms, emotion is your brain's ability to organize patterns and analyze disruption to patterns. It then prompts you to take certain responsive actions. By understanding the elements of emotions we can begin to understand how to manage them, particularly when operating under pressure. So let's begin.

The 4 main fundamental elements of emotion are arousal, feeling, motivation and meaning. So let's look at each one individually and then address the role they play in the mind and body of a trader.

1. Arousal. This is when you begin to feel your muscles tense up and your heart beat faster. In some cases your mouth may go dry, your breathing may become heavier and you may start to feel butterflies in your stomach.

2. Feeling. This is when you feel the emotional chemistry rushing through your body. The initial arousal gradually turns into a full on emotional rush.

A good way to conceptualize the main difference between arousal and feeling is to think of a firework. When a firework is lit it begins emitting sparks as it burns through its fuse. This can be considered the arousal phase.

Once the fuse has been consumed the gun power ignites and the firework shoots off at high speed. This is when we feel the emotion whipping through us. The important thing to note here is that this is the point where the emotional right brain hijacks the rational left-brain.

You need to learn to recognize when this is occurring so that you can take immediate measures to disrupt the emotion before it takes off and begins influencing your decision-making.

3. Motivation – This is essentially the action your brain tells you to take in response to the emotion. Once motivation comes into play your brain will prompt you to either fight or flight.

4. Meaning – This refers to your individual beliefs and how they drive your perception. If you recall earlier, I said that all traders project their beliefs onto the markets and then receive feedback on the effectiveness of that belief through their trading account balance.

Once you take time to understand the elements of emotion you can then begin developing emotional intelligence. In other words you can learn how to manage them more effectively and foster a mindset that is more adapted to the arena of trading. You need to bear in mind that emotional intelligence is far more important than cognitive intelligence when it comes to trading.

So in summary, emotional intelligence is about.

1. Understanding that you are an emotional being.
2. Understanding that emotions cannot be suppressed or "left at the door".
3. Understanding that emotions are biologically embedded in you therefore they have to be managed.
4. Understanding that your brain has default wiring that will cause you to behave a certain way in certain situations.
5. Understanding that the emotional right side of your brain will impact your decision making by influencing the rational left side of your brain whenever it perceives potential danger.
6. Being able to recognize when you're progressing from a state of emotional arousal to emotional feeling.
7. Having the mental capacity to disrupt these emotional transitions before they cause you to make irrational decisions.
8. Understanding that your success has very little to do with knowledge of trading. It is primarily dependent on your emotional intelligence.
9. Taking an active measure to strengthen and develop your emotional intelligence.
10. Progressing from unconscious incompetence to unconscious competence.

CHAPTER 12:

Mimic Them

Many of us have limiting beliefs about things like money, hard work, and success. One thing that sets millionaires apart from the rest of us is not just how much money they have but how they think. This mindset is not exclusive to how they think about money but also encompasses how they think about themselves, the people around them, and life in general. In short, they have a mindset that gears them for success rather than for mediocrity or survival.

They have a positive mindset.

We have all heard about the power of positive thinking. Turning negative phrases, such as, "I don't want to eat spaghetti for supper," into, "I want to eat a hamburger for supper," can completely change a person's mindset and attitude. This positive attitude isn't just a way to survive a mediocre day but is actually one of the keys to millionaire-type thinking.

There are a lot of negative phrases about money. You have probably heard plenty of them. Some examples include:

- Money can't buy happiness.
- Money is the root of all evil.
- Wanting a lot of money makes a person selfish.
- Money and wealth bring loneliness, isolation, and misery; just look at how unhappy lottery winners are.

If the majority of millionaires really believed these sayings, they wouldn't work so hard to be successful! Instead of looking to these maxims to justify your lack of money, try changing how you think. Move from negative views about money, success, and wealth to positive affirmations about yourself and the world around you.

- I have everything that I need to become the person that I want to be.
- I have the creativity and work ethic to create the prosperity that I want.
- I can accumulate wealth and resources.
- I can live in wealth and prosperity rather than in debt.
- I can be the successful person that I envision myself becoming.

Even better than this is practicing the art of gratitude and thankfulness for what you already do have.

- I am thankful for the house that I have and the people around me.
- I am thankful for my job and income.
- I am thankful that I am able to put money into savings.

You can substitute these statements for any that apply to your own life and circumstances. Just remember to leave all negativity and complaining at the door and practice positive thinking!

They Have Mentors

Most millionaires didn't become rich on their own. Rather, they found people whose lifestyles they wanted to emulate and followed what those people did. In other words, they found mentors.

Mentors are people who have already been there and already done that. They've already made mistakes and broken barriers. While their success won't become your success, they can show you what works and what doesn't. On the road to financial success and wealth, you don't have to fail in the same ways that other people have failed. You can find someone to show you how to do things more efficiently and how to make better financial decisions.

Try Success On For Size

How would you do things differently if you were a millionaire? I'm not talking about what you would buy or what house you would live in. I'm talking about the day-to-day choices that you would make, especially concerning how you interact with people and with yourself. Start making those choices now. You will be amazed at the change in how people see you and in how you see yourself.

Would you dress differently? Maybe you fancy yourself wearing an Armani suit every day. Maybe you would style your hair nicely and put on makeup and jewelry every day. Start doing those things now! Maybe you can't afford an Armani suit; if you can't, buying one would be a silly decision. But start dressing for success. Wear a tie and sports jacket. Wake up 10 minutes earlier than you are used to so that you can do your hair and makeup. Dress and present yourself as if you are millionaire material.

How would you treat people if you were a millionaire? Would you be more generous? There is no need to wait to be generous and kind to others. Maybe right now, you can't afford to give $50,000 to charity, but you can give $50 or volunteer somewhere. You can tip your waiter or waitress generously.

How would you treat yourself if you were a millionaire? If you have a lot of negative self-talk — in other words, if you wouldn't talk to your best friend or family members the way that you talk to yourself — you may envision that you would talk to yourself and see yourself differently. Don't wait until you have a lot of money to see yourself in a different light. Replace the negative self-talk with positive affirmations about yourself and your abilities.

Changing the way that you see yourself and the people around you will create changes in how other people see you. When your co-workers see you walk into work dressed nicely and polished every day when your friends and family see you treat others and yourself with respect, when you see yourself as a kind and generous person, you are on your way to having a millionaire mindset.

They Focus on Earning

If you are like most middle-class Americans, you probably see your income as limited to a certain amount (you may get a Christmas bonus and a yearly raise, but for the most part, you are stuck at a certain earning level). You are also probably looking for ways to hoard and save your money for the fear that it might one day run out, should a catastrophic event like job loss or severe illness occur. You may be looking for nickel-and-dime ways to save money, such as spending hours every month looking for coupons or switching to a phone plan that is $10 cheaper. While living within your means is a worthy goal, this mindset of hoarding will keep you from using a millionaire mindset to earn true wealth.

Millionaires think differently than most of us when it comes to how they see money. Instead of focusing on how to hoard their wealth, they focus on how they can earn more money. Of course, they understand the value of saving. However, they are less concerned with modest gains, such as a 1% interest rate on a savings account, than they are with finding where the big money is. They may decide to invest their money in the stock market or in a business venture, giving it the opportunity to grow even more rapidly, rather than socking all of it away in a savings account. Instead of focusing their mental energy on living as frugally as they possibly can, they look for creative ways to earn big money.

They Know How to Leverage

Many middle-class people know very well the value of hard work. They go into work every day, rarely missing a day unless absolutely necessary, and work tirelessly until the time comes when they can go back home. When they see their paycheck, they can feel proud because this is money that they earned. They may not have had to sweat for it, especially not if they work in an air-conditioned office, but they worked hard for it.

While millionaires understand the value of hard work, they also understand the value of leverage. Leverage is using your resources, contacts, and network, and time in such a way as to maximize results in every aspect. If one aspect of the business isn't fruitful, either prune it or use your network of people to find a way to make it fruitful. Focus your efforts on what works best, and leverage it as best as you can.

Keep in mind that leverage is not the same as using people to get what you want. While some millionaires undoubtedly use people, this is a way to create enemies and alienate people so that they will not be there when you need them. When leveraging people, always look for ways to give back to them and let them know that you are not merely trying to use them for personal gain.

They Don't Equate Money and Time

If you are like most middle-class people, how much money you earn is probably directly connected with how many hours you spend working. Even if you are in a salaried rather than an hourly position, you won't make much more money at work, except through raises and bonuses, unless you invest more time. This paradigm creates a linear view of money in which the amount of money you make is basically fixed without significantly more time invested.

Millionaires don't equate money, especially not big money, with time. They know that the best financial decisions can happen through creativity and problem-solving — things that don't happen on a 9-5 schedule — rather than through working more hours. Ideas and creativity are limitless; therefore, so is the amount of money that you can earn. The right idea activated at the right time can create a fortune virtually overnight.

Instead of thinking about money in linear terms, in which time and money are directly correlated, think of it in exponential terms, in which ideas can generate unlimited wealth.

They Have an Action-Based Mentality

Many middle-class Americans who want to become rich are taking passive steps at best towards wealth and financial success. They may be buying lottery tickets or putting in resumes for a better job, one that they may not even be qualified for. So may simply hope and pray that prosperity will one day find them.

Millionaires, however, are constantly looking for how they can take action. Instead of buying lottery tickets, they are looking for a good and better investment options. Instead of looking for good and better jobs, they are looking for business ventures that can bring in big money.

Millionaires aren't looking for a hero to rescue them and bring them financial success. Instead, they recognize that their wealth is in their hands and that they must be their own heroes if financial prosperity is to be theirs. They take action and take responsibility for their actions. They are constantly moving forward and looking for new, creative ideas.

CHAPTER 13:

The Trader's Winner Psychology

The absolute strongest asset that you have in your trading career, and the foundation of everything, is you. When it comes to getting involved in making trade deals, you are the one that you are going to have to rely on to make the best possible choices about what trades you should make, when you should make them, and how you should manage those trades. Without being in the right state of mind, and without the right level of confidence in yourself and your decisions, you are going to find yourself creating a mess out of your trades that will ultimately get worse over time.

I suggest that before you ever begin trading, and during every single trade you make, you place a large emphasis on your mindset to ensure that you are always harnessing a winner psychology that will ultimately help you succeed with your trade deals. We are going to look into depth about how you can manage your psychology and your emotions so that you are ready to get involved in trading. I cannot stress enough how important it is that you take this seriously, as many traders overlook it out of excitement and find themselves rapidly spiraling out of control due to emotional errors early on. Your emotions can and will try to take over and prevent you from making logical, positive moves in the marketplace. You are going to doubt yourself, you are going to experience fear, and you are going to experience attachments to your money along the way. If you are not prepared to experience these emotions and thoughts, and if you do not make the right decisions right now, you are going to find yourself rapidly being consumed by them and making poor judgments.

We are going to go into depth about what you will likely think and feel along the way, and how you can effectively manage these thoughts and emotions so that you are ready to deal with them like a pro. Even if you find yourself not feeling too overly affected in certain trades, I recommend putting these strategies into play anyway so that you are training yourself to have that winning mindset. Believe me when I say you will be grateful that you took this action proactively rather than waiting for something to happen, as it will go a long way in keeping your head above water in the stock market.

You Are Going to Experience Stress, Period

One of the most important things that you can do for yourself right now, before you get involved in anything to do with the stock market, is accept that you are going to experience stress. Trading on the stock market is stressful because you have personal assets tied up into it and it is a volatile place. You are going to watch the market constantly rise and fall, and you are going to wonder if you are making the right decisions to do your investments justice. You are going to be afraid that you have not done enough research and that you have invested your funds into a bad deal that could cost you money in the long run. You are going to be terrified of your funds hitting the stop loss rather than the profit target. And, when they do, you are going to start to doubt yourself and your ability to even make trade deals in the first place. When it comes to the stock market, especially early on, you are going to find yourself constantly obsessing over every little thing and worrying that you have not done enough to prepare for your deal and set yourself up for success. Even if you are excited right now, and even if you find yourself staying excited throughout the first few trades you make, you are going to experience fear and stress at one point or another.

After three years in the market, I still experience stress to this day when it comes to making trade deals and investing my money in a new stock. Even stocks I have invested in countless times in the past create fear in me, as I worry that I have not done my research enough or that things are not going to go as I expected. This is *normal.* If you can accept that you are going to experience fear and stress along the way, you can prepare yourself to reasonably manage and deal with that fear as you go. As a result, you are going to have a much easier time managing your emotions and staying in the mindset of a winner.

You Need to Remain Flexible

When you go into the stock market, it is crucial that you hold no attachment to your trades, that you are willing to change your opinion right away as needed, and that you are focused on the present moment.

You also need to follow your intuition, which will grow stronger and more reliable as you increase your experience in trades. With the stock markets, there is no way to guarantee anything, and so you have to remain flexible at all times. If you are unable to remain flexible and willing to change your approach on a moment's notice, you are going to find yourself extremely stressed out as you attempt to cling to strategies or plans that are no longer fitting the approach that you are trying to take. Rather than desperately clinging to your initial plan, you need to be willing to adapt your approach and make changes along the way as new information presents itself and the market begins to change. You will protect your assets, and your mindset, far more reliably by being flexible with the market than you will by trying to force everything to stay the same. Remember, the market is a volatile place which means it is ever changing, and you are playing its game, not the other way around. If you are not prepared to or capable of staying flexible, you are going to completely blow up your own trade deals and destroy any profitability that you may have been able to create otherwise.

You Must Be Willing to Implement Strategies

As you start trading stocks, it is crucial that you are willing to implement your strategies at all times. It can be extremely easy to let your emotions get the best of you in the stock market and make trades that ultimately destroy your chances at succeeding. You may find yourself selling before you reach your stop loss for fear of the market dropping too low, or attempting to push past your profit target to follow a growing stock. While this may seem like a good idea at the time, unless it is founded in fact-based information that you feel strongly justifies the move, you should never make it. In fact, it is a good rule of thumb to simply avoid making these decisions at all once you have chosen your strategy and position in the market. Doing so ultimately puts all of the research you had done out the window and results in you exposing yourself to massive risks based on willingness to attempt to gain more, or prevent yourself from losing more. You need to be willing to create strong strategies that you can stand behind, and then stand behind them no matter what once you enter a trade deal. This level of discipline will earn you more than it loses you, so stick with it every single time.

You Have to Stay Focused on the Bigger Picture

In addition to looking at long term trends in trades, you also need to look at the bigger picture in general. This means that, in addition to following long term trends in the specific stock that you are planning on investing in, you are also looking at long term trends of the industry itself and the market in general. Typically, the entire market will follow similar trends that bring it upward or downward, causing virtually every stock in the market to follow that trend. Although they may follow at slightly different times, you can feel confident that nearly every stock on the market will follow the same trends. Believe it or not, staying focused on the bigger picture is as much about your psychology as it is about strategy, when it comes to trading. It can be easy to get so fixated on a single stock that you become attached to the idea that it has to behave in a certain way, no matter what the market is doing. When, in reality, it can often be tracked in relation to the market and the bigger picture itself is frequently an excellent indicator of what is going on overall. Do not become so fixated that you cost yourself capital because you believe that you are right and you are arrogant to the reality of how the market tends to behave. Trust me when I say, you will always wish you had followed the market in the long run because it knows more than you do, and it will always be this way.

You Will Make Mistakes

Just like you need to accept that there is going to be stress and fear related to getting involved with the stock market, you also need to accept that you are going to make mistakes, and that this is completely unavoidable. Even at three years in, I make mistakes from time to time where I make an incorrect judgment that results in me missing out on profit that I thought was a sure thing. In fact, just a couple of weeks ago I lost out on a few hundred dollars because I invested into a stock that I was certain was going to increase, but it did not go as planned and so almost immediately after I invested it went on a downtrend. Every few weeks or so I find myself making these mistakes and losing out on profits because of it. At the end of the day, the best thing that you can do when you make a mistake is to commit to learning from it so that you can hopefully avoid making that mistake again in the future. This is where I keep my notebook handy and I write down how the mistake was made, what contributed to the mistake happening, and what I could possibly do differently in the future to avoid making a similar mistake. Then, I show gratitude for the opportunity to learn and improve my trading style in order to do even better going forward.

CHAPTER 14:

Use These Time Tested Sayings to Transform Your Trading Psychology

Abandon Ship

When you next find yourself in a trade that isn't working don't hang on in the hope that it will work out and start moving your stop loss further away, that money could be put to good use in another trade that would work out.

Just say to yourself when the trade isn't working 'Abandon Ship' and exit the trade.

Actions Speak Louder Than Words

Are you always promising yourself to do something that would improve your trading performance but never get around to it because it's boring or difficult?

When was the last time you thoroughly back tested your system?

Have you back tested every part of your system to make sure that each moving part works the best it can?

The next time you promise yourself to do something connected with improving your trading remind yourself. 'Actions Speak Louder than Words' and like Nike says, Just Do It!

All That Glitters is NOT Gold

Often when you are waiting for a trade setup or in some other trading situation, a tasty looking opportunity presents itself, that is outside your system and tempts you into a trading behaviour that you know in the cool light of day will be against your best interests.

The next time that happens, say to yourself

"All That Glitters is NOT Gold" to remind yourself of the consequences of following that tempting path and avoid taking the trade and if necessary close down your computer.

All Work and No Play Makes Jack a Dull Boy

Have you become obsessed with trading?

Are you spending hours in front of the computer at the expense of health, family and life?

Successful trader's lead balanced lives, losing your health and relationships are not the answer to being a successful trader. It's vital to balance screen time with family life and self-care to become successful in trading. After all success is so much more than just having money in the bank.

When you feel that tug towards the charts taking you away from spending with your family or friends just remind yourself of this useful truism 'All Work and no Play Makes Jack a Dull Boy',

About Face

In life we don't value people who switch direction at 'the drop of a hat', we call them flaky or unreliable. So people try to act consistently with their beliefs because they like to seem to themselves and others as a 'stand-up guy'.

In trading however you may need to 'spin on a dime' if you are trading in a direction and price keeps moving against you.

If that happens you may need to say 'About Face' and trade in the opposite direction.

A Watched Pot Never Boils

This saying can help you to avoid micro-managing your trades.

Watching and worrying about the result of your trades after you have placed them can be counterproductive and leads to exiting too early and moving stops closer or further away.

In effect, undoing the research that got you into the trade into the first place.

Use this saying to remind yourself to give the trade time to work.

Are You a Man or a Mouse?

You see the trade, it's a perfect setup for your system, you have confirmed it exactly as you should, but you are hesitating to pull the trigger on a trade, at that point then ask yourself

Are you a man or a mouse?

And place that trade!

It's a phrase that reminds you that when it comes time to take action we need to be brave and go for it!

An Ounce of Prevention is Worth a Pound of Cure

Have you done the correct trading preparation for your trading day?

Successful traders have a routine and repeat that routine every day that they trade.

The proper preparation is vital for making sure that when that trade comes you can take it knowing that every part of the trading analysis has been done. Off the cuff trades are a no-no for a successful trader.

Remind yourself if you need to do your preparation early and you are tempted to skip it, 'An Ounce of Preparation is Worth a Pound of Cure' and what the potential results could be of taking trades which have no proper preparation behind them.

Back From the Dead

Ok so you blew out your account, let yourself down and traded like a maniac.

It took weeks to recover your emotional equilibrium. It's happened to lots of great traders and they come back from it.

You've refunded your account, put in place strategies to make sure you never repeat the old mistakes and it's 'onwards and upwards' you are 'Back from the Dead'!

Back Seat Driver

Don't be a 'Back Seat Driver' when trading, also known as trying to micro manage your trades.

You've done the analysis and placed the trade, now don't hover over the trade (unless that is part of your strategy)

Let the market do its work, there are only three outcomes, a win, a loss, or break even and your trade should have those three outcomes built in.

Let the trade have room and time to develop, remind yourself when you are tempted to interfere with the trade, don't be a 'Back Seat Driver'

Back to the Drawing Board

So you have bought a system or seen a system on a forum that looked great, other people have been making big money with it and you were full of optimism, the only problem is you can’t trade it.

The system may be a day trading system and you don't have the patience or time to do it.

It may be an end-of-day system and you don't have the money it would take to cover your trades.

For whatever reason the trading system does not work for you

So it’s 'Back to the Drawing Board' to find the right methodology that suits your personality and life style,

Just don't let that search for the right methodology turn into another trading cliché the search for the trading Holy Grail, for the system that never loses and will make you a million bucks.

It doesn't exist, but there is the option of finding a system that is a perfect fit for you, and it's worth going 'Back to the Drawing Board' time and again until you find it.

Better Safe than Sorry

This saying applies to those traders who are tempted to take trades that are risky.

If you are often taking trades that fall outside your risk parameters, use this little saying as a mental short-cut to remind you to stay safe in your trading.

Bad trades can spiral out of control, and what starts off as 'a bit of a punt' can end up losing half your account as you try to compensate.

'Better Safe than Sorry' is a valuable truism for your trading.

A Bird in the Hand is Worth Two in the Bush

This is a common belief amongst traders and can work for or against you. If you are regularly exiting trades too early then this saying is not for you.

If however you are losing profits you could have taken because you are letting the trade run on too long, then use the saying 'A Bird in the Hand is Worth Two in the Bush' to remind yourself to take your profits.

Bite the Bullet

Sometimes in trading as in life there comes a time when you have to 'step up to the plate' and take a risk.

If entering trades is a problem for you or it is time to scale up your trades, or you have any other trading issue where timidity is stopping you from taking action, then remind yourself to 'Bite the Bullet'.

Take the action however uncomfortable it may feel at first. It will get easier the more often you repeat the action until you no longer have to steel yourself up to it and it just becomes routine.

The Buck Stops Here

In trading there is no substitute for taking personal responsibility for everything that happens. If you feel yourself tempted to blame outside events for your trading difficulties then 'The Buck Stops Here' could be an apt reminder.

Ok, so a news announcement may have spiked price past your stop, taken you out and moved in the correct direction, but the real question is does your methodology take these events into account.

For all trading events however random there needs to be an accompanying strategy to deal with that event and no blaming attached to anything outside in you.

When you take responsibility for everything that happens then you are on the road to greatness and can find a way of dealing with the problem.

In trading as in life, 'The Buck Stops Here'.

A Bump in the Road

In trading there will be constant setbacks, but it is the way you view these setbacks that will determine whether you have what it takes to succeed in trading.

If you expect constant setbacks and look at them as a way of making improvements to yourself or/and your system you will soon come to regard them as just another 'bump in the road' to successful trading.

For traders who are always getting upset because of trading setbacks, then using the saying 'It's a Bump in the Road' can help take a longer view and put things into their true perspective.

Curiosity Killed the Cat

One of the emotions that can derail traders which is not often mentioned, is that curiosity can lead to staying in trades too long to see what happens.

That sense of curiosity can turn a good profit into a break-even or even a losing trade.

Sticks to the take-profit you have chosen and don't let curiosity cause you to stay in the trade to 'see what will happen'.

Use the phrase "Curiosity Killed the Cat" to remind yourself not to give in to curiosity and to exit trades when the profit is there to take.

Call it a Day

Many day traders get so caught up in the thrill of placing trades they can't walk away from the charts.

They trade to failure by keeping on trading during times that aren't suitable for their system or psychology and start losing money.

They then start trying to get their money back from the market and at the end of the day find themselves exhausted and holding a large loss, when if they had just 'Called it a Day' after hitting a target or getting a couple of wins under their belt they would have finished the day early and in profit.

'Call it a Day' when you hit your target not at the end of the 'working day', that is Job Thinking,

In trading you ideally want to finish while your mind is still fresh before tiredness sets in.

CHAPTER 15:

Investing Dynamics

What Is Investing?

Investing is a way to make money work for you. Normally, people spend lots of hours just to work for money. When you learn how to invest, it becomes the other way around: Money works for you. This is the ideal state of earning money, and this is also why so many people these days are eager to learn just how to make the right investments. However, just as there is a possibility for you to make a profit, there is also the risk that you might lose your investment. Hence, it is important that you learn the 'rules' of investing in order to increase your chances of success.

Unlike keeping your money in the bank where it grows a small interest, you can earn much higher when you put your money somewhere else. Well, the truth is that keeping your money is a bank is also an investment. However, there are other investments that you can make where you can make a much bigger profit.

Investing is the way for people to escape the rat race or the long hours you spend in the office. If you want to increase your money, then you have to learn how to make a successful investment. Unfortunately, many people jump into making investments without understanding what it is, and so many of them end up disappointed.

Where Can You Invest?

Just where exactly do you put your money in? There are many things that you can invest in. The question is being able to identify the ones that will give you positive results. Do not worry, we will teach you profitable options that you can consider, such as investing in penny stocks, cryptocurrencies, real estate, and blogs, among others. Investing is about putting your money in something and then getting it back at a profit. Hence, you do not really 'spend' your money when you invest.

If you just think about it, almost anything can be turned into an investment. It is about putting your money into something and making it grow. Thanks to technology, it is now very easy to make investments with just a few clicks of a mouse. But then again, take note that it is not just making an investment that matters, but being able to make a profitable investment. This is the tricky part as it is not always easy to spot a good investment. Not to mention, even a highly profitable investment today can end up as a bad investment in the future. Indeed, making investments, specifically good investments, take more than just having money. More importantly, you need to have the right foundation and skills.

How Much Should You Invest?

There are no hard and fast rules as to how much you should invest. But, it is strongly suggested that you should only invest the money that you can afford to lose. Even though investing can make you a big amount of profit, you must not ignore the possibility that an investment can turn bad and end up in losses.

Is it still a good idea to invest a big amount of money? This depends, but since you will be earning a percentage of your investment, then the more that you invest, the bigger is your potential return. Hence, many people like to invest a big amount. For example, if you invest $1,000, and you profit by 100%, then you will gain $1,000. If you only invested $20, even if you gain the same percentage profit of 100%, then you will only earn $20. Still, there are investments that will allow you to earn a profit of more than 100% of your investment.

As a basic rule, it is worth repeating that you should only invest the money that you are comfortable with spending, which is the money that you can afford to lose. Feel free to invest as much as you want or as little as you want. Do not worry, you are free to add more investment money as many times as you want. If you are just starting out, especially if it is your first time making an investment, then it is advised that you start with just a small amount.

Busting The Myths

Unfortunately, there are people out there who have wrong view or understanding of what it is to make investments. To give you a better idea of what making investments really is, let us bust down the myths about it one by one:

- You need to have lots of money to make an investment

Although you can invest a big chunk of money and indeed there are people out there who spend millions and thousands of dollars on their investments, you are still free to make small investments. In fact, you can invest even $1 if you want. Again, there are no hard and fast rules as to how much you should invest. Many people start out small and then gradually make their way up as they earn more money. But, one thing is clear: you do not need lots of money first before you can make an investment. Rather, you can make lots of money by making profitable investments. In fact, most people make investments not because they already have lots of money, but because they want to earn money. As you can see, financial capability should not be an obstacle. In fact, it is something that is within your reach when you make an investment.

- It is complicated

Okay, take note that the only thing that makes investing complicated is when you do not understand what you are doing. For example, you might try to invest in cryptocurrencies but then fail to take efforts to even understand what cryptocurrencies are and how they work. In this case, then it does get complicated. But, this should not be the case. In fact, if you still think and feel that something is complicated to you, then that only means that you should not make any investment yet. You should only invest in something that you understand. This way you can increase your chances of making the right investment decision.

- It is an easy and quick way to become rich

Sadly, people always want an easy way out, but such a thing does not exist unless you get really lucky. Professional investors watch their investments very closely and spend hours in research and analysis to identify the best possible investment opportunity. As a true and professional investor, you do not just place your money in something and hope that you earn some profits out of it. Professional investors do not rely on luck. They spend time and effort to ensure that they make the right investments. If you are not willing to put in time and effort in what you do, then perhaps investing is not for you. Take note that investing needs plenty of hard work for you to be successful. Still, it is nonetheless one of the best ways to make money and even attain financial freedom.

- It is only for a chosen few

There are those who think that investing is only for some chosen people as if there is a special class that you should belong to. However, this is not true. Anyone can invest, as long as you are of legal age. With the help of technology, you can now make different investments with just a few clicks of the mouse in the comfort of your home. This is one of the reasons why you should seriously consider making an investment since it is now easier to make an investment than ever before.

- Is it for you?

Do you have what it takes to be a successful investor? The good news is that investing is something that you can learn and practice. Just like any other craft, the more that you learn and practice it, the better you will get. If you are the type who is willing to face some risks and challenges for a nice possible return, the investing is for you. If you are tired of your office job and want to earn more income, then investing is for you. If you want to buy your way to financial freedom, then investing is definitely for you. Simply put, if you want a better life and be in a better financial standing, then you should definitely learn and invest in something. Still, the best way to find out if this path is for you or not is by giving it a try. So that you will not be pressured, you may want to begin by investing just a small amount and see how it goes. Do not worry; you can always add more money if you want. So, is it for you? Well, it is time for you to find out.

CHAPTER 16:

How to Manage Stress in Investing?

Trading is a process that revolves mostly around three major factors. These are money management, trading strategies, and psychology. You need to keep in mind that the markets can be a very emotional place, so it is crucial that you remain focused and disciplined. If you do not stay disciplined, then you will lose out, and others will very likely take advantage of you.

What you really need to do in order to trade successfully is to have a solid strategy, follow the strategy, and stick to it. If the strategy does not follow the intended plan, then simply quit and come up with another strategy.

If you have a strong mindset, you will be able to understand when to pursue a losing trade and when to quit. If you lack discipline, then one of two emotions will take over. These are greed and fear.

You Are Going to Experience Stress, Period

One of the most important things that you can do for yourself right now, before you get involved in anything to do with the stock market, is accept that you are going to experience stress. Period. Trading on the stock market is stressful because you have personal assets tied up into it and it is a volatile place. You are going to watch the market constantly rise and fall, and you are going to wonder if you are making the right decisions to do your investments justice. You are going to be afraid that you have not done enough research and that you have invested your funds into a bad deal that could cost you money in the long run. You are going to be terrified of your funds hitting the stop loss rather than the profit target. And, when they do, you are going to start to doubt yourself and your ability to even make trade deals in the first place. When it comes to the stock market, especially early on, you are going to find yourself constantly obsessing over every little thing and worrying that you have not done enough to prepare for your deal and set yourself up for success. Even if you are excited right now, and even if you find yourself staying excited throughout the first few trades you make, you are going to experience fear and stress at one point or another.

After three years in the market, I still experience stress to this day when it comes to making trade deals and investing my money in a new stock. Even stocks I have invested in countless times in the past create fear in me, as I worry that I have not done my research enough or that things are not going to go as I expected. This is normal. If you can accept that you are going to experience fear and stress along the way, you can prepare yourself to reasonably manage and deal with that fear as you go. As a result, you are going to have a much easier time managing your emotions and staying in the mindset of a winner.

Sometimes traders trade on a whim and keep posting random trades. Rather than take this approach, you really should focus on a successful strategy which you will pursue until you need to exit. You should also have good trading skills and proper money management plan. With these in place, you will be able to focus better and think in terms of probabilities and risk-reward ratios. This way, you will not leave room for emotional trading.

You also need to accept any possible failures. Sometimes your strategies will not work out, and you will lose some trades. This happens to all traders, even experienced ones. If you assume that you must succeed on each attempt, then you will be setting yourself up for failure.

There are other things that you need to also keep in mind. For instance, you need to develop and stick with good trading habits. As a trader, you need to note that a winner is one who is persistent and consistent. You should develop the habit of closely studying the markets, conducting your analysis, and position sizing.

Position sizing is common, especially in a volatile market. As such, you need to take care of your downside risks and ensure that you position the size appropriately. You should also envision the end game. Come up with a vision of where you want the trade to head then prepare to make any necessary adjustments.

You also need to accept any possible failures. Sometimes your strategies will not work out, and you will lose some trades. This happens to all traders, even experienced ones. If you assume that you must succeed on each attempt, then you will be setting yourself up for failure.

Investing Mindset

Traders may also learn different mindsets from other traders. By researching extensively and hearing how other people conduct their trades, there is much to learn. By increasing knowledge, the investor may decrease their negative emotional reactions. They will further understand the stock market and how it operates, and this will help to eliminate such reactions.

Although it is important to stick to one's plan, traders must adopt flexible mindsets. They must be willing to try new tools, buy and sell new stocks, research new companies, and trade differently. There is no "correct" way to trade. There are simply many different ways of doing so. Some may be more profitable than others. Some may work well for one trader and not well for another. Traders should be willing to slightly experiment to see what the best way for them to trade is. This may also decrease emotion when it comes to stock.

Investors should also be critical of themselves and view their trading from a logical stance. There will be certain ways to trade that will result in greater returns. Traders must be willing to reflect on their performance and see what resulted in gains and what didn't. There is always room for improvement, and traders must recognize that. Perhaps for one time period, the trader wasn't researching as thoroughly and missed certain aspects that they should have spent more time on. Perhaps the trader did let emotion influence their trades.

By recognizing potential bad habits, the trader will be able to work on improving themselves and making themselves a more profitable and skillful trader for the future.

Traders must use technical analysis to drive their investing decisions. There are various ways of doing so. Perhaps the trader wishes to focus on charts. This can prove highly beneficial for seeing a visual representation of performance. The trader may have a group of investors that they seek advice from with their trades. They may have a journal to write their plan in. There are programs to use to help with investments. Whichever way the trader prefers that they conduct their business, there should be some sort of support to help logically analyze their decisions. There must be a guide.

Patience is also crucial for traders. Fear and greed, combined with a lack of patience, can truly harm the trader's ability to think quickly and make the right decision. By practicing patience, the trader will be able to decide better when the right time for buying or selling a stock is. Otherwise, the trader might be willing to jump into or out of the market despite the bad timing of doing so. Practicing patience can improve one's ability to time the market better and hold onto investments that will perform better with time while letting go of investments that have had their time.

CHAPTER 17:

Secrets for Success

Allow Yourself Time

Traders get into the market with so many expectations about the market. They imagine that they will enter the market, put some money and the next minute they are swimming in millions of money. Trading is profitable when done right, but it also needs time before you finally enjoy your benefits. Allow yourself time to adapt to the market, to know how trading actually works, and even understand the many risks you are likely to incur. Allowing yourself time to just adjust to the market without so much greed for the money will make you a very great trader who will succeed in the long run. It is better to make small profits for a long time than to make huge profits for a short while. Not being ready is essential for a trader; it will give him the patience to wait and work towards being great traders rather than just focusing on being short term traders. It will also make the trader love their trading experiences because they are not rushing themselves or putting too much unnecessary pressure on themselves.

Have a Network of Fellow Traders

Like all other businesses, traders are supposed to create friendships among themselves. These fellow traders will not only inspire a trader, but they will offer help to the trader when the trader needs it. It is good to have friends doing the same thing as you are as you get to hear their experiences, and you can compare them with your own experiences. Having friends who been in trading longer than you have will give awareness of what awaits you in the long run. You can get some things to copy from a friend who has been doing this ahead of you. Having friends who are in the same industry will also give you a friend counselor or mentor who will help you in making various trade decisions. You can make this advisor your mentor whom you will consult from time to time. A mentor will help you avoid making bad trading decisions that could cost you a lot of money and also help you identify how to work out your weaknesses. A network is generally crucial because even other than having people who will offer you help, you also have people who can give you future connections in the market.

Love the Trading Market

To love the trading experience means that you enjoy the process more than your love for the money that comes along. By doing this, it means that even when you don't get so much money from the process, you will push on with the trade because you love the thrill of trading. The benefits are vital without them; there would be no reason to do trading. However, the benefits will not be very rewarding for someone who does not enjoy the process of getting them. This is even more so because you may lose all the money you had invested in trading, but if you love the process, you will know how to pick yourself back up. The rewards are not very fulfilling for a trader if the trader does not enjoy his journey and keeps waking up to make the trade just for the money. Enjoying the process gives you reasons to take more risks that will yield you more profits. But when you do not enjoy the process, you only play safely to maintain the same earnings as you make every day. If you are able to maintain a standard point, you do not really care for anything else. Loving the process means that you get to explore more to understand the market and also to find ways that will make you enjoy your work more. When you love trading, you are not like to be as exhausted when working as people who do not enjoy it. When you enjoy the trading process, you are likely to adjust to the market quickly and even succeed more than traders who have been doing it for long.

Stick to What You Know

The trading market is diverse, stick to what you are comfortable in rather than wasting your time going for different strategies. It is good to be open to new methods, but if the ways just spend your time or slow your progress, it is good to stick with what you know. Take time to modify what you have because that may be more beneficial for you as a trader. The art of mastering the industry involves that you deal with the little you know and work on it until perfection. When you have perfected one area, you can then pick another area and work on it. In short, it is good to subdivide your trading schedules and work on them individually than picking a big task that will not yield you much result.

Keep Practicing

It is good for a trader to first try by practicing to ensure that they are more comfortable in the market before investing their money. Practicing before you finally get to put your money will give you security because you already know what you are about to face. You may achieve this by using a trading simulator, which will help you get a feel of the real work awaiting you. When you finally are convinced that you are up to the task, then you can venture into trading. Then when you eventually become a trader, it is good to keep putting into practice all the different methods you learn along the way. Every opportunity as a trader should be used to perfect on your skills, and the way to perfecting is by ensuring that you are not lazy but keep learning.

Don't Be Too Excited

Excitement is good, but in trading, it will cost you a lot. You may be too excited and end up making rushed decisions that will make you losses. Sometimes the market works too much in your favor that you begin to think you are perfect. You may keep getting it right, but you still need to be careful because getting too excited may make you make a small mistake that will bring you down. Your strategy may be working, but that does not make you an overnight prophet that you now think your predictions are always right. You will still need to keep observing the market; you will still need to keep trying different strategies because there is no guarantee that you will keep winning. Losing several times, on the other hand, does not make you a definite failure. You don't have to keep taking bigger risks to ensure that you recover your money. Take your time and strategize your moves and see where you are going wrong instead of crucifying yourself. Do not be too hard on yourself simply because a few times. The plan didn't work out for you. But also, do not let the excitement make you too overconfident as overconfident is most likely to bring you down. When you can seem to strike a balance, it is good to take a break from trading and relax. Continuing like this will be more harmful to you than if you had relaxed.

Create a Routine

It is essential that as a trader, you have a routine that you follow strictly. A routine will give you the discipline to do things in a more streamlined way. A routine will remind the trader of various things they need to follow each day, and therefore the trader doesn't end up wasting time. A routine will help you meet your objectives as a trader because it will act as a reminder of the tasks you are supposed to accomplish within the day.

Have the Proper Tools for the Trade

This includes having the right tool to conduct your trading. Some traders prefer having a computer while others find using a mobile phone more comfortable. But as a trader, you should have either of the two to be able to trade. A computer or a mobile phone has to be connected to an easily accessible internet as you need to be connected to the market. You also need software that will facilitate your trading. Without one of these, trading is impossible, and therefore, it should be anyone's priority to get the right device before getting into trading.

Have a Strategy

You already know your goal, and you already know your strengths and weaknesses. It is now essential to have a well laid out plan of how you intend to accomplish your strategies. The strategy should consider factors like when you intend to make your entrance into the market. A trader with a plan knows that entering the market without considering the timing is almost useless. A good plan should also include the intended time a trader plans on making an exit. Do you, as a trader, intend to be in the market as a short term or long term, and what precisely do you mean by the two. Knowing this will keep you in check on your intended goals so that you do not exit too hastily.

A good plan also ensures that a trader has gone through their trading strategy and therefore knows when to stop a loss and when to close a profit. This well-planned strategy of preventing losses will, therefore, keep the trader on his toes as he tries to find technological systems that will alert him beforehand. A good strategy also ensures that the trader not only knows the potential risks in the market, but he also knows what to do in case the risk actually happens. A good strategy is what tells the trader if they are indeed ready to be in the market. It is not enough to have the capital to start trading, you also need a strategy, and it should actually come first. If you invest money without the right strategy, you are likely to lose your money. You may even enter into the market and keep going in circles trying to find out where to lean on as a trader because you did not have the right strategy when you began.

A good strategy saves a trader time because they already know what they want, how they want it, and when they need it. A person who does not have a strategy spends most of their time figuring this out, and therefore, even if he makes good returns, he will not identify when it's time to exit. A good strategy is also a source of motivation; the trader can always see what they are aiming to achieve. Therefore, when times get hard, and you feel like quitting, you will remember the plan you had and keep moving ahead. A good plan also has the power of calming a trader when the trader thinks they are achieving too much. A trader may be getting a lot of returns, but they may not be what he was initially after. This will help calm him so that the only time he gets excited is only they have achieved their overall objective and are about to exit the market.

CHAPTER 18:

Technical Analysis and It's Basics

No matter the kind of vehicle you choose for your actions, there are some basics that you have to be familiar with. This fundamental knowledge is mostly connected to the behavior of the markets. If you learn how to recognize the way they behave, you will be able to anticipate the movement of the prices more accurately, thus make smarter decisions while trading. It can be interesting to note that regardless of the value that is traded on the market, some concepts can always apply to the prices and their way of performance on the market.

This can be explained by independent traders and investors being responsible for short-term price fluctuations. We can say that the price depends on the actions of the people who invest or trade values on the market and that prices react in a similar way when they are given similar input or stimuli. The study that is dedicated to researching the ways of price behavior is called technical analysis and understanding its basic is one of the most essential education points that you will need to be able to make correct financial decisions on the market.

The basics of Technical Analysis

Technical analysis represents a huge topic. If you decide to enter the market and become an investor, there is a high possibility that you will catch yourself coming back to studying and learning something new many times for as long as you intend to work as a trader. That is why every person knowledgeable in options trading would advise that a basic understanding of technical analysis is a very important step for every person involved in the market. However, you don't need to know everything about it right away. Since it is a large area of research, it is ok if for some aspects of your business you just research parts of the technical analysis that you are particularly interested in for that concrete project. For instance, the technical analysis offers more than a hundred indicators for analyzing the market. In reality, traders usually use three or four, mostly the most popular ones or just those that they were familiar within the first place.

If you don't limit yourself only to option trading but you do trading in general, you will realize that technical analysis can be applied to any financial instruments such as futures or stocks for example.

We can say that their basis is in psychology and human nature in general and how they behave in practice. For better understanding, we will overview some of the main topics in technical analysis. These topics will be:

Technical analysis' foundation; how to chart principles and trends; patterns in technical analysis; technical analysis through the movement of the averages, and Indicators in technical analysis.

Technical analysis' foundation

The main basis of the technical analysis is found in the term known as " market action". Market action represents a whole personal knowledge about the trading market, and it doesn't include information that you might obtain from an insider. It can be simply defined as a study that determines: "the way that the price moves over time". If possible, it also examines its volumes and how they change over time too.

Still, the fundamental concept of technical analysis is based on the premise that the behavior of the market is a reflection of everything that happened and will happen with the price at a certain moment. Many things can have an impact on the price, and the amount of the impact depends on the market in which the trade is made. That's where technical analysis comes in, it cuts across all of those possibilities and states that all the things that can be known about the price are basically already included in the price that we see at the moment we want to trade.

This means that you shouldn't worry too much about the things that influence the price, as according to this it is enough to follow how the price changes over time and you will get all your answers. At first, many people wondered if this kind of principle can work because it sounded rather easy. If you had any doubts, the answer was already proven and it says that yes, technical analysis is successful although this kind of definition doesn't seem that complicated.

However, there is one very important point coming out from all of this. Technical analysis doesn't guarantee the behavior of the price. It can tell you that the price will increase or decrease for a certain period, but that doesn't necessarily happen. It may or it may not. The reason for this is that regardless of the calculation that the market has to do something, it is impossible to be 100 percent sure that it will. The market has its own ways and eventually does what it wants. So what technical analysis does is that it gives you the indication that shows what will be the most probable outcome, which means that the only certainty that you get is to know if the law of probability is on your side or not.

You can do a large number of average trades and hopefully make some profit, but you should never invest an amount of money or some valuable goods such as your house or your car if you can't afford to lose it. It is not recommended especially if one successful trade makes you confident that just one is enough to be a good technical indicator for certain gain. This is one of the reasons why the first task of technical analysis is to improve your chance for success by analyzing the prices and the way they behave on the market.

The second reason for the analysis is the fact that prices almost always change using certain trends. For instance, if the price increases its trend will be to rise until there is something that disables it from further growth. In comparison, we can say that prices act like Newton's motion law, which says that: "a body in motion will stay in motion unless acted upon by an external force." Of course, to prove this to be true, it has to happen over time. If this wasn't the case the price charts represented in many analyses wouldn't be the way they are. They would be illustrated as a random movement of the prices. The third reason is that technical analysis supposes that history will, as always, repeat itself. If certain situations happened in the past, and you see them happening once again in the present than it is highly expected that the same thing will happen in the future too. Since people are not expected to change in this equation, the second logical conclusion would be that their results will be the same too. In a nutshell- this was a very foundation of technical analysis. Don't forget that one of the most efficient ways to become good in trading and to increase your chance to become a successful investor is to be able to use most of the things that this analysis can give you.

There are a few arguments that you can hear against the use of technical analysis. Still, the only proof that you really need is the fact that this analysis works and that at least it can improve your chances to get more percentages while trading. However, we will point out some of the attitudes toward technical analysis:

One of the traders said: "Charts only show what has happened in the past, how they can reveal what hasn't happened yet?" The answer to this is quite simple, there is evidence from earlier trades and those pieces of evidence are used in technical analysis with the premise that history will repeat itself. This way you can anticipate at least with some fair certainty what is the next thing that will happen with the price on the market. In comparison, it works in a similar way as the weather forecast, if they say that it will rain on the TV, you know that it might not rain even though they said it will, but you take your umbrella with you anyway. The same principle applies with the technical analysis and that is how you can predict the future by using the past events.

Another trader noted: "If the prices already incorporate everything there is to know, then any change in price can only come from new information that we don't know yet." This kind of idea doesn't only appear in trading options, it is present in all financial markets. It surfaces in many areas and even academics are still discussing it. Differently, from the opinion that is popular between the traders, this concept doesn't actually say that the price that is currently on the market is the correct one. It just states that it isn't possible to establish if that current price is too low or too high. That is why the smartest choice to deal with this concept is to prove in which way technical analysis really works. In the end, if everyone supported this kind of idea then we would have zero analysis and the price would be always the same. We can imply that technical analysis has self-fulfilling characteristics.

This means that if the majority of traders do the analysis and estimate that the price has to increase all of them would become buyers on the market, which would mean an increase in demand, thus price that went up. The same principle applies to the price that is supposed to go down. This is one more example in which technical analysis showed that it works. Of course, there can always be some doubts but does it really matter to prove why the price went in the direction that you thought it would? Additionally, if a large number of traders who are not well educated and they just want to make quick profit fail, it can be seen as a sort of evidence that the idea of having a massive amount of traders regardless of their knowledge and dedication is somehow wrong from the beginning.

CHAPTER 19:

Stubbornness

Stubbornness has long been a problem with some traders who refuse to change their views, even though the situation changes for the better or worse. Often, we make decisions based on what we think is right i.e. emotionally led rather than relying on the hard facts presented to us during a trade.

What You Can Do

There are several ways to overcome stubbornness as a cognitive bias. It requires one to not hold on to any long-held beliefs, but instead focus on analyzing data and executing based on what the market is telling you. Cutting your losses may be admitting defeat, but limiting the damage is far more important than protecting your ego. This also frees up an opportunity to reinvest somewhere else. It is far easier to recoup your losses in a trade when a stock has momentum, as opposed to waiting for the tide to turn on a sinking ship.

Anchoring Bias

Case Study

Bob starts off his trading day by spotting a bullish trend in the market. He is convinced that the bulls will take full control for the rest of the day. Although the market shows signs of exhaustion later on, Bob is essentially anchored to the information glimpsed from the strong bullish thrust first seen at the start of his day. After many trades, he finally realizes that he has only spent the day fighting the market, all because he was anchored to the positive start.

You're Learning Curve

Does anchoring affect traders? It absolutely does! Everything we do is based on price and value, and we're constantly trying to determine and evaluate the price of our chosen trade and if it's going up or down.

Anchors such as the first piece of information we get stuck with get in the way of our objectivity, much like a horse wearing blinkers. When we see a particular stock gaining momentum at the beginning, we think the only way is up.

Listen to what the market is telling you. Strike a balance between looking back in time for support and resistance when executing technical analysis, but also look for additional clues and indicators that may turn the tide. This can be a delicate balancing act, one that requires you to analyze historical data. Just remember, always use past information as a guideline, not an unwavering fact that cannot be altered.

Take control of the anchors themselves. Forget about profit targets, maximum losses, best entry prices, or any other price-based numbers. Even if a trade works exactly the way you want it to go, it doesn't guarantee that any of these targets will be reached. Learn to anchor on execution instead.

Confirmation Bias

Case Study

Bob is trying out a new trading strategy, and decides to increase his variance by participating in ten trades. Among the ten, 8 are losers, and 2 are winners. Subconsciously, Bob downplays the significance of the losers, focusing purely on the 2 profitable trades. Bob convinces himself that the new strategy works and that the losers will eventually recover, even though the bigger picture says otherwise.

You're Learning Curve

Confirmation bias is an example of selective perception, a way of filtering information. But instead of seeking out the negative, it glorifies the positives and makes the success larger than life. Everyone loves being right, so naturally we seek out any information that reiterates that the move that was executed was the right move.

In its logical conclusion, confirmation bias lets traders see trades that just aren't there. The slightest hint of something that looks like a winner already has you jumping in with both feet, diving head-first. But this bias hides the real truth, convincing you that the long trade you just made is really working out, and that the falling price is nothing more than a retracement.

So how do you beat something you are inherently blind to? Flipping charts help – and I mean really physically flipping them. Imagine entering a trade but it doesn't go the way you expect it to. According to your detailed strategy plan, you should pull out and exit, even if it means taking a loss. Flipping a chart helps you see what is really there, instead of what you want to see. By doing this, you are confusing the bias, allowing you no more excuses to stay in the trade. You can quickly exit with a small loss, rather than letting the trade get away from you and turn into a potentially bigger let down.

Post Purchase Rationalism

Case Study

Bob waits patiently and observes the market intently. He refrains from making sub-optimal trades, convincing himself that if he waits long enough, he would find that one perfect trade of the day.

And then it arrives. Bob takes it without hesitation. In his mind, he is convinced that he is the epitome of an ideal trader – patient, calm, observant, and strategically wise. But after getting into a long position, post-purchase rationalization comes in. Bob has placed a considerable amount of time and effort into finding this trade; so much that he forgoes the warning signs from the very start. He refuses to accept that while it did have a potential chance to shine; it is slowly shaping up into a losing trade. As a result, he gave up many chances to exit with smaller gains. In the end, the market plummets, and the small gains became a substantial loss.

You're Learning Curve

After buying something, traders tend to rationalize and prove that the purchase is right. This is especially true for expensive purchases. We do not want to admit that we purchased in bad judgment after spending all that time and effort to research. Do not try to rationalize your trade only after you've made the purchase. That justification should have been done before entering a trade.

CHAPTER 20:

Characteristics of Losing Traders

Harvey is a brilliant engineer with an advanced degree from an Ivy League university. He has a lot of confidence because his career has been marked with great success and he is highly respected in his field. However, it would be a mistake to assume that his success in engineering will automatically translate into a profitable career as a day trader, because the two endeavors require different skill sets. Success requires going through a learning phase.

There is nothing wrong with being confident. In fact, confidence and belief in a trading plan are essential to longer-term success. The problem occurs when an individual becomes so intent on perfection and controlling everything that they do not use common sense. In fact, if a trader feels a need to consistently self-validate how smart they are, they are setting themselves up for disappointment.

In other words, big egos can be advantageous in day-to-day living and when trying to climb the corporate ladder, but when dealing with financial markets, a big ego is usually a ticket to a quick exit.

Successful trading comes from managing imperfection and surrendering to what we cannot control. It is not possible to control where prices are heading next or how the market—the unruly beast—will react from one day to the next. The winning trader focuses attention on the things that can be controlled.

Harvey is not coachable, because he thinks he is smarter than his coaches. He cannot accept being wrong, and, since he cannot concede defeat, he holds losing positions too long. Harvey does everything in his power to control the outcome of the trade. In the end, he cannot get out of his own way to transform into something different: a winning trader.

What Harvey is really doing is asserting his over-embellished ego to validate how smart he is, which is not going to end well, because trading to prove your self-worth is not the right reason to trade.

Trading is hard, very hard. That is why losing traders far outnumber winning traders. Harvey fails because his ego gets in the way. Losing traders fail for a multitude of other reasons, including (but not limited to) the following:

Unrealistic Expectations

Most new traders dream about making large amounts of money in a short amount of time. When that does not happen, frustration sets in. They have a choice: work hard to grow and develop their trading skills, or quit. Most quit.

A third choice is to throw the baby out with the bathwater and begin chasing down a new trade strategy. We call that chasing performance. They might have a winning tradeplan or strategy, but they cannot see the forest for the trees. They are trying not to get crushed by a few falling trees and are unable to elevate high enough to see that their plan can and will grow their forest larger.

They actually do possess the keys to the kingdom, but they do not know how to use them to open the door, or they do not even recognize the door that is right there in front of them. Just put the key in the lock, open the door, and walk through it.

In trying to survive as humans, we often do the wrong things as traders. Losses hurt and represent a risk to our survival (in trading). So we do what humans would do to avoid the pain: we try to fix the losing trade. But the losing trade does not represent a risk to our survival as traders if it is part of a winning trade plan, which will accomplish our goals if we stay the course.

We have instincts, as humans, to want to survive and not become extinct. Understanding that survival is your first goal is probably the best way to approach trading.

That does not mean trying to avoid the random losing trade. But it does mean not taking random trades at all. Any trade should have the odds stacked on your side and be within the context of a proven trade plan. The trade could still lose, but within such a context it is not going to threaten your survival as a trader. Let the odds do the heavy lifting for you. It is a pure numbers game.

Your account will grow over time. But even then, it will not grow in a straight line. You will have periods of wins and losses. Your account will go up, go down, go up again, and go down again. To succeed, upswings must be larger than downswings.

I will show you how to prove your trade methodology and help you achieve your goals before you ever risk any real money. Once you prove it to yourself, you can begin to solve the emotional and psychological issues that haunt all would-be traders.

Emotional Decision-Making

Losing traders tend to get excited or fearful when a trading situation develops. The excited ones often get in prematurely and the fearful ones often miss the trade entirely.

If the trade is profitable, the excited trader may hold on to it too long in hopes of a greater profit—only to see the market reverse course and erase much of the original profit.

The fearful trader, after missing out on what would have been a winner, will pull the trigger too quickly on the next trade. Often, that second trade will be a loser.

Trading objectively and without emotion is the hallmark of good traders, and trading emotionally is the hallmark of poor traders. Which do you want to be?

Chronic Hesitation and Second-Guessing

After a few unprofitable trades, the average trader becomes hesitant about entering the market again, because he or she fears the next trade will be a loser too.

Often these traders will try to find a new indicator that they can add to their system that would have prevented them from getting into those losing trades. This can become a continuous cycle that ultimately leads to "paralysis by analysis." They are looking at so many indicators that they are unable to make a decision about whether to trade.

Inadequate Trading Plan

Unsuccessful traders usually don't think through their trading plan. Or, worse, they don't have one at all! They take a haphazard approach to the markets they trade, the hours they devote to trading, and their daily preparation.

Often, they keep no records of their trades and never ask themselves what they did right or wrong at the end of the trading day.

Proper planning and preparation provide a solid foundation that allows traders to exercise the necessary patience and discipline to trade well.

There is an old saying: "Failure to plan is planning to fail." That is absolutely true in trading.

Unproven Strategy

Unsuccessful traders usually do not thoroughly test a trading system, whether it is a system they developed on their own or a system they picked up from another trader. As a result, they lack conviction in implementing the system and are prone to making a variety of trading errors.

Building a trading system that works in the real-world markets over long periods is no simple matter. We go through the building blocks together, step by step. If you execute this system consistently and correctly, it will put you in the best position for success as a trader.

Poor Money Management

Money management is probably the most underappreciated part of successful trading. For every trade you enter, you should know exactly where you will get out for a profit and where you will get out for a loss. If you choose instead to play it by ear, you will probably end up losing more on your losers than you win on your winners. That is a recipe for failure.

Unsuccessful traders frequently will risk too much on a single trade. Sure, you may win big the first time. But eventually some of those big trades will go against you and you will have a very tough time coming back. Simply put, minimizing losses is critical to successful trading.

Let's say you have a $100,000 account and you lose 20%. You now have $80,000. You'll need to grow the account by 25% to get back to $100,000. If you lose 50% and have $50,000 left in the account, you'll need to grow the account by 100% to get back to where you started. Growing your account by 100% just to get to the break-even point is a lot harder than it sounds.

Money management is a foundation for trading success. There are different levels of money management and techniques that need to be learned.

CHAPTER 21:

Physical and Mental Health

As traders, looking after our physical and mental health could not be more important. Trading can be a wonderful experience when your trades are coming in and the profits are following. However, as we all know, there's nothing worse than when you hit a bad patch. You follow your strategy and your analysis, you know losing trades is part of the game, but losses still hurt!

I myself have been through a rough patch with trading. Losing a number of trades in a row, getting more and more stressed out by it. I was seeing my account drop, all my lovely profit disappearing, and losing money more often than I was winning. Although I like to think I have my emotions in check when it comes to trading, I started to struggle this time. The pressure was building and with each new trade I placed, the anxiety grew. If I didn't have my 'escapes', then I honestly believe things could have gotten a whole lot worse. Luckily, I'm a much better trader now than I was then. I have everything in place to stay in a positive mindset. I learned from my mistakes and made changes to my strategy.

I share this story with you because I believe that three of the most common mental health issues can affect traders the most. These are depression, anxiety, and stress. Let me explain why:

when you're working with numbers all day long, winning, losing, and looking at charts and screens, stress can build up. When you have a bad day/week/month, losing more trades than you're winning, depression can kick in with seeing those losses grow. This then leads on to anxiety growing each time you place a trade or have a trade running. Will it come good? What if I lose again?

Now, a lot of full-time traders out there have their emotions fully in check no matter what! And fair play to those that do - in my opinion, it's one of the hardest things to accomplish; especially if trading is your full-time career and you rely on trading to make you money. Now, from my experience, the majority of traders still struggle with their emotions, whether they like to admit it or not.

So, what can we do about this? Well, luckily, I would say 95% of what is in your control will help you keep your mental health positive; this comes in the form of self-care. Diet, exercise, and rest. Now, I'm not here to turn this into a self-help, fitness book. I'm simply here to give you some basic structure that you can take away and develop into something which works for you. In return, you'll see a more productive, happier, and healthier you which is a recipe for increased success.

Before moving on to physical health and what we can do each day to take care of ourselves, I wanted to share some quick statistics about mental health.

- Approximately 1 in 4 people in the UK will experience a mental health problem each year
- 676 million people are affected by mental health issues worldwide
- 70-75% of people with diagnosable mental health illness receive no treatment at all
- Mental illness is the largest single source of burden of disease in the UK
- Suicide is the biggest cause of death in men under 35

Now, physical health is another area of our lives which must take priority. Without looking after ourselves physically as well as mentally, we can't hope to perform at our best. Imagine you owned a £200,000 supercar. You're not going to run it on a tight budget, putting the cheapest wheels on, using cheap petrol, and sourcing discounted second-hand parts. Your body needs to be the same. Take care of yourself and you will reap the rewards.

How do we take care of ourselves physically? You already know the answer to this; it's called exercise. Physical activity has a huge number of benefits for the body. One thing a lot of people don't understand, though, is that physical exercise is one of the best things you can do to support your mental health. Let me give you an example: when you get filled with anger, what is a 'normal response' for a lot of people? Punching a wall? Swearing/shouting? How about a bit of boxing as a better release of all that anger? When I used to work as a personal trainer, I mostly trained people who worked stressful 9-5 jobs. They would often come into our session stressed out, angry at their boss or whatever. Before our session would start, I would get out the pads and tell the client to just hit them as hard as they could for 2 minutes. After doing so, you could see all that stress just go away.

That's the beauty of physical exercise; it benefits both your body and your mind. Many people don't know that the endorphins that your body release after exercise is one of the strongest chemical reactions in the body. That's why people get hooked on exercise - it can become a healthy drug. Sure, it takes effort, but once it's set in stone in your routine, just like eating food or getting dressed, then it really doesn't take much to be consistent.

Let's relate this to trading. You're sitting at your desk working the charts for a couple of hours each day at least. You hit some losses and suddenly, you're stressed out; you try to work harder, spend more time on the charts, and do more research and learning. You lose another trade, so the stress grows again. Now, rather than trying to force some wins, try taking a break. Go and do some physical exercise for even just 15-20 minutes. Let your mind take a rest.

How about we look at it a different way: purely the time spent sat down working on the charts. It's easy to spend 3 or 4 hours without even moving. Think about what that does to your body. Every trader should have some form of exercise as part of their daily or weekly routine. I'm not just talking about going down the gym and lifting weights; it can come in many different forms. Below I have given you some examples of gym and non-gym splits that you can follow. You don't need to become super healthy and super fit, I'm not suggesting that! What I'm trying to help you do is spend a little more time on yourself so that you perform better and ultimately progress with your trading career. That's the end goal, right? Being in good health is a key foundation to growing yourself as a business.

Below are some benefits of physical exercise followed by some examples of how you can add physical and mental activities into your routine. These are just guides on how to add exercise into your routine.

Those who may have specific physical goals, like weight loss or bodybuilding, are best off sticking to your current routine. This is aimed at those who perhaps don't do much or any exercise at the moment. Before doing any physical exercise, I recommend you consult an exercise professional.

Benefits of physical exercise:

- Increased energy
- Improved heart strength - reduce the risk of a heart attack
- Endorphin release
- Increased motivation
- Muscles strength and endurance
- Better weight management

Weekly workout example 1: Gym based - To get the best bang for your buck at the gym, it's best to train your body with a mixture of weights and cardio work. If you aren't a member of a gym, I recommend visiting your local one in the near future and asking to be shown about. There are a lot of gyms out there nowadays which cost less than £20 per month.

Monday - Upper body weights and cardio (45mins weights, 15mins cardio)

Tuesday - Lower body weights and cardio (45mins weights, 15mins cardio)

Wednesday - Cardio only (30 - 40mins intensive cardio work, such as boxing or an exercise class)

Thursday - Upper body weights and cardio (as before)

Friday - Lower body weights and cardio (as before)

Saturday and Sunday - REST

Weekly workout example 2: Non-gym based - There are more than enough activities you can do which don't require a gym membership.

Workout classes, sports, bike rides, walking, running, swimming, and exercises at home… the list goes on. I recommend mixing high impact exercise 2/3 times a week with a lower impact style of exercise 2/3 times a week. I have given some examples below.

Monday - high impact home workout (full body focus, 30-45mins)/workout class

Tuesday - low impact walk or bike ride (45-60mins)

Wednesday - low impact walk or swim (30-45mins)

Thursday - high impact home workout (upper body focus, 30mins)/workout class

Friday - high impact home workout (lower body focus, 30mins)

Saturday - low impact walk/swim/bike ride (30mins)

Sunday - REST

The best place to find 'at home workouts' is on YouTube. Simply type in 'upper body home workout' or 'lower body home workout'. Most of these will be body weighted circuits which require little to no equipment but can still give great results.

Can you see how a small amount of time spent on yourself each day can make a huge impact to your wellbeing? There are no excuses when finding the time. Everyone can find 30 minutes to go for a walk or a run. The time you allow for certain activities in your day is usually determined based on what you see as important. For example, spending time on the charts looking for your entries is important; it's how you make money. Therefore, you allow a lot of time for this. When you view your wellbeing as a priority in your life, then you will naturally find the time to do something which benefits you. I promise that if you commit more time your physical and mental wellbeing, you will see increased results in all areas of your life. Give it a try and let us know how you get on!

Mental Health Tips

- Sleep - The best single thing you can do for your mental health, in my opinion, is to ensure you get a good night's sleep. This gives your body and mind time to shut off and reset. Aim for 8 hours.

- Meditation - Often overlooked by many people, meditating or other similar activities such as yoga have countless mental benefits. Your mind can wander into almost spiritual places and your body can strengthen from within. 'How To Meditate For Beginners - A Definitive Guide' by Improvement Pill is a great place to start. Search it on YouTube.

- Reading - A must for every aspiring trader/entrepreneur/individual. Reading is vital for your self-development, but it's also great for your mental health. It gives you a chance to zone out and get lost in the book. If you're reading a business or self-help book, then it's great for getting your mind thinking in a positive, productive way. A great book that I read recently is 'The Art of War by Sun Tzu.

CHAPTER 22:

Having the right Mindset for Trading

Trading is more of a mental game than really anything else. The best tactic or the technical indicators is going to be useful to help you see a good way into the market. But they will be worthless if you do not bring in the right mental approach to the game. It all starts right in the rain before you ever placed any of your trades.

Being mindful the whole time you were in the trades, and even before you enter the trades, I hope you make the best trades and can keep your mind clear of any emotions that may get in the way. If you were a bit worried about how this is going to work and whether you can make your mind smart enough to go through these trades, there are a few simple questions that you need to ask yourself before you ever even consider working with options contracts. The three main questions that you should consider include

Why Am I Making This Trade?

When we get started with trading, no matter what kind of trading, that is, there are a ton of strategies that you can use to make this successful. Things like price action and the fundamentals of the market can be enough to make anyone feel like they are overwhelmed in no time. This is completely normal no matter who you are. No matter what tools we want to use, we have to make sure we remember why we got into the trade to start with, and then make sure you stick with these tools and only make trades that fit with your strategy.

Let's take a look at an example of how to make this happen. If you want to trade using the strategy known as moving average crossovers, you have to look at the charts and tools you have and see if there are actually any averages that are crossing. If you want o trade options when there are periods that have a lot more volatility, it is IV at a level that seems to make the most sense.

There are a ton of strategies, and you can pick out any that you would like. No matter which one you go with though, we have to make sure that we only place trades based on information that is objective. Never make a trade just to be in the market. Only be in the market and make a trade when it looks like it will actually make you money.

How Much Will I Risk on the Trade?

Risk management is going to be one of the most important things that we need to consider no matter what kind of investment we choose to work with. Before you choose to place any trade, you need to find out how much you are willing to risk on that trade. Knowing this risk from the beginning will make it easier to maintain your objectivity during the trade, especially if it ends up not going the way that you want. Never get into options or any kind of trade without really knowing all about the risks before starting.

Each trade should have a minimal amount of risk. The only way that you can completely eliminate the risk is to make sure that you never enter the market. But the best way to lose all of your money is to take all that is in your account towards one trade without saving some back. Neither of these is good risk management strategies, so we need to find something that is a little bit better.

A good idea is to find out what percentage of your account you are willing to risk on each trade. It is best to stay under ten percent as a beginner. As your account starts to grow more, you may want to consider going with maybe three to five percent. You won't be able to put as much money towards the trades you do, but it can definitely help you to avoid risking too much and ending up with nothing to work with any longer.

When you keep your risk down to only ten percent, and sometimes less, of your account at a time, you will find that you aren't as emotional about the trades. Even if it goes south, your whole account is not lost. You can still enter into other trades, sometimes at the same time, without having to worry that your whole account will be wiped out with one wrong decision. Considering that even professional traders can have trouble with some of their trades occasionally, this is a good thing to look into.

How will I Manage My Trade?

During this process, we need to consider how we will manage our trades. If you find that a trade will move in your favor, think about how you plan to manage that trade. There are a lot of theories of thought on this idea, and none are necessarily the best ones. Some work best for a few traders, others are preferred in some cases, and so on. You have to determine which one is best for you to help make sure you manage the trades well and get the profits you would like.

For example, there are many traders, new and professional, who like to set up a profit target when they first enter a new trade. Others will use trail stops to help them because it ensures they will capture some of the larger moves or larger trends that are potentially going to happen. Sometimes you may find yourself in a situation where you want to add to a winning position. This is more a personal preference, so you have to see what works best for you. But it is still critical to see how you would properly manage a winning strategy ahead of time. This ensures you make as much as possible without staying in the market so long you lose out.

The strategy you choose will make a big difference in how you manage your trade. A good strategy will help you to know how to enter the market, and when it is time to exit. They can often help us to learn how to read many of the charts that are out there, which makes it so much easier to pick the right time to get into the trade. If you pick a strategy, use the steps and tips it talks about to help you manage each trade you use it on. This helps to take the guesswork out and can help you get some profits.

While it may seem like these are really simple questions, and we shouldn't even need to ask them, remembering what they are and asking them during each trade will be the trick you need to make sure your options contracts are as successful as possible. As a beginner, you may ask these questions of others and be surprised at how many never even think about them at all.

Consider the Emotions

As we go through all of this, we must make sure that we can accurately handle all of our emotions along the way. If our emotions start to come into any trade, we instantly lose all of that critical thinking and start making some really poor decisions along the way. This is easy to do, which is why a good strategy and some strong stop-loss points can help.

About these stop-loss points and strategies, they basically allow you to make a good plan for your investment right from the beginning. You won't get caught up in emotions because you know exactly when to enter and when to leave ahead of time. Before entering the trade, you have no skin in the game, so you aren't worried about things going well or things going poorly. You make sound and rational decisions, which will help you along the way. If you wait to make these decisions later on, then it is possible the emotions will sneak in and can ruin even the best trade.

With a good plan in place, you know exactly when to enter the market, and exactly when to get out. Emotions will allow you to stay in the market too long, and add more risk than is necessary to any trade you are doing. You can pick one of the strategies that we talk about later on in this guidebook to help you get started on this and to make sure that you are set up with options contracts that will actually make you money.

Remember that it is just fine to take a break from trading if something is going on. If your head is not in the game or you find that things just aren't going along with the plans that you have, and it is making you frustrated, then it is fine to take a step back and stop trading for a few days, or even a few weeks. We can fall into the trap of thinking that we need to trade all the time. If we are in the right mindset and feel good about our trades, then we can keep on going. But if we just aren't feeling it or we find the trades are getting us down, and then it is best to take a step back.

You can always come back to the trading. Sometimes a little break is a perfect solution to getting your mindset back and helping us to get back into it. A few bad trades, especially when we are beginners, can be enough to throw us off all our hard work. But a few days of not focusing on the trades or worrying about them may be just what the doctor ordered.

The right mindset is going to be so important when you want to earn money in the stock market and with options. In fact, this mindset is going to come into play with many of the trades that you do, no matter which underlying asset you choose to have along with your contract. If your mindset is not in the right place, you will not understand how these contracts are meant to work, and you can lose a lot of money in the process. If you allow those emotions to get into the game, then you may as well kiss your money goodbye.

What If It Is Just Not Working Out?

With a little bit of time and practice, you can make options trading work well for you. It is possible that you will see more losses than you would like when you first jump into this. It is hard to get a feel for how the market behaves and how these contracts work, and mistakes can be made. Though taking some steps to minimize these mistakes, it is still possible that at least a few of your contracts will go downhill, and you will lose money.

With some practice and some time making these trades in the market, you should start to get a feel for how things work. This will help you to improve your skills in investing and can make it easier for you to get more profitable trades than you did in the past.

CHAPTER 23:

Creating your own Day Trading Strategy

As you start to get more into day trading, you may decide to develop your own strategy. There are a lot of great trading strategies that are out there. There may be some market conditions or other situations where you need to be able to develop your own strategy. Or, after trying out a few different things, you end up finding a new strategy, or a combination of strategies, that ends up working out the best.

Over time, it is important that you find your own place inside the market. As you go through, you may even find that you would rather be more like a swing trader rather than a day trader just because of the different methods that are available. The good news is, there is a market for any kind of trader, and there are a million types of strategies that you can use based on your own personal preferences along the way.

Before you jump into the market as a beginner with your own trading strategy, it is important that you start out by picking one of the strategies that are in this guidebook (or another proven strategy that you have researched). You need to have some time to try out a strategy and tread through the market a bit before you start coming up with your own strategy. Even if you have invested in the stock market before, you will find that working with day trading is completely different compared to some of the other methods available, and you do not want to pick a strategy that may have worked with one of your other trades, but will make you fail miserably with day trading.

It is all about spending some time in the market and getting familiar with the market. You will want to get familiar with how the day trading market works, how to recognize good stocks and so on before you make a good strategy that can help you. After spending some time in the market, working with one or two strategies that you like, you will be able to learn the patterns that you like and what to watch out for, and it becomes so much easier to make a strategy that will actually work.

But no matter where you are as a trader, it is so important that every trader has a strategy of some sort to help them get started. It is so easy for beginners to just pick out a stock and then start trading, without having a plan in place at all. This is a dangerous thing to work with. It pretty much leaves the decisions up to your emotions, and we all know how dangerous this can be when you are first starting out. You should never leave your trades up to the emotions; this will make you stay in the market too long or leave the market too early, and you will end up losing money.

In addition, you need to pick one strategy, whether it is one from this guidebook or one that you made up on your own, and then you need to stick with that strategy. Learn all of the rules that go with that strategy, how to make that strategy work for you, and exactly how you should behave at different times in the market with that strategy. Even if it ends up leading you to a bad trade (remember that any type of strategy and even the best traders will end up with a bad trade on occasion), you will stick it out until the trade is done. You can always switch strategies in between trades, but it is never a good idea to switch your strategy once you are already in the market.

Switching strategies can seem tempting when you are a beginner in the market. You may see that things are going south or may realize once you are in the market that you should have done a different strategy from the beginning. But as you look through some of the strategies that are in this guidebook, you probably notice that they are a bit different, and they need some different requirements before you can get in and out of the trade. Switching in the middle is not going to work and will lead to an automatic loss.

The most important thing that you can remember when you become a day trader is that all traders will fail at some point. Many beginners will fail because they do not take the time to learn how too properly day trade or they let their emotions get in the way of making smart decisions. But even advanced traders will have times when they will fail and lose money as well. The market is not always the most reliable thing in the world. Even when you are used to reading the charts and looking at the market, there will be times when it does not act as expected and a trader will lose out. Or the advanced trader may choose to try out a new strategy, and it does not work that well for them.

There will be times when you will lose money, and this can be hard to handle for a lot of beginners. This is also why you need to consider how much you can actually afford to lose on a trade before you enter the market. You do not want to go all out on your first trade because it is likely you will fail and lose that money or maybe more depending on the trade.

If you are worried about getting started in the market or you want to mess around and try out a few of the strategies ahead of time to see how they work, especially if you are using one of your own strategies, then you should consider working with a simulator. Sometimes you will be able to get one of these from your broker to try out and experiment with the market, and sometimes you may have to pay a bit from another site to use this simulator. However, this can be a valuable tool that will help you to try out different things, make changes, and get a little familiarity in the market before you invest your actual money. As a beginner, if you have access to one of these simulators, it is definitely worth your time to give it a try.

Picking your trade based on the time of day

Before we move on, we will take a look at which types of strategies seem to work the best at different times of the day. As you get into the market, you will notice that each time period of the day will be different and there are some patterns that seem to show up over time with them. We will work with three times of day, the open, the mid-day, and the close. If you want to be successful with day trading, it is not a good idea to use the same strategy at all three times of the day because these strategies will not be successful at all times of the day. The best traders will find out what time of day they get the most profitable trades and then they will make some adjustments to their strategies and their trading to fit them into these profitable times.

First, let's talk about the open. This time period will last about an hour and a half, starting at 9:30 in the morning on New York Time. This is a busy time of the day because people are joining the market for the first time or they are making adjustments based on how their stocks had done overnight. Because this time is so busy, it can also be a really profitable time period if you play the game right. It is a good idea to increase the size of your trades during this time and do more of them because you are more likely to make some good money during this time.

The best strategies to use during the open will be the VWAP trades and the Bull Flag Momentum.

Next session is the mid-day session, and this will start at 11 in the morning and go for about four hours. This is a slow time in the market, and it is considered one of the more dangerous times to trade during the day. There is not going to be much liquidity or volume in the market. Even a smaller order will make a stock move quite a bit during this time, so you really need to watch the market if you are holding onto your stocks. It is more likely that you will be stopped with unexpected and strange moves during this period.

It is common for many traders, both beginners and those who are more advanced, to have a lot of trouble during the mid-day. Many decide that it is not the best idea to work in the market during this time. But if you do decide to trade, it is important to keep the stops tight and also to lower your share size. You should also be really picky about the risk and reward ratio during this time. You will find that new traders will often do their overtrading during this time, and it may be best to simply avoid trading during this time period altogether.

If you do decide to trade during the mid-day, it is best to watch the stocks as closely as possible, get some things ready for close, and always be very careful about any trading decisions that you try to do. You will find that support or resistance trades, moving average, VWAP, and reversal strategies work well during the mid-day.

And finally, there is the close, which starts at 3 in the afternoon and goes for about an hour. These stocks are considered more directional, so it is best to stick with those that are going either down or up during this last hour. It is possible to raise the tier size compared to what it was at in mid-day, but you do not want to go as high as you were at open. You will find that the prices at closing are often going to reflect what the traders on Wall Street think the value of the stocks is. These traders have stayed out of the market during the day, but they have been closely watching things so that they can get in and dominate what happens during the last little bit of trading.

It is also common to see that many market professionals will sell their stocks at this time and take the profits because they do not want to hold onto the trades overnight. As a day trader, you will be one of these professionals because you need to sell all of your stocks on the same day to be a day trader.

CHAPTER 24:

Extraordinary Skill Set as Trader should Have

If you spent a year staring at the chart and looking at the chart the same way after a year, you are not paying attention. If you don't discover a different trick to trade each month you trade, you are not doing your homework. If you are doing the same strategy that you learned or discovered 2-5 years ago, you will not prosper.

All financial markets evolve. The Forex market is not an exemption. It is actually one of the fastest markets that mutate. Price movement behavior, patterns, and/or speed of a certain currency pair may change in a span of 24 to 60 months. Some may change faster. The impact of a certain type of news on the market may not be the same as it did 2 years ago. Price patterns or indicator patterns that you have been using for the past 3 years may not be as profitable as before. Continuous market research and strategy development is a must for a successful trading career in the long-run. Working with your strategies should be a passion. It should be exciting and fun for you. If not, you will lose your shirt eventually. If the only inspiration you have in doing it is that you will earn big time in a short period of time, you will lose all your shirts.

So what are the extraordinary skills that a trader needs?

Thorough Engagement

Problem-solving is cognitive. Meaning, it is a process of acquiring knowledge and understanding through thought, experience, and the senses. But the thorough engagement on problem-solving is a motivated one. One should be willing to engage the problem no matter how hard it takes, no matter how long it takes. One should be willing to take time to experience everything about it. A Forex trader should have this attitude towards learning on successful trading. If after a few failures on using a strategy, you are quick on dismissing it or changing it. Then your success will take longer. Engage more. Understand why every step is essential. Extraordinary attention to detail is a must. Experience every possible situation that you may encounter in using it. Immerse your thought into how to make it work after every test that didn't work.

Imagination

As Albert Einstein said, "Imagination is more important than knowledge". Though imagination is not the only tool you need to be a successful trader, it is one of the most important tools. You have to have it to be a good one. Imagination can lead you to something you haven't tried before. Most of the time, it gives you a picture in your mind that illustrates the idea or solution you need. Sometimes it gives the solution in an unexpected time or place. You just have to be good at catching those ideas. Take note of these ideas and try it the next time you sit in front of the chart.

Contemplation

More than imagination, contemplation is about deep reflective thought about your strategy. You have to answer these five questions when trading.

What may happen?

How do you feel when it happens?

How do you prepare yourself to switch the bad feelings into more appropriate feelings when it happens?

Can you avoid it to happen?

Most importantly, what to do when it happens to avoid disaster?

Problem Simplification

Some traders want to be portrayed as an intelligent trader rather than being a real intelligent trader. They are accustomed to intellectualizing it. They present their trading plans in the most complicated manner so that others will think they make the cleverest analysis of the market. They haven't got the faintest idea that the sure way to become an intelligent trader is by simplifying the overall trading analysis to come up with the best profitable solution. The best mathematician is the one that solves a tough mathematical problem by not using a mathematical formula.

Learn How To Learn. When I was an engineering professor, I used to tell my students a story about learning. Here's the story: A first-grader Math teacher "Addition" to his pupils. In detail, he talked about the concept behind "Addition". As an example, he gave "1 plus 2 is equal to 3" (1+2=3). After the discussion, to see if the pupils understood it, he asked 2 of them to stand. He asked them "2 + *1?*". The first one answered "3". The second one guessed "4" and said, "I'm not sure about my answer because you haven't tackled that one in our discussion". Sounds familiar? The first pupil really went over deeply on combining the numbers by the teacher. The second one relied on the example and memorized it but didn't bother to understand why it got the answer. This is a very simple case of learning the wrong way. Most people are actually like this. Most traders also have this trait. They scratch only the surface. They see the chart but they don't bother to understand what's behind the chart. They use an indicator but don't spend time to understand the formula behind it and what it makes it behave that way. Most traders memorize the "1+2=3" equation but never able to answer correctly the question "2+1".

Off-System Money Management

Off-system money management is considered as one of the skills to become a regular earner. It is not part of the overall technical trading plan. Not part of the trading system. It is more of a habit. This money management is literally a way to manage your money before trading and after a cycle of trades. It can make you earn regularly even if you fail on some trades or get a totally burned account. It is simple but very powerful. It will allow you to win overall even if you lose at some point.

What You Need First?

You have to have a good working trading strategy. It can be a conservative one or an aggressive one. You can use all the strategies

- It is something you tested on a demo account that reached at least a 100% profit. More than that is better.

- It is the strategy that you have experienced the worst-case scenario. Either it happened to you and found out how to bring it back to life or you got burned after reaching 100% profit or more. It is not uncommon for a good aggressive system to reach 200% to 10,000% and get burned on the last few subsequent trades.

You have to know the minimum capital needed to start the strategy, and you have the money at least three times bigger than what is needed. For example, if the minimum capital needed for a strategy is $200, you should have at least $600. If you want to fast-track your earnings and want to start with a bigger amount than the minimum requirement, let's say, you want to start with $1000, you have to have at least $3000 or more available anytime.

You need 1 trading MT4 account and 1 repository MT4 account. The trading account is the one you will use for trading. The repository account is for storage only. I will tell you why you need a repository in a moment.

The most important one before you start using this method is you should have a hardcore discipline to follow it. In this money management, you are required not to put all your money into your trading account. You will understand why in a moment.

Steps On Earning Regularly Even If You Fail Sometimes

The best way to explain this is by example. If you will use a strategy that needs a minimum capital of $200, you have to have $600. Split the money into two. Put the $200 into the trading account. Put the rest, $400, in the repository account.

You can start trading anytime. But the best time to start this is on Monday. At the start of the Tokyo Market, 12:00 AM GMT.

Depending on the system that you use, if you use a conservative system, you may earn just a few dollars or cents after your first week. If you use a moderately aggressive one, you may earn a bit higher than the first one. If aggressive or very aggressive one, 10% to 100% profit, or more a week is not impossible. Some will say, "Oh don't do that. That's too risky. " Yes, that is true, it is way too risky than usual investment. This is the reason why we have this money management in place to fight for that risk. Remember "High-Risk is High-Reward". If you can manipulate the risk, you may still have the reward even if you jeopardize the account. One important thing that you need to make sure is that the system that you will use is really working.

Before the weekend, find a way that the system can close all trades before the last trading hours of Friday. This way, you will see the exact profit that you have for the week.

Transfer all profit from your trading account to your repository account. Every week you will do this until you reach 100% or more of your initial capital in your trading account. So if you start with $200 in your trading account, you need to get a total transferred amount of $200 or more after a few weeks or months.

Your repository account now has $600 or more. The next step is to continue trading and earning while you are not yet getting in the Truth-Moment (points B and C), the worst-case scenario.

Every weekend, transfer half of your profit in the repository account. This way, you increase both your trading account and repository account. It is a safe play to make sure that your trading account is increasing. The money in your repository, which is also increasing, is now the source of possible income that you can withdraw, in case you decide to withdraw some. If you decide to withdraw weekly, just be sure that you do not withdraw the money more than the money you transfer in the repository per week. This will still make the repository grow. What's the use of the money in the repository account? That is your safety net. As I have said, all good strategies have a worst-case scenario. In case it happens to you. Your account gets burned. You can easily transfer $200 in your trading account and start trading again. One important thing that you should remember if your trading account is in bad shape, do not transfer right away some money from the repository. You need to do only one thing. Try to succeed in that difficult moment. Do everything not to get burned. Two things will happen; 1) You will recover all losses and/or floating losses, 2) You will get burned. Once you get burned, that's the time that you need to transfer $200 into your trading account from the repository account. If you have a good system, it will win back all the losses and more than that.

CHAPTER 25:

Attitude and Rules

With a correct attitude towards forex trading, you can be sure to achieve your goals. Here are a few suggestions that can help you develop the correct attitude and mindset for forex trading and trading in general.

Be Objective

In forex trading, one is required to be objective and not trade with emotions. As stated earlier, a forex trader should keep the eyes on the final product, that is, his financial goals. Being subjective or acting on emotions is disastrous for any business and learning to act by the book is key to a successful forex trading career. This means that you should not also listen to people who claim to be Pros in the game and trust your trading patterns instead of sheepishly following the crowd. This doesn't however mean that you should not trade on mass thinking but if you do, always keep in mind that the masses are not always right.

Be Realistic

Just like any other business, one should be real and expect a particular profit according to the capital traded-in. Always remember that forex trading is not like Lotto or betting where one can win a jackpot of a million dollars by stalking just a little money. It takes time to build up your skills, your knowledge and your confidence and secure good profits with forex trading. Therefore, one should expect the right amount of returns on investment and what comes with it. By not giving up, being disciplined and patient, and doing your research, you might end up achieving your goals and reaching top-level in the forex world. This mentality also helps one to limit the number and types of transactions or operations on a daily or weekly basis and to stay in the game even after losing a small percentage of the initial investment. This is a business opportunity just like any other.

With all said and done, there are rules to abide by in order to reach your potential and most importantly realize your potential in terms of profit. Below are 12 rules that can help you achieve your goals in forex Trading.

Trust the Process

Forex trading is a business and needs time and effort to grow and consolidate which means that there is more than just waiting for profits. Profit oriented businesses can end badly if the thresholds one has set are not met and the overall approach is not thoroughly planned. Any business is not only buying and selling as it involves huddles and logistics to make the whole institution work and doable. Some profit oriented forex traders tend to give up easily if they don't meet their target after a few operations or a short period of time. However, one can set a timeline and work towards meeting the set target without having to achieve a specific point which might turn to be the opposite. To achieve your goals, some points are process-oriented and help in reaching the high note in forex trading and are outlined.

Outline Daily Activities

Day to day activities can only be achieved when put down on paper for a specific task in forex trading. Having in mind the right thing to do on a specific day is good as it helps avoiding distractions and other things that may get in the way on a business day. This means that the more you know what you are doing on a busy day, you will not waste time doing other things that do not help achieve your goal and the needs you want to build your forex trading skills.

Analyze the Market

As pointed out earlier, trading with emotions is bad for business as it does not go by the plans and strategy but with the reaction of business gone wrong or even a big win. Being greedy is so bad in forex trading and it is advisable to analyze the market first before trying out forex trading and giving a shot on the most promising patterns. When you play by the rules, you train the mind to follow the right procedures and even helps in becoming more discipline in forex trading. Training the mind helps in a vulnerable situation which will make you hold on when there is a crisis.

Be Defensive

This is another important rule to follow in forex trading for it is the core purpose of joining the business and what will keep you survive storms that will come your way in one way or the other. This simply means that you should not trade everything including your capital, defend your initial capital and aim at making profits. When you make a target and do not meet it, then at least you tried, but trading profusely just to meet the target with limited time is not good at all as it is an offensive approach. You should always protect your capital as it is the only thing keeping you in the business and one mistake can send you to factory reset, i.e; going back to the drawing board wondering when the rain started beating you.

Have a Trading Plan

Just like any other venture, Forex trading needs a business plan that has been tested to be working and giving impressive results. The plan involves things that you need to do from A-Z, this may include the rules of engagement, trading pattern, market analysis, and other key aspects that make the business run well. After making the trading plan, you can test it virtually to see if it will go well with the market and if it is good, then give it a green light and start the forex trading. But make sure that you outline the plan as it is the backbone of the whole venture.

Know That Trading Is a Business

Forex trading is like a business and should be treated as such for one to get the best out of it by giving the attention it deserves. Other researches have talked about not comparing trading with job opportunities or hobby to be done on leisure time. This means that one should not expect a salary and works on getting profits and give attention and not only focusing on it when you are free. With this, a forex trader will learn to prioritize forex trading just like any other business.

Outline Risk

Make sure that you point out the risk you intend to get yourself into and do not give it too much until you are out of business. Do not risk an amount that you cannot afford, risking is only for the amount you are capable of and not anywhere near initial capital. Remember as said earlier, if you lose capital that means that you are out of business and you will not want that to happen to you. Only risk an amount that you know if they go then you will not struggle with bringing back the business into living.

Use Technology

The modern era of inventions and innovations can be a plus in forex trading as it helps improve the outcome of a venture. Technology has played a big role in forex trading, thanks to innovators who come with new things every day to enhance the world in bringing people closer. With technology, one can trade anywhere in the world monitor charts using a computer or even mobile phones. This means that one can travel all over the world as well as working at the same time. This has been evident for bloggers and travel entrepreneurs who blog for a living and promote products online while they travel. This can be the same for forex traders and it helps in even having a good time and relaxing the mind while working.

Have a Stop Loss

This is somehow similar to outlining risk but specifies the amount that one should be willing to lose in particular trading. In Forex trading, you should only lose what you afford and it is very important to outline the amount or percentage that one should only lose in trading. This also acts as a disciplined mode as it helps in controlling the mind and emotions not to surpass the limited amount of possible risk.

Focus On the Bigger Picture

What is the purpose of starting forex trading? Can you make the business to be aligned in that direction? Are you getting some profits and losing sometimes? then you are on the right track heading to greatness in forex trading. Business is not about just making profits but making impacts on a personal level and getting more skills. So what is your bigger picture? To have gained at least 10 per cent in the financial year 2020-2021? Having this in mind, then you can be sure of aiming in the right way as compared to only focusing on maximizing profits.

Keep Learning Markets

Forex trading is an ongoing process even after mastering markets and getting out of an amateur venture. One does not stop learning at anything and things keep changing in the forex world this is important to keep an open mind in everything to do with business. Some of the skilled forex traders can fall prey of crowd psychology and some markets are unpredictable making forex trading a learning experience every time one is trading.

Be a Progressive Trader

Every forex trader wants to earn profit as it is the main reason for venturing in forex trading in the first place, but are you only profit-oriented the first day in the market or you are moving forward? Learning also can be a huge progress as it helps one avoid making similar mistakes and open ways for more profit in the future. A progressive trade is the one that celebrates every win either small or big as long as it is a victory. Just like a child, you learn to sit then start crawling and in no time you start taking a few steps and eventually running. The same applies to forex trading, you gradually move from one stage to the other and you cannot jump directly to only making profits. You either win or learn. After making a trading plan and testing it, one can join the trading business and encounter ups and downs as it shapes the ultimate goal of forex trading. With this progress, one can be sure of securing a future in forex trading full of experiences and lots of encounters that can prepare you to any hard hurdles that one might come across during your trading experience.

So are you setting up your mind on winning and achieving your goals? If so I suggest you follow the suggestions outlined above and start winning small until you fully master the art of forex trading and rejoice looking at your bank account after meeting your ultimate goals. Remember, forex trading is not a walk in the park and you have to make the right choices.

CHAPTER 26:

How to Think Like an Expert Trader

Know when to go off book: While sticking to your plan, even when your emotions are telling you to ignore it, is the mark of a successful trader, this in no way means that you must blindly follow your plan 100 percent of the time. You will, without a doubt, find yourself in a situation from time to time where your plan is going to be rendered completely useless by something outside of your control. You need to be aware enough of your plan's weaknesses, as well as changing market conditions, to know when following your predetermined course of action is going to lead to failure instead of success. Knowing when the situation really is changing, versus when your emotions are trying to hold sway is something that will come with practice, but even being aware of the disparity is a huge step in the right direction.

Avoid trades that are out of the money: While there are a few strategies out there that make it a point of picking up options that are currently out of the money, you can rest assured that they are most certainly the exception, not the rule. Remember, the options market is not like the traditional stock market which means that even if you are trading options based on underlying stocks buying low and selling high is just not a viable strategy. If a call has dropped out of the money, there is generally less than a 10 percent chance that it will return to acceptable levels before it expires which means that if you purchase these types of options what you are doing is little better than gambling, and you can find ways to gamble with odds in your favor of much higher than 10 percent.

Avoid hanging on too tightly to your starter strategy: That doesn't mean that it is the last strategy that you are ever going to need, however, far from it. Your core trading strategy is one that should always be constantly evolving as the circumstances surrounding your trading habits change and evolves as well. What's more, outside of your primary strategy you are going to want to eventually create additional plans that are more specifically tailored to various market states or specific strategies that are only useful in a narrow band of situations. Remember, the more prepared you are prior to starting a day's worth of trading, the greater your overall profit level is likely to be, it is as simple as that.

Utilize the spread: If you are not entirely risk averse, then when it comes to taking advantage of volatile trades the best thing to do is utilize a spread as a way of both safeguarding your existing investments and, at the same time, making a profit. To utilize a long spread you are going to want to generate a call and a put, both with the same underlying asset, expiration details, and share amounts but with two very different strike prices. The call will need to have a higher strike price and will mark the upper limit of your profits and the put will have a lower strike price that will mark the lower limit of your losses. When creating a spread it is important that you purchase both halves at the same time as doing it in fits and spurts can add extraneous variables to the formula that are difficult to adjust for properly.

Never proceed without knowing the mood of the market: While using a personalized trading plan is always the right choice, having one doesn't change the fact that it is extremely important to consider the mood of the market before moving forward with the day's trades. First and foremost, it is important to keep in mind that the collective will of all of the traders who are currently participating in the market is just as much as a force as anything that is more concrete, including market news. In fact, even if companies release good news to various outlets and the news are not quite as good as everyone was anticipating it to be then related prices can still decrease.

To get a good idea of what the current mood of the market is like, you are going to want to know the average daily numbers that are common for your market and be on the lookout for them to start dropping sharply. While a day or two of major fluctuation can be completely normal, anything longer than that is a sure sign that something is up. Additionally, you will always want to be aware of what the major players in your market are up to.

Never get started without a clear plan for entry and exit: While finding your first set of entry/exit points can be difficult without experience to guide you, it is extremely important that you have them locked down prior to starting trading, even if the stakes are relatively low. Unless you are extremely lucky, starting without a clear idea of the playing field is going to do little but lose your money. If you aren't sure about what limits you should set, start with a generalized pair of points and work to fine tune it from there.

More important than setting entry and exit points, however, is using them, even when there is still the appearance of money on the table. One of the biggest hurdles that new options traders need to get over is the idea that you need to wring every last cent out of each and every successful trade. The fact of the matter is that, as long as you have a profitable trading plan, and then there will always be more profitable trades in the future which mean that instead of worrying about a small extra profit you should be more concerned with protecting the profit that the trade has already netted you. While you may occasionally make some extra profit ignoring this advice, odds are you will lose far more than you gain as profits peak unexpectedly and begin dropping again before you can effectively pull the trigger. If you are still having a hard time with this concept, consider this: options trading are a marathon, not a sprint, slow and steady will always wins the race.

Never double down: When they are caught up in the heat of the moment, many new options traders will find themselves in a scenario where the best way to recoup a serious loss is to double down on the underlying stock in question at its newest, significantly lowered, price in an effort to make a profit under the assumption that things are going to turn around and then continue to do so to the point that everything is completely profitable once again. While it can be difficult to let an underlying stock that was once extremely profitable go, doubling down is rarely if ever going to be the correct decision.

If you find yourself in a spot where you don't know if the trade you are about to make is actually going to be a good choice, all you need to do is ask yourself if you would make the same one if you were going into the situation blind, the answer should tell you all you need to know.

If you find yourself in a moment where doubling down seems like the right choice, you are going to need to have the strength to talk yourself back down off of that investing ledge and to cut your losses as thoroughly as possible given the current situation. The sooner you cut your losses and move on from the trade that ended poorly, the sooner you can start putting energy and investments into a trade that still has the potential to make you a profit.

Never take anything personally: It is human nature to build stories around, and therefore form relationships with, all manner of inanimate objects including individual stocks or currency pairs. This is why it is perfectly natural to feel a closer connection to particular trades, and possibly even consider throwing out your plan when one of them takes an unexpected dive. Thinking about and acting on are two very different things, however, which is why being aware of these tendencies are so important to avoid them at all costs.

This scenario happens just as frequently with trades moving in positive directions as it does negative, but the results are always going to be the same. Specifically, it can be extremely tempting to hang on to a given trade much longer than you might otherwise decide to simply because it is on a hot streak that shows no sign of stopping. In these instances, the better choice of action is to instead sell off half of your shares and then set a new target based on the updated information to ensure you are in a position to have your cake and eat it too.

Not taking your choice of broker seriously: With so many things to consider, it is easy to understand why many new option traders simply settle on the first broker that they find and go about their business from there. The fact of the matter is, however, that the broker you choose is going to be a huge part of your overall trading experience which means that the importance of choosing the right one should not be discounted if you are hoping for the best experience possible. This means that the first thing that you are going to want to do is to dig past the friendly exterior of their website and get to the meat and potatoes of what it is they truly offer. Remember, creating an eye-catching website is easy, filling it will legitimate information when you have ill intent is much more difficult.

First things first, this means looking into their history of customer service as a way of not only ensuring that they treat their customers in the right way, but also of checking to see that quality of service is where it needs to be as well. Remember, when you make a trade every second count which means that if you need to contact your broker for help with a trade you need to know that you are going to be speaking with a person who can solve your problem as quickly as possible. The best way to ensure the customer service is up to snuff is to give them a call and see how long it takes for them to get back to you. If you wait more than a single business day, take your business elsewhere as if they are this disinterested in a new client, consider what the service is going to be like when they already have you right where they want you.

With that out the way, the next thing you will need to consider is the fees that the broker is going to charge in exchange for their services. There is very little regulation when it comes to these fees which means it is definitely going to pay to shop around. In addition to fees, it is important to consider any account minimums that are required as well as any fees having to do with withdrawing funds from the account.

CHAPTER 27:

Mindsets of a Master Trading

Invisible Success

You've probably seen trading commercials on YouTube where people are driving their Lamborghini saying how they could improve your trading.

These presentations are easily visible, and people quickly understand and see success from this visual representation.

You'll see this in many areas of life like fancy cars, boats, and private jets. All these things that you see are known as external success, and it is visible to everyone.

But external success is not real success.

Real success is about having the knowledge, the skills, and experience that takes years to attain.

Real success is internal. Real success is invisible. People may only see it when they get to know you at a deeper level.

It's because of this invisible success that allows you to have external success.

External success would not be possible without internal success.

The average person that you run into on a day-to-day basis is attracted to fake external success. It's why many people buy into fake stories about sports cars, mansions, and private yachts. They want that dream too.

Unfortunately, at times, external success is a mirage placed in front of your eyes. To give you some perspective, one of my good friends worked in banking for many years. He mentioned that most people who drive fancy cars have very little money in their bank account and are frequently late on their payments.

If you saw these people on the street, you would think they are successful, but they aren't.

For them to feel successful, they want to drive a fancy car. Unfortunately, since they don't have the cash, they have to take out a loan, and then they struggle to make the monthly payments.

However, these people get a feeling of success at least externally. Unfortunately, this is not real success. Real success is when you possess knowledge.

For a trader, it's when you know how to trade correctly.

Real success is when you know how to manage your risk and your money. It's about knowing how to adjust your positions properly.

Real success is internal. It's your knowledge, your education, and your experience.

If you have real success and someone stole all your money, you would be able to earn it back. That's because real success can't be taken away.

With real success, you can turn a little bit of money into more money. You can buy a bigger house or even a fancy car.

If you don't have real success, you have first to earn the knowledge, skills, and experience, and then external success will follow.

As you progress in your trading journey, don't get caught up in the lavish things. If you're successful internally, then you are wealthy, and the external riches will follow.

Mental Overload

If I gave you a list of numbers, could you close the book and remember them?

827 - 950 - 063

If you did well, how about another try with a series of numbers that are a little bit more complicated? Give this next batch a try:

2951 - 4397- 89 -195 - 3918 - 49428 - 30057 - 892994

That was a tough one! You're probably thinking: could I remember this, and what's the point?

The thing is, these numbers are simply bits of data that's thrown at you. It's not much different than the world around us.

You might say that in the real world, the information is more significant. If you were genuinely trying to remember and regurgitate the numbers above, then you made them important.

The problem with remembering all these numbers is it's too much data in a single instance. You were overloaded.

Now if you practiced for memory competitions that might be a different story, but for the average person, this exercise is challenging because it's a lot of information for us to process.

Mental overload happens in many situations, from driving your car to taking tests at school and even the stock market.

When it comes to trading, we tend to overload our brain in multiple ways. I've seen sensory overload happened in a few various ways, such as:

- Following too many stocks
- Trying too many strategies
- Using too many indicators
- Managing too many trading accounts
- Following too many people
- Trading too much capital
- Having too many positions

- And many others

The stock market has a constant flow of data. In other words, the information never stops, which makes it easy to be overwhelmed with information.

It's difficult for the mind to do what it needs to do with the data. Typically it has to do a few things, and those are:

1. Input and receive the data
2. Interpret or digest the information
3. Sort the information
4. And then if needed, find out the best course of action to take

With all this data and information coming from the stock market, it's easy to exert your mind and become overloaded with trading.

Eventually, this leads to a mental shutdown or burnout.

In trading, this is when losses continue to spiral out of control. It's when people start chasing to make their money back and put on riskier trades with no plan.

Don't trade while overloading your brain. Take a step back and work at your pace, which will help you stay in the flow.

From our earlier example, instead of trying to soak in and absorb all of the numbers similar to how people attempt to digest every bit of stock market data – simplify it.

Make it a point only to remember one number.

2951 - 4397- 89 -195 - 3918 - 49428 - 30057 – 892994

Why not just aim to remember: 89 if that's the number that sticks out for you?

You'll be trading with less stress, and it will be effortless.

Guidance in Coaching

When you're traveling to a new destination, a guide is not needed to see all the different sites.

If you were visiting Germany, you might be interested in seeing the Brandenburg Gate, Cologne Cathedral, and the Neuschwanstein castle.

You could see all the sites on your own, but the problem is we frequently get distracted. We get pulled into multiple directions as we take our journey.

As you travel from one thing to another, you might miss a turn, you might want to stop at a flea market to see local offerings, or you may want to explore a beautiful view.

All these detours are distractions that slow you down from your more important destination.

Having a guide helps you get to your destination faster without getting distracted.

A guide is not necessary to have an excellent time, an adventure, or to reach your destination. In fact, I see this all the time with people who are learning to trade the markets - they do it on their own without any help or any direct guidance.

They use the resources that they have available to them like reading free online articles, watching YouTube videos, and attending free webinars.

Eventually, they start experimenting on their own with paper trading until they get the grasp of things. Later they start trading real money, and through this journey, they tweak their strategies and continue to evolve.

With time you could say that they have reached their destination of trading successfully on their own. It's not that you can't do it without a guide, but it may take longer.

Other people who have decided that they would like guidance can save time, energy, and headaches.

A guide can help them stay focused and will give them a direct path of what they should learn, focus on, and exercises they should do. A guide can show them the bigger picture of things they may not have seen before.

This is exactly what I work on with my coaching students!

I guide them through the process so that they can see the fine details that they may miss on their own.

As a coach and mentor, I help them save time by giving them a learning plan specific to them. A learning plan might outline for them the exact steps they need to take to move them forward. This plan might include videos they should watch, books to read, the courses to study, and the exercises to do.

It's not that you can't learn to trade on your own. Many have learned to trade stocks on their own for years, but it takes longer.

However, if you are interested in getting to your destination faster, a coach or mentor can help cut out the distractions.

Trading Knowledge vs Wisdom

I've often had one-on-one coaching sessions with people who have studied many courses and read dozens of books.

They have attained a lot of knowledge, and it's fresh in their brain. Their ability to spit out knowledge may even be superior to mine.

Sadly, their trading still suffers, and they aren't happy with their results.

Their results aren't at the level that they expect, not because they lack the knowledge, but they lack wisdom.

Knowledge is not wisdom. Knowledge is simply information.

You can know a lot about trading, but if you've never executed a trade, then how much experience do you have? How fluid and dynamic are you in various trading situations?

When I see new traders who are exceptionally knowledgeable, they often wear the curse of knowledge badge on their chest.

The curse of knowledge is the point where a person is too knowledgeable to recognize that they are flawed.

It's the point where listening stops.

An exceptionally knowledgeable person knows the right answers, but this creates errors in their decision-making.

Knowledge is excellent because it's the first step to moving forward and getting you to your desired goal, but it's theory.

You have to take that theory and make it your own. The only way to do that is to attain wisdom.

Wisdom is distinct from knowledge in that it grows internally. Wisdom must be earned - it cannot be given.

Everything that I teach and give to you is from my knowledge and wisdom. Unfortunately, you are only able to receive information in the form of knowledge.

To attain wisdom, you have to grow it for yourself.

I can guide you on different trade setups, trading strategies, and show you multiple ways of managing your trades. But you have to spend countless hours behind a trading screen.

You need to experience real losses, face problems, feel the fear and greed, and struggle through managing positions to gain wisdom.

You can learn a tremendous amount about trading from books, videos, and courses. Even with all your knowledge, your trading may still suffer until you attain wisdom.

CHAPTER 28:

Get Rid of the Bad Behavior

Some of the worst things that new or intermediate investors can do is to look at successful investors who model bad habits. We will go through some of these habits below in hopes that they can be modified or avoided completely to ensure you have greater success than those who engage in them. Having a healthy mindset creates stability and also helps to drive well-informed decisions that are not based on emotions. Basically, there is no room for emotions in a financial numbers market. Here is a list of what to do/not do.

1. Do not start off by sticking to one particular stock.

You need to cast off the emotions of being tied to a certain stock. The best investors may do well for a long while, and accrue considerable wealth, but every stock has its end, and the best investors also know when it is time to cash out. Emotionally, it is hard for some people to let go of the thought that a stock is something to ride out through thick and thin.

This is generally a good framework, and it keeps you from short-term sales, but even when a stock does well it also has its glory days and they will fade so get out while it is good. By selling your favorite stocks you can also think of it as investing the assets you have gained into something else. Nothing lasts forever, so you need to move and be flexible. Some people may choose to stay with a losing stock on the other hand. That is entirely a different factor!

You also want to avoid selling stocks when it is not the right time. Selling either too soon or too late are other problems. Many people do this based on emotion as well, and not necessarily based on their actual performance.

2. Do not try to chase the stock if it loses

Some investors are gluttons for punishment and cannot accept the fact that a particular stock is a losing stock. They may try to chase the loss by coming back at a later time to repurchase the same company's stock. Some think of this as "I'll show you" type thinking; a semblance of punishment to the stock itself that demonstrates to the investor that they can and will beat the market this time.

Irrational thinking is a huge barrier to success in the market and it will catch up to you every time. Some call it mythological thinking. People have fantasy notions, distorted beliefs about why a stock works or did not work. None or little of that may be true. Allow the numbers and histories of the stock speak to you. As a beginner, you learned how to read and analyze stocks. Sometimes a refresher is needed, to stay objective and to avoid this fantasy thinking.

3. Do not hold onto dead weight.

Although a good rule of thumb is to forget anything you have sold there are times when you may want to revisit an old stock. If you are in a position where you are holding dead stock you will only see its value spin downwards and it will not come back up most likely, so selling it would be a good choice. However, some investors think that losses are due to bad timing and luck.

Some people delude themselves into thinking until they sell their failed stock they haven't really lost anything, and besides, it may return!! If it comes back then mentally it may seem that it was a wash, or a win. This is also irrational thinking. Additionally, wishing, hoping, thinking and praying that a stock revive itself will not make it a reality.

4. If a stock you finally sold off had lost but then bounces back, forget it unless it has completely recovered and is super strong.

Not all stocks bounce back. Most of the major company's stocks that are reflected in stock market charts show a comeback that is evident in graphs. Smaller or lesser known companies do not always follow these trajectories and they may bottom out. This is often overlooked as well. The big guys tend to follow different patterns.

5. If you do mess up it is best to own up to it and move on.

How to Become a Patient Trader

We are here to demystify the often-complex subject of trading psychology and provide simple and effective strategies to improve your trading. The reason this is important is that most trading psychology books seem to have been written for academics, by academics, and while they are great for increasing your understanding of the processes that are taking place internally, which lead to self-sabotaging trading behaviors, they fall short of giving simple, easy to implement procedures to make fast and effective change. Is it necessary as a trader to understand all the complex processes that are taking place in our psychology? After all when we drive a car we don't need to know how the car works, we just want to know how to operate the car and how to drive. I recently conducted a survey with my students and readers to find out what were the main issues still holding them back in their trading. One of the key issues was a lack of patience. This came disguised in many forms such as not letting profits run, not waiting for the proper entry setup before entering a trade, exiting trades before they had a chance to develop, trying to trade too many systems and time frames (impatient to make money), and other types of behaviors such as not committing to the vital preparation that is needed to ensure profitable trading, such as keeping and analyzing detailed records and regular back-testing.

Personal change can be a long and trying process when using willpower and self-discipline.

Instead of asking the trader to use willpower and discipline to increase their store of patience, using metaphors from the world of NLP (Neuro-Linguistic-Programming) and hypnosis, combined with tapping sequences using EFT (Emotional Freedom Technique), which aims to change your beliefs about trading and enable you to effortlessly improve your trading performance. For example, by using simple techniques such as 'reframing', reframing in NLP parlance is to put a different frame around a troubling issue so that the issue is perceived differently, and change naturally takes place.

I truly believe that by adjusting the way you think about trading, you will find it unnecessary to use willpower to control your impulse to act outside your system, and will naturally adjust your behaviors to reflect what is needed to trade successfully, thereby making lack of patience a non-issue in your trading.

CHAPTER 29:

Knowing when Enough is Enough

We discuss a person's mental well-being clinically we use a thing called the biopsychosocial model. This is used all throughout medicine and in this context it says that a person's well-being is determined by biological, psychological and social factors.

We will look at trading while you are impaired and I will try to encourage people not to do it. We will discuss how some people's relationships with their family and friends are adversely effected and finally we will discuss how your place in society overall can change and how to some extent it might be better for your overall well-being to try to resist this.

Trading while Impaired.

I feel on some level that I should be stating the obvious but obvious or not I think it needs to be said for completeness and also because, in spite of it clearly not being a good idea, people do trade and make decisions when they are less than 100%. For people who feel this is OK it will be hard to persuade them otherwise but I will do my humble best.

Never ever trade whilst under the influence of alcohol or drugs. Some drugs act as stimulants increasing impulsive behavior, risk tolerance and regardless of how it feels both stimulants and sedatives reduce cognition and analytic ability. Likewise do not trade whilst hungover or experiencing withdrawal.

Many members of the public believe professional traders behave like this from the way the role is portrayed by the entertainment industry. Remember, even if this were true, they are trading with someone else money, you are trading with your money.

Additionally do not trade whilst in need of sleep. There is road safety evidence that driving whilst sleep deprived may be equivalently risky to driving after consuming alcohol. Motor insurance cost is often higher with some professions associated with sleep deprivation because they crash more often. It seems likely that trading performance would also be reduced.

Finally judge your mood. If you have had a particularly bad day and you are angry, sad, worried or similarly emotionally compromised do not trade as you will not focus on it as you should. Take an hour or two out, go to the gym or go for a run, exercise has proven benefits for mood but until you feel better and can give your decision making the focus it deserves do not trade.

If you feel you may be suffering from a clinical mood disorder like depression go to your family physician and again take some time off from making important decisions.

Remember, if you make an investment and it goes wrong and falls by 20% it will require a 25% increase to restore the original amount. If it falls by 50% it will require a 100% increase to restore the original capital. Future gains have to be more impressive than losses to restore the original amount.

If you feel you are impaired but feel compelled to trade try to engage in negative visualization, the opposite of what athletes do where they picture “making the shot”, visualize in your head the consequences of the trade not going well.

Impact on Family/relationships

If emotional fallout from trading starts impacting on your relationships with your family it is time to find a new line of work.

Everyone feels stressed or annoyed about the outcome of an investment from time to time but it should not become a regular occurrence that impacts on your relationships.

I tend to be fairly philosophical about trades gone wrong. I can do this because when I make an investment I know that even if I lose all the money invested I will still be able to meet my financial obligations. I only use money I can afford to lose. Additionally I feel confident that over time my wins will outnumber losses, this is my trend and it must be this way if someone is to be capable of supporting themselves financially by trading or investing.

We have said before that family and good relationships with other people are things that psychological research indicates do positively impact on happiness whereas wealth has less of a correlation with happiness. Happiness should be the overall goal and trading just a means to an end.

At the start of the book we talked about the importance of knowing why you wanted to be a trader. Whether it was due to a desire for riches, just a means to pay the bills or due to lifestyle flexibility factors. Whatever the reason was, trading is not as unique as a career that other jobs might not let you achieve the same result, hopefully with lessor stress.

Your role in society

At the start of the book we raised the question of why you wanted to be a trader or investor? One of the possible answers to the question, and I think that this is the best answer, is that you wanted to be able to maintain your lifestyle in an independent manner where you would have a lot of personal control over your decisions, the hours you work and your geographical location.

One of the potential problems that can develop is that as you become increasingly successful trading and need to spend fewer hours working at it you end up with an increasing amount of time where you don't really have that much to occupy your thoughts or give your day meaning. Some people may roll their eyes as I say this but you do need to find something socially meaningful to do with this time.

The nature of happiness we said that a lot of things that are proven to bring satisfaction with one's life are social in nature. Additionally, if you are now able to meet your financial needs with minimal interaction with the rest of society then, over a period of time, skills that you had used to support yourself will diminish and on some level your personal development may start to regress.

To this end I would encourage readers when they are hitting certain financial targets that, even if they do not wish to engage in traditional employment, they might consider engaging in volunteer work in some social cause they find meaningful. Consider doing this in a manner proportionate with your financial success. For a person's long term mental well-being my view is that this would be better. If you find something to do that you love you will never work a day in your life.

Conclusion

Well, you've made it to the end. Either way I hope you got something useful.

There is no simple winning system that "just works". It's you who has to put the work in every single day to keep up-to-date on what is driving the market and what the future outlook is. You have to weigh the information and decide how it affects the current market conditions, if at all. You have to determine where others have their orders positioned and how the market will react to this. Every day is a new day.

You still have a lot of work ahead of you, but with trading there's always something new to learn. New type of events will happen that you will have to familiarize yourself with. Banks will make announcements that you will need to understand. There's always new things coming your way that you will have to digest so that you can stay on top of what the market is doing and what's driving prices up and down your charts.

If I have put you off trading, great! If I have made you even more hungry to trade, great! If you still aren't sure one way or another then that's cool as well; Sooner or later you'll decide if trading is for you or not. It isn't for everybody; Trading isn't for most. As long as you see and understand there's no secret system, and ongoing hard work is the key to success, then you already have a better chance than most retail traders who are only looking for easy riches.

Open a demo account and see how you go. If you aren't successfully capturing pips and growing the account while employing excellent risk and money management 100% of the time then don't go live - you aren't ready for live. There is no reason at all to lose your hard-earned money to your broker.

The world of FOREX trading can be a mirror that reflects and highlights all of your good and bad traits and you will almost certainly learn more about yourself in the process of learning how to trade. Your trading will reflect if you are diligent or lazy, persistent or easily surrender, cautious or reckless, shrewd or able to be misled, patient or quickly frustrated. Your trading will reveal if you are a gambler or a trader and if you have self-control or are controlled by emotion! When you observe your FOREX peers you'll see the same traits being revealed in them - it can be fascinating to watch.

You need to find the truth for yourself and find what works for you. See what others have to say, but listen with a critical ear and read with a critical eye. In the end it's not their money that is at risk here, it's yours.

Throughout your ongoing learning you will discover exceptions to every rule, but that doesn't mean you have to toss-out the rule nor what it aims to achieve just because it doesn't cater to every possible situation. If you are going to go against what you believe and understand to be good advice then you need a good reason to do so; No, have a GREAT reason to do so. Don't be put-off by the few people doing everything wrong yet still making stupid amounts of money. Dumb luck is dumb and not something to emulate.

If what I have presented is all new to you then maybe you are a little overwhelmed. After testing ideas and applying what you know it'll all come together and make sense. You will learn by doing - practice makes perfect.

If you are fortunate to have friends that are also interested in FOREX but who are stuck in their trading like every other retail trader then this could be your chance to form your very own think-tank where you bounce ideas off each other and help each other grow. Success is often a collaborative effort. We hope it was informative and able to provide you with all of the tools you need to achieve your goals whatever they may be.

The next step is to apply everything that you have learned. It is time for you to open an account with a trustworthy broker and start trading. Once you are confident enough, then it is your time to turn the forex market into a goldmine.

Trading currencies can be a very lucrative career. It is not a secret that many professional traders consider this activity as their full-time profession. They were able to quit their 8-hour employment and now engage in forex trading as a living. This is also possible for you. However, you should understand that this is something that you cannot do without making sacrifices. You need to spend time and put a lot of effort into learning how to trade effectively. This would mean spending hours doing careful research and analysis. You should also develop and test your trading strategy countless times. As a professional trader, you are responsible for all your actions. Therefore, you need to be careful, especially when trading using real money.

Being a forex trader can be a very fun career. Of course, if you get really good at it, then you might even be able to make your way to financial freedom. Every day, many professional traders around the world are making a decent profit. If you think that you have what it takes to be a successful FX trader, then it is time for you to take positive actions and change your life.

So, here we are at the end, but for you it is just the beginning. It's now up to you to find what works and continue learning every day. Good luck on your journey, and I hope you catch some pips along the way!

STOCK MARKET INVESTING FOR BEGINNERS

How To Approach Trading To Make Money With Forex And Options. Train Mentally To Improve Your Psychology To Build A New Stream Of Income With The Most Profitable Strategies

WARREN DOUGLAS

PART ONE

Introduction

Before the invention of online trading platforms, people could only engage in stock market trading through brokerage firms, financial institutions, and other trading houses. As more inventions related to the internet were made, it became easy for individual traders to invest in the stock market. One way you can make money on the stock market is through day trading.

Day trading is one technique that can help you gain a lot of income if used properly. However, it becomes a challenge for those who have little information or those who lack the right trading strategies. Sometimes, even the most experienced traders end up losing a fortune because of inadequate knowledge and planning.

Day trading refers to a technique of stock trading that involves buying and selling of security or assets within a single day. Although day trading takes place in most marketplaces, it is more common in forex and stock trading platforms. For you to succeed in this kind of trade, you must have enough capital. The main goal is to leverage the profit on every slight price movement.

When day trading, you must ensure that each position you open closes by the end of the same day. This means that you cannot hold a position overnight. Instead, you must close the position in the evening and reopen it the next day. It is the opposite of long-term trading where you purchase stock, hold it for some time then sell it off at a profit. That is why day trading is not considered as a form of investment.

Individuals who engage in this kind of trade are known as day traders. As a day trader, you must master how prices move in the marketplace. This is important if you want to make a profit from each short term price movement. A trader can make an unlimited number of trades within a single day. However, beginners can limit themselves to one or a few trades depending on the amount of capital and time available. If a trade does not seem quite profiting at the end of the day, you may decide to let it continue to the next day. However, you will be required to pay some fee to your broker for this to happen.

How long each transaction lasts depends on the trader. Some complete trades in a matter of seconds or minutes while others take several hours. Traders who purchase and sell multiple times within the same day usually end up with high-profit volumes. Some traders prefer selling their stock as soon as a good profit has been realized. Others prefer to wait until the close of the day to end their positions.

Qualities of a Good Day Trader

Day traders who engage in the business as a career always seek to improve their skills each day. They possess in-depth knowledge of the market as well as the strategies required to make good cash from the market. So, who is the right person to engage in day trading? Let us look at some of the characteristics one should possess.

Market Experience – if you happen to engage in day trading without the requisite knowledge of the market, you may lose all your capital. You must be good at reading charts and carrying out technical analysis of the prices and market trends. You must also be able to carry out all the due diligence required to ensure you maximize the profits you realize from the trade.

Adequate capital – like any other trade, you need sufficient amounts of money to day trade. You must understand that this should be risk capital that you are ready to lose in case the market does not perform in your favor. Preparing yourself this way will save you the emotional torture associated with loss of cash in the trade. You must invest large capitals if you want to make more significant returns.

A good strategy – several strategies are involved in day trading. You need these strategies to stay ahead of other traders on the market. Before you start trading, you must understand how to apply these strategies in your transactions. When used correctly, these strategies ensure more consistent returns and fewer losses.

Discipline – it is essential to be disciplined as a day trader. Without discipline, it becomes difficult to record any successful transactions. Day trading depends on the volatility of stock prices. Traders are often interested in stocks whose price changes a lot in the course of the day. However, if you are not disciplined enough in the way you select your shares, you may end up losing a lot despite the substantial price changes.

This trait is particularly crucial because the stock market has uncountable trading opportunities. You may decide to trade on several industries, products, and assets, but the truth is – not all these opportunities are good for making a profit. If you are disciplined enough, you will spend time analyzing opportunities before investing in them. You will also open and close trades at the right time, and this will ensure that you minimize losses.

Patience – day trading involves a certain level of waiting. You need to time when to enter the market and when to exit. Getting into the market blindly always results in a lot of problems. You must be patient enough to get into trades in good time.

Besides being patient, you also need to adapt to the changes taking place in the market. For instance, how a market appears at the beginning of the day is not the same way it will be at midday. You must be able to adjust your strategies to accommodate market changes accordingly.

Most successful day traders always seek to acquire these characteristics as a way of improving their business. Doing this requires a high level of mental as well as financial flexibility. You must be thick-skinned enough to risk your capital and accept any losses that come along. Remember, the main difference between successful and unsuccessful day traders lies in the profits. More profits depict you as a successful trader while fewer profits display you as one that is on the losing end. However, losing trades should not make you focus less because even professional day traders started by losing.

CHAPTER 1:

What Financial Markets are Today?

Trading in Stocks

The thought of trading in stocks scares away many investors. Individuals who have never traded are terrified by the fact that one can easily lose money with wrong decisions. The reality is, stock trading is a risky activity. However, when approached with the right market knowledge, it is an efficient way of building your net worth.

So, what is a stock? A stock is a share. It is also termed as equity. Basically, it is a financial instrument which amounts to ownership in a particular company. When an individual purchases a stock or shares, it means that they own a portion or fraction of the company. For instance, say a trader owns 10,000 shares in a company with 100,000 shares. This would mean that the individual has 10% ownership of the stakes. The buyer of such shares is identified as a shareholder. Therefore, the more shares one owns, the larger the proportion of the company which they own. Every time the value of the company shares rise, your share value will also rise. Similarly, if the value falls, your share value also declines. When a company makes a profit, the shareholders are also bestowed with the profits in the form of dividends.

Preferred stock and common stock are the two main types of stocks you should be aware of. The difference that lies between these stocks is that with common stocks, it carries voting rights. This means that a shareholder has an influence on company meetings. Hence, they can have a say in company meetings where the board of directors is elected. On the other hand, preferred shares lack voting rights. However, they are identified as "preferred" shares or stocks because of their preference over common stocks. In the event that a company goes through liquidation, shareholders with preferred shares will be preferred to receive assets or dividends.

Far from the information provided about the varying kinds of stock, a day trader doesn't necessarily have to understand the difference. Remember, you are only a day trader. Thus, you will only buy shares for a short period before selling them on the same day.

Basing on the factors pointed out above, the stock market could be evaluated as follows.

Capital Requirements

According to the Pattern Day Trading Rule, the minimum brokerage balance you are required to maintain for you to trade in stocks is at least $25,000. Without a doubt, this is a lot of money to start with. Surprisingly, there are tons of traders who began with a lower amount than that. To understand how this rule applies, you need to know what it means to be a pattern day trader. This is the type of trader whereby they execute more than four traders within five business days in their margin accounts.

Leverage

There are two ways of trading in stocks. You could either choose to trade using a margin account or a cash account. With the margin account, it gives a trader the opportunity of buying their stocks on margin. Conversely, with cash accounts, you only buy the stocks for the amount of money present in your account. In other words, you will be trading with a leverage ratio of 1:1.

The notion of trading on margin implies that you will be seeking funds from your broker. This means that you will be able to buy more stocks far beyond what you can normally afford. To use a margin account, a trader will be required to have at least $2,000 as their starting capital. However, some brokers will demand more. Once your margin account is open, you can get a loan amounting to 50% of the buying price of the stock.

In a real-life example, say you make an initial deposit of $10,000 to your margin account. Since you deposited about 50% of the buying price, it means you are worth twice as much, i.e., $20,000. In other words, your buying power is worth twice what you deposited. Therefore, when you buy stocks worth $5,000, your buying power will reduce to $15,000. Your leverage ratio is therefore 1:2. Traders with a good trading relationship with their brokers could have this ratio increased to even 1:8.

Liquidity

With regard to liquidity, you can be certain that trading in stocks is not a bad idea. There are over 10,000 stocks present in the U.S. stocks exchanges. Most of these stocks are traded on a daily basis. Dealing with these stocks guarantees that you evade the common issues of slippage or manipulation.

Volatility

A trader shouldn't worry about the volatility of the stocks market as they often go through cycles of high and low. This is not a bad thing as a trader simply needs to study when the markets are rising and be wary of instances when markets seem to fall.

Basing on these factors, it would be true to argue that stocks have got good volatility and liquidity. The only issue with stocks is that they have a high capital requirement.

Trading in Forex

Most traders would argue that trading in forex is quite complicated. However, it's not. Just like any other form of trading, you have to stick to the basic rules. In this case, you need to buy when the market is rising and ensure you sell when the market is dropping. Basically, trading in forex involves the process of trading in currencies. In simpler terms, a trader exchanges currency for others based on certain agreed rates. If you have traveled to foreign countries and exchanged your currency against their local currencies, then you should understand how trading in forex works.

At first, it could seem confusing to choose the best currencies, but a trader should simply go for major currencies. Some of the frequently traded currencies include the U.S. dollar, Japanese Yen, European Union Euro, Australian dollar, Canadian dollar, and Swiss franc. An important thing you ought to understand about forex trading is that you need to trade in pairs. This means that when you are buying one currency, you should do this while simultaneously selling another. If you do some digging, you will notice that currencies are quoted in pairs, i.e.

USD/JPY or EUR/USD. Below is an image showing how currencies are quoted in pairs.

Often, the most traded forex products include:

- USD/JPY
- EUR/USD
- GBP/USD

An important thing to keep in mind with regards to forex trading is that the market is highly volatile. This means that a trader could easily lose a lot of money within a single day. Before venturing into this market, a trader should take time to understand this market in detail.

The forex market could be evaluated as follows.

Capital Requirements

With the number of brokers over the internet, it is relatively easy to begin forex trading. The best part is that different brokers will require varying amounts of capital from you. Hence, you could settle for the best depending on how much you can afford. You can trade in forex with just $1,000 as your starting capital.

Leverage

Typically, leverage in the forex market stands at 1:100. This implies that if you have $2,000 in your trading account, you can trade $200,000. The ratio varies depending on the forex trader you deal with. There are traders who offer leverage of 1:200.

Liquidity

Liquidity is not an issue in the world of forex trading. The only problem is that a trader doesn't have access to real-time volume data simply because the market is decentralized.

Volatility

Considering the fact that there is high leverage in forex trading, it implies that little movement in the market could earn one huge profit. The market's volatility is quite impressive but not as volatile as the stock market.

Basing on these factors, trading in forex is a smart move. A trader can begin trading with as little as $1,000. Also, with the high leverage present in this market, it is easy to earn huge returns with the right moves.

CHAPTER 2:

Technical Terms to Know

In order to succeed in day trading, you need to ensure that you understand the terminologies that are used. From the basic ones to the complex ones; this includes the ones that beginners can understand to the advanced ones.

Day Trading: This is the act of buying stocks or shares and planning to sell them within the day.

Professional Day Trader: This is an individual who does day trading for a living, as their source of income. They are licensed to do the trading, and they pay costly in order to trade. That is why when opening an account you will need to indicate if you are a professional trader. As for day traders, they do not need to be licensed, since you are using your money to trade.

Swing Trading: This type of trading involves holding the trades overnight. They are required to hold their trades for a minimum of a day. They are investments on a short term basis.

Bull or Bullish: This refers to the strong market when the stock is moving up. It is also used to know the position a trader is trading on. When the market is considered bullish, it means the stock goes up.

Bear or Bearish: This is known as the weak market. Most traders think that the stock market is expected to go down. When they are considered bearish, they end up selling their positions.

Initial Public Offering: This is when a company offers its IPO. Then they offer a fixed number of the share to the open market, the reason to make money. For example, a company, have 1 million shares, and when the shares cost $10 each; then the IPO is expected to rise to $100. The money is then invested in the company's growth.

Float: These are the outstanding shares that are available to trade with. They normally come up after the IPO and shares are released.

Share Buy Back: This is when a company can buy shares back after they were sold at an IPO. This will end up reducing the shares available to trade and the shareholders will then increase their value. This will also reduce the float.

Secondary Offering: This is the offering that is given after IPO and it will help in increasing revenue and sell more shares. The share value will be decreased and the share supply increased. This is normally not preferred by most traders.

Day Trade: This happens when a trader opens and closes a trade the same day and the same stock. They are supposed to follow special rules when trading.

Beta: It is used for fluctuation measurement and it is used as a numeric value. It measures the stock fluctuation against the changes and movement in the stock.

Freeriding: This is a situation where an investor will buy security and then dispose of them before knowing the original price.

Crossed Market: This is a situation that is considered temporary; where the asset-bidding price is considered more than the asking price.

Dividend: This is the money that shareholders are paid after holding the company's share. This is termed as sharing company success.

Divergence: A trading concept that is formed when the price of the stock separates with the oscillator momentum and it is considered as a reversal.

Earnings per Share: This is part of the company's profit that is set to an individual's share and is what is used for analysis.

Market Cap: This measurement is used to identify the size of the company. The sizes are set as small, medium and large, and it's based on the market value to the total shares.

Merger: This is the union when two companies come together and become one company. There are different reasons for mergers to take place.

Penny Stock: This is any stock that is below the $5 mark and they are considered as security.

Profit and Loss Ratio: This is the ability of measurement that a trading system has. It helps in profit generation instead of loss and it is on a percentage basis.

Return on Investment: This is the system that is used to measure loss or profit that comes from an investment.

Shares Outstanding: These are the company stock that is with the current shareholders; they are categorized as institutional and restricted shares.

Market Trend: It is referred to as the direction that the market is taking for a set time. This trend can be from several days to months or years.

Volatility: This is how the security ability is measured and it is normally calculated over a set period as standard deviation.

Support Level: The level when the security demand is strong and will prevent any price decline.

Resistance Level: This is the level whereby selling security is considered strong and will help in eliminating price increase.

Stock: This is the asset that will give individual ownership in a company. You will be able to claim the assets and any other earnings.

Price Target: This is what is projected as the recommended financial instrument price. It is always given by an analyst and will be used to know of any stocks that are under or overvalued.

Recession: It is the time when the economy of a country is experiencing a decline. This is caused by different factors over a certain period.

Mutual Fund: This is when individuals pool all their funds and invest in securities. Securities like bonds or stocks.

Cryptocurrency: This is digital security that uses the cryptography concept for security purposes. An individual can send to other people anywhere in the world.

Equity: It is referred to as the ownership of the asset after liabilities and all the debts are settled. This is also considered as the share ownership in all the public companies.

EFT: This is the acronym for exchange-traded fund. A security that is marketable for tracking bonds and any commodities.

Ex-Dividend: This is the date that that is important when owning a stock. This is because it is the date you need to hold stock in order to receive dividends.

Blue Chip: They are the companies that are worth a lot in billions, they also pay out dividends and are known to have reliable and stable business operations.

Bond: They are debt in terms of investments, they are funded to corporate and government as loan for a period and charged interest.

Capital Gains: When a stock or option is sold at a price higher than the original cost price.

Bull Market: This is a situation when the market is serving on an upward trend.

Capital Loss: This is when a day trader sells its assets at a price that is lower than the asset's cost price. This is the direct opposite of capital gain.

Cash flow: This is the money that comes in and out of the company's account. It can be for the whole business or for a single project.

Stock Market: This is the trade whereby individuals are able to buy or sell their stock and companies can issue stocks. Stock is what represents the company in terms of shares and equity. The main purpose of any day trader is to make money.

Annual report: This is a report that is prepared by the company to give the financial position of a company. It normally includes the company's information

Arbitrage: This is when there is selling and buying of shares to different markets and at different price points. A good example is when the stock market is at $20 on market A and $25 on market B. A day trader could decide and buy several shares at $20 from market A and sell them at $25 at market B and pocket the gain.

Averaging Down: This is when an investor decides to buy more stock when the price is going down. This means there will be a price decrease on the cost price.

Beta: This is what is used to measure the relationship between the stock price and the market movement. For instance, when a stock has a beta of 2, this means that for every two points that the market moves and the stock will move 2 points.

Blue Chip Stocks: These are large stocks belonging to large companies; they are known to give good dividend payouts and are of sound financial position.

Broker: This is an individual who sells and buys an investment on behalf of another person at a fee paid as a commission.

Bid: This is the amount of money that a trader needs to pay for every share for any given stock. There is a balance against the asking price and is what a seller will want for every share.

Close: This is the time when the stock exchange operating hours closes. That means no trading will happen at that time, the official closing hours is normally 4 pm. There could be an extension called after hours that could go up until 8 pm.

High: This is a milestone in the market whereby a trade will reach the maximum point in terms of price as opposed to. When there is a record of highs, it means that a stock may not have reached the current point in terms of price.

Index: This is known as a reference marker that is used by traders as a benchmark. For instance, when there is a 10% return, it may seem better. But a 12% market index may not be considered good. And the conclusion would have been, it is better to invest in the index fund rather than in trading.

Leverage: It happens when you borrow shares with the intention of increasing the profits. You collaborate with your broker when you sell at a price higher than the cost price, you make a profit and keep it.

Low: It is the lowest point in the stock price.

Margin: It is an account that traders use to get funds from brokers in order to buy an investment. The difference between the loan and the security price is what is referred to as margin. It is considered a dangerous way of trading because when you are not sure of the outcome it can lead to losses. It is a requirement to have a minimum balance on the margin account.

Moving average: The average of the stock and price per share known for a certain period. The common time frames known for moving average are 50 and 200-day.

Open: It is the time when traders start trading; it is normally from 8 am. The pre-market hours are from 4:30 am

Order: When an investor places a bid to buy or sell a stock is what is called an order. It is a requirement to put in an order to be able to buy or sell the stock.

Portfolio: This is a collection of investments that an investor owes that is what makes up a portfolio. There is no limitation to the number of stocks a trader can have in a portfolio.

Quote: A quote is the stock current trading price. It can sometimes be delayed unless you use the trading platform used by a broker.

Share market: This is the market where there is buying and selling of shares.

CHAPTER 3:

What Is Day Trading?

Day trading is a strategy of trading financial securities, such as stocks and currencies, where positions are taken and closed within the same day. Also called short trading, it involves buying financial securities and selling them before the trading day closes.

How short can day trading last? It can be as short as buying and selling in a few minutes, or even seconds! The point is to end the trading day with a square position, i.e., neither long nor short on any financial security.

It doesn't matter how many trades you do during the day. You can trade just once a day or 10 times a day...it doesn't matter. The defining characteristic of day trading is ending the day with a square position.

Day trading can take place in any market, but the most common ones are the stock market and foreign exchange or forex markets.

When you start day trading, you'll need to start looking at financial securities from a different vantage point. For example, if you're used to swing trading or a buy-and-hold approach to stock market investing, you'll need to look at stocks differently when you day trade if you want to profit from it.

Instead of having a longer-term perspective on stocks, you'll need to reorient it to a very short-term one. In particular, you should shift your focus from a company's possible growth over the long term to its possible immediate price actions during the day.

Another area where you'll need to reorient your thinking is gains. Instead of looking at substantial gains, e.g., 10% or more, you'll need to scale down. Given the short time frame, you may have to make do with gains as low as 1% to 2%. This is because day trading involves trading at a higher frequency but with smaller gains, which accumulate over time.

How to Choose Your Day Trading Market

There are several things to consider when choosing your day trading market. One of the most important factors is your own financial position. For example, if you can't afford to start trading $30,000, you'll have to skip the stock market and settle for the futures, cryptocurrency, or foreign exchange markets instead.

Another factor to consider is the trading system required to day trade. If you don't have the necessary equipment or software to day trade, you'll be very hard-pressed to succeed in day trading.

Another factor to consider is the time zone. You see, the United States isn't the only day trading market that can provide profit opportunities. There are other day trading markets around the world, i.e., different time zones. If you're a night owl, maybe financial markets from the other side of the pond may be more suited for you. If you're a day person, you shouldn't have a problem day trading the United States markets.

And lastly, your personality and interests may also play important roles in your ability to day trade successfully in certain markets. You'll have an easier time learning the ropes of successful day trading markets that you're very interested in compared to markets you don't like.

And when you have finally chosen your starting market, make a commitment to stick to it for the foreseeable future. Why? Flipping back and forth between different markets isn't just stressful, but it can also impede your ability to master a particular market. Focus is key.

Markets Where You Can Day Trade

For most people, especially the uninitiated, day trading equals stock market trading. They're not entirely wrong because most day traders trade in stocks listed in major stock exchanges. They're not entirely right, too, because there are other markets where day traders also make money. But that being said, let's look at the stock market first, considering it's the most popular market for day trading.

If you'd like to start day trading in the United States' stock market, you'll need a minimum of $25,000 in your broker's account at all times. This means if your equity balance falls below this amount at any point, your day trading privileges may be suspended until you put in more money to meet the minimum amount.

Your equity balance includes your cash balance and the current market value of the stocks you're holding. If the market values of the stocks you're holding plunge to the point that your total equity balance falls below the minimum, you'll be compelled by your broker to put in more money to bring your equity back up to minimum levels.

Considering the highly volatile nature of day trades, you'll be better off starting with an equity balance higher than the minimum. A good amount to start with would be $30,000, which is $5,000 more than the $25,000 minimum most brokers require. With a $5,000 leeway, you won't have to worry about having to frequently put in more money in case the values of your stocks fall.

Another popular day trading market is the futures market. As the name implies, this is the market to trade futures contracts, which are nothing more than formal agreements to buy or sell a specific number or amount of specific assets at a fixed price, regardless of what the price of such assets is in the future.

Day traders can make money day trading futures the same way they do with stocks, i.e., they buy futures contracts at a lower price and sell them at a higher price within the same trading day.

Compared to day trading shares of stocks, day trading futures contracts require less capital. If you want to start day trading the futures market, you'll only need between $3,500 to $5,000 to begin day trading S&P 500 Emini (ES) contracts, which is one of the best futures to day trade.

Trading hours for futures markets aren't as fixed as those in the stock market. They depend on the kind of contracts involved. For this reason, you must pay close attention to the actual end of the trading day for the kind of contracts you're trading to avoid carrying an open position to the next one.

Other day trading markets include the foreign exchange, commodity, and cryptocurrency markets.

How to Day Trade

Once you start day trading, you can use a myriad number of techniques and methods to execute trades. For example, you can choose to trade based solely on your "gut feeling" or you can go to the other extreme of relying entirely on mathematical models that optimize trading success through elaborate automated trading systems.

Regardless of the method, you can have limitless day-trading profit potential once you master day trading. Here are some of the strategies many expert day traders use profitably.

One is what's called "trading the news", which is one of the most popular day trading strategies since time immemorial. As you may have already gleaned from the name, it involves acting upon any press-released information such as economic data, interest rates, and corporate earnings.

Another popular day trading strategy is called "fading the gap at the open". This one's applicable on trading days when a security's price opens with a gap, i.e.

"Fading the gap at the open" means taking an opposite position from the gap's direction. If the price opens with a downward gap, i.e., below the day's lowest price, you buy the security. If the price opens with an upward gap i.e., It opens higher than the day's highest price, you short or sell the security.

Traits of a Day Trader

Now that you are envious about becoming a day trader, there are several traits of a day trader that you should be aware of.

Market Experience

A day trader should have sufficient market knowledge. Failing to study and understand the market will only make you fail in your day trading activity. As such, it is imperative to take time to understand the securities that are worth buying and those that you should stay away from.

Sufficient Capital

Also, with day trading, you have to gather enough capital before venturing into the activity. Traders are often advised to risk what they can afford to lose. The advantage of having sufficient capital is that it cushions them from financial ruin. In this case, a trader can easily capitalize on rising prices for particular securities.

Strategy

Besides having the right market experience and capital required, you also need to have a working strategy. Which strategy will you be employing to buy or sell securities? The different strategies that these materials include arbitrage, trading news, and swing trading. A good trader should refine their strategies to the point where they earn consistent profits. It goes without saying that the best strategy is one that will limit the number of losses incurred.

Discipline

Another important trait that should be evident in a successful trader is discipline. To be successful in day trading, discipline is a must. You should stick to your day trading goals without being swayed by attractive securities. In line with this, a trader should know their limits. When a day goes wrong, they should know when to stop to avoid incurring further losses.

CHAPTER 4:

Difference between Option, Day, Swing, Forex and Stock Trading

Option Trading

Options are not restricted to the stock market. The name option gives us a clue as to what these financial instruments are, however. An options contract is one which enables the buyer to have the *option* to do something. Options contracts can exist in any context where you are interested in buying something. The proverbial example that is used is the option to buy a new home.

Let's say that Jane is moving to her new job in Houston, Texas. She is interested in buying a new home in a good neighborhood that is reasonably close to her job. She has two kids, so she's also interested in buying a home in an area with a low crime rate and good schools.

She finds out that there is a new housing development near her job. She also finds out that it will take about 4 months to have a home ready for her to move in. Because of the high demand in the area, home prices are changing rapidly. She'd like to lock in a price for a home but wants to look around in the meantime. How can she do that? The answer is she can enter into an options contract with the developer.

The type of homes that Jane is interested in are currently going for $350,000. Jane tells the developer she is willing to buy a house at this price, but she needs 120 days to decide. The developer knows that prices are rapidly increasing, but to make a deal. He offers the possibility for Jane to lock in a lot and home for $360,000. She must buy the home on or before the date the contract expires 120 days from the date, she signs it. If she fails to close by that time, the contract expires, and the developer is free to sell the lot to someone else at market prices.

Jane is not taking too much risk because she is not forced to buy the home; she has the option. If prices end up dropping, she can simply let the option contract expire. If prices stay about the same or keep rising and she doesn't find another home she is interested in, Jane can go ahead and exercise her rights under the contract and buy the house for $360,000. This is true even if the price of new homes in the area has jumped to $400,000 at the time the contract expires. So, by locking in a price, Jane may have put herself in a position where she could save a significant amount of money yet get the home (investment) that she wanted.

While laws may vary based upon the given specific contract type, though generally speaking, the contracts themselves can be bought and sold. The contract itself becomes valuable because of the *underlying* asset (in this case, the home), and the ability to buy that asset at the fixed price. In an environment of rising prices, this can provide a big advantage to buyers. In many cases, the buyers won't go through with the contract. Actually, executing the contract is called *exercising* the contract. Of course, if home prices in the area were to rise to $400,000, it would be worth it to exercise this options contract.

Jane may not want to do so. Maybe she found a different home more to her liking. However, since the contract has obvious value, she could sell it to someone else. Ever since financial instruments were invented, secondary markets were created soon afterward, where people traded them. Options are no exception.

Since an option derives its value from an underlying asset that is not directly traded or even owned by the person who buys the option, it is called a derivative. The media often talks about derivatives as if they are extremely exotic and complex, but it is really nothing more than that. A derivative is a financial instrument or contract that derives its value from an underlying asset.

Day Trading

Day Trading is not investing, which, in simple words, is the process of purchasing a stake in an asset with the hope of building a profit over time. Time, in this case, is subjective; however, investors can hold on to an asset for years or even decades.

Investors usually invest in organizations that pay off debts, make good profits, and have a good range of popular products and/or services. On the other hand, Day Trading is the process of purchasing and selling assets within the same day, often using borrowed funds to take advantage of small price shifts in highly liquid indexes or stocks.

Swing Trading

If you are not familiar with it, swing trading is a simple trading philosophy, where the idea is to trade "swings" in market prices. In a commonsense kind of way, there is nothing special about swing trading because it's a buy-low and sell-high method of trading with stocks. You can also profit from a stock when the price is declining by "shorting" the stock.

So, what distinguishes swing trading from other types of trading and investing? The main distinction that is important is that swing trading is different from day trading. A day trader will enter their stock position and exit the position on the same trading day. Day traders never hold a position overnight.

Swing traders hold a position at least for a day, which means they will hold their position at a minimum overnight. Then they will wait for an anticipated "swing" in the stock price to exit the position. This time frame can be days to weeks, or out to a few months' maximum.

A swing trader also differs from an investor, since at the most, the swing trader is going to be getting out of a position in a few months. Investors are in it for the long haul and often put their money in companies that they strongly believe in. Alternatively, they are looking to build a "nest egg" over a time period of one to three decades or even more.

Swing traders don't particularly care about the companies they buy stock in. They are simply looking to make a short-term profit. So, although swing traders may not be hoping to make an instant profit like a day trader, they are not going to be hoping for profits from the long-term prospects of a company. A swing trader is only interested in changing stock prices. Even the reasons behind the changes in the stock prices may not be important. So, whether it's Apple or some unknown company, if it is in a big swing in stock prices, the swing trader will be interested.

The chart below shows the concept of swing trading. If you are betting on falling prices, you can earn profit following the red line in the chart. If you are betting on increasing prices, you would follow the upward trending blue line. A bet on falling prices is often referred to as being short, while a bet on rising prices means you are long on the stock. This, of course, is another difference between swing trading and investing; investors don't short stock.

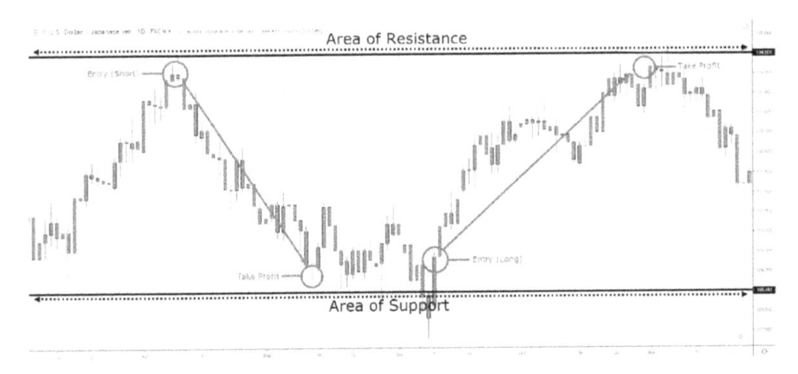

Swing trading can be used in any financial market. In the chart above, we are actually showing a chart from the Forex (currency exchange) market. The principles are the same, so the specific market we are talking about doesn't really matter, which is why it works with options.

What Is Forex Trading

The word 'forex' is short for 'foreign exchange.' It involves the process of converting one currency into another currency for reasons including tourism, trading, and business.

Although a person can participate in foreign exchange by traveling to a different country and exchanging his or her currency for the foreign country's currency, the foreign exchange market is more significant than that. The foreign exchange market is a global forum for exchanging substantial national currencies against each other.

Due to the international spread of finance and trade, the forex markets experience high demands for foreign currencies, which makes the market the most significant money market in the world.

When multinational companies intend to buy goods from other countries, companies need to find the local currency first. That exchange will involve vast amounts of currency exchange. As a result, the local currency value will move up as the demand for that currency increases. With that exchange going on around the world, the exchange rate always changes.

When global traders exchange currencies, currencies have a specific exchange rate, the price of currency changes according to the law of supply and demand; the higher the demand, the higher the supply and the higher the exchange rate.

The foreign trading market has no centralized marketplace for foreign exchange. Foreign exchange bureaus operate electronically through computer networks between traders all over the world.

Therefore, foreign trading goes on for 24 hours a day, six days a week in leading financial centers of major capital cities around the world. Investment and commercial banks carry out most of the Forex Trading in the international marketplaces in place of clients and investors.

Stock Trading

Stock Trading is what I have referred up to this point as speculation. It is a way of seeking short-term gains from the financial markets by attempting to predict the future movement of prices of a financial instrument such as a stock. Traders are not concerned with the intrinsic value of an asset or its long-term performance. The only concern of a trader is how he or she can make a profit from the movement of prices. Since traders are mostly concerned with the movement of prices, the classic tools used are technical analysis tools and trading systems. A trader will rely on things like charts, trend lines, moving averages, and many others. These tools are built into any trading software you will get out there. The beauty of becoming a trader or speculator is that you can make a profit whether the market goes up or down; a trader can buy or go long when the market is going up and sell or go short when the market goes down. Since traders operate with this kind of flexibility, they are thought to have access to more opportunities as compared to investors. Based on the time a trader can hold an investment alone, traders can be put into four different categories.

CHAPTER 5:

Tips and Tricks

Have a plan with you:

A trading plan is a set of policies that guides a trader on its activities. It is a necessary tool needed by all individuals. You always need to have a plan for everything you are working on. As a beginner in day trading, you also need to have a plan on how to do your trading.

A plan entails how, when and why to do your day trading. It will guide you on what action to implement to attain a certain number of sales or even profits for your trading. A trading plan will alert you when you are on the wrong path and you will be able to correct yourself so quickly before it is too late.

Make use of demo accounts.

Most day trading software normally provides mock accounts for their traders. You should take full advantage of them. Before getting into the real accounts, practice trading with the demo accounts, at least they provide virtual cash. They also provide tools such as charts which you can read on the price fluctuations. Charts improve the performance of a trader a lot. Know the tricks in trading using these accounts and perfect your skills. After that, you can confidently create a real account with a broker and ace day trading.

Have a routine for day trading.

Have yourself a routine on how to do your trading. Routine is a set of scheduled activities for any individual. Check your market trades effectively and efficiently and make sure they align with your trading plan. Scheduling yourself will make you organized and you will be able to correct the mistakes that may arise.

Never get tired of learning.

Trading keeps evolving with time. As a trader, you should not be left behind. Be alert with all that is evolving. Do a lot of research, learn from articles and videos and also be alert with the trends in trading. Study on the price fluctuations to be up to date. Big losses and market risks will affect you when you stop learning. Though do not overwork yourself to research everything all at once. Go at your own speed and have the basic knowledge on day trading.

Be responsible.

Responsibility and self-discipline are a must to succeed in day trading. What I mean by being responsible is by taking the correct actions on the mistakes that arise and learn from the mistakes. Never ignore the mistakes, you will terribly fail. Also, make sure that what you do is what is included in your trading plan. If it is still not working out, go back to your trading plan. Make changes to it and try again. By doing this, your day trading business will have no complications and issues.

Begin with little cash.

Do not be so overexcited when starting day trading. Day trading involves lots of risks and not being careful with trading risks can make you fail terribly. When starting off day trading, begin with little cash. Using lots of cash as a beginner can contribute to huge risks to the business. Little and reliable cash guarantees you with good profits unlike risking a lot of your money and end up losing. Always remember this trick in order to succeed in day trading.

Shun losses.

Losses are everywhere. They can be a nuisance sometimes in business when they occur. Some manage to be cautious enough to beat these losses but for the faint-hearted, they end up just giving up. I do not want this to happen to you as a beginner in day trading. In day trading, you need to weigh and select the securities that are safe for you. If a market trade does not bring any benefit to you, leave it and look for the one that is good for you. This will enable you to shun the losses in day trading.

Utilize resources.

You need to take advantage of the resources provided to you by the brokers. The resources can be research tools, news feeds, and tools for analysis, charting tools and also back testing tools. Select software with abundant tools for easier trading. Research as much as possible to be up to date.

Read and follow up the charts to have good data on the prices fluctuating in the market. Also, utilize the news. News will keep on updating you on the market changes in terms of the prices of the securities. Analyze the different markets with the tools provided. Weigh options and definitely select the best market you can handle.

Have the basics for day trading?

The basics for day trading include a good internet connection, a stable trading platform, a cheaper and a legit broker and also try your best and own a desktop or a laptop.

- Purchase for you a strong internet be it wired or wireless connection. This will promote fast and good quality trade executions. It will also save you a lot of time. Slow internet will slow down your trade executions and you will not be up to date on the market changes.

- A trader is advised to have at least two desktops. You can have one laptop at the start if money is an issue but the idea of having two monitors is the most advised one. If one of the desktop crashes at crucial moments while trading, you would at least have a backup and you will lose no profit. Having one monitor can be so risky and will affect your trading performance.

- Trading platforms are essential for all-day traders. Select a trading platform which is of ease of use. Choose software with a friendly user interface since you spend your time mostly in here. Also, consider the cost and stability of the platform. Unstable trading platforms can crash down anytime, and you will lose all your profits and data.

Choosing platforms that are expensive for you to afford is a very bad idea. Select the software with the cost that you are comfortable with to avoid spending much than the profit. Also, select a trading platform with sufficient tools. The tools will ease the trading process and will increase your performance.

- A day trading broker can be legit or fake. Know how to distinguish the two. Be aware of the legit brokers and make a connection with them. Choose a legal broker with reliable software and less commission. Some brokers can be hard on you by charging a high commission on your trades. You need to put your profits into consideration since the main aim of all businesses is to make a profit. Also, select a trading broker who is near you or within the same country so that you can get assistance whenever you are in need.

Have a time schedule for your trades.

As a beginner, you need to sit down and have a schedule for the time you will be day trading. Different markets have different times of trading. It depends on the type of trading you are working on. Here is a time schedule for forex, stock and future type of trading.

- For forex traders, you can trade within 24 hours. Though the best time to trade in forex markets is around 6.00 am and 5.00 pm GMT.

- For the stock traders, the best time to trade comes in two ranges of time. You can decide to wake up early and trade around 9.30 am – 1.30 pm EST or around 1500hrs-1600hrs of EST.

- For futures traders, the appropriate time for your trade is around 8.30 am- 11.00 pm EST.

So be aware of the best time to make your trades to be able to grab the best opportunities. Do not just trade anytime you feel to.

Have a trading strategy.

As a beginner, do not rush to learn everything all at once. Have at least one trading strategy for yourself. It is healthy this way other than struggling to learn everything ending up losing everything. That one trading strategy will help you grow, learn things with the right speed, correct your mistakes and you will definitely make it in day trading.

Set your entry point.

Identifying your entry and exit points is a crucial thing to consider as a beginner in day trading. An entry point is a price spent by a trader to purchase or sell a market trade whereas an exit point is its vice versa. A trader should ensure there is a big difference between an entry and an exit point to promote growth in trading.

Set realistic profits.

Do not set high-profit targets and you are just a beginner. Set reasonable profits that are realistic to achieve with little experience in trading. Focus on how to improve your trading skills and perfect them. Trading needs patience, so relax and do it the right way. Do not rush. Beginners who rush for bigger profits end up failing in trading.

Shun distractions.

Distractions are part of the game. With a working trading strategy, try your best to avoid all kinds of distractions. Distractions can come from analysts or even articles and they will mislead you on how to do things. Kindly watch out and be on the move always.

Have a strong trust for yourself.

Trusting yourself is a crucial necessity for any trader. Trust the process you are facing, and all will be well. Do not over read articles and watch too many videos, you will lose hope during this journey. Have the one trading strategy you normally implement at your fingertips and do what you have to do.

Learn from experience.

Losses are normal in businesses. Do not be a trader with a faint heart. When things do not turn out of what you expected, breathe in. Learn from the mistakes you made and improve. You will progress by learning from your mistakes. So, do it. Do not mind what others will tell you.

Be calm.

Do not panic or stress a lot when the stock market begins acting crazy. Be hopeful and courageous enough to handle it in order to be successful. Fear of failure should not be part of you. Do what you have scheduled yourself to do according to your trading plan and all will be alright. Invest in other stuff in your life, do not focus too much on trading.

Take control of your greed.

Greed normally affects traders so much. For instance, you can make a trade of around $30 and set your profit target at $45. You, fortunately, hit this target at first trading. You then think of setting the target a bit higher to earn more but you, unfortunately, fail terribly at the second time ending up making big losses. My point here is that you need to be patient in trading. As time goes by, profits will increase. Set profit targets according to your trading plan and avoid losses.

Develop a good attitude.

Day trading is not an easy thing. Many have lost hope and gave up on it, but you should not be part of them. Develop an amazingly positive and winning attitude that you will make it no matter what. Make sure to concentrate on what is to be done and what is according to your trading plan.

CHAPTER 6:

New Trading Products

Today, most traders prefer to trade in futures due to their associated advantages. Trading in futures is quite flexible and diverse. The good news is that a trader can employ almost any methodology to trade. Some traders shy away from this form of trading due to their limited knowledge about futures. Also, others are discouraged from trading futures because they think that it is difficult. Well, to some extent, this is true. Comparing trading in futures to trading in stocks, the former is very risky.

There are different forms of futures contracts, including currencies, energies, interest rates, metals, food sector futures, and agricultural futures. The best futures contracts you will find in the market are briefly in the following lines.

S&P 500 E-mini

Most traders will fancy the idea of trading in the S&P 500 E-mini because of its high liquidity aspect. It also appeals to most investors because of its low day trading margins. You can conveniently trade in S&P 500 E-mini around the clock, not to mention that you will also benefit from its technical analysis aspect. Essentially, the S&P 500 E-mini is a friendly contract since you can easily predict its price patterns.

10 Year T-Notes

10 Year T-Notes are also ranked as one of the best contracts to trade in. Considering its sweet maturity aspect, most traders would not hesitate to trade in this futures contract. There are low margin requirements that a trader will have to meet when trading in 10 Year T-Notes.

Crude Oil

Crude oil also stands as one of the most popular commodities in futures trading. It is an exciting market because of its high daily trading volume of about 800k. Its high volatility also makes the market highly lucrative.

Gold

This is yet another notable futures contract. It might be expensive to trade in gold; however, it is a great hedging choice more so in poor market conditions.

Capital Requirements

The amount of money required to begin trading in futures will vary. Some brokers will require a trader to have about $5,000. However, there are those who would require only $2,000. It is vital for a trader to choose the best broker who is flexible enough to allow them to trade with the little capital they have.

Leverage

Leverage will also vary depending on the type of futures you trade in. The contract value will also have an impact on the amount of leverage that you will have.

Liquidity

Just like leverage, the liquidity aspects of futures will also depend on the futures you are trading. Accordingly, it is important for any trader to regularly check the respective volumes of contracts before trading with them.

Volatility

Futures are volatile. The advantage gained by using high leverage ensures that a trader makes a good profit with little price changes in the market.

Keeping the above factors into consideration, futures are a good market to trade. A trader can easily day trade with as little as $2,000. The high leverage ratio will also guarantee that huge profits can be earned.

Trading in Stock Options

Trading in stock options is almost similar to trading in futures. Here, a trader also buys stocks at a pre-established price and sells when prices rise.

Capital Requirements

Stock options trading is also affected by the Pattern Day Trading Rule. This means that your minimum capital requirements will be $25,000. If you engage in more than four trades in a particular week, then you should have about $30,000 in your trading account.

Leverage

Since there are many options to choose from, leverage will vary. The exciting aspect of stock options is that they have high leverage amounts.

Liquidity

With regard to liquidity, stock options are not that liquid. A keen eye on this market reveals that a few options are traded on a regular basis. The low volume of trades is affected by the many options that traders can choose from. Fortunately, stock options are rarely manipulated by the market. Their values are not influenced by supply and demand.

Volatility

Stock options are highly volatile.

From the look of things, stock options have similar pros and cons like trading in stocks. Most new traders will shy away from this form of day trading due to its high capital demands. Its high volatility could be scary to most investors as it makes the market to be unpredictable. This makes this form of trading to be very risky. Therefore, it is not recommended for new traders.

CHAPTER 7:

How to Use Different Tools

The main tools you'll need for day trading are an online broker and an order execution platform. It goes without saying that you'll also need a very good internet connection and a computer on which to execute your trades on the platform. And if you're not part of a day trading community yet, you'll also need a stock scanner.

The Broker

You'll need a very good broker, who'll be your access to the securities market you plan to day trade in, e.g., the stock market. Take note that your broker can't just be good: it has to be very good. Why?

Since you can't access the stock market or other securities markets directly, you'll need to go through a broker. Even if you choose your SIPs correctly, you can still lose money in your trades if your broker's slow to execute your order at your target price or if their system suffers from frequent glitches.

It can be challenging to choose a broker because there are many of them out there. Some offer top service but are expensive while some charge very low fees but their service is crappy. Worse, some are both expensive and crappy!

Minimum Equity Requirement

The United States Securities and Exchange Commission (SEC) and the Financial Industry Regulatory Authority (FINRA) enforce rules on people who day trade. They use the term Pattern Day Trader to qualify those who can engage in day trading with stock brokerage firms operating in the United States.

The qualify pattern day traders as those who day trades, i.e., takes and closes positions within the same day, at least four times in the last five business days. The SEC and FINRA require that pattern day traders must have a minimum equity balance of $25,000 in their brokerage account before they day trade. When the equity balance falls below this amount for one reason or another, brokers are compelled to prohibit pattern day traders from executing new day trades until they're able to bring their equity

back up to at least $25,000.

Many newbie day traders, especially those who only have this minimum amount, look at this rule as more of a hindrance to day trading glory rather than a protective fence against day trading tragedies. They don't realize that it's mean to keep them from taking excessive day trading risks that can easily wipe out their trading capitals in a jiffy because of their brokers' commissions and fees.

While this rule is the minimum requirement under the law, many brokers and dealers may use a stricter definition of a pattern day trader for purposes of transacting with them. The best thing to do is to clarify this minimum equity requirement with your chosen broker to avoid confusion later on.

If you can't afford the $25,000 minimum equity requirement for day trading, you can opt to trade with an offshore broker instead. They're brokerage firms that operate outside the United States such as Capital Markets Elite Group Limited, which operates out of Trinidad and Tobago. Because these brokers operate outside the jurisdiction of FINRA, they're not subject to the pattern day trader rule. This means you're also not subject to the same minimum amount.

But before you think of trading with offshore brokers, keep in mind that these brokers are beyond the juridical reach of the SEC and FINRA. This means if anything goes wrong, you can't count on the Federal Government to help you out. If you really want to use them to avoid the pattern day trader rule, just make sure to limit the amount of day trading equity you'll place with such brokers to an amount that you're comfortable risking or losing.

Direct-Access and Conventional Brokers

Conventional brokers normally reroute their customers' orders, including yours, to other firms through some sort of pre-agreed upon order processing scheme. Thus, executing your orders through conventional brokers involve more steps and can take significantly more time. And when it comes to day trading, speed is essential.

Conventional brokers are often referred to as full-service brokers because they tend to provide customers with other services such as market research and investment advice, among others. Because of these "extras", their commissions and fees are usually much higher than direct-access brokers. Conventional or full-service brokers are ideal for long-term investors and swing traders because they're not as particular with the speed of trade executions as day traders are.

Compared to full-service or conventional brokers, direct-access brokers focus more on the speed of trade executions than research and advisory services. And because they often skip the extra services to focus on providing fast and easy access to the stock market, they charge fewer commissions and fees. This has earned many of them the alias "discount brokers".

Direct-access brokers use very powerful computer programs and provide customers with online platforms through which they can directly trade the stock market, whether it's the NASDAQ or the NYSE. And while they provide the necessary trade execution speeds required in day trading, they're not perfect and they have their share of challenges.

One such challenge is the imposition of monthly trading volume quotas. If you fail to meet their minimum monthly trading volume, they'll charge you an "inactivity fee", which often serves as their minimum monthly commission from your and all their other clients' accounts. However, not all discount brokerage firms impose inactivity fees.

Another challenge particular to direct-access brokers concerns newbie day traders, i.e., familiarity with direct-access trading. With conventional brokers, all a newbie trader needs to do is tell their broker the details of their orders and the broker will be the one to take care of all things related to executing their orders in the market. With direct-access brokers, the day trader him or herself executes the orders through the broker's online platform or software.

This can be quite challenging for newbie day traders because apart from choosing their SIPs, they also need to know how to execute their orders on the platform properly. But since day trading is a more sophisticated form of stock market trading, the chances are high that newbie day traders have enough experience with direct-access trading already.

But just in case you're new to both direct-access brokerage trading and day trading, your best bet would be to practice on a broker's trading simulator before you even consider opening and trading a real account with that broker. That way, you'll have one less thing to think about when you finally start to day trade.

The Trading Platform

A trading platform pertains to the computer program or software that you'll use to day trade. This is different from the direct-access broker itself, but many traders make the mistake of thinking they're one and the same.

The trading platform is what you'll use to send your orders to the stock exchange, which the direct-access broker will clear on your behalf. While it's different from the direct-access brokers, it's not unusual for such brokers to develop and have their clients use their own proprietary trading platforms to trade stocks in the exchange.

The number and quality of the features of trading platforms influence the price direct-access brokers charge their clients for their services. The more features a platform has, the higher the commissions and fees may be and vice versa.

A very important feature that you should look for in a trading platform is Hotkeys. Without them, you may not be able to execute trades fast enough to make them profitable. Considering that day trading focuses on stocks with relatively high volatility, being a second or two late can spell the difference of taking and closing positions at the ideal prices and missing out on profitable day trading opportunities.

Real Time Market Data

Unlike long-term investors and swing traders who only need end-of-day price data that's available for free online, day traders need real time data as the trading day unfolds because they need to get in and out of positions within a matter of hours, minutes, or even seconds. And unfortunately, access to real time intraday price data isn't free and you'll need to pay monthly fees to your direct-access broker or the platform owner (if different from the brokerage firm) for them. Just ask your direct-access broker for details on their monthly fees for access to real time day trading data.

Two of the most basic types of data that you'll need to look at as a day trader are the bid and ask prices. The bid prices are the prices at which other traders and investors are willing to buy a particular stock. The ask prices are the prices at which other traders and investors are willing to sell a particular stock.

The bid and ask prices are arranged such that the best price is at the top. The best bid price is the highest one, i.e., the best price for sellers is the highest price at which buyers are willing to buy. The best ask price, on the other hand, is the lowest price at which sellers are willing to sell. It's considered the best price from the perspective of buyers. Bid and ask prices also indicate the number of shares that other traders and investors are willing to buy or sell them at specific prices.

The bid prices are usually listed on the left side while the ask prices are usually listed on the right such that the best bid and ask prices are right beside each other. If you want to execute your buy orders immediately, you "buy up" the best ask price. If you want to immediately execute your sell orders, "sell down" at the best bid price.

The Day Trading Orders

The three most important types of day trading orders are market, limit, and marketable limit orders.

Market orders refer to orders to buy or sell stocks at their current market prices for immediate execution. If you remember from earlier, these refer to buying up at the best current ask price or selling down at the best bid price.

Depending on market conditions and subsequent price movements during the day, market orders may be the worst or best prices to trade in. For example, if you send a market order to sell when the bid-ask prices are $1.00-$1.05 and the by the time your order hits the market, the bid-ask prices shift to $0.95-$1.01, your sell order will be done at $0.95. In this example, your sell proceeds get cut by a minimum of five cents multiplied by the number of shares you sold.

On the other hand, let's say you sent a buy market order when the current bid-ask prices are $1.10-$1.15. If the bid-ask prices change to $1.12-$1.17 by the time your market order reaches the market, you'll end up paying $0.02 cents more for every share of that stock.

Only market makers and professional traders with a lot of day trading expertise and experience can benefit from market orders. For retail day traders like you and me, we should avoid market orders as much as possible. Why?

CHAPTER 8:

New strategies and Tactics: Which Current Strategies to Use

Anyone who wishes to make money with the stock trading should have a better strategy on how to predict the trend in prices of the stock in order to maximize profits. The charts show the trends that have different patterns that a new person in the trade cannot easily interpret. The patterns in the trend have meanings that give signals to the trader on when to make a move by either buying or selling stock.

The ABCD Pattern

This is a harmonic pattern that is used to derive the other patterns of trade. This pattern is made up of three swings that are made up of the AB and CD lines, also known as the legs. The line BC is known as the correction line. The lines AB and CD are almost of the same size. The AB-CD pattern uses a downtrend that indicates that the reversal will be upward. On the other hand, the bearish pattern uses the uptrend than indicates there will be a reversal downward at some point. When using this pattern for trade, you have to know the direction of the trend and the movement of the market. There are three types of ABCD pattern: the classic ABCD pattern, the AB=CD pattern, and the ABCD extension.

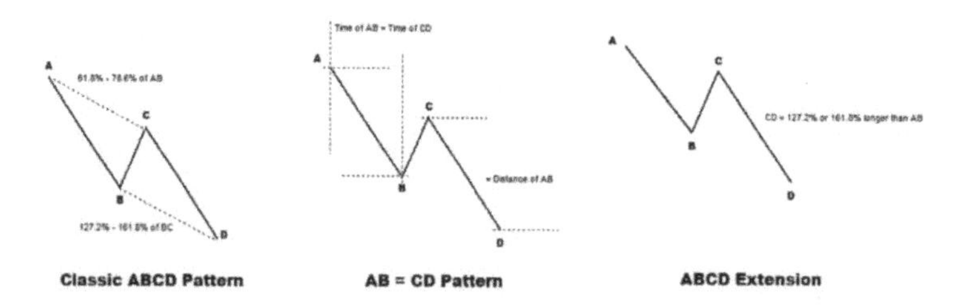

Classic ABCD Pattern AB = CD Pattern ABCD Extension

When using this pattern, remember that one can only enter the trade when the price has reached point D. Therefore, it is important to study the chart o at the lows and highs; you can use the zigzag indicator, which marks the swings on the chart. As you study the chart, watch the price that forms AB and BC. In a bullish trade ABCD, C should be at the lower side of A. The point A, on the other hand, should be intermediate-high after B that is at a low point. D should be a new point that is lower than B. as mentioned earlier, the entry is at point D, but when the market reaches point D, you should not be too quick to enter the trade, consider other techniques that would make sure that the reverse is up when it is a bullish trade, and down when it is a bearish trade.

Flag Momentum

In a trading market, there are times when things are good and the traders enjoy an upward trend, which gives a chart pattern that represents a bull flag pattern. It is named as such because when you look at the chart, it forms a pattern that resembles a flag on a pole. The trend in the market is an uptrend, and therefore the pattern is referred to as a bullish flag. The bull flag pattern is characterized by the following; when the stock makes a positive move with a relatively high volume, the pole is formed, when the stock consolidates on a lighter volume at the top, the flag is formed. The stock continues to move at a relatively high volume breaking through the consolidation pattern. The bull flag momentum is a trading strategy that can be used at any given time frame. When it is used to scalp the movements of price, the bull is used only on two instances of time frame: the second and the fifth minute time frames. The trading bull flags also work well when using daily charts to trade and can also be used effectively when swing trading.

It is simple to trade, but it is challenging to look for the exact bull pattern. This problem can be solved using scanners that help to look for stocks on the upward trend and wait for them to be in a consolidation position at the top. The best and free scanners that can be used to locate bull flags are Finviz and chart mill. There are tips that can be used to indicate a bull flag. When there is an increase in stock volume that is influenced by news, and when the stock prices remain high, showing a clear pattern for a pullback. At this point, you can now check out when the prices break out above the consolidation pattern or on high volumes of stock. To make a move, place a stop order at the bottom of the consolidation. At this point, the ratio of risk to reward is 2:1, and it is the best time to target. The strongest part of the pattern is the volume of the stock, and it is a good sign that there will be a major move and a successful breakout. On the trend, it is also good to look at the descending trend as it gives a sign on the next breakout. This can be seen in the trend line that is found on at the topmost of the flag.

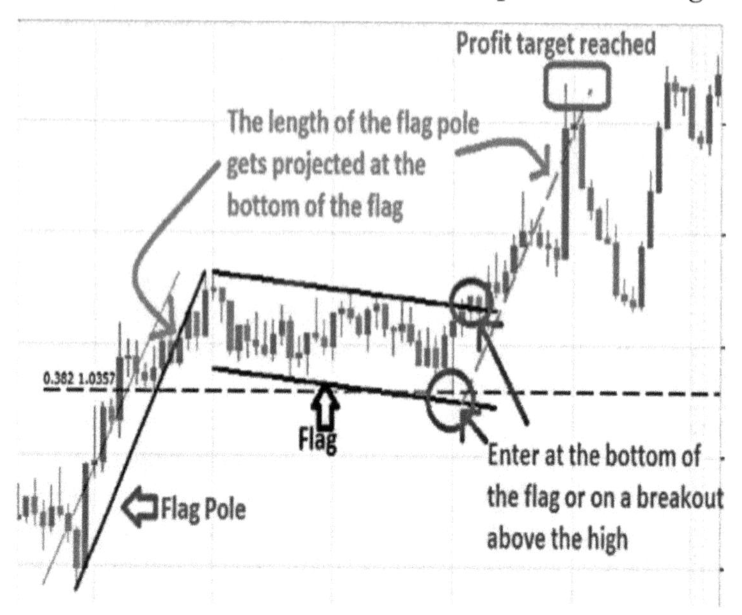

When used well for trading, the bull flags are effective tools of the trade; however, things can go wrong, and therefore one must be ready with an exit strategy. There are two strategies, one is placing a stop order at a point below the consolidation area, and the second method is using a moving average that is monitored for within 20 days. Within the 20 days, if the price of the stock is below the moving average, then it is time to close out the position and try out other trading routes.

Reversal Trading

Reversal trading, also known as a trend reversal pattern, is a trading strategy that indicates the end of a trend and the start of a new one. This pattern is formed when the price level of stock in the current trend has reached a maximum. This pattern provides information on the possible change of trend and possible value of price movement. A pattern that is formed in the upwards trend signals that there would be a reversal in the trend, and the prices will go down soon. Conversely, a downward trend will indicate that there will be a movement of the prices and it will be upwards. For you to recognize this pattern, you have to know where specific patterns form in the current trend. There are distribution patterns that occur at the top of the market; at this point, traders sell more than they buy. The patterns that occur at the bottom of the markets are referred to as accumulation patterns, and at this point, traders buy more than they sell.

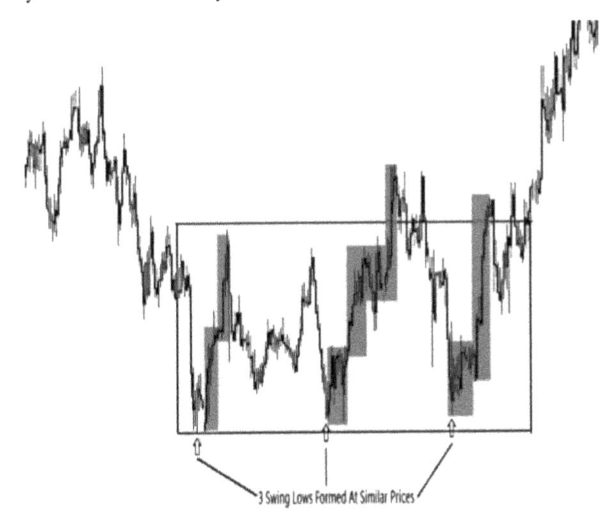

Reversal trends are formed at all time frames, and it is because the bank traders have either place trades are taking profits off the trades. The trend can be detected when there are multiple up and down formations that are fully formed; they should be at least two upswings and two downswings indicating a bearish pattern. The swing highs of lows on the trend line depend on which reversal pattern is formed.

The highs or lows form at a similar price because the bank traders want to appear as if they are causing a reversal in the market, by getting all their trades places at the same time. In the real sense that is not the case because they appear at different points of the trend. Therefore, as a trader, you should wait for a clear and steady trend upward for you to sell in the case of a bullish trade and a steady trend downward for the case of a bearish trade for you to buy.

There are different types of reversal patterns. The double top reversal pattern is a pattern that has two tops on the chart. It looks like "M." The double top has its reverse type known as the double bottom pattern that resembles "W." The double bottom has two bottoms located either on the same support or at different supports.

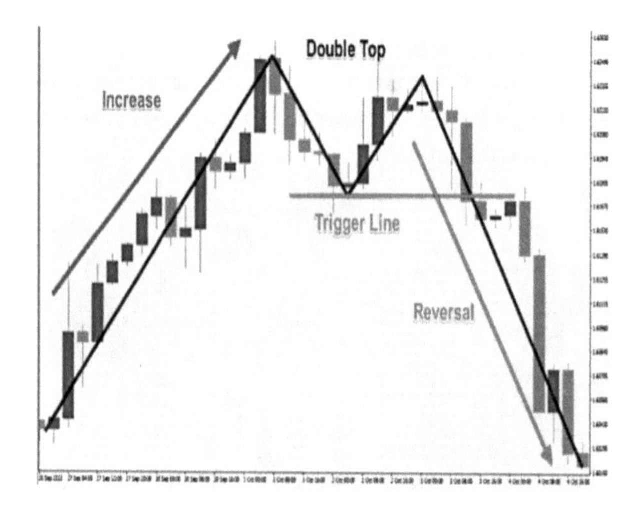

Another reversal pattern is the head and shoulders; this pattern resembled two shoulders and ahead. The two shoulders are tops that are slightly below the other top that is known as the head. The head and shoulders can also be represented in a descending pattern whereby the tops become bottoms.

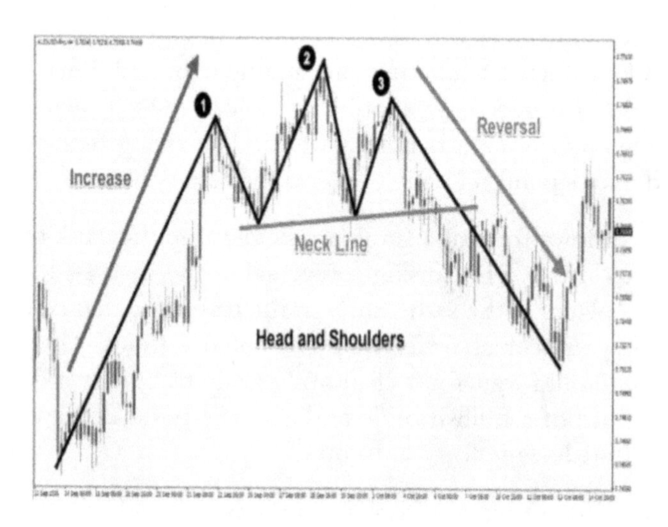

Moving Average Trend Trading

This strategy of trading is common among traders and it uses technical indicators. A moving average helps to know which way the price is moving, if the moving average is inclined upwards, then the price is moving up, and if it is inclined downwards, then the price is going downwards. Moving average can also help to show resistance or support of the trend, but this depends on the amount of time of the moving average. Support is shown when the trend of the price is downward, and at this point, the selling pressure reduces, and buyers start to step in the market. Resistance is shown when the trend in the price of the stock is upward. At this point, buying of stock reduces and sellers step in. it should be noted that the prices of trade stock do not always follow the moving average, but it is good to know that when the stock price is above the moving average of the trend, then the price trend is upward. Conversely, if the price is below the moving average, then the trend of the price of the stock is downwards.

Moving average is a powerful tool of the trade as it is easy to calculate, which makes it popular among traders. This tool of trade enables the trader to understand the current trend and identify any signs of a reversal. It also helps the trader to determine entry into the trade or an exit, depending on whether it offers support or resistance.

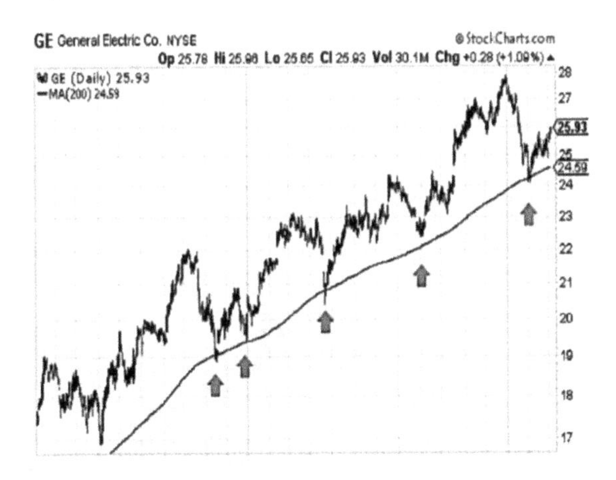

There are different types of moving averages. The simple moving average, which sums up five recent closing prices and calculates the average price, another one is the exponential moving average, whose calculation is a bit complex because it applies more weighting to the data that is most recent. When the simple moving average and the exponential moving averages are compared, the exponential moving average is affected more by the changes in prices that the simple moving average.

VWAP Trading

VWAP is the volume-weighted average price. It is a trading strategy that is simple and highly effective when you are trading in a short time frame. For it to work for you, you must use different strategies, and the most common strategy is the waiting for a VWAP cross above and enter long. A VWAP that is across above gives signals to the traders that buyers would be entering the market, and there would be an upward movement of price. The bearish traders might short stock giving it a VWAP cross below, thus signaling the buyers to leave the market and take profits. VWAP can also be used as a resistance or support level for determining the risk of trade; when the stock trades above the VWAP, the VWAP is used as the support level, and when the trading is below the VWAP, the VWAP is used as a resistance level. In both cases, the trader is guided by the VWAP to know when to buy and when to sell.

CHAPTER 9:

Manage Risk

Understanding Margin Trading

Brokerage firms and financial institutions that allow day trading on their platforms, provide margin facility to their clients to trade stocks or other financial assets at a fraction of the original cost. This called margin trading, and it is usually restricted to intraday trade.

With the margin facility, a trader with $20 can trade a share that costs $200. Trading on margin is borrowing funds from the brokerage firm, and trading on that borrowed money for far many times then your money will allow, is not a good idea.

Margin trading allows day traders to trade multiple times in a session with a small investing capital. For prudent day traders, it is a good facility that they use for their profits. But for beginners, it may turn into a trap, making them greedy and losing money by over-trading. Margin facility gives a false sense to day traders of having more money than they have. During trading, they forget that they're trading on borrowed money and sometimes, accumulate more losses. Also, the brokerage charges pile up and total losses for them become higher than the money in the account. In such situations, traders get a call from their brokerage, demanding to deposit money in their accounts to cover the deficit. This is knowns as the "margin call' is and is a signal that the trader is accumulated losses.

Like nuclear power, margin trading can be good in experienced hands and destructive in the hands of novice traders who become greedy for its power.

Therefore, margin trading should be done in a calculated way. Traders should keep an account of how many trades they have done in a single session and how much loss or profits they have made.

Margin facility is good for those traders who have strict rules for money management and control over their trading habits. By trading carefully, they can increase their profits with just a small investment. Trading on margin increases a trader's trading power because with the help of margin they can trade for a greater amount than the money in their trading accounts will allow. If your brokerage firm offers merging facility for day trading, consider and plan carefully how you will use it before making any decision.

In margin trading, all open positions are squared off before markets close for that session and traders are not allowed to carry forward positions that have been opened using the margin facility.

Manage Market Risk

When people think of day trading, they only think of potential profits, not losses. Therefore, day trading attracts so many people that don't see the risk of losses. In stock markets, various events can trigger losses for investors and traders, which are beyond their control. These events can be economic conditions such as recession, geopolitical changes, changes in the central bank policies, natural disasters, or sometimes terror attacks.

This is the market risk; the potential of losing money due to unknown and sudden factors. These factors affect the overall performance of stock markets, and regardless of how careful one is while day trading, the possibility of market risk is always present, which can cause losses. The market risk is known as the systematic risk because it influences the entire stock market. There is also a nonsystematic risk, which affects only a specific industry or company. Long-term investors tackle this risk by diversification in their investment portfolio.

Unlike investors, day traders have no method to neutralize market risk, but they can avoid it by keeping track of financial and business events, news, and economic calendars. For example, stock markets are very sensitive to the central banks' rate policies and become highly volatile on those days. Nobody knows what kind of policy any central bank will adopt in its monetary meeting. But day traders can check the economic calendar and know which day these meetings will take place. They can avoid trading on those days and reduce the risk of loss in trading.

Therefore, knowledge of stock markets and being aware of what is happening in the financial world is essential for day traders. Many successful traders have a policy of staying away from trading on days when any major economic event will take place, or a major decision will be announced. For example, on the day when the result of an important election is declared; any big company's court case decision comes in, or a central banks' policy meeting takes place. On such days, speculative trading dominates stock markets and market risk is very high. Similarly, on a day when any company announces earnings results, its stock price fluctuates wildly, increasing the market risk in trading of that stock.

For inexperienced day traders, the best way to tackle market risk is to avoid trading on such days.

Risk Management Techniques

In day trading, there is always a risk that you will lose money. Now, if you want to start day trading as a career, learn a few techniques that will reduce and manage the risk of potential losses. By taking steps to manage the risk, you reduce the potential day trading losses.

To stay in the day trading business for the long term, you must protect your trading capital. By reducing the risk of losses, you open the possibilities of future profits and a sustainable day trading business.

If you plan well, prepare your trading strategies before starting to trade; you increase the possibility of a stable trading practice which can lead to profits. Therefore, it is essential to prepare your trading plans every day, create trading strategies and follow your trading rules. These three things can make or break your day trading business. Professional day traders always plan their trades first and then trade their plans. This can be understood by an example of two imaginary traders. Suppose there are two traders, trading in the same stock market, trading the same stock. One of them has prepared his trading plan and knows when and how he will trade. The other trader has done no planning and is just sitting there, taking the on-the-spot decisions for buying or selling the stock. Who do you think will be more successful? The one who is well prepared, or the one who has no inkling of what he will do the next second?

The second risk management technique is using stop orders. Use these orders to decide to fix your stop -loss and profit booking points, which will take emotions out of your decision-making process, and automatically cut the losses or book the profit for you.

Many a time, profitable trade turns into loss-making because markets change their trend, but traders do not exit their positions, hoping to increase profits. Therefore, it is necessary to keep a profit booking point and exit the profitable trades at that point. Keeping a fix profit booking point can also help you calculate your returns with every trade and help you avoid taking the unnecessary risk for further trades.

Taking emotions out of day trading is a very important requirement for profitable trading. Do not prejudge the trend in stock markets, which many day traders do and trade against markets, ending with losses.

Using Risk-Reward Ratio

Day trading is done for financial rewards and the good thing is, you can always calculate how much risk you take on every trade and how much reward you can expect. The risk-reward ratio represents the expected reward and expected risk traders can earn on the investment of every dollar.

The risk-reward ratio can excellently indicate your potential profits and potential loss, which can help you in managing your investment capital. For example, a trade with the risk-reward ratio of 1:4 shows that at the risk of $1, the trade has the potential of returning $4. Professional traders advise not to take any trade which has a risk-reward ratio lower than 1:3. This indicates, the trader can expect the investment to be $1, and the potential profit $3.

Expert traders use this method for planning which trade will be more profitable and take only those trades. Technical charting is a good technique to decide the risk-reward ratio of any trade by plotting the price moment from support to resistance levels. For example, if a stock has a support level at $20, it will probably rise from that level because many traders are likely to buy it at support levels. After finding out a potential support level, traders try to spot the nearby resistance level where the rising price is expected to pause. Suppose a technical level is appearing at $60. So, the trader can buy at $20 and exit when the price reaches $60. If everything goes right, he can risk $20 to reap a reward of $60. In this trade, the risk-reward ratio will be 1:3.

By calculating the risk-reward ratio, traders can plan how much money they will need to invest, and how much reward they can expect to gain from any trade. This makes them cautious about money management and risk management.

Some traders have a flexible risk-reward ratio for trading, while others prefer to take trades only with a fixed risk-reward ratio. Keeping stop-loss in all trades also helps in managing the risk-reward ratio. Traders can calculate their trade entry point to stop-loss as the risk, and trade entry to profit as the reward. This way, they can find out if any trade has a bigger risk than the potential reward or a bigger reward than the potential risk. Choosing trades with bigger profits and smaller risks can increase the amount of profit over a period.

CHAPTER 10:

How to Save Money and Time

Time Management

Time management, a key aspect in forex trading, is one of the determinants of the gains and losses a trader is to make from the opening and the close of a trading period. It is therefore paramount that a trader has a solid plan in his or her time management in trading to reap off gains. A trader has to know when to enter and exit the market when to get the necessary information on trading patterns.

Match your personality and your trading pattern with the time you have

It is suicidal for a trader to operate on the basis of a trading pattern that does not suit their personality and goes against them at all odds. The personality type being referred to in this case is major whether the trader is patient or not. An impatient trader will want to have instant results and gains for trades made and will therefore not tarry around for trading systems that are long term. Such traders do not find the trade analysis tools that are long term to be useful to their course. Impatient traders are mostly associated with swing traders who get antsy and do not stay put to trade for the long term. Analysis tools that evaluate for long term trade may not be suitable for such traders. Short term analysis tools are mostly preferred for such traders and will work perfectly to their trading plan. The plan also has to mindful of the time available for the swing trader, which is very limited in most cases, and they, therefore, have to come up with a strategy that works in the available time that they have to trade.

Analysis tools and trading patterns that work for the long term are applicable to those whose personality is being patient. Long term strategies work for these kinds of people. They should, however, take caution not to be blind to current events that may drastically and completely change the trading pattern in existence and therefore results in losses for them. Their strategy also has to be within a time frame that they are comfortable trading in. On the other hand, swing traders are on the disadvantage that they have the tendency to overdo and overexert themselves in analysis of the trading patterns all the while trading for just but a short period of time. An advantage to the long term traders is that they can concentrate on other works while at the same time still trading. It is therefore of great importance to match one's personality with their trading pattern, choosing the one that will work for them.

Consider the important trading analysis

Irrespective of the type of trader that you are, critical and important analysis on trading patterns and factors affecting trading of forexes is not to be ignored. Just a small bit of information may change the trading scales to either make profits or losses. Even when a trader is pressed for time, never make a trade on a pair of currencies without thoroughly evaluating them to avoid regretting later. For the long term traders, an important analysis is to trigger you to make a change in the currency pairs for a profitable trade. Make use of the little time, if you are a swing trader, and do a proper analysis on the currencies before putting your money at stake for a loss. Many traders have failed to do so where their efforts to pairing profitable currencies came to naught. Only make a trade when you are confident enough that your currencies ae a go after employing your time in a wise manner.

Unplug from distractions when analyzing trading patterns

Distractions such as social media, the TV, background noise and many others are to be avoided when making an analysis. They tend to eat up a lot of time when it could have been spent wisely in analyzing and not miss out on an opportunity to make a trade that could have resulted in profits. Unplug from social media for a while trading and shout out all the noise in your surrounding and fully concentrate on evaluating the currencies and making wise decisions on pairing them. This saves a lot of time that otherwise could have been used in multitasking trading and other activities all the while not fully concentrating on each activity.

Come up with an information sorting strategy

There could be information overload on forex exchange and a lot of unnecessary news regarding the same that waste time for a trader goes through all that in a bid to make a successful pairing of currencies. There are also a lot of sites online that offer updates on forex trading and if a trader could subscribe to all of them, then all they could be doing is analyzing trading forexes and doing zero trading at all. Sort out the relevant information that only has effect on your currency pairs. It is also advisable to have reliable sites to get information from and not a lot of them or some bogus ones. This is a strategy that could save a lot of time, especially to the new traders who jump into every forex trading bandwagon.

Sync your preferred trading time with profitable trading widows

In forex trading, timing goes a long way. It is everything. A trader should, therefore, come up with a strategy that ensures that their available time is also a profitable window to trade-in. It is not always that the free time you get and available to trade in will result in profits. Choose the most appropriate window and execute a trade. However, a trader should also be able to enjoy his or her free time and also at the same time make money through forex trading. This cannot be reiterated enough, sync your 'available time' with profitable trading windows.

Money Management

Money management strategies are important to a forex trader to ensure that the trades made are profitable and reduce the chance of a loss happening to the bare minimum. Forex can be a game of chance to the traders who are not so keen on learning about managing their money in this type of trade. New traders lose their money when pairing the wrong currencies, and even made the correct currencies by the trading patterns but at the wrong time. The rules on money management reduce the chances of having a negative account balance when it could have been avoided.

Avoid overexcitement of the forex market

This is mainly applicable to the new traders who get overexcited on the trading patterns and tend to trade currencies in a rush with no proper analysis of the currencies and the market, thereby leading to huge losses. This should be avoided where the habit can turn out to be more of a game of chance or betting rather than wise trading. You don't have to make a new trade when an opening presents itself every hour. It can prove to a fateful and damning idea where the profits made and accumulated may be lost in an attempt to reach for more. Don't be afraid to lie low for days when waiting for an opportune time to make a good trade that may have huge profits. Being antsy for quick money and chasing the forex market will most of the time result in losses. Most assuredly it will. Analyze the market, an opening for a profitable trade will surely come. A trade made in an overexcitement of the market will not equate that made after a careful analysis of the trading patterns. Very few trades will be lost when this strategy is put into employ, especially to the new traders. No opportunities to trade and make profits, then no trade at all, a philosophy that should be a guide in making decisions in the forex market. Overexcitement for the market can also be displayed by opening a lot of trades in a short period of time, which may work against you should the tables turned. This habit, coupled with other equally poor money management strategies in forex trading, has left traders' accounts on the negative balance, wiping off a lot of profits. Let several necessary trades work for you.

Take caution to trade on leverage

Leverage might be a great way to make money, double money, as is the thought of many new traders. This is however not the way leverage tends to work. It may turn against your trade wiping all your profits. While on the one hand, large leverage might increase your money when one pair of currency is making profits, it can also create losses in a very quick way. A trader has to look into ways how they can protect their startup capital before making huge profits on the same capital. Leverage can either work for the good or work for the worst where your money in trading forex is concerned. It is therefore advisable in choosing the level of leverage to trade in, putting in mind that it may go either way and when it doesn't work, the losses are steep, especially on large levels of leverage. Being a cautious trader, you'll look into the balance that you have in your account before making the decision on the level of leverage you'll have on your capital. Other factors to put into consideration are such as the risk per trade and the stop loss distance. You have to look at how fast the system can respond to the cut of loss before running a lot of losses. When considering the risk per trade, carefully analyze whether the trade you are about to make will profitable and whether it is worth your money, or whether there is a change of a loss occurring, especially when you have a high level of leverage on your money.

CHAPTER 11:

What the Trend Is and How It Can Be Exploited

Trends are supposed to be a trader's friend, or so we've been told repeatedly by every single trading book out there. I agree with this thought. However, the issue is that very few traders can actually identify what a trend really is and how friendly it is in the moment.

Ask a beginner trader what a trend is and they're likely to point their arms at a 45 degree angle, either up or down, and call that a trend. The truth is that this is just one type of trend. Trends have varying degrees of strength attached to them and the 45 degree trend is just one of the many forms trends take. It also happens to be the friendliest.

One of the most difficult aspects of trading trends is that they can run away from you before you can take advantage of them. Prices move very quickly when trending and this is why, contrary to popular perception, trends are not very friendly to beginner traders. You need to be quick and decisive when entering a trend and both of these attributes are in short supply when we speak of beginner or unsuccessful traders.

However, by learning to identify the nature of the trend currently prevailing in the market (its strength), you'll be in a much better position to understand how you can take advantage of it. All trends go through three phases: The beginning, middle and end.

The three phases of trends have certain characteristics to them which you need to look out for. One of the reasons why it is extremely important for you to be able to identify these characteristics is that you'll know how much longer the trend is likely to proceed. By doing this, you can let your profits run as much as possible and get out before the trend ends and prices move in the other direction.

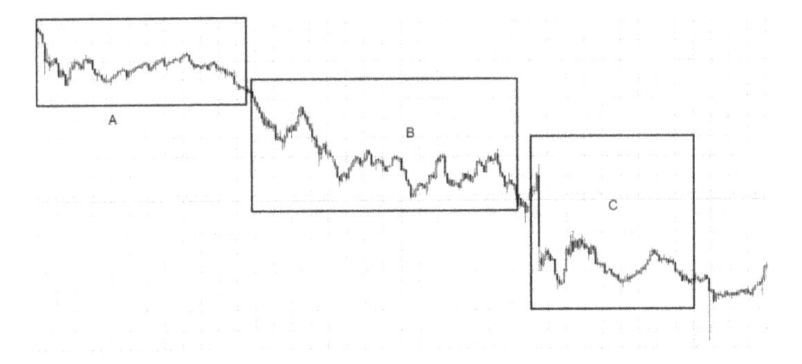

The Three Phases of Trends

The Beginning

The box labeled A is the one that comprises the beginning of the trend. This is where price begins to trend in a certain direction. Generally the exact moment a trend begins is tough to pinpoint but happily, you need to do this in order to trade successfully.

Trends begin from within ranges and this makes the beginning portion of a trend a little difficult to identify. You can't see this, but portion A is actually the end of a larger range. Don't worry about what a range is at this point. Just keep in mind that you don't need to get in on the very first bar of a trend. In fact, the best time to enter a trend is not at the beginning but during the transition period between the beginning and the middle.

The beginning of a trend doesn't usually look like one and in real time; it is unlikely you'll be able to spot it. However, there are some telltale signs to watch out for. The first is that price will begin to show definite bias towards one particular side of the market. Notice how the huge bearish bars to the left are not challenged by bulls. Price keeps meandering downwards, even if it does so while moving sideways for the most part.

Another telltale sign of the beginning of a trend is the sluggish nature of price movement that occurs after rapid changes. Box A is a perfect example of this. A few sharp bearish bars are followed by a bunch of small bars that take price nowhere. It's almost as if the price is in two minds: It isn't sure whether to move down or move sideways. This kind of hesitation is caused due to bearish (in this case) traders absorbing any remaining bullish pressure before getting ready to push the price down.

Lastly, notice the big bearish bars at the start of A. These bars are decently sized and aren't met with much support. The price drop is relatively smooth. What I mean is that price doesn't jerk downwards as much as it flows down. Keep this feature in mind for later.

The Middle

The middle is where the fun really is. This is where you'll make the most money if you can correctly identify the phase the trend is in. At some point towards the end of the first phase (the beginning) of a trend, the traders (bears in this case) decide enough is enough and apply pressure on the market.

This results in price tumbling downwards. You can see this happen quite clearly towards the end of A and in the first half of B as the bears are pretty much unchallenged. In the first quarter of B, we see a massive upswing but this is the same upswing that was highlighted (the higher time frame SR.) As such, this is an anomaly. Notice that price moves down quite forcefully and that bullish presence is negligible.

The second half of B is another story altogether. Here, we see the brakes being put on the trend as price begins to move sideways. The general movement is still towards the downside but there's no doubt that the bulls are reasserting themselves. Every bearish push is met with a counter bullish push, even if it isn't as strong as the downward pressure.

Towards the second half of the middle, the counter trend traders (in this case the bulls,) begin to find their voice so to speak. They assert themselves to a greater degree as they find that the bears aren't as strong as they once were. All of this sets things up nicely for the final phase of the trend.

Before we move to the end, I'd like to point out certain characteristics of the middle of a trend. The first half of the middle is dominated by the with trend side. The transition period from the beginning to the middle is a crucial phase where you need to prepare to enter. Even if you miss the transition phase, the middle of a trend will still give you ample opportunities to enter.

So where and how should you enter? Well, recall what you learned about SR levels. Can you spot a few SR levels where you can enter short (that is sell before buying the instrument back at a lower price?) Can you spot any levels which are retested from the opposite side once broken? In addition to this, there are a few price patterns that are printed as well which you'll soon learn about.

At this point, don't worry about figuring out where to enter. Your job is to understand and explore the phases of a trend. If you can spot a trend that is still in the beginning or in the middle, you will know that any counter trend pressure is likely to be short lived and that the correct thing to do is to ride the trend for as long as possible, until it starts displaying characteristics that indicate it is coming to an end.

The End

The end of a trend is marked by two types of price behavior. We do see instances of both although this will not always be the case. The first type of behavior is called exhaustion. Exhaustion is when the growing counter trend (in this case bullish) pressure starts alarming the with trend traders (bears.) This causes them to gear up and seek to completely smother the bulls.

There's just one problem: The bulls are much stronger now and are not going to go away. Hence, the bears put even more effort into their push and in the process produce a huge downward move. The flip side is that in doing so, they exhaust themselves and have nothing left.

You can see this manifest as a huge bearish bar. This looks impressive but notice how nothing follows after this. A series of smaller bars follow and the bulls are still there. Sure, they don't immediately push back but remember, we're still in a bearish trend. Trends don't end on a dime and flip back in the other direction. There is a transition period.

Contrast the exhaustive downward movement with the bearish push at the beginning of the trend. While in the beginning, the downward moves were smooth and didn't have much push back, here, bearish moves are jerky and if they aren't huge enough, they are immediately wiped out.

The second type of price behavior you will see towards the end of a trend is increased sideways movement. Whereas the beginning sees a general decrease of such movement, the end witnesses an increase. Notice how after exhausting itself, price moves sideways in little bars.

Also notice how the bears try to push prices further down but they aren't able to do so. They just have no strength left.

The end of a trend is the best place to get out of your short position (or long in case of a bullish trend.) Ideally, you'll want to wait for the exhaustion but it doesn't always manifest as I mentioned earlier. Watch out for a lack of with trend progress and increasing sideways movement. Whatever you do, don't try to squeeze the last few bits of juice from the end of a trend.

Many traders fall into this trap and only end up wasting their time and energy. It's far better to instead prepare for the new state the market is moving into: A range. Before getting into ranges though, I'd like to point out a few things:

1. Conventional wisdom identifies just the transition period between the beginning and the middle as being a 'trend.' As you can see, a trend is much larger than that and contains ample sideways movement.
2. Don't worry about the exact transition period between phases. All that matters is that you understand the major characteristics and learn to watch out for them.
3. There is a difference in the sideways movement in the second half of the middle and in the end. The middle sees negligible counter trend progress. It's more about slowing the trend down. The end sees negligible with trend progress. Here, the counter trend traders might not make progress but neither do the with trend traders. This is because they're being absorbed by the other side.

CHAPTER 12:

Set your Budget

Money management is a term to refer to the many ways people manage their financial resources. It ranges from budget planning in regards to their income. Money management involves planning and purchasing items that are important to you. Without planning well and lack of money management skills, the amount a person has will always not be enough for them.

Before anyone starts on the money management journey, you need to be aware of the assets and liabilities that you have. Some of the examples of Personal assets and properties are cars, home, retirement, investment, and bank accounts. On the other hand, personal liabilities are loans, debts, and mortgages. To be able to know your net worth, you should see the difference between your assets and liabilities. When the liabilities are higher than the assets, then you have a lower net worth. Having excellent money management skills, you will be able to avoid this.

Goal setting helps in Money management. Without goal setting, you will be worried about daily bill management; this can adversely affect your long term goals. With goal setting, you can have a clear view of the expenses needed to, and which needs to be cut out. When budgeting, you will have multiple accounts to manage. For example, you may have an emergency fund and saving accounts. By doing this, you will avoid the temptations of spending the funds on impulse buying. The retirement plan should be kept separate from the other accounts. There is different software that you can use to assist you in money management. An example of money management software is Quicken; it helps in tracking your various accounts and ensuring your saving and spending goals are on the right track.

The different aspects of money management include analyzing, planning, and executing a financial portfolio. The financial portfolio includes investment types, taxes, savings, and banking. In business management, there are economic variables that might affect your business finances. The best Money Management skills are to be able to access and control all the factors that might affect your financial position.

You can achieve your set goals through excellent money management. A dream of owning a home without using student loans, and be able to have a stress-free life from debts. Have a better plan to be able to deal with unpredictable events that can affect your finances, like loss of employment, serious illness. With Money Management, you will be able to have some savings that will cover your unexpected events.

The Internet is a global computer network that contains information and provides communication. Banking, investment, and insurance needs did not exist before. In the past days, customers had restrictions on decisions making in their financial matters, with less information on their options in their local areas. With the lack of internet connection, there was limitation and restrictions on where to find the right information. People had to go shopping for different items, like furniture and electronics. And also the purchasing of mortgages and insurance policies.

Money Management Skills

Do you know your income expenditure? Do you know your shopping, clothing and entertainment expenses?

Money Management is a life skill that is not in the school curriculum. Most people learn it from our parents on how to handle money. Since most people didn't learn about financial skills in school, you can still learn them now. Here are some of the Money management skills that you can follow to improve your skills.

Set a Budget

Track how you spend your money. Do you spend on food, movies, entertainment, and clothes? Do you frequently have an overdraw of your bank account? If this is true, then set a budget. Check your bank statements and note down how much your expenditure is categorical. You will find out how much wastage of money you are not aware of.

Spend wisely

Have a shopping list when you go to the grocery store? Do you first check the price of an item before putting the thing in your basket? Use coupons if available. Use online resources and mobile apps to stay focused on your expenditure.

Monitor your spending! By not being attentive to these small tips, you will keep on losing money. It takes time to get coupons, and it takes some effort to find coupons and writing a shopping list and checking the price of an item before buying. It will all be worth it in the long run.

Balance your books

Most people rely on going online to look at their bank balance. By doing this, you won't be able to know how much you are spending at the moment. The best advice is to be accountable by recording all your expenses; you will have avoided over-spending.

Set a plan

You must have a plan for you to accomplish anything. For you to go from location A to B, it won't be possible without a GPS to show the routes. You will end up driving aimlessly going nowhere.

This is similar to not having a financial plan. You will always be broke and not knowing where your money is spent on. "Where did that money go?" With a great plan, you will be able to track your money and expenditure.

Make a budget and also see a financial adviser to learn how to invest your money. You must ensure that you have the same financial goals and stay focused.

Save Money

Have a strong commitment to saving your money and securing your future. You can improve your financial situation and make it better! But you need to start with the decision to do so. Decide to start saving your money and improving your management skills.

Importance of Money Management

Sticking to a budget and living within your means – is proper money management. Look for great price bargains and avoiding bad deals when purchasing. When you start earning more money, understanding how to invest will become an essential way of reaching your goals, like having down payment for a home. Understanding the importance of excellent money management will help you achieve your plans and future goals. Some of the importance of Money Management is:

Better Financial Security

Being cautious of your expenditures and saving, you will be able to save enough for the future. Saving will give you financial security to deal with any unexpected expenses or emergencies like loss of employment, your car breaking down, or even saving for a holiday. Having savings, you will not have to use a Credit card to settle crises. Conservation is a crucial part of money employment as it helps you build your financial security for a secured future.

Take Advantage of Opportunities

You may encounter opportunities to invest in a business to make more money or an exciting experience like a good deal on a holiday vacation. A friend may inform you of a great investment opportunity or get a great once-in-a-lifetime dream holiday vacation. It can be frustrating not having the money to jump right to these opportunities.

Pay Lower Interest Rates

With excellent money management skills, you can determine your credit score. The highest score means you pay your bills on time and with low-level total debt.

Having a higher credit score, you can save more of what you have and have a lower interest rate for car loans, mortgages, credit cards, and even car insurance. And there is the chance to brag to your friends about your high credit score at the parties.

Reduce Stress and Conflict

Paying your bills on time can have a relieving feeling. But on the other hand, being late in paying your bills cause stress and have a negative impact like shutdown in your gas and water supply. Always being broke before your next paycheck can bring conflict and a significant amount of stress for, couple. And, as we all know, stress brings health problems, experts say, like hypertension, insomnia, and migraines. Being aware of how you can manage your finances, so you have extra cash and savings can put your mind at ease. You will enjoy a stress-free life.

CHAPTER 13:

Start to Invest Step-by-Step

Build a Trade Plan

Set the Rules for Exit

One of the main mistakes that most traders fail to understand is that they usually concentrate over 80% of their efforts in trying to look for signals showing buy. They, however, fail to look at where and when they should exit a trade. Most investors will not risk selling if they are down because they are usually not ready for losses. You should get over it or else you will never make it in the trading world. Don't take things personally, especially when you are making losses. It only indicates that your predictions were incorrect. Keep it in mind that professional/experienced traders often have more losing trades that the winning trades. You will still make profits if you are able to manage your investments and limit your losses. Therefore before entering a trade, clearly know yours exists. For every trade you do, ensure that you have at least two exit points. The first exit point is the stop-loss which will tell you to exit in the event that you are trading negatively. You should ensure that you have a written exit spot and not memorizing them. Second, ensure that you have a profit target for each trade you perform. However, don't risk more than the percentage that you have set in your portfolio. Here are exit strategies you can choose;

Exit Strategy: Traditional Stop/Limit

The most effective way to keep your emotions in check is by setting targets or limits and stops the moment a trade is entered into. You can use the DailyFX to research into the over 4o million traders. You will realize that most of the successful traders set their risk to reward ratio to at least 1:1. Before entering into a market, you have to analyze the amount of risk you are willing to assume and then set a stop at this level, while at the same time, place your target at least many pips away. This means that if your predictions were wrong, your trade would be closed automatically, and this will be at an acceptable risk level. If your prediction is correct, the trade will be closed automatically after having your target. In either way, you will still have an exit.

Exit Strategy: Moving Average Trailing Stops

This exit strategy is also referred to as a moving average. This strategy is effective in filtering the direction a currency pair has trended. The main idea behind this strategy is that traders are usually busy looking for buying opportunities, particularly when the prices are above a moving average. Traders will also be busy looking for selling opportunities, especially when the prices are moving below the average. Therefore this strategy also considers the fact that a moving average can also be a trailing stop. This means that if a moving average cross over price, the trend is considered to be shifting. When you are a trend trader, you would consider closing out the position the moment a shift has occurred. It is preferred that you set your stop loss based on a moving average, as this is very effective.

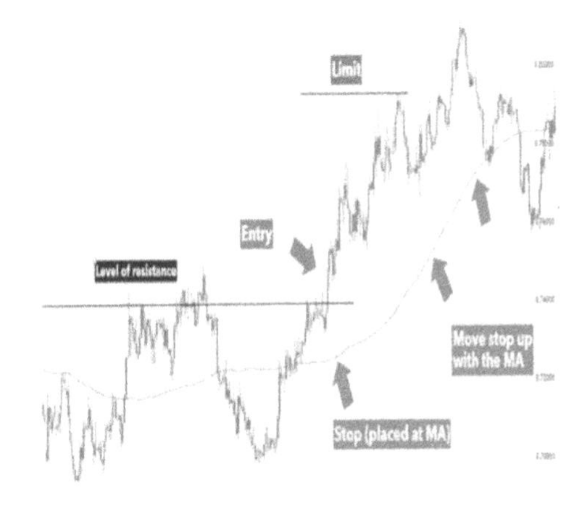

Exit Strategy: Volatility Bases Approach Using ATR

This technique involves the use of the Average True Range (ATR), which is designed to determine market volatility. It calculates the average range of the last 14 candles found between the high and low and thereby tells a trader the erratic behavior of the market. Traders can, therefore, use this to set stops and limits for every trade they do. A greater ATR on a given pair means a wider stop. This means if a volatile pair can generally be stopped out early, and thus will have a tight stop. You can adopt ATR for any time frame; a factor that makes to be considered as a universal indicator.

Set Entry Rules

We have set the exit rules to come before the entry rules for a reason. The reason is that exits are very important compared to entries. The entry rule is basically simple. For instance, we can have an entry rule like: "Given that signal, B fires up and we have the minimum set target is suggested to be three times the stop loss, from the fact that we give that we at service, buying Y shares or contracts here is appropriated and allowed." In as much as the effectiveness of most of these systems is determined by how complicated they are, it should also be simple enough to enable you to make effective decisions quickly. In many cases, computers usually make better trade decisions than humans and this is the reason why nearly 50% of all trades occurring today are generated on computer programs.

Computers have powerful information processing capabilities and will not want to think or rely on emotions to make decisions. If a given condition is met, then they will automatically enter. They will exit when the trade hits its profit target or when the trade goes the wrong way. Each of the decisions made by a computer is based on probabilities. Otherwise, if you rely alone on your thoughts, it will difficult for you or almost impossible to make trades.

Building an effective watch list requires three basic steps. The first step is collecting a handful of liquidity components of leadership in each of the major sectors in the market. Secondly, you will scan through stocks that meet the general technical criteria fitting your approach to the stock market. Third, do a rescan on the list nightly to be able to identify and locate setups or patterns that can generate opportunities in the session to follow while at the same time culling out the issues you don't have interest on may be due to their technical violations or secondary offerings, etc.

Building a Watch list

The U.S stock exchanges, for example, list more than 8,000 issues. However, a fund manager or a typical trader only accesses just a fraction. Why? because they have failed to come up with their effective watch lists. The main reason behind this failure is because the identification of stocks that can fully support working strategies needs some skill sets, which is usually lacking in most participants. It is therefore wise that you learn this because it will mark a trading edge that is a lifetime. For you to have a well-organized watch list, you should have a proper understanding of the modern market environment; you need to have an understanding of how different capitalization levels impact on price development. Lastly, you should also understand how different sectors are likely to react to different catalysts over time. When choosing the candidates you want to follow, be it on a daily, weekly, or monthly basis, you have to consider economic cycles, seasonality, and sentiments.

Guidelines for Building a Watch list

The requirements of a watch list depend on the amount of time a trader has to do trade and as well follow the financial markets. For instance, if you are a part-timer who only plays a few positions each week, daily, you can have a simple culling list having 50-100 issues to track. Otherwise, if you are a professional trader, you have to spend more time on the task. You should build a primary database containing 350 - 500 stocks. You should also have a secondary list fitting your trading screens. Note that each trading screen should be able to accommodate between 20 and 75 issues, but this will depend on the space that charts, market depth, scanners, and news sticker's windows will take. It is appropriate that to trade well, one screen should be devoted to stickers and each entry of these stickers should display just a maximum of three fields like the percentage change, the last price, and the net change.

Execution

This refers to the completion of a sell or buys of an order for a security. Order execution occurs when the order gets filled and not when an order is placed by an investor. As an investor, when you submit the trade, the trade is sent to a broker. The broker determines the best way with which this trade can be executed. The law requires that brokers give the best execution possible to the investors. There is an established commission, referred to as the Securities and Exchange Commission, where brokers report the quality of their executions. Brokers are also required to notify customers whose orders were not routed for best execution. The growth of online brokers today has made the cost of trade execution to reduce significantly. Today, many traders offer a commission rebate to their customers for some set monthly targets for these customers. This can be very important for the short-term trader who tries to keep the execution costs as low as possible.

There are high probabilities that you will be able to settle at the desired price if you have placed a market order or any other order that is relatively easy to be converted into a market order. However, this does not apply for all cases because there are orders that may be too large and will require that they be broken down to come up with several small orders and this might be very difficult to execute and get the best possible price range. To solve this, you can involve the use of risk in the system. Execution risk is the lag between order placement and settlement.

CHAPTER 14:

Building your Portfolio

The next logical step towards sound stock investment is to build a portfolio that suits your financial needs. It is very important to understand that an investment portfolio is not a mere collection of a few stocks, but it also must reflect your long-term financial goals.

There are some key things that should guide the structure of your investment portfolio.

Age: This is a very important factor in many ways. If a person who is still in his/her teens starts investing, even a small amount of investment will lead to big returns in the long-run as the time is by the side of the investor, and the compounding effect of interest will come into play. On the other hand, an investor in his/her middle age might have to invest more as there will be less waiting time at hand. Therefore, the kind of portfolio you can have will depend upon the age in which you begin investing. The sooner, the better.

The Maturity Time: Even if a small principal amount is left for a longer time, it will become a big amount due to the compounding effect. If you want to make your investment big, the first option is to invest large sums of money. The second option is to invest comparatively smaller amounts for longer periods. The more time you give your money to grow the greater the returns would be. So, you'll have to build your portfolio keeping in mind you are ready to give your money to grow without expecting returns.

Your Risk Tolerance: This is another big factor that would determine the kind of stocks you'll be putting in your portfolio. If you want to build a low-risk portfolio, your collection of assets would be different. In case you want to grow your money fast and have some ability to take risks, your asset portfolio will be entirely different. This would again have a very deep impact on your portfolio.

4 Major Categories of Investment Portfolios

You need to understand a very important thing that any kind of investment in this world bears some degree of risk. To mitigate that risk, we do investment planning. Even the money kept in your savings bank account is not free from risks. There are several internal and external factors that can affect your net-wealth. The purpose of portfolio designing is to cater to this risk. Even if you have picked only stocks for your portfolio, it doesn't mean you are gambling your money. To mitigate the risk further, we take the help of another tool called diversification. This means that you don't put all your money into one stock. You spread your money across various segments and industries. You can then further diversify your investment portfolio by investing in various classes of assets.

Aggressive Portfolio

This is a portfolio for the people with a great fire in their belly and the ability to bear risks. Young investors with a lot of time on their hands and very few responsibilities on their shoulders can adopt this portfolio strategy. In this, you can invest 100% of your money into stocks. This is a bit risky strategy as stocks involve a degree of calculated risk as compared to bonds and debt funds, but they also give you better returns. You can put your money in stocks for a few years and let it grow fast.

Conservative Portfolio

This is the kind of portfolio you can pick when you don't want to put all your money into risky assets. In this, you can put 75% of your funds into stocks and 25% of the funds in bonds. The investment in bonds may bring slower returns as compared to stocks, but it also has lower risk exposure. Building such a portfolio ensures that you will get more than your initial investments in any case, even if most of the things in your financial planning fail.

Balanced Portfolio

This is a portfolio that suits the people investing in their middle age. In this, you can invest 50% of the fund in stocks and the remaining 50% in bonds. This brings greater security and also keeps half of the money on a faster growth track.

Safe Portfolio

This is an investment portfolio people usually pick up late when their risk appetite has gone down completely, and they simply want their money to grow at a steady path. In this, you can invest 100% of your funds in bonds and completely relax and market fluctuations will have little impact on the growth of your investments.

Popularly only the stocks are known as the main asset that you can have for investment. However, that's not true these days as investors have a wide variety of assets that give you greater security and growth opportunities.

Various Types of Assets

Stocks: This is the hot potato that gets the most part of the limelight. The main reason behind its popularity is its ability to grow fast. There is a higher risk in stocks as compared to other assets, but you can mitigate it by diversifying your investment. You can pick stocks from large-cap, mid-cap, and small-cap industries. Maintaining a balance among these sectors usually brings good returns.

Bonds: When governments and big corporations need money, they issue bonds. The bonds are mostly risk-free as they are free of the effect of profit or loss on the enterprise which has issued the bonds. However, the rate of growth in bonds is slow as they take the loans at lower rates of interest. When you invest your money in bonds, you will have to keep in mind factors like the kind of bond you are investing in, the maturity period of the bond and also the rating of the issuer along with the offered interest rates.

Mutual Funds: Mutual funds are the mixed bag of assets managed by qualified fund managers with a wide experience of the market. Qualified fund managers with long-exposure to market choose a portfolio that has assets from various classes like stocks and bonds. They keep rebalancing portfolios from time to time to reduce your risk exposure and increase your returns. Mutual funds are a great idea for people who want to invest safely and don't want to pay a lot of attention to the investing business. However, you'll have to keep in mind that a substantial part of your investment will also go towards the expenses of managing the fund.

Exchange-Traded Funds (ETFs): This is another interesting class of assets that can be explored by the beginners. They are comparatively safer as they have the cushioning of the market. They basically function like mutual funds but are less expensive and more industry-specific. ETFs can be a great addition to your portfolio as they have better growth prospects and the chances of risk in the long-term are generally low.

Change is Eternal

This is an important lesson that every investor must have in mind all the time. A stock that has been performing extremely well for years isn't a guarantee that it will keep doing so forever. The bankruptcy of big names like Lehman Brothers has taught this important lesson to everyone.

Therefore, when you invest your money in stocks, it becomes imperative that you keep an eye on the overall performance of your stocks. These days this is an easy thing to do. Gone are the days when you had to scan the newspapers daily or hunt for news aggressively. These days you can easily get alerts, news, and tips about your specific stocks online. You must remain updated about industry news and take proactive steps if there is any concern in any stock with your investment.

The best thing to do when one industry is experiencing any specific stress is to do rebalancing. You simply need to reduce your risk in specific equities under stress and reinvest them in safer areas. However, this decision must not be taken in haste, and you must take a qualitative decision while doing so.

CHAPTER 15:

The Time Horizon for Your Goals

It is generally accepted that goal-setting motivates us and improves achievements. However, psychological research on this topic shows that it is not so simple. The most important thing is HOW you have formulated your goal. Depending on this, it may be for your good or vice versa. Leading forex trainers can set goals to help achieve brilliant results. Let us turn to their invaluable experience.

Some studies show that goals affect our performance in several ways:

Guidance

Goals direct our actions along the highest priority path, past all that is excessive and unnecessary.

Activation

Goals motivate us to solve specific problems. This aspect is especially useful if solving these problems requires some super-extra-effort from us.

Tenacity

When our goal is significant for us, for the sake of its achievement, we will break into a cake. Undoubtedly, this cannot but affect the performance in a positive way.

Cognition

Goals activate our knowledge and skills, without which we cannot reach the top of the trader.

But these peaks will obey us only when we understand that our goals are our children. We must value them above all. We must entirely give them everything that we have. Researchers note that dedication to all of one goal is a beneficial thing, entailing additional effort and powerful commitment. And do not forget about self-confidence. Your goal should be adequate for your capabilities. Avoid too simple and too complex goals.

Goals alone are not particularly useful. Mountains of research (including practical) on goal-setting once again prove this. What matters is not the goal itself, but how you analyze the process of achieving it while gaining experience and motivation. Very often, traders set a goal, then to put it in the long box, thinking that the act of goal-setting in itself will be enough. This is not true. All the salt of the goal is how it will direct your efforts in the right direction. But this will happen when you begin to work on this goal. Tracking this process, creating new sub-goals based on regular feedback is the essence of everything we are talking about!

And remember: the most effective goals are short-term. They quickly form the direction of your efforts and give fast feedback (feedback). I do not want to belittle the dignity of long-term goals. But a smart trader will always split a long-term goal into several short-term ones. This is perhaps the most effective approach.

Also: try to set flexible goals. "Flexible" - that is, those that do not require the radical result of "all or nothing." Always leave yourself one more chance. For example, a “flexible” goal may look like this: reduce losses to a certain number of ticks per period. And when you set yourself a certain amount, which you must, no, MUST earn in a week or a month - this is "all or nothing." In trading, this will not work. Such a goal depends only on market conditions, and a trader cannot influence them. Flexible goals are aimed at what the trader can control directly. They always stimulate our faith in ourselves.

Setting goals, taking feedback into account, and creating new frontiers is precisely what you can brilliantly use your trading diary for. And if suddenly keeping a journal and an endless race for goals become a burden to you - probably you are merely setting yourself the wrong goals. Ideally, targets should motivate us to new achievements and increase trading skills.

CHAPTER 16:

How to Understand and Analyzed Charts

Have you ever checked out the chart of a commodity or a stock? For most people, this is a daily activity. Most of the traders that analyze charts take a look at the price movements for a period of time – quarter, moth, year, etc.

For a majority of traders and analysts, charts show the beginning of all the potential analysis. Even the traders that do not love technical analysis use charts as well. They do this because charts give a lot of information in just a short period of time.

For instance, looking at a five-year chart of a company can give you an insight into what the company has done over the period. Based on these movements, you can tell if a company's worth over the phase or lost.

Using the chart information, you can also determine how volatile the shares of a company have been by just looking at the price movements. A company that shows fluctuations over a short period is obviously more unpredictable than one whose stock moves efficiently.

The Need for Charts

Before computers became the main tools for determining trades and other tasks, charts were the mainstay of determining trading strategies. However, creating charts by hand was tough because each chart is to be drawn by hand, the chart designer adding a data point each close of day.

The advancement in technology has seen increased popularity in the use of technical analysis, making them vital tools used by traders.

Charts display a lot of information that you can use to determine the direction of a trade. Charts usually tell you what is going on between the buyers and the sellers. Charts are an ideal way to come up with signals, and they can form the lone tool you need as a trader.

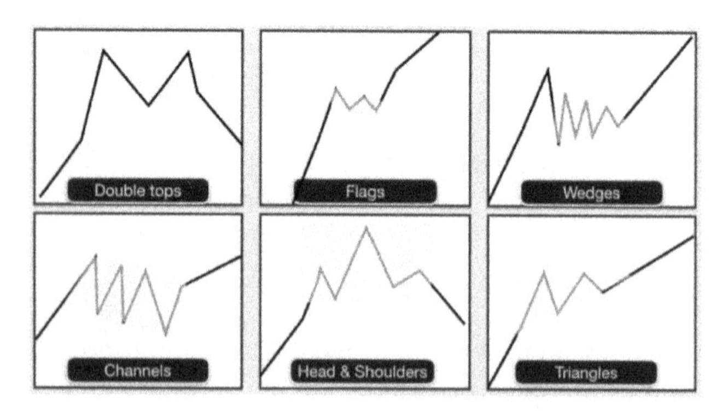

Chart Patterns

Chart patterns tell the trader that the price is expected to move in a certain path or the other after the pattern ends.

There are several patterns that you need to know – reversal as well as continuation. A reversal pattern tells you that the preceding movement will turn around when the pattern completes. On the contrary, a continuation pattern shows that the preceding pattern will maintain when the pattern completes.

Before you go ahead and look at specific chart patterns, you need to understand a few concepts. The major one is the trend line that is drawn to show a level of support or resistance for the commodity.

A support trend line is a level at which the process has difficulty going below. A resistance trend line shows the level at which a price has a hard time going beyond.

Here are the different patterns that are used by chartists:

Head and Shoulders

This pattern is a popular one and also reliable for most traders that use technical analysis. As the name implies, the pattern resembles a head that has shoulders.

This is a reversal pattern that shows that the price will possibly move against a preceding trend. The pattern signals that the price will most likely fall when the pattern completes. The pattern usually forms at the peak of the upward trend.

The pattern also has another form, an inverted head, and shoulder facing down. It signals that the price might rise and usually forms during an upward trend.

Head and Shoulders Top

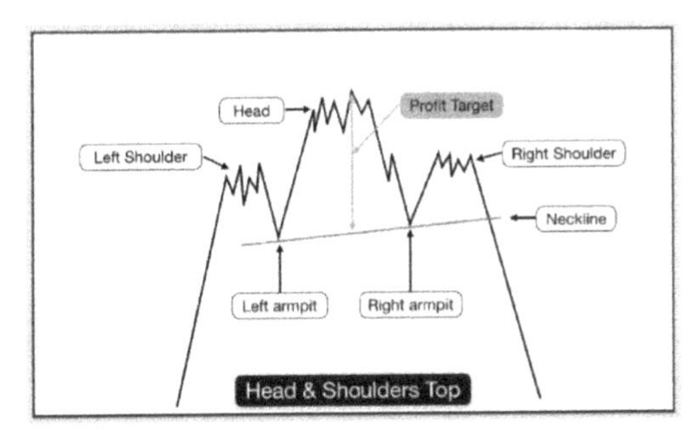

This tells the chart user that the price of a security will likely take d downward trend. It usually forms at the peak of the upward trend and is a trend reversal pattern.

The pattern has four main stems to complete and show a reversal:

The formation for the left shoulder – comes about when the commodity hits a new peak then drops to a new low.

Creation of the head – after reaching the peak, the price retracts to the formation of the other shoulder.

Formation of the right shoulder – occurs when a peak is lower than the peak in the head.

Neckline – the pattern finished when the price goes below the neckline.

Head and Shoulders Bottom

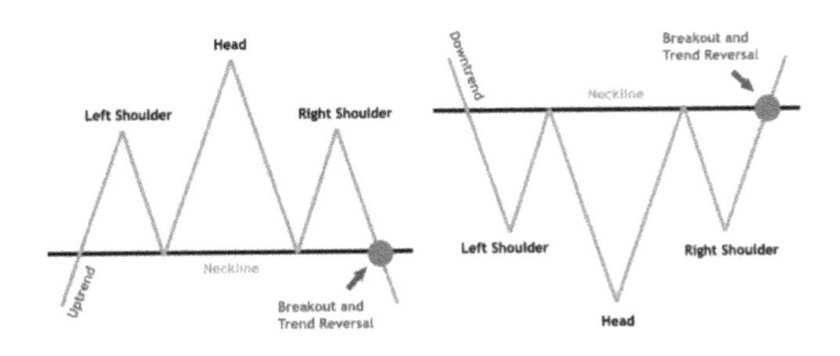

Head and Shoulders Top and Head and Shoulders Bottom

This is exactly the reverse of the earlier pattern. This signal tells you that the scrutiny will make an upward move soon.

The pattern usually comes when the downtrend ends and is considered a reversal pattern with the direction going high after pattern conclusion.

Steps include:

Configuration of left shoulder – happens when the price drops to a new minimum and then to a new high.

Head formation – when the price goes below the preceding low, then it jumps back to the earlier high.

Right shoulder – these experiences a sell-off, ending at a low price but higher than the earlier one with a drop to the neckline.

Neckline – the return to the earlier level forms the neckline.

This pattern is complete when the price goes above the neckline.

Cup & Handle

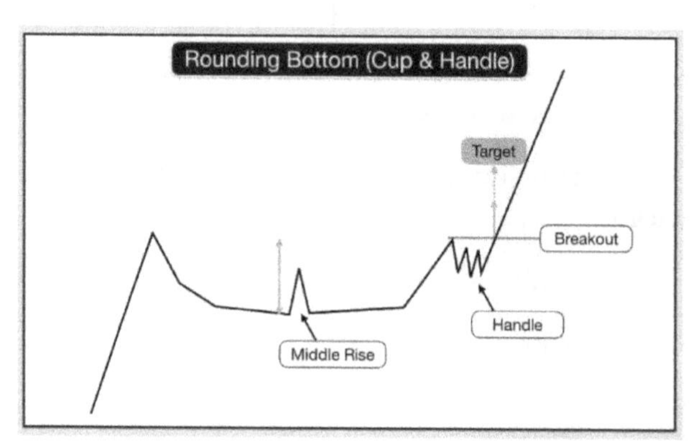

This looks like a cup on the chart. The pattern shows a bullish persistence pattern whereby the rising trend pauses then traded downward, after which it continues in an upward trend upon conclusion of the pattern. It can run from numerous months up to a year, though the common form remains constant.

This is usually preceded by an increasing move, which then stops and sells off. This is the start of the pattern, after which the security trades flat for a long time without a definite trend. The final part of this pattern, called the handle, is a downward move that resumes the earlier trend.

The Components

The cup and handle has several components that you need to know of.

First, you need to know that an upward trend occurs before the trend forms. The longer, the earlier trend is, the lesser the possibility for a huge breakout after completion of the pattern.

The construction of the cup is vital – it ought to be nicely rounded, more of a semi-circle. The cup and handle pattern signals that weaker investors are leaving the market, and buyers are staying for the commodity. If the shape is too sharp, it shows a weakening signal.

You need to focus on the handle as well because it signals the completion of the pattern. The handle represents a descending move by the commodity after the increasing move on the right part. During the move, a downward trend line can be drawn to form a breakout. A move above the trend line shows that a prior upward trend is soon starting.

As with most of the patterns, you need to consider volume so that you confirm the pattern.

Double Top & Double Bottom

These indicate a reversal. They indicate the desire for security to continue with an existing trend. When this happens, especially with numerous attempts to run higher, the inclination reverses and begins a fresh trend all over.

Double Top

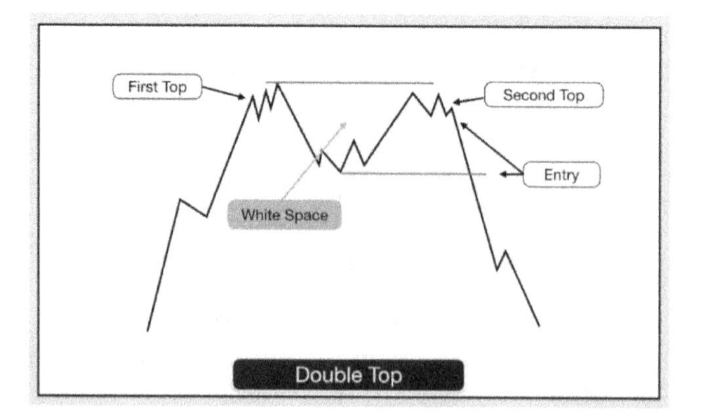

This occurs at the peak of an upward movement, and it shows that the earlier trend is failing, and buyers aren't interested in the trend. Upon the conclusion of the pattern, the movement shows reversal, and the commodity is supposed to go down.

The last phase of the pattern is the formation of new highs in the rising trend, after which the price starts to go towards the stage of resistance. The pattern completes when the price falls lower than the support level established in the preceding move, marking the beginning of a downward trend.

When using this pattern, it is vital that you wait until the price breaks below the critical level before you place a trade. Doing this before the signal forms can lead to catastrophic results because the pattern is only set up for a reversal.

The pattern illustrates a pull between sellers and buyers. The buyers are trying so hard to shove the commodity through but are getting opposition, which prevents the rising trend from proceeding. When this continues for some time, the buyers decide to give up, and sellers take hold of the commodity, pushing it down on a new downtrend.

Just like before, you need to consider volume before you make a decision as you need to look at the volume of the commodity when the price falls below a certain level.

Double Bottom

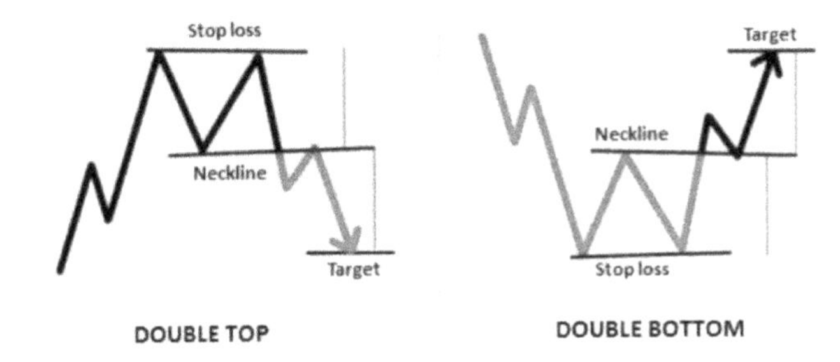

The double bottom shows a reversal to an uptrend. The pattern forms when the existing downtrend goes to a new minimum. The move finds all support, which then prevents the commodity from going lower. When the move finds the right support, the commodity will hit a new high, which in turn creates the resistance point for the commodity. The subsequent stage takes the commodity to a low.

However, the commodity finds some support then it changes the direction. You confirm the pattern when the price goes over the resistance level it encountered before the move.

For definite reversal, the commodity needs to get through the support to show reversal in a downward trend.

CHAPTER 17:

Technical Analysis

Technical analysis is increasingly becoming a favored viewpoint to trading, gratitude in part to the development in trading platforms as well as charting package. Nonetheless, a new trader comprehending technical analysis as well as how it can assist in foreseeing market trends can be challenging and daunting.

Technical analysis basically involves studying the manner in which prices move within a market, in such a way that traders use patterns from historic charts and indicators to foresee the impending market trends. It is a visual reflection of the present and past performance of a given market and it enables traders to make use of this information in the fashion of indicators, patterns, as well as price action, inform and guide forthcoming trends before getting into a trade.

Here, we focus on the basics of technical analysis and consequently how it can be put into use in trading.

Comprehending Technical Analysis

The technical analysis mainly involves interpreting patterns in charts. Traders use historical data that solely depends on volume and price and consequently use the information they acquire to spot lucrative opportunities to trade based on familiar or habitual patterns in the market. Charts are exposed to a variety of indicators to establish points of entry and exit to enable traders to maximize the potential of a trade at a ratio of good risk to rewards.

In as much as the people who support fundamental analysis have a belief that economic factor mainly contributes to market movements, technical analysis traders insist that olden trends are helpful in foreseeing price movements in the future. In as much as these styles of trade vary, comprehending the disparity between technical and fundamental analysis as well as how to collaborate them can be very advantageous in the long run.

How Technical Analysis Can Help Traders

Numerous trades have approved technical analysis as an instrument for managing risks, which can be a major setback. As soon as a trader comprehends the principles and concepts of technical analysis, he/she can use it in virtually any market, thus making it an adjustable analytical instrument. As fundamental analysis seeks to identify a market's intrinsic value, the technical analysis seeks to spot trends that can suitably be caused by basic fundamentals.

Technical analysis has the following benefits:

•It can be used as an independent method.

•It is applicable to any market using any timespan.

•Technical analysis enables traders to spot patterns in the market.

Using Charts in Technical Analysis

Technical analysis is centered on charts. This is simply because the only way to gauge a market's past and current performance is by analysis the price; this is where you kick off the process of analyzing the ability of a trade. It is possible to represent price action on a chart because it is the most censorable indicator of the impacts of the price.

Charts are useful in finding the general trend, regardless of whether there is a downward or upward trend over a short or long term or to discover rage bound circumstances. The most known types of technical analysis charts include candlestick charts, line charts, and bar charts.

Whenever you use a bar or candlestick chart, every period will feed the technical analyst with information on the high and low of the period, the price where it started and also the close. Candlestick analysis is preferable the patterns as well as how they are interconnected can help in predicting the direction of the price in the future.

As soon as a trader comprehends the fundamentals of charting, they can use indicators to help in predicting the trend.

Technical Analysis Indicators

Technical traders use indicators whenever they are looking for windows of opportunity in the market. In as much as there are very many indicators, price, and volume-based indicators. These are useful in finding out the levels of resistance and support are, how they are breached or maintained as well as determining how long a trend is.

A trader has the ability to see the price as well as any other indicator by doing an analysis of numerous time frames ranging from a second to a month. This, in turn, gives the trader a different view of the price action.

The most known indicators in regard to technical analysis are:

•The corresponding strength indexes

•Moving averages

•Moving average divergence as well convergence

The last two indicators in the list above are usually used to spot market trends whereas the corresponding strength index is basically employed in finding out probable points of exit and entry. Indicators help traders in conducting an analysis of the market, finding entry points and doing validation of how trades have been set up.

Limitations of Technical Analysis

The major setback to the authenticity of technical analysis is the economic aspect of the efficient market hypothesis (EMH). EMH asserts that market prices are a reflection of all past and current information; therefore, there is no way to exploit mispricing or patterns to get more profits. Fundamental analysts and economists who have a belief in efficient markets have no belief that any sort of information that can be acted on is contained in volume data and historical price, and in addition, that history does not repeat itself, instead, prices shift like an unplanned walk.

Technical analysis is also under criticism because it is applicable in some cases only because it contains a self- actualization prophecy. For instance, most traders will position their order to stop loss under the two-hundred-day motion average of a given company. Considering that a variety of traders have done that and it happens that the stock gets to this price, then the number of sell orders will be enormous and it will shove the stock downwards, approving the movement that traders were anticipating.

Thereafter, other traders will notice the reduction in price and also opt to put their positions up for sale, consequently improving the robustness of the trend. This selling pressure that is generally short-term can be regarded as self- fulfilling, however, it will have very minimal direction on where the price of assets will be a couple of weeks or months to come. To sum it up, if people employ similar signals, it could result in movements foreseen by the signal, but eventually, this main group of traders becomes incapable of steering price.

The Main Features of Technical Analysis

Technical analysis of options trading always shows how a successful options trading has become and what normally leads to its success. It lists the number of successful trades on the option and what contributed to the success of these traders. Definitely, there are guides and trading techniques that a trader should always consider for them to achieve success. The analysis of options trade has always shown different features and the main feature we are going to discuss below.

First and foremost, we are going to talk about discipline. This is the key to any successful trade or even a project. As a trader, you need to be highly disciplined about what you are doing. It is however not so easy being disciplined up to a certain point in options trading but still for you to be successful, you must always exercise discipline in your field. You need to be highly committed to what you are doing for you to achieve the best that you need. You don't necessarily have to concentrate on one thing the whole day but the commitment that you show is very important.

You also need to learn from the losses that you encountered in the past. It is normal for all traders to record a loss at some point during the trading session. This does not mean that trading should stop. You learn from the loss, pick up and move on. No shortcut. You should be in a position to accept the losses and carry on with trade because of everyone's losses and if everyone was to panic and quit there would be no trading that would be proceeding until success is recorded. If you trade, lose and give up, there is no progress.

You should also be ready to learn. You are new in the market and you don't have a full idea about what you are doing. You just allow yourself to take lessons from the experts and be ready to apply the same tactics for you to carry on successfully. Watch what others do. How they carry out trade and respond to different matters is very important. You will realize you are gaining more and being well prepared to go for what you want. Technical analysis shows that if you are not well experienced in the field of options trading, you are only subjected to making mire errors than you work to succeed.

Be the decision-maker in your trading. Don't wait for others to decide for you what to do. Being your own decision maker allows you to carry out your trade successfully without putting blames on anyone. Learning for yourself is very important as much as you feel you need to take lessons from what is happening where you are. Nothing should influence you and dictate the decisions that you make. Take lessons but be independent in selecting what is best for you. This is the only way you can keep moving forward. Following what someone else is doing only leads you to a destination that was never meant for you.

A trading plan is another important feature of technical analysis of options trading. You should always have a trading plan of your own. Plan yourself well and decide what is best for you. You know exactly what you can handle and what you cannot handle and this means if you let someone plan for you, you risk straining to do something that is not within your level capacity. This only makes trading boring for you and that's why most traders quit and divert their attention to something else or blame someone for making them fail.

Watch how you react. Don't just react because you are supposed to react. The careless reaction is the number one cause of failure in any world of trading. You may face losses in your trade or some difficulties that come unplanned. How you react to them is what is more important. How do you handle losses? How do you respond to your client when something is not right? Being proactive helps you build good customer relationship with your clients and also help you to remain positive to keep moving on despite the challenges. Understand the market and making decisions based on your trading plans. Letting emotions take over you and control how you react will only interfere with how you participate in the market.

Develop a broad scope of learning. Don't just stick to one idea and think you are good to go. Everything needs a wide view so that you know how to attack everything from a different angle. When you have more ideas on what you are doing, you will find it easy switching to another plan when one fails. Being in a position to have several options helps you as a trader to be at room temperature with all types of trades. Open up your mind to convince different ideas in different fields.

CHAPTER 18:

Fundamental Analysis

Fundamental analysis is a type of market analysis that tries to derive the underlying value of a financial instrument or asset by studying and assessing economic data. In this approach, the traders do not need to look at the charts to determine the future of the market. Rather, they seek all the relevant data about the instruments they are trading and then use the information to make their trades. Some of the economic data that traders look at closely include inflation, employment, GDP, exports, imports, interest rates, central banks' activities, and so on.

- The objective of fundamentalists is to use economic reports as indicators to predict the overall conditions of the market. Out of this analysis, they hope to spot trading opportunities that promise high returns and minimum risk. In a nutshell, fundamentalist traders interpret present economic data and then use the information to decide whether an instrument is likely to gain or lose value in the future. For instance, they know that if a report comes out about Facebook launching a new product and the public being highly anticipative of it, the value of the Facebook share (stock) is likely to appreciate in the future. As such, they will buy stocks in anticipation of the growth in value.

Here are some of the economic data that fundamentalists focus on.

- The economy

The status of an economy directly affects the value of a country's currency, imports, exports, and other factors. If a country's economy is doing well, then its currency will grow stronger. Its exports will cost more, and the imports will be cheaper. For instance, when the price of oil increases, the value of all the currencies that produce and export the commodity will grow. Similarly, if the growth of an economy is reported to have dropped, the value of its currency and export commodities will decrease.

- Political stability

Political stability leads to increased confidence in the commodities or currencies of independent countries. On the other hand, political instability erodes investor confidence, leading to less investment and deterioration of economic performance. A good example was in 2018 when Facebook was entangled in the Cambridge Analytica scandal, where it was accused of interfering with the electoral process in Kenya, an East African country. On the first day of the report, Facebook shares lost close to $18 billion. By the time the scandal had stabilized, the company had lost over $134 billion. In this case, any trader that had sold the stock made a lot of money.

- Government policies

Government policies, such as interest rates, have significant effects on the general performance of currencies and commodities. When interest rates are increased, this curbs inflation and slows economic growth. Similarly, reducing interest rates stimulates economies by promoting investment. Other aspects, like fiscal policies, also affect the movement of the market. For example, high taxation slows economic performance and discourages business.

- Observing market makers

There are traders who wait for the big players in the market to make their moves; then they will jump in and flow with the tide. They base their decisions on the assumption that since the big players have the ability to move the markets. If they can spot the big moves as they start, then they can reap big profits. Such traders will, therefore, place their focus on hedge funds, governments, central banks, and other huge financial institutions.

- Reports and news events

Do you remember 9/11? If so, then this point will be easy to understand. When the tragic news went live, the dollar plunged immediately. In about 5 days, the US economy had lost over $1.4 billion. In this case, anyone who had bought the EURUSD would have made a lot of money. Similarly, any trader who had sold the USDJPY would have made handsome profits as well.

Another event is when, in 2019, a Boeing 737 MAX crashed in Ethiopia a few months after a similar plane had crashed in Indonesia. Both flights killed all the passengers and crew. Controversy emerged that the plane model was unsafe. In just a few days, the shares of Boeing sunk by 12%, which is close to $27 billion from the market. A trader who had analyzed this event and sold the Boeing stocks would have made a lot of money from the decline in price.

Advantages of Fundamental Analysis

- First, since fundamentalists seek to predict the movement of the markets before, they happen, they can easily explain why a movement occurred. This fact alone is enough to increase one's predictive ability and profits.

- Second, studying economic data can help a trader to know the long-term position of price. In short, they can place trades and know where to anticipate the market to reach in the future. This improves their confidence when they have active trades.

- Third, due to the amount of data that is collected and analyzed, a trader gains a better understanding of the markets. As such, they can predict the markets more accurately and reduce guesswork.

Disadvantages of Fundamental Analysis

- The biggest downside of fundamental analysis is that it lacks definite timing. A trader might know that the price of a stock will decline in the future, but they have no specific time when the fall will start. This is very risky when trading.

- Second, due to the lack of proper timing, this approach is not suitable for short-term trading, such as day trading or scalping. However, there are some types of fundamentals that can be used for day trading.

- The third disadvantage is that collecting too much economic data can lead to information overload. When this happens, the trader is unable to process the information. In the long run, they might make wrong decisions that can lead to losses.

- The final disadvantage is that interpreting economic information might vary. One trader might believe that a market will ascend while another interprets the same data in the opposite direction. A wrong interpretation can lead to inaccurate analysis and losses.

CHAPTER 19:

The Most Common Mistakes to Avoid

As a beginner, there are a lot of things that you need to learn to do well with swing trading. Learning all the strategies, learning how to read the charts and making smart decisions when it comes to picking out stocks to work with can be a challenge. As you are getting used to the whole process, it can take some time and effort, and you are likely to make some mistakes along the way.

These mistakes are pretty normal when you are a beginner, but no beginner wants to deal with them. They want to be able to make as much money as possible, without losing a lot of money as they start to learn how things work. Let the emotions get in the way

One mistake that almost all beginners will make is that they let their emotions get in the way of their decision making. They see that they are about to lose out on a trade or they see that the profits will keep reaching a higher value, and they want to stay in the market longer, despite what all their research and their strategy told them before. This will end up disastrous and is one of the leading reasons that beginners lose so much money and end up having to stop at day trading.

You need to learn how to keep the emotions out of the game. If you are a highly emotional person, swing trading is not going to be the best option for you to try out because things can change in an instant. The good news is that there are a few techniques that you can use to help keep the emotions out of the game so you can reduce your risk and increase your chances of profit.

First, make sure that you use stop points and that you stick with them. These stop points will ensure that you enter and exit the trade at the right times to either limit your losses or to help limit the risk that you have while gaining a profit. They aren't always full proof, but if you stick with them, you are less likely to have issues later on. Picking a good strategy, asking for advice, and really doing your research before you begin are all good ways to ensure you can keep the emotions out of your trading.

Forget to use stop points

The stop points will be so important when you start out as a swing trader. These points will tell you when to get out of the market, whether the market is going up or down and can reduce your risk. You need to have a stop loss point, which is the point you will get out of the market if you lose so much money, and you need a stop profit point, which is where you will get out of the market once you earn a certain profit.

Both of these are important to ensure you cut down on your risk and that you make as much money as possible in the process. For the stop loss point, you are figuring out how much money you are comfortable with losing in the market. Once the market goes down to this point, you need to get out. It is highly likely that the market will keep going down and if you don't get out at your stop loss point, you will potentially lose a lot of money in the process. This takes the emotions out of the game. You simply see that the stop point was reached and cut your losses until the next trade.

You also need to have a stop point for the profits that you want to earn. This may seem silly because you want to earn as much profit as you possibly can with each trade. But emotions can come into play here again too. Without the stop point, you may end up staying in the market too long, and make some costly mistakes. The market can turn around just as quickly as it went up, and if you are still in the market, you may lose all your earnings instead of gaining anything.

For this stop point, what you can realistically make on the trade. Where do you think the market for your stock will go over the next few days based on the trend that you are setting? Put the stop point there and then as soon as the market reaches that point, you will take your earnings and withdraw from the market.

Putting in more money than you can afford to lose

With any investment that you work with, you need to be careful about the losses that you are dealing with. If you take on too much risk, you will end up losing all your money and never getting a chance to give it another try. Coming up with a good risk to reward ratio will help to limit your losses, but you also must make sure that you never put in more than you are willing to lose.

A good place to start is to put some savings behind for your swing trades. Never use money that you would need for rent, food, and other necessities. The second you do this, you bring the emotions into the game, and you are more likely to lose it all. Starting a savings account right now with the money you can use for swing trading allows you to have a little cushion without having to eat up all the money you need for other things.

When you are using the extra money, rather than money that you really need elsewhere, you are ensuring that you will spend it wisely. You won't stay in a trade too long in the hopes of recovering that money. No one wants to lose money along the way when they are trading, but it is much easier to cut your losses when it was just a little saving rather than if that money was your rent payment for the month.

Not understanding your strategy

If you do not understand the strategy that you are using, it can be impossible for you to get results when you get started with swing trading. Your strategy will outline exactly how you will behave in each trade situation. It will tell you how to look at the charts, how to pick out the stocks, when to enter the market, and when to exit the market. Each strategy has the potential to be successful, but you need to understand the strategy and use it properly.

When you get started in swing trading, it is always best to start with a simple strategy. Yes, there are some more complex ones that may sound fun, but since you are already learning about the market and how it works, why add in more complications with a hard strategy. There are a lot of great strategies that are simple, and some even designed for the beginner, that will make you just as much money as the more complex strategies, without all the work.

Picking a strategy is really important when it comes to doing well in swing trading. Before you pick out one, make sure to read through them all and fully understand what you will need to do to make it successful. You want one that is effective and easy to follow, as well as one that you will not want to switch out of in the middle of the trade. There is nothing wrong with trying out different strategies to see which one you like the best in between your trades, but if you switch strategies while in the same trade, you are setting yourself up for failure.

Not having the right tools

As a trader, you need to have some of your own tools in place if you would like to get started with swing trading. This can be a very difficult method when it comes to investing, and without the right tools, you will miss out on some important information that can help you see trends and make smart decisions along the way.

The first place to go for some tools is to talk to your broker. Often the broker will have a variety of unique tools that they can give to you as part of their fees. If you don't know how to use some of these tools, make sure to ask questions and learn how to make it all work or you will miss out.

You can also bring in some of your own tools to the game as well. Find charts about the market, look online, and ask questions. Remember, the best way to notice a trend is when the same information starts to show up on more than one chart or tool so always strive to have as many of these tools available as possible.

Following others rather than learning your own way

When you first get started, it can be tempting to find a mentor or a group and then just follow along exactly with what they do each time. This is really tempting if you see that they are making a lot of money and you want to join and make that money as well. But in the long run, no one knows the trading style that you like, and there are times when even an advanced mentor will get things wrong.

Instead of following along blindly with what someone else tells you, it is better to learn your own way. There is nothing wrong with talking to a mentor and others who have been in the market for some time, but you need to learn your own methods, your own strategies, and how you want to behave in the market. This will help you to stay on track with your trades and will ensure that you don't get misled by others who may not have your best interests at heart.

Not cutting your losses

Even the best swing traders will make mistakes at times. They will misread the market, they will try out a new strategy that doesn't work for them, or the market just doesn't behave in the manner that they had hoped. And when this happens, the trader will lose out on their money. As a beginner, it is more likely that you will earn a loss at some point. The important thing is to learn how to cut your losses, rather than staying too long in the market.

Some beginners will see that they are losing money on one of their trades and so they will try to regain that money. Even with the market going down, and no signs of reversal, they will stay in the market and hope that things will reverse. This is dangerous because it results in you staying in the market way too long and you will lose way too much money in the process.

CHAPTER 20:

Financial Freedom

What is Financial Freedom?

While there are many things that you may dream to accomplish in your life, you will find that almost everyone is interested in gaining financial freedom. Being free financially means that you are able to maintain the lifestyle that you want without a regular paycheck. It is like having a retirement where you are able to live comfortably and maybe go out and have some fun without having to worry about stretching yourself too thin.

There are actually a lot of stages that come with gaining financial freedom. It is not really a single point in time, but rather four stages that will lead you to this. The four stages of financial freedom that you should follow include:

No freedom

Everyone is going to start out the journey at the same place. During this stage, you will rely on your monthly paycheck. You will see that a job as well as the reliable income stream that it provides is required so that you are able to pay the bills. If something happened to your income and you no longer received that paycheck, your savings would be depleted quickly, and you may end up defaulting on our monthly expenses. This is not the best place to be financially, but it is the starting point and you will be able to work from here.

Temporary freedom

In this second stage, you will still need your income on a regular basis, but you are able to spend less than what you earn. You can then turn the extra over into a pool of savings. You want to get into this stage so that you can build up a good savings, otherwise, you will end up with working forever because your lifestyle will depend on all the money that you earn. As you start to save some of your income, even if that amount is small in the beginning, you may want to consider investing your savings into a diversified investment that will provide you with a stream of income when it grows. Or, you have the possibility of starting a business on the side so that you can create a second source of income.

You will find that your freedom is going to grow along with your savings. Over time, you will have saved enough money so that you are comfortable. You may decide to take some time to travel for a year, go back to school, start your own business, switch jobs or do other things that would be hard if you worked a full-time job. These are big changes in your life, but these are not permanent changes. The freedom that comes with this stage is going to be temporary. Your income will usually exceed your expenses with this one and you will not be able to remain free for too long.

Permanent freedom

When you get to the third stage, the non-employment income that you make will be higher than what your total expenses are. You would be able to quit working your regular job and still have enough from your business or your investment that you are still able to pay all your bills. You should have a reliable income that keeps coming in so that you are able to enjoy life and gain a permanent freedom, not one that will be gone quickly.

Yes, if you have a side business, you are still going to put in some labor to make it work. You will still be trading your time for money. But it is much different compared to what you would do working for someone else. The side job that you take over should represent your passion and be something that you really enjoy doing. This means that while you may be working at a side job, you will enjoy it and you will feel like you are free.

Having fulfillment is the entire point of financial freedom. Just because you have freedom in this matter does not mean that you have to retire completely, unless you choose to. It's all about having independence to choose how your daily routine is going to go and it will allow you to design a better life while being able to spend your energy, money, and time in a way that is more meaningful. This could include investing, starting a side business, or doing something else that you enjoy that brings in money.

Luxurious freedom

This is a stage that is not going to be achieved by very many people. This is where you are able to have enough of a passive income that you are able to spend it freely. Your income is going to exceed the expenses that you have by a large margin so that you are able to live the lifestyle that you would like without having to put in much more work.

This one is going to take some time to accomplish. You will have to work hard at your passive income, and perhaps have a few different sources of this income, so that you can earn enough to make this work. You have a choice. You can choose to get your passive income to a point where you can cover the bills and then stop and hope you don't go backwards in the stages. Or you can work a bit longer and end up with the luxurious freedom that we just talked about.

Do you want financial freedom?

To start with this, there are three main questions that you should ask yourself. These include:

- Are you happy with the lifestyle that you have right now?
- Have you found a job that has a good work to life balance?
- Do you enjoy the job that you do and enjoy the purpose of your daily routine?

These are hard questions that you have to answer, but they will help you to determine what your thoughts are about gaining financial freedom. There are three categories that you can split these into. First, you have to check whether your work is meaningful. There are some individuals who like their jobs and who see no reason why they should stop working. This is just fine because you are able to work while also being financially free.

The second category is that work is okay for you. You do not particularly enjoy the job, but it is something that you do because it is something that you don't completely despise, which will pay the bills. You will have some good days and bad days, but you are pretty neutral about the job.

If you are in this second situation, your preferred level of freedom financially should be inversely related to the amount of disdain that you have for your work. It is up to you to work harder to increase the amount of savings that you have so that you can have more control and even change careers if you would like.

And finally, you could fall into the third group where you find work to be boring and somewhat terrible. For this group, financial freedom should be really high on your priority list. If you really hate the job you are in, it should be easy to make sacrifices to find a way to escape. This would include working a second job, moving somewhere that has a lower cost of living, and cutting out the unnecessary expenses. You should spend this time saving all the money that you can so that you are able to change jobs.

By focusing on this freedom, the perspective that you have is likely to change. You will go from sludging through many more years at a job you don't like to design the life that you would like to have. If you put your mind to it, you will be able to devote all your energy, time, and money to that goal, and you are more likely to see success.

During this point, time, rather than money, is the most valuable asset that you have. If your time at that job is making you miserable, it is time to save money so that you can quit your job.

CHAPTER 21:

What Strategies Do Not Follow If You Are Expert Trader

An expert counselor can be portrayed as a definitive trading robot, which consistently screens markets and settles on an arrangement of trading choices for the trader. A genuine Forex EA will yield a great deal of money for the trader, while counterfeit EAs will plunge him/her into monetary ruin. There are numerous strategists who are building their unique EAs that perform uncommon trading stunts to yield results that may look great when they are really phony. There are different methods for spotting counterfeit expert consultants.

Instructions to spot Expert Advisor tricks:

• Check most extreme drawdown detailed in the back-test report of the mechanized trading framework;

• Check if the part measures are expanding. There is a probability the strategists are utilizing martingale trading style to recuperate from misfortunes.

• Check if the Forex robot utilizes the matrix style of trading, whereby there is a great deal of purchasing and selling simultaneously. Such a strategy uncovered the record into a lot of risks and ought to be dodged.

• Check if Forex EA closes the exchanges merely seconds. Such trading bots are utilizing scalping strategies and they, for the most part, don't deal with some other trading account since they are delicate to spread changes;

• Check if EA utilizes stop misfortune. Expert guides that don't utilize stop misfortune can't shield traders from misfortunes and are in this manner not worth looking at.

• Check if exchanges are held open for quite a while. EAs that hold strategies for quite a while or those that nearby exchange seconds (scalping strategies) regularly produce incredible value bends, yet have no genuine pertinence in genuine trading.

Which sorts of Expert Advisors you ought to keep away from

In the first place, we should discuss the sorts of Expert Advisors and trading strategies that you ought to stay away from. Expert Advisors are significant with regards to robotized trading. Numerous individuals have been directed to budgetary ruin just on the grounds that an EA came up short on a little piece of detail. Everything about right now significant and ought to be taken into key thought.

Avoid strategies with very high drawdown.

Think about this backtests:

The outline speaks to a strategy report

For a great many people, this is a phenomenal trading strategy. Be that as it may, regardless of having an upward value bend and a 99% displaying quality (a great many people judge strategies by these two coincidentally), the outcomes are a long way from great. This is shown by the drawdown, which is at around 31% – a high add up to lose. Much more terrible, the relative drawdown is at 93%. In live trading, this strategy would not make due, as demonstrated by the relative drawdown.

Numerous traders are tricked by backtests basically on the grounds that they don't have the foggiest idea where or what numbers to take a gander at.

The value bend may trick apprentice traders or expert traders who have recently set out on an excursion to extreme trading utilizing expert counsels; however, for an expert, this backtests has not been progressed admirably.

Let us take a gander at the parcel sizes to appropriately clarify the imperfect idea of this backtests.

Avoid strategies with unthinkably large parcel sizes.

The exchanges start with 0.44 part sizes, and afterward, they keep on 8 parcels. When the strategy gets its first effective exchange, the part measures move again to an extremely modest number and afterward moves to parcel size 8. At that point, they hop to estimate 43. It is stunning that the parts continue expanding they go to 200, to 900, and afterward, they settle in thousands. No normal agent would permit his/her customers to exchange with 1000 parcel sizes.

For it to be even conceivable, the trading record ought to be incredibly large for it to have the option to execute such trading positions. More or less, these backtests glances great in its value bend, yet in all actuality, it is finished rubbish.

In this way, additional safety measures ought to be taken when managing strategies that twofold their parcel sizes. The motivation behind why swindlers utilize enormous parcel sizes is to endure the strategy tests and to make their strategies look great on the screen.

The graph speaks to the strategy with huge parcel sizes.

Avoid strategies that long open exchanges for madly extensive stretches.

Moreover, strategies that hold exchanges for significant stretches of time are bad. There are traders anyway who contend that they exchange for the since quite a while ago run, which is excellent.
Long haul exchanges stop to bode well when they keep going for quite a long while. They should keep going for half a month or months all things considered before they are shut.
From the model underneath, one trading strategy goes on for 1287 days, which is around three and a half years. Sensibly, who might ever hold a solitary exchange for over three years?
Precisely, no rational individual would show restraint enough to hold an exchange for a long time when there are such a large number of exchanges that could be made over a similar period.
It could be accepted that the proprietor of the strategy wouldn't like to lose any exchanges and needs to have the same number of wins as he/she can have, regardless of whether they are ludicrous.
There are other extraordinary exchanges that last between 300 to 900 days.

Before receiving such a strategy, you ought to ask yourself: why clutch a strategy that guarantees yearly returns when you can have the same number of exchanges as you need in the equivalent time period?
The outlines a strategy that holds exchanges for a significant stretch of time.
To additionally feature the issue of long haul exchanges let us take a gander at a trading report beneath:
The outlines a value bend with numerous drawdowns.
At the point when you appropriately take a gander at the value bend, you see that there are numerous drawdowns (pointed by the red bolts). The drawdowns speak to exchange places that have been held for an extensive stretch and afterward wound up in misfortunes. As much as the strategy picks up benefits, the quantity of drawdowns is high.
Besides, the reputation of the record isn't checked. This could imply that the strategy is created. Truly, OK, sit tight for that long and hold your losing position when you realize that they may wind up in misfortunes?
Avoid scalping strategies since they are touchy to spread changes.

Shouldn't something be said about scalping strategies? Is it accurate to say that they aren't among the most mainstream expert counsels?

The facts demonstrate that they are famous as prove by the number of individuals who use them to scout for well-known markets. The issue with scalping strategies is that the greater part of them doesn't work.

You might be tricked by the attractive exchange results. However, like different strategies, they can be effortlessly created to deliver results that may tempt traders.

Moreover, scalping strategies are delicate to value changes. Along these lines, they, for the most part, don't chip away at most merchants.

Investigate the length of the exchanges the model given underneath:

The length of most exchanges is zero seconds. The Pips are running in the hundreds in only zero seconds, and the average holding time is somewhere in the range of zero and three seconds. This is totally crazy. It is dubious that this strategy works in any genuine trading other than the demo account that it began from.

Avoid strategies with a massively enormous stop misfortune

Strategies with immense stop misfortune should likewise be maintained a strategic distance from except if you ensure your MetaTrader 4 record (MT4) with Equity Sentry Expert Advisor. Stop misfortune is fundamentally the capacity of a trading strategy to totally end trading positions when they begin making misfortunes. Along these lines, envision a strategy that doesn't utilize stop misfortune and the money related ruin that anticipates a trader that utilizations such a strategy.

A few people may contend that they don't utilize stop misfortune since they utilize shrouded stops. In the event that that is the situation, at that point, for what reason don't they utilize hard stops too?

Hard stops may be set to be two or multiple times greater than concealed stop misfortune, yet for a situation Internet association issue, you would not lose in excess of a hard stop misfortune. Along these lines, you have a higher possibility of controlling losing exchanges while utilizing shrouded stops and hand stops simultaneously.

For what reason would anybody consider utilizing strategies with no stop misfortune on the off chance that they posture such a substantial hazard to his/her benefits? There ought to be some degree of assurance at any rate against misfortunes, regardless of whether it is only half of it.

So if an EA doesn't offer hard stop arrangements like an assurance of the record's value, debilitating Autotrading, and shutting the exchanges, at that point, it ought to be disposed of.

Avoid framework trading Expert Advisors.

In conclusion, there are those strategies that utilization matrix trading style – this style includes making loads of purchasing and selling exchanges simultaneously with the point of making immense benefits. Making various purchase stops and sell stops simultaneously opens the record to high hazard and a bit nearer to catastrophe.

Protecting your MT4 account with the Equity Sentry EA

Value Sentry EA (or ESEA for short) is an extra for the MT4 account. It secures trading accounts by observing record value/parity and open exchanges.

Value Sentry EA will initiate 'security trigger' if:

• Equity/balance reaches or drops to a specific level;

• Open exchanges (skimming misfortune/benefit) arrive at a specific level;

• Closed exchanges + open exchanges arrive at a specific level. ESEA can likewise investigate the history of the exchanges and aggregate benefits up to the finish of the end exchanges;

To spare your record capital, EA will:

• Close all exchanges/orders (Hard Stop);

• Disable all EA to keep them from trading (Close and Stop);

• Close MT4 terminal totally;

• Send email cautions and MT4 Mobile notices. This permits the client to get moment alarms of what's going on in his/her record;

Value Sentry EA bundle

CHAPTER 22:

Why Day Traders Fail

With the numerous benefits that can be gained from day trading, it begs to question why most day traders fail. If the activity is as lucrative as it sounds, why do most of these traders fail? Understanding why traders fail gives you some insight on the common mistakes that traders fail which makes them lose money. Accordingly, you will be better placed to trade wisely by avoiding common pitfalls in such trading. Here is a look at some of the reasons why traders fail.

Relying On Random

Let's assume we have a new trader in the market called John. John has some knowledge about the market just because he always watches the news more so on stock markets. , However, John has never traded. Since he has some basic market knowledge, he feels that he can try out day trading. To this point, John has never sat down to write down some strategies which he could implement to trade on stocks. So, he opens up an account and purchases 400 shares without thinking.

Fortunately, to his advantage, the stocks rise during his lunch hour period. After lunch, John decides to sell off his shares. His first sale earns him a $100 profit. His second attempt also earns him $100. Now, John has the feeling that indeed he is a good trader. In just a day, he has managed to earn $200.

After a careful analysis of John's situation, an experienced trader would argue that John's day trading activity could easily be short-lived. In John's example, he faces the risk of losing money if at all he gains the perception that his strategies are working. Interestingly, he might be tempted to increase his shares because he knows that he will earn a profit. It is important to understand that John's strategies are untested. Therefore, there is no guarantee that his trading activity could earn him returns over the long-run.

The danger that John faces here is that he believes in his formulated and untested strategies. Consequently, he might overlook recommended trading techniques that would have helped him avoid common mistakes. In the end, when he loses money, he will be disappointed arguing that day trading is not lucrative. This is the trap that most newbies enter into. Their first luck in online trading blinds them from realizing the need for constant learning in this activity.

Abandoning Strategy

Assuming that John learned his mistakes and corrected them in his future trades. Now, he relies on a strategy that helps him find success in day trading for about a year or two. At this point, John feels that he has found the right strategy that works for him. However, there is another problem that ensues. John realizes that his plan has led him to losses for more than six times now. He is in a huge dilemma wondering what to do since he cannot continue making losses.

So, what does John do; he decides to adopt another strategy. Regardless of the success that he enjoyed using his plan, John now feels that it is time to switch to another strategy. Ideally, this is a new and untested strategy that he will be adopting. One thing that you should realize here is that John is going for a strategy that is not tested. He is abandoning a strategy that has worked for about two years now. The risk here is that John could find himself where he started. He could incur losses because of his abandoning strategy.

Here, you should learn that randomness can lead to profits and that it can also drive a trader to incur losses. To ensure that such randomness is avoided, it is recommended for a trader to have a solid plan that they stick to. This is a plan that will define how they trade. A good plan ought to lay their entry and exit strategies. Also, the plan should stipulate the money management technique which will help a trader use their money wisely.

Lack of Knowledge

A major reason why most traders fail is their lack of market knowledge. By failing to educate themselves about stock markets, they find themselves in a ditch. You cannot count yourself as a trader just because you buy and sell shares. Certainly not! You have to learn how to analyze the securities which you will be buying. Your broker might not give you all the information that you need to become a good trader. So, don't assume that reading magazines and newspapers will get you the market info that you need.

A prudent trader knows the significance of working with a profitable trading plan. They understand why it is imperative for them to analyze stocks effectively to determine whether they are buying profitable stocks or not. More importantly, a wise trader should know of ideal strategies that they will employ to manage their finances shrewdly. Don't believe day trading myths circulating over the internet. Do your homework by researching and educating yourself about stock markets.

Unfitting Mindset

We are human beings with emotions. However, being overly emotional can be dangerous in an uncertain trading environment. To become a successful trader, you need to work on your emotions. Dealing with your emotions will have a huge impact on whether you close your day with losses or profits. Hence, it is very important that you keep your emotions in check.

Rigidity to Market Changes

One thing that you can be sure of is that trading markets will always change. There is no guarantee that a particular market will rise steadily throughout the buying and selling period. If this were the case, then everybody would have been traders. The best traders will always adjust to market changes. They will know when to buy and when to sell. Before jumping to purchase a particular stock, it is advisable to conduct scenario analysis. Afterward, you should devise strategic moves which will ensure that you make profits while lowering the chances of incurring losses.

Learning from Mistakes

You often hear people say that failing is part of succeeding. Well, this is true. Unfortunately, it stands as one of the main reasons why day traders fail. Learning by making mistakes here and there will cost a day trader a lot of money. Engaging in trial and error is what discourages most traders from every trying to put their money in stocks. Some even end up arguing that day trading is a form of gambling. To circumvent this problem, one should learn from other experienced traders. This way, you will reduce the chances of making losses. Equally, you will learn the tricks which can be utilized to take advantage of market volatility. Therefore, do not choose to learn how to trade through trial and error. You will only lose a lot of money beyond your expectations.

Unrealistic Expectations

Take a breather! Indeed, day trading is a profitable activity that can earn you a living. Nonetheless, this should not blind you from realizing that losses can also be made. You cannot get rich overnight with day trading. However, it is a slow and gradual process that will see your money multiply. Traders fail because they try to force returns to cover for the huge losses that they have made. Having the right plan and sticking to it will help you in toning down your expectations. Deep inside, you should have it in mind that you are trading for a living. Therefore, patience is important.

Poor Money Management

The effort that you put in finding a working strategy is the same effort that you should put in managing your finances. A trader should stick to a plan that defines the amount of money that they will risk on a regular basis. The money risked should give the trader the satisfaction that it is worth the rewards they anticipate. Having enough funds set aside for the trading activity should not give one the impression that they need to splash their money on stocks. As a matter of fact, the more you have as capital, the more you should preserve.

The bottom line is that traders can deal with their possibilities of failing by sticking to a plan. Sticking to a trading plan will mean that you are discipline enough to know the exact amount of money you will risk. It also implies that you will employ a buying and selling strategy that works for you. Most importantly, you will also give yourself time to learn what there is to learn about day trading.

CHAPTER 23:

How to Keep a Day Trading Journal and Why It's Important

As was already stated before we started our discussion on specific advanced day trading strategies, it might be necessary for you to go back and reevaluate the key points of each one before you actually start to use it in a real-time setting. Now that you have a basic understanding of two advanced strategies that many day traders use on a regular basis, we are going to turn attention away from the technicalities of strategies and towards the idea of recordkeeping. One of the things that many experienced day traders tout is the importance of keeping some sort of trade journal. Let's take a look at what you should be including in your trade journal, and then we will focus on why it's important to create one and upkeep it.

What Should You Be Including in Your Trade Journal?

1. Did Your Trade Work as You Expected It To?

One of first aspects that you need to consider as you look to write entries into your trade journal is whether or not the trade worked out in the same way that you originally thought it would. Often times when trading on the stock market, things have a tendency to not go as planned. If you find that this is the case when you're making deals for yourself, then you need to address the areas that strayed from what you had in your head before the trading began. While you're documenting this information, it's important to keep in mind that often times the strategy behind your trade can differ from what actually happens when there's money as stake. Again, this could be for a variety of reasons, including the fact that emotions could be influencing the trades that you're making. Be open to being honest with yourself about whether or not a trade went right or wrong. This will help you to see not only your areas of weakness but also your areas of strength and this will help you in your overall long-term stock strategies

2. What are Your Stop Limit and Why Did You Set It There?

Once you've documented whether or not your trade strategy work out as you intended it to, the next concept that you should be documenting is your stop limit. Your stop limit is the amount of money that you're willing to lose in a trade. Often times, even seasoned investors in the heat of the moment will stray from their stop limit because they are eager to make money where it doesn't exist. Documenting what your stop limit is, the reason why you set it there, and whether or not you stuck to your stop limit can help you to out how disciplined you are in sticking to your stock market strategy over the course of the day and whether or not you need to check yourself as the day progresses. Another reason why documenting this type of information is important is because it will most likely ultimately lead you to realizing that you need to have a firm grasp on how much money you're going to be spending throughout the day on each investment. Again, this aspect of the trading journey is mostly there to reinforce the idea of discipline into your trading strategy.

3. What Did You Choose to Trade and Why?

Lastly, one of the key elements that is included into any successful and serious investor's trade journal is documentation of which stocks they traded throughout the day and why. So many investors back up their investment strategies with reasons that include that the price of a particular stock has risen or fallen to the amount that is "just right", without backing it up with any substantial information. This isn't a good type of strategy, and writing down your reasoning for purchasing a particular stock will help you to see whether or not your stock choices are grounded in substantial logic. What's even worse is that sometimes traders will choose to purchase and sell stock out of merely a feeling of boredom. This too can end up having disastrous consequences. It's likely that a trader may not be aware of the fact that he or she is trading out of boredom or because the market is moving "just right" for them, and often times having a trade journal will force these people to be awakened to these types of facts. This is yet another reason why a trade journal can be beneficial.

Why is a Trade Journal Important?

Hopefully after reading this, you will be able to see why you need to start using one. One of the great things about the prevalence of computers is that you can easily create templates for yourself and quickly insert this information at the end of each trading day. Even if you are not that thrilled about documenting your experience as a day trader at the end of each trading day, you should still be willing to do it at least once a week. Now that you have hopefully come to understand the type of information the is generally found in a trade journal, let's take a look at some of the reasons why a trade journal can be beneficial to you.

Reason 1 Why You Need a Trade Journal

Some of the best day traders go over their trade journal in the morning before they start their trades for the rest of the day. By doing this, they are clearing and focusing their mind on the mistakes and good things that they did the day before. Another good tactic that the top traders typically implement is that they will write down key notes that they learned at the end of the day for that particular day. Over time, you will be able to simply look at the key information from each day, and this will eliminate the need to sift through entire pages of information when you've for what you're looking. Over time and day-by-day, you will be growing and educating yourself as an investor, and this activity only takes a few moments each morning.

Reason 2 Why You Need a Trade Journal: Improvement

The second reason why you really should be considering keeping a trading journal if you're not already is because it gives you the ability to improve upon areas of yourself and your trading patterns.

Reason 3 Why You Need a Trade Journal: Emotional Check

The last reason why you should consider keeping a day trading journal is so that you can keep your emotions in check. Emotional trading is often one of the aspects of trading that many investors forget about, but it can also be the silent killer that causes deals to go south. It might even be beneficial for you to document each day the emotions that were surrounding particular decisions, so that you can focus some of your energy on eliminating these feelings over time.

CHAPTER 24:

Red Flags to Consider with Day Trading

When it comes to day trading, there is a lot of potential that you are able to work with. You will be able to utilize this form of investing to make a lot of money, but only if you are willing to put in the time and the attention that is needed to get this done. This is not always as easy as it seems, and there are plenty of people who have gotten into day trading and were disappointed by the results that they got in the process. With this in mind, many of them are going to badmouth and talk down about the benefits of day trading and say that it is all a big scam to watch out for.

There are a lot of benefits to working with day trading, and you are certain to enjoy quite a few of them when you get started. However, there are times when day trading is not going to work out as well for you as you might like, and there are a few red flags that we are able to watch out for as well. Some of the red flags that we need to consider when it comes to starting out with day trading and figuring out if this is the right move for you includes:

Do you let your emotions get the best of you?

If you are a highly emotional kind of person, then day trading is not going to be the best option for you. You will stick with bad trades and go too long on some of the good trades, and it will never go well for you at all. Emotions are going to get in the way of sound judgments, and this is going to really harm you as you go. But when you are able to hide those emotions and limit them as much as possible, you are more likely to get some good profits when you work with day trading and investing.

Emotions can harm us, whether the market is doing well or not. If the market isn't doing well, it is common for the emotions to get the best of us, and we get fearful about losing money and other issues along the way. We may stay in a trade, hoping that it will all turn around, just to find out that this is one of the worst things to do, and we just end up losing a lot of money in the process.

On the other hand, it is possible that even when we are making money, we are going to get into a good deal of trouble along the way. We may see that we are doing well and then turn around and throw our plans out. These results in us losing money because we stay in the market for too long, and we lose money in the process because the trade goes back on us.

Having some of the stop loss points that we talked about earlier is one of the best ways to do this and ensure that we get into and out of the market at the right places each time. In addition, it is going to be a good idea to determine the amount of money that we are willing to spend on these trades ahead of time, and then sticking with the limits. Remember here, the more that you are able to keep the emotions out of the game, the easier it is going to be to keep things organized and ensure that we are not going to end up with a lot of trouble and losing a lot of money in the process.

Are you able to put aside the right amount of money to do this ahead of time?

Before you even start with day trading, you need to make sure that you have some money set aside in order to do the trading. Don't' dip into the account that you use for your paychecks and to pay your bills. Doing this is going to be one of the fastest ways to get yourself into trouble because before long, all of your money will be gone, and you won't have anything left to put towards food and bills at the end of the month.

A better option is to go through and a few months before you decide to day trade set up an account. Put the money that you can afford to lose in this account and only trade with that. When that money is gone, then you are done and can no longer do trades. This way, even if things do not go the way that you want, you will still have the money you need to pay bills and get food without harming your livelihood or increasing the risks as you go.

Do you struggle with gambling or addiction?

Another thing that we need to consider is going to do with you personally. If you are someone who gets swept up in gambling or have trouble with turning away when things are too good or going against your plan, then day trading is not going to work for your needs. Day trading is not a form of gambling, but some of the decisions that you have to make, and the fast-paced nature of the whole thing is going to be a struggle to deal with as well.

For those who already struggle with these kinds of addictions, day trading may prove to be too similar and can bring out the emotions. You could get stuck in wanting to ride things out, not wanting to lose any money and holding onto the position for too long or holding onto a winning position too long and losing it all. If these are conditions that you are dealing with, then it is time to walk away and not do this kind of trading.

Does the offer seem too good to be true?

Day trading on its own can sometimes seem like it is too good to be true. Make a purchase of stock at some point in the day and then at another point on the same day sell it, all while making a profit? It does sound like it is made up and a scam. But for the most part, there are no promises with this one, and it is possible that you can risk a lot of money in the process if you don't do the right amount of research and dedication to the work at hand.

With this in mind, though, there are going to be a lot of scammers who show up and try to just take your money. Some people don't perform the right amount of research or pay attention enough, and scammers love to sink their teeth right into them. They will go after these people with lots of promises of guaranteed money and how this is the best opportunity out there.

There are benefits with day trading, and we can make a lot of money, but there is no guarantee that you are going to earn money with this method. Everyone has the chance to fail, especially if they don't know much about the market or how this all works. If someone is giving you an offer that seems like it is too good to be true, or they promise that you will make money no matter what, then it is time to run the other way.

Can you devote the time and attention to this?

Day trading is going to be time-consuming. At the very least, you will need to spend half the day watching the stocks and seeing if you can break even. Some of the most successful day traders, though, are going to spend all day watching the market and entering and exiting trades as they can make profits along the way. If you are not ready to dedicate this much time and attention to the work, then day trading may not be for you.

The good news here is that there are a few different things that you can do along the way to make this easier. Maybe choose just one or two days a week where you will devote to this, around your regular schedule. Or, as we mentioned earlier, you can often get the trading done in the early morning before things start slowing down and just do day trading for part of the day.

Either way is going to help you to gain some profits if you do it well. But there are many traders who get into this who are not aware of the amount of time and commitment that they are putting in, and get overwhelmed. This is not a kind of trading strategy where you put it in and forget about it for years, and hope there is money at the end of it all. Instead, it is a strategy where we are going to need to devote a good amount of time and attention to in order to see the best results.

Is someone asking for money to get started or to learn the secrets?

It is possible to get started in day trading without having to spend a lot of money. In fact, outside of paying to purchase the stocks and a little bit in fees to the brokerage firm that you use (usually on a flat rate per trade or based on the amount of income that you earn). But outside of these amounts, you should not have to pay for anything to get started.

If someone is coming up to you and offering to show you the secrets or promising that you will make money overnight, but they need a huge fee from you before even starting or doing a single trade, the know that this is a scam and you should run fast in the other direction. This is going to be one of the worst ideas, and these kinds of scammers are a big reason why so many people are against day trading in the first place.

You will have to put up some money in the first place. The stocks that you are handling are not going to be for free. And the broker who is handling some of the trading for you and offering you some features to watch the stocks and work with charts and graphs will need to make something as well. But there is a difference between paying a bit where it makes sense and paying because someone else wants to make money off you.

There are a lot of times when we will find day trading is a great option to go with, and it is going to provide us with some good quality returns if we know what we are doing. However, there are also times when this may not be the best course of action for everyone, or times when the market is just not going to behave in the manner that we want, and it may be time to back out of it all.

CHAPTER 25:

Strategies for New Traders: Long vs Short

Short Term Strategy

The use of a short-term strategy is intended to make as much money as possible in the short run, meaning on a day to day basis, or in periods of about a week. On the whole, "short term" refers to anything that's less than a month. Of course, there are some investors who plan their moves on an hourly basis. So, the concept of "short-term" does have varying degrees. It should be noted that short-term strategies are quite popular with novice investors as they are able to reduce the likelihood of risk by entering and exiting trades before any serious market fluctuations take place. As investors gain more experience, they can get a better feel for the way markets behave thus allowing them to stay in the game longer.

20-Day System

This is one of the techniques we use to make some short-term gains. If you look at the stock that has recently gone up, chances are it will go down drastically within 20 days. 99% of the time, this is the case, which is why we like to wait 20 days before we make any investment on a stock. If you wait 20 days, you will hit the lowest price point of that particular stock. When it is at its lowest, it is ideal that you invest your money into that stock. Chances are the stock will go up again; many top traders have been using this technique with fantastic success. The trick is to wait 20 days at least before you make a trade. Depending on the company, the stock prices will drop down within 20 days of it going up drastically. And on the 20th day, this is when you invest your money into that stock and see it grow. You can see capital gains within ten days of the spending that money.

To execute this strategy, it's a great idea to become very familiar with the 10-day moving average of the particular stock or asset you are looking to invest in. The 20-day strategy is two 10-day moving average periods. By observing this measure, you can determine where the trend of the stock lies. In this manner, you can estimate for the where prices may rise or fall. Although, an important thing to keep in mind is that you shouldn't account for trades lasting longer than a week. The reason for this is that 5 days is exactly half of the 10-day moving average. As such, you can come in and out well before markets recalibrate at the end of the week and then at the start of the week. It's always a good idea to get in the start of the week and be gone by Friday afternoon.

Don't sell until the Stock Price Hits Back up to Its All-Time High

After understanding the basics of the 20-day strategy, you need to know that you should not sell your stock unless and until it has gone back up to its highest stock price in those 20 days. Most of the time, when the stock hits its all-time low, it will rise again up to its all-time high if not higher, which is why it is advised that you wait for the stock to grow back up to its highest point or above. Meaning that you should not sell your stock unless and until it is leveled back up to its highest price point. A great rule of thumb would be to wait another 20 days after you've invested your money. Once you do that, except for the stock to climb back up, once it climbs back up to a price where it was at the highest or even higher than that, then you can most definitely pull out that money and enjoy it. We understand that you are always very emotional with the money you're investing.

A great piece of advice for novice investors is to avoid becoming emotionally attached to a stock or a particular deal. This is why options can help you take out the emotional component from trading. The reason for this lies in the fact investors feel that if they hold on just a little bit longer, then can offset their losses and recoup some profit. This is a flawed strategy. As such, it's always a good idea to cut your losses and move on when you can.

Look at the Trend

They must start looking at the pattern when you are trying to achieve short-term capital. Always look at the trends that are taking place and invest your money accordingly. If you have a feeling that a particular stock will go up in a short period, then make sure that you invest in that stock. If you look at the transcript history, then it shouldn't be hard for you to see which stocks will go up soon and which won't. This will allow you to make fantastic capital gains with your options trading. However, when following trends, you must keep an eye on your stock. As trends go, they will go up quickly, and they will go down even quicker. This is why it is ideal they keep checking up on your stock as much as possible and pull the trigger when you think its right. As always do not get emotionally attached to your stocks and if you feel like it is slowly dropping down then perhaps sell the stock.

Control Risk

Risk is an inherent factor when it comes to trading. Consequently, it is imperative for you to manage risk in such a manner that you can cover yourself if, and when, markets suddenly turn. While this isn't all that frequent, there is always the possibility of a sudden event which can cause investors to sell off right away. In addition to purchasing options as a means of hedging your investments, never put in more than 2% of your investment capital into a single trade. What this does is that it spreads out the risk among the various deals you have going on at any one time. So, if one deal goes sour, the most you could potentially lose on that deal is 2%. On the contrary, if you invested, say, 50% of your capital on one deal, and that deal went sour, you'd lose half your investment capital. Needless to say, that would devastate your portfolio.

Target Stocks Which Will Make Big Moves Very Soon

Similar to looking at Trends, this is one of the long terms / short-term strategy options. The strategy can be both used in a long-term and short time. However, its right to a short-term options trade and you'll need to focus on stocks that have a history of making significant moves in a short period.

Long Term Strategy

We will talk about technical analysis and explain to you what it is and the same thing with the fundamental analysis. And then we will help you understand which method works better for what, once you've been able to understand this you will be in a much better position in terms of making more money with options trading.

Technical Analysis

To put with technical analysis, it is a way Option Traders finds a framework to study the price movement. The simple theory behind this method is that a person will look at the prices and the changes, hence determine the current trading conditions and the potential price movement. The only problem with this method would be that it is philosophical meaning that all technical analysis is that it is reflected in the price. The price reflects the information, which is out there, and the price action is all you would need to make a trade. The technical analysis banks on history and the trends, and the Traders will keep an eye on the past, and they will keep an eye on the future as well and based on that they will decide if they want to trade or not. More importantly, the people who are going to be trading using the technical analysis will use history to determine whether they're going to make the trade or not. Essentially the way to check out technical analysis would be to look up the trading price of a particular stock in five years. This is what many Option Traders used to determine the history and the future of the capital, and whether or not they should trade using technical analysis. There are many charts you can look up online to out how technical analysis takes place. However, we have given you a brief explanation of what technical analysis is.

Fundamental Analysis

Fundamental analysis is more realistic and feasible in the long term. The whole premise behind the theoretical analysis is that you look at the economy of the country and the trading system that's going on to determine whether it is a good trade or not. More focusing on economics, that's why it helps you to which dollar is going up or down and what is causing it.

One of the greatest things you can do when it comes to Options Trading is to understand why a dollar is dropping or going up. Once you're able to understand that, you will be in a much better position for gaining profits in your Option Trading endeavors. When using the fundamental analysis, you will be looking at the country's employment and unemployment rate also see how the training with different countries overall sing the country's economy before you decide on whether you should try it or not. Many successful Option Traders solely believe in fundamental analysis, as it is factual, unlike technical analysis. Even though technical analysis is accurate, it is not guaranteed like the theoretical analysis. Instead of looking at the trends, you will be looking at what is causing the highs and the lows. Not only that, based on the highs and lows, you will be able to determine the country's current and future economic outlook, whether it is good or not. One rule of thumb to look into with be how good the state is doing, the better the state is doing, the more foreign investors are going to take part in it. Once starting the piece in it, the dollar or the stock in that country will go up tremendously.

The idea behind fundamental analysis is that you need to look at the countries economical, and you also need to look at it. To make you understand, what fundamental analysis is it is mostly when you invest in a country is doing good in the economy, and not invest in a company when they're doing wrong in the marketplace. Which makes sense since the economy dictates how high are low prices going to be per dollar? Most of the time, investors will invest the money as soon as they see the dollar going up. The reason why they will do that is that they know the dollar will keep climbing up since the economy is getting better. One of the great examples would be when the US dollar dropped in 2007 2008, and the Canadian dollar took up, at that point, a lot of investors are investing in Canadian dollars of the US dollar.

CHAPTER 26:

Fundamentals of a Profitable Day Trading Plan

Ask any day trader to share a copy of their plan and you will realize that it is a closely-guarded secret. Now let's look at the elements of a winning trading plan which you can create to boost your trading experience.

Know the Number of Trades to Use to Evaluate Your Performance

For most people, time represents the main driver for evaluating their performance. For instance, you find companies issuing reports every quarter of the year.

As a trader, how long do you take to evaluate your performance so as to come up with the best plan? The answer is simple – don base your evaluation on the time that has passed rather base it on the number of traders you place. Time is highly irrelevant in trading, and one year of best trading can be overshadowed by a week of poor trading.

You need to identify the number of trades –for most traders; the magic number is 10 trades. This is regardless of the duration it takes to run these trades.

Know Your Key Performance Metrics

You need to measure your trading performance to make sure you know what to expect. There are a few metrics that you can use to measure your performance. These include the R score, which is a ratio of your lucrative trades divided by non-profitable trades. The ratio you get translates to the profit you get when you run the trade. For instance, if the ratio is 3, then you will get triple the profit.

The opportune time of Day for You to Trade

You need to find the right time to trade, though it is best to limit your trading activity to a certain time. For most traders, 9 am to 12 pm is their optimal time.

Identify the Stocks to Trade

Come up with a standard methodology to identify the different plays. You need to identify the stock depending on the time horizon of the trade. Day traders usually focus on stocks that occur in the news. Regardless of your trading approach, go for stocks that have the maximum profits.

As a day trader, you need to focus on the major companies, because they provide you with the best chance to locate stocks that are trending. The market movers also provide the top list of trades that are gaining and losing instantaneously.

Once you get the stock that you feel will give you the profits you desire, it is now time to add them to your list so that you can monitor its performance.

Determine your Stop Loss

Stop losses keep you in trading over the long haul. For instance, you can place a threshold of 3 percent. The percentage is based on how volatile the stocks are. If you realize that the stop loss is being hit consistently, check the unpredictability of stocks that you are interested in.

Understand When to Let Go

You need to know when the run has come to an end. There are many traders that don't know when to exit a trade and end up losing out a lot. To avoid such scenarios, you need to have a strategy to exit the trade. Keep the exit strategy easy – for instance, if the value goes below the moving average that you have set.

The Investment Per Strategy

Without the proper management of money, you won't make money in trading. The best way to determine how much you can invest is to look at your performance. If your key indicators are low, then invest less money so that you minimize damage to your account balance.

When to Take a Break

You might not read about this in other books, but taking a break is essential if you wish to make things work for you. But the real brainer is when to take the break. For most traders, taking a break is something they never think about. All they do is run trade after trade, day after day.

You need to take time to take a break so that you relax. Taking a break also allows you to take control of the market.

Sample Trading Plan

Davy'
What is the number of trades to gauge my trading performance? 20
What time should I place new trades? 9.30 am to 10.30 am
What time do I exit the market? 12.00 pm
How much do I risk each day? 3 percent of the position
How much do I invest in each position? 10 percent of my buying power
How do I get stocks? Use scanners to get top players for the day
How long do I take a break? 2 trading days

As you can see, you have set down the rules to follow so that you know what to do at any particular time.

Skill Assessment

Are you ready to be a trader? And not just any trader, but a serious one as such. Have you tested the system and found it working the way you expect it to do? Can you track the signals with no hesitation? Trading is all about give and take, you need to have the right skills to trade, the time as well.

Mental Preparation

Before you can make money trading, you need to be ready for the challenge. If you aren't psychologically ready, don't start otherwise you will lose out.

This happens when you are preoccupied, irritated or unfocused from the trading task waiting for you.

Do Your Homework

Before the trading market opens, you need to know what is happening around the world. Check out the index futures so that you gauge the mood of the market before it opens.

Consider the various economic reports so that you decide which one is ideal to follow. For the majority of traders, it is vital to wait for a report rather than jumping into the foray and taking the risk.

Trade Preparation

Whatever the kind of trading program you use, make sure you set it up properly before you start trading. Label the various resistance and support levels, set alerts, have clear signals and make sure you monitor them.

KEEP RECORDS

All good traders keep records of what they do. More importantly, if you win your trade, you need to know exactly why I went through and how. Write down various aspects such as targets, time, entry and exit points, and daily open range. Record comments beside each trade on the reasons you have learnt.

Make sure you save the trading reports so you can revisit them and scrutinize the P&L of the particular system.

CHAPTER 27:

Day Trading with Options or with Shares-What is the Difference?

Everybody understands that purchasing something now and offering it later on at a greater cost is the course to earnings. That is not great enough for alternatives traders since alternative costs do not constantly act as anticipated, and this space in understanding might trigger traders to leave cash on the table or sustain unforeseen losses.

Among the significant problems for brand-new choices, traders develop originates from them not truly comprehending how to utilize alternatives to achieve their monetary objectives since alternatives trade in a different way than stocks.

Whether you are a financier or a trader, your goal is to generate income. Your secondary goal is to do so with the appropriate minimum level of threat.

Choices are unique financial investment tools, and there is far more a trader can do than merely purchase and offer specific choices. Choices have qualities that are not readily available somewhere else in the financial investment universe.

Binary alternatives traders "gamble" on whether or not a possession's rate will be above or listed below a particular quantity at a defined time. Day traders likewise try to forecast cost instructions. However, losses and revenues depend on elements like entry rate, exit rate, size of the trade, and cash management methods. Like binary choices traders, day traders can go into a trade understanding the optimum gain or loss by utilizing revenue targets and stop losses.

An alternative is a monetary derivative that offers the holder the right, however not the commitment, to either purchase or offer a set quantity of a security or other monetary property at an agreed-upon cost (the strike cost) on or prior to a defined date. A binary alternative, nevertheless, instantly workouts, so the holder does not have the option to purchase or offer the hidden possession.

A binary choice is a type of choices in which your profit/loss depends totally on the result of a yes/no market proposal: a binary alternatives trader will either make a set loss or a set revenue. Revenue or loss for a day trader relies on a variety of factors, comprising of entrance rate, departure expense, and amount of securities, deals, or lots sold and bought by the dealer.

The Greeks Statistical Methods Professional commodity traders don't buy stock all the time. For certain situations, they appreciate giving brief wanting to profit as the cost of product declines. A lot of beginner alternative traders do rule out the principle of offering alternatives (hedged to restrict threat), instead of purchasing them.

Binary choices are offered on a range of underlying properties, consisting of stocks, products, currencies, indices and even occasions, such as an approaching Fed Funds Rate, Jobless Claims and Nonfarm Payrolls statements. An alternative binary position a yes/no concern: for example, Will the cost of gold be above $1,326 at 1:30 p.m.? The cost at which you purchase or offer the binary alternative is not the real cost of gold (in this example) however a worth in between absolutely no and 100.

If you can determine danger (i.e., optimum gain or loss) for a provided position, then you can likewise lessen it. Translation: Traders can prevent nasty surprises by understanding just how much cash can be lost when the worst-case circumstance takes place.

Traders should understand the possible benefit for any position in order to identify whether looking for that possible benefit is worth the threat needed.

A couple of elements that alternatives traders utilize to assess risk/reward capacity:

Holding a position for a particular time period. Unlike stock, all alternatives decline as time passes. The Greek letter "Theta" is utilized to explain how the passage of one day impacts the worth of choice.

Delta determines how a cost modification, either greater or lower, for underlying stock or index impacts the rate of choice.

She continued to cost modification. That is another method of stating that the choice Delta is not consistent, however modifications.

It is extremely various for stock (no matter the stock cost, the worth of one share of stock constantly alters by $1 when the stock rate modifications by $1), and the idea is something with which a brand-new choices trader should be comfy.

In the world of choice, altering volatility plays a big function in the prices of the alternatives. Vega determines how much the cost of alternative modifications when approximated volatility modifications.

Hedging with Spreads

Choices are typically utilized in mix with other alternatives (i.e., purchase one and offer another). That might sound complicated. However, the basic concept is easy: When you have an expectation for the hidden property habits, such as:

Technical Analysis vs Fundamental Analysis

Generally, day traders are more interested in a stock's cost action, whereas financiers are more focused on the underlying business. Day traders might likewise use take advantage of for a greater concentration of shares to pocket a smaller sized relative rate motion rate gain.

Commissions

A day trader could get several times in a single day into and out of a position, while the financiers could keep positions for years or months. Contrary to this, day traders often move in and out of roles and profits will quickly add rising.

- Bearish
- Neutral (anticipating a range-bound market).
- It is ending up being far more, or much less, unstable.

The number of possible mixes is big, and you can discover info on a range of choices techniques that utilize spreads. In exchange for accepting restricted earnings, spread out trading comes with its own benefits, such as a boosted likelihood of making cash. Stock traders have absolutely nothing comparable to choice spreads.

Choice trading is not stock trading. For the informed choice trader, that is an advantage due to the fact that choice methods can be developed to make money from a variety of stock exchange results, which can be achieved with minimal danger.

Contrary to this, financiers are based on large industry: industry this they believe can expand in the years to come. Although uncertainty is beneficial to a day trader, to a financier, it may reflect chaos. Financiers tend to search for much safer stocks from the more genuine business.

Threat Exposure

Drawback danger can form from global markets and occasions while U.S. stock exchange is closed, leading to futures gapping down, which eventually triggers most stocks to likewise open with space down. Investing thinks these are simply little missteps in the general photo of the long-lasting viewpoint.

Day traders have various requirements than financiers when looking for stocks. Day traders are more focused on technical analysis than basic analysis. Day traders look for stocks with momentum and volatility.

Stocks can respond strongly to the business profits report and assistance. Years of earnings can be lost in a single session for missing out on agreement expert quotes and assistance. Financiers normally will choose whether to continue holding a position based on these outcomes where basic analysis plays a crucial part in the decision-making procedure.

The details are being provided without factor to consider the financial investment goals, danger tolerance, or monetary scenarios of any particular financier and may not be ideal for all financiers. Investing includes danger, consisting of the possible loss of principal.

The primary distinctions between day trading and investing are the activity levels and position holding times. Day traders focus on short-term trades consisted of in a single trading day using direct-access trading platforms.

CHAPTER 28:

Trading Business Plan

Aside from carefully evaluated day trading plans and strategies, here are other tips that can help optimize your day trading success.

Practice with a Trading Simulator First

These days, pilot trainees learn to fly airplanes on a simulator first before flying a real one. Why? By practicing with a flight simulator first, the risk of a pilot trainee crashing the plane becomes much lower. It's because flight simulators allow pilot trainees to experience how it is to fly a plane and how planes respond to controls without having to actually leave the ground. In case they commit major and potentially catastrophic mistakes during flight training, there will be no serious consequences other than low grades.

Day trading with real money on real stock or securities exchanges without first experiencing how it is to day trade is akin to learning how to fly a plane in a real plane in the sky! The risks of losing money are simply too high for a beginner to handle. By using your trading platform's trading simulator before day trading real money, you can afford to lose money as part of your learning process without actually losing money!

Stick to Your Daily Limits

While knowing how much capital you're willing to risk in day trading as a whole, you'll also need to have sub limits, i.e., daily limits. If you don't have such limits, it can be much easier to wipe out your entire trading capital in a day or two. A sensible guideline for your daily limit is to cut your losses when your daily trading position registers a maximum loss of 10%.

Avoid Becoming Attached to Your Stocks

As a newbie trader, your chances of becoming emotionally attached to your chosen SIPs are high. That's why a big chunk of the trading strategies enumerated earlier involve using numbers as triggers for entering and exiting positions in SIPs. Numbers are objective and if you stick to them, you can prevent your emotions from hijacking your trades.

Feel the Mood of the Market

Technical analysis, via candlestick charts and technical indicators, are very good ways to gauge the market's mood. However, they're not perfect and you may need to validate their readings by interacting with actual traders.

Trade Patiently

Only fools rush in, as the saying goes. However, it can be very easy to rush into trades, especially for newbies, when a significant amount of time has passed without any trades. It's because it can seem that one is wasting time by not trading.

The truth is, time will be wasted, as well as trading capital, by rushing into trades for the sake of making them. Remember, the point of day trading is to make money and not to simply trade. If no good opportunities are available, there's no need to force a day trade. Be patient and wait for trading signals to appear before taking positions.

Befriend Your Losing Trades

Nobody's perfect. That includes day traders. Even the very best still get into losing day trades, albeit their total trading profits significantly exceed their total trading losses.

Knowing that even the best of the best still have their share of losing trades should make you feel much better about losing trades. Even better, why not look at them from a different perspective just like how Thomas Edison looked at his "failed" experiments.

When asked about the first 1,000 failed experiments on the working light bulb, Edison corrected his interviewer by saying those weren't failed experiments. They were successful experiments because each of those first 1,000 light bulb experiments showed him how not to make the light bulb and in so doing, brought him a step closer to making a working version of the bulb.

Choose Your Broker Wisely

Many newbie day traders choose their brokers without really giving it much thought. Probably it's because they're overwhelmed with so many new things to learn that they fail to pay attention to the brokers they choose. Don't make the same mistake because remember, you'll be entrusting your precious day trading capital, which in the United States is a minimum of $25,000. And that's a lot of money to entrust, which means choosing a trustworthy and excellent day trading broker is a must.

With so many new online brokers popping up on the Internet these days, it can be quite challenging to sift through the reputable and not-so-reputable ones. Fortunately, there are many online resources and forums on which you can glean information on online brokers' reputations and quality of service.

Part of choosing the right broker is platform or order execution speed. Remember, day trading success is very dependent on how fast you can execute your orders in the market. So, choose a broker that's not just reputable but has a fast order-executing platform.

Don't Scrimp on Technology

I can't emphasize enough the importance of speed when it comes to day trading, where a mere few seconds can spell the difference between profitable and losing trades. For this, you can't afford to settle for the cheapest hardware and software, which most likely be too slow for consistent day trading success.

Now, I'm not saying you should get the most expensive, top-of-the-line computers for your day trading activities. It'll be like trying to kill a fly with a shotgun. However, your primary consideration for buying a computer and choosing Internet service providers should be technical specifications. Price should only be the secondary factor and fortunately, you don't need to buy an iMac or a MacBook Pro just to day trade with sufficient speed.

Also, make sure that you have either a landline or a cellular phone line to reach your broker in the event that your Internet connection acts up for one reason or another. Better to err on the side of caution than on the side of negligence, don't you think?

Focus on Price Movements and News Triggers or Catalysts

Day trading relies on technical analysis and very little on fundamental analysis, except for news catalysts or triggers. And by nature of its reliance on technical analysis, it doesn't bother itself with a company's financial data and the like.

Why am I reminding you of this? One way you can sabotage your day trading success is by overanalyzing your stocks or securities. When you extend your research and analysis on a company's balance sheet and income statement items, as well as industry and economic trends, you'll spend too much time on things that aren't really important to day trading. Fundamental analysis is crucial for swing trading and long-term investing but with day trading, all you need to focus on is price movement and significant news announcements.

Stick to those two only so you can make the most out of your day trading time and so that you can enter and exit positions on a timely basis.

CHAPTER 29:

Average Income of a Day Trader

Imagine a scenario where I revealed to you that while exchanging salary has numerous factors, by applying some essential research strategies. You can go to a reliable gauge of what an informal investor can make dependent on their area, beginning capital, and business status.

I am going to share various sources that can give you clear gauges that you would then be able to use to decide your potential benefit potential.

Let's face it, a significant number of are thinking about going out without anyone else and are not hoping to find a new line of work.

Anybody that discloses to you a conclusive range for a day exchanging pay is likely pulling your leg.

I may as was well be conversing with one of my children about Yo Gabba (it was one of their preferred shows on Nickelodeon).

Presently, for all you corporate individuals that can go to destinations like converse with your insider companions to check the amount you can make in an exchanging work, kindly don't anticipate hard numbers from any of these sources.

The reason being, there is a large group of outside variables that play into how a lot of cash you can make. In this article, we will tear through all the lighten on the web and get down to cold hard certainties. Sit back, unwind, and get some espresso.

A Decision You Should Not Take Lightly

You ought not to trifle with this choice, and you should gauge the upsides and downsides. First of all, exchanging for another person will permit you the chance to use the devices and systems of an outfit that is ideally beneficial.

A portion of the positives of exchanging for another person is evacuating the weights of distinguishing both a triumphant framework and a tutor that can help you end route.

It is On the off chance that you are not beneficial "enough," be set up to have a more significant number of rules tossed at you than when you were in sixth grade.

This degree of administration over your exchanging action is because of the reality you are utilizing another person's cash, so profit or become acclimated to somebody revealing to you how to relax.

The one significant upside for day exchanging for another person is you will get pay. This pay is likely insufficient to live on; however, you do get a check.

At the point when you go out alone, there is no pay. You are a financial specialist wanting to make payments

Licenses

On the slim chance that you choose to work for the firm and are exchanging customer's cash or conceivably interfacing with clients, you will require your Series 7 and perhaps your Series 63 permit.

Arrangement 7

The Series 7 will give you the permit to exchange. Last I checked, the test cost $305 and relying upon the outfit will be secured by the firm.

Arrangement 63

The Series 63 is the following test you should take after the Series 7. This test licenses you to request orders for stock inside a point of view state.

A straightforward perspective about this is the 7 gives you the privilege to exchange on a government level, and the 63 enables you to work inside the limits of state laws.

I don't anticipate covering the theme of day exchanging for somebody finally because I haven't lived it.

From what I do know, you are required to finish some in-house preparing programs for the firm you speak to. For venture houses, you will get a not too bad base pay, enough to keep you at the lower white-collar class extend for New York.

Need to know the best part?

Your base stock merchant pay could go from 50,000 - 70,000 dollars US, which is only enough for you to take care of your link tab, feed yourself and perhaps take a taxi or two. In any case, this not the slightest bit covers meals, vehicles, excursions, tuition-based schools, and so on.

In this way, I surmise you can rapidly observe that for you to be fruitful, you're going to need to make your reward. There is only one catch; you need to profit day exchanging. Superficially, this sounds sensible because you bring down your hazard profile by having another pay stream of a base compensation; in any case, you need to perform to remain utilized, and will just get around 10-30%% of the benefits you get from your exchanging movement.

In light of these numbers, you would need to make about 300k in exchanging benefits to break a 100k in compensation.

Most likely about it, the advantage of exchanging with an organization is, after some time, your purchasing influence will increment, and you have none of the drawbacks dangers since it's the organization's cash. The key is ensuring you have a lot of money under administration.

As should be evident in the infographic over, the way to making genuine cash is to begin dealing with different assets. You, in one way or another, draw that off, and you will make by and large 576k per year.

Indeed you read that right.

I realize the 576k looks engaging; however, recall it is out and out hard labor to get to the highest point of the mountain.

The other brings up to get out from the infographic is that the usual reward is beginning to drift higher and if things go as conjecture will surpass the downturn top not long from now.

Along these lines, on the off possibility that one of your objectives is to profit, you are looking in the right business.

Regular Income Trading for a Company

The widely appealing individual can hope to make somewhere in the range of 100k and 175k. In conclusion, it is on the off chance that you are beneath normal, hope to get a pink slip.

In any case, pause - there's additional.

Certainty, if we broaden our exploration past New York, you will see the regular pay for a "Merchant" is $89,496.

Try not to trust me?

Open Trading Firms

Be that as it may, I can consider many employments where you can make near $89k, and it doesn't require the degree of responsibility and hazard taking required for exchanging.

You might be thinking, "this person just revealed to me it could go as high as $250k to $500k in case I'm better than expected, where does $89k become an integral factor."

What I have talked about so far are the pay rates for traded on an open market organization.

Good karma attempting to get precise information for the first-class universe of private value brokers. What you will discover is regularly the top brokers from the Chase and Bank of America's endeavor out to flexible investments, as a result of the opportunity in their exchanging choices and the more significant compensation potential.

Here's the most significant part, with the general population firms, corporate objectives will frequently drive a segment of your other targets.

The magnificence of the multifaceted investment world is while there are still organization objectives, you have the chance to eat a more significant amount of what you slaughter.

It's nothing for a top broker to out-acquire their chief on the off chance that they carry enough an incentive to the firm.

What amount do you could make?

Advantages of day exchanging for an organization

1. Pay
2. Medical advantages
3. The renown of working for a venture bank or fence investments
4. No danger of individual capital
5. Climb the corporate positions to deal with various assets
6. A drawback of day exchanging for an organization
7. Must connect with customers
8. Office legislative issues
9. By and large, you get 20% of benefits (Public Firm)

Day Trading for a Prop Firm

Day exchanging for prop firms can feel similar to living on the edge.

Like exchanging for an organization, you will get some preparation before the prop firm enables you to trade with their cash and approach their frameworks. From that point forward, all likenesses between exchanging for a prop firm and an organization contrast.

Try not to expect any human services of paid downtime. You won't have a base compensation or yearly audits. The prop firms will expect you to store cash to begin utilizing their foundation.

The advantages are the prop firm will part benefits with you anyplace from a third and up to half. The drawbacks are again no compensation, and you bear a portion of the torment with regards to misfortunes.

However, here's the rub, the explanation prop firm merchants make not precisely those for the speculation houses is access to capital. Since you are likely exchanging the exclusive firm proprietor's cash, the pool of assets you approach is constrained.

I would state a better than an expected broker for a prop firm can make about 150k to 250k every year. The typical broker will do somewhere in the range of 60k and 100k, and underperformers will have such huge numbers of position limits set for them, they are fundamentally rehearsing and not profiting. These underperformers will probably expel themselves from the game because rehearsing doesn't take care of the tabs.

Advantages

- Split benefits with Prop Firm
- Low commission rates
- No Boss
- Increment Margin

Negatives

- Utilize your cash-flow to begin
- Loss of individual riches
- Constrained preparing
- No medical advantages or paid downtime
- No vocation movement
- Just cause cash off what you to acquire

CHAPTER 30:

Best Day Trading Platforms

Introduction to Trading Platforms

Trading platforms can be defined as software designed from entering and exiting trades at the stock markets. The software enables traders to manage positions, open and close them on behalf of a trader. This is often performed through an intermediary such as a broker.

Today, most day trading platforms are online and are a service provided to traders by brokers at a fee. Sometimes the services are available at a discounted rate, especially for active, long-term traders.

Trading Platform Basics

Trading platforms enable traders and investors to access the stock market and place different trades. Traders can purchase or sell all kinds of securities, such as currencies, stocks, futures, and options. However, most brokers tend to specialize in a given security. For instance, a broker may wish to provide options trading only to clients. This way, clients will then sign up to only trade in this specific security.

There are generally two distinct types of trading platforms. We have commercial platforms, and then we have the prop platforms. Commercial platforms are more suitable for retail investors and day traders. These are often simple to use, easily accessible, and come with numerous additional features that make investing and trading much easier. These additional features include charts and news feeds amongst others.

We also have prop platforms which are customized to suit the needs of clients who can afford the cost of customization. Such clients are usually large brokerage firms and other organizations where professional traders have certain specific needs. The development is undertaken by brokerages together with software developers in order to meet the needs and trading styles of large professional traders.

There are certain considerations that need to be made when determining the most appropriate trading platform. Traders need to consider things such as fees charged, features provided, accessibility, customer service provided, and other crucial matters. Some traders are more focused on customer service and access to the broker while others prefer platforms that are easy to use and come with a variety of features.

As a day trader, you will most likely be using commercial platforms provided by different brokerage firms. Even then, there are some things that you need to be on the lookout before choosing one. For instance, what are the included features? How about costs and fees charged? Also, different traders will require different tools on their platforms. There are certain tools that are suitable for day and swing traders, while others are more suitable for options and futures traders.

When selecting a platform, always watch out for the fees charged. As a small-scale, retail day trader, you want to trade on one that charges low and affordable fees. However, sometimes, there are certain trade-offs. For instance, some platforms charge low fees, but they lack certain crucial features or provide poor services. Others may seem expensive but provide crucial features, including research tools and excellent services. So you will need to consider all these factors before eventually selecting a suitable trading platform.

There is another crucial point to keep in mind when selecting a trading platform. Some platforms are available only through specific brokers or intermediaries. Other platforms are universal and work with different brokerage platforms and intermediaries across the board. Traders also select trading platforms based on their own personal styles and preferences.

You should find out if there are any particular requirements or conditions that require to be fulfilled. For instance, some platforms require traders to maintain at least $25, oo0 in their trading accounts in the form of equity and possibly cash as well. In this instance, a trader may then receive approval for credit, which is also known as margin.

Examples of Day Trading Platforms

1. The Home Trading System

The home trading system is an algorithm and trading software designed to improve performance. Using this system, you can expect to make smarter, faster, and better trading decisions. This particular platform comes with innovative features and a custom algorithm that combines seamlessly to provide a real-time, fully integrated trading platform. You are bound to benefit from this platform and experience the benefits of seamless trading complete with all the features that you need.

The platform is completely compatible with some of the most dynamic and highly reliable charting tool. It is able to work with all kinds of markets, from stocks to Forex and indices. The platform is compatible with a variety of bars such as range and momentum bars as well as tick charts.

The designers of this platform took great care to consider all the different kinds of traders. This is why this specific platform is suitable for day traders, swing traders, Forex traders, retail investors, and long-term traders. The Home Trading System constitutes a modular platform that consists of different core features. A lot of these features can easily be switched off and on depending on the situation or to suit a particular requirement.

One of the advantages of this platform is that it endeavors to make trading extremely simply. For instance, the algorithm automatically colors the candlesticks or bars a red or blue color in order to provide a clear view of the market conditions and trends. The system will continue following the trends and mark any major changes in a contrasting color. For instance, whenever there is a trigger bar, these will appear in a different color so that it is clear to you the trader that there is definite variation in the trend.

This color feature not only makes trading easy but also improves your trading psychology so that you can trade with very little worry. Other desirable parameters that are essential to your trades are also provided on the platform. For instance, you need accurate and reliable trading signals delivered at the right time. Fortunately, the Home Trading System is designed to provide these signals in a timely and accurate manner.

When there is a turning point in the momentum of stock in the markets, then this will be detected, and a change of color will clearly indicate the turning point. You will be able to see a blue color with contrasting orange color pointing out areas of interest. The dots will indicate the entry points, exit points, collect profit points, and so on. A stopping point is also indicated just in case the trade does not work out as planned and you need to exit.

2. The Entry Zone Platform

We also have a trading platform known as the Entry Zone. This platform has been around for a while but has recently undergone a complete overhaul. It has received a new design to specifically address the needs of day traders. There is no trader in the entire world who wants to join an over-extended market even when it features a large stop-loss point.

One of the main benefits of this platform is that it helps eliminate the challenge of entering an overly extended market. It starts by first checking for a pullback. It does this by accessing the 60-minute timeframe. This way, you will be protected from accessing the markets at the worst moment. The algorithm is able to proceed and track the markets so that you eventually get to find out the best market entry points.

3. Able Trend Trading Platform

This is another platform designed with day traders in mind. One of its most outstanding features is its ability to instantly identify changes in the trend. Trend direction is first indicated by a distinct color. When the signal is headed upwards, then the color is blue, and when it heads downwards, it changes color to red. If there is any sideways movement, then the color changes once more to green.

This platform, therefore, makes it pretty easy to observe the market trend and keep abreast with it. Additional information will then enable you to make the necessary trade moves that you need to as a trader. For instance, you will notice red and blue dots on your screen. These indicate the various stop points. When there is a downward trend, then the red dots will indicate your sell points while blue dots will indicate your buy points on the upward trend. These stop points ensure that you partake of the large market movements but with very little risk or exposure.

The reasons why this system is so successful is that it comes with state of the art features. It generates dot and bars colors that you can choose for the different bar charts. These include the 5 minutes, 1 minute, daily, tick, and weekly charts. Many traders have termed this platform as both robust and functional. It is a universal platform that can work with different trading systems.

You can make large profits if you can enter the markets and join the trend at an early stage. Identifying the trend is easy when you have this software. Remember that the trend is a friend of day traders. Therefore, spend some time at the beginning of your trades to identify the trend and then move on from here. Identifying the trend at an early stage is what you wish to do. The risks to you are minimal at this stage. This platform helps you identify the trend and provide you with additional crucial information that even large investors do not have.

You can operate in any market so that you are not limited to trading stocks only. If you wish to trade in options, currencies, and other instruments, then you are able to do so. The platform is suitable for all trading styles, including day trading, swing trading, and position trading, and so on.

4. Interactive Brokers

This is a popular platform that has been recently revamped. It is highly rated software because of the useful tools available to traders. Some of these tools are extremely useful to sophisticate or seasoned traders who need more than just the basics.

This platform is able to connect you to any and all exchanges across the world. For instance, you may want to trade markets in Hong Kong, Australia, and so on. The software is able to seamlessly connect traders so that you have great trading experience.

This platform has seen the addition of new features which make trading even easier. These are, however, more suitable to seasoned traders who are more sophisticated than the average retail investor or small trader.

One of the attractive features of Interactive Brokers is that it is a very affordable platform. It is especially cost-friendly to small scale traders, retail investors, and the ordinary swing trader as the margin rates are low and affordable.

The platform supports trading across 120 markets located in at least 31 countries and deals in more than 23 different currencies. It also supports traders who execute trades pretty fast.

Conclusion

Day trade is relatively straightforward; the fact of the matter is that it is an extremely complex process requiring the successful use of a variety of tools and skills that not everyone will be able to follow through on reliably. As such, this list of pros and cons should make it easier for you to determine if this type of trading is one that you are interested pursuing in the long-term in search of your ultimate financial goals.

Pros: The biggest pro when it comes to day trading is the potential for gain when everything goes according to plan. The average successful day trader tends to buy a large number of shares at a time to ensure that they stand to make a serious profit from even an extremely small amount of movement. Additionally, they have the potential to work for themselves, only trading when they feel the urge or when the market is in a place that is too good to pass up.

Another major benefit to day trading for certain types of traders is the amount of excitement they can expect to see on a daily basis. As they only ever trade in the absolute shortest timeframes, the average day trader sees far more action than most other types of traders would in the same amount of time. What's more, day trading provides those who are up to the challenge with the opportunity to face off with many of the best traders in the world, dozens, if not hundreds of times each day. If you are the sort of thrill seeker who is sure to appreciate a good spike of adrenaline then day trading might be for you.

Another benefit to day trading is that you can teach yourself as easily as you can pay someone else to teach you what to do, making it one of the few ways you can get a job in the financial sector with a formal education. As long as you are willing and able to put in the time and dedicated enough to see it through to the end, then there is no reason you can't acquire the skills you need on your own and then hone them through countless hours of practice.

Cons: The biggest downside to day trading has to do with the wide variety of costs associated with being able to do so successfully. As they are dealing with very small amounts of movement, day traders need a sizeable amount of trading capital just to get off the ground. An amount of around $20,000 should be enough to let you get started in a truly productive fashion. Beyond that, the numbers of daily trades being made means that the costs paid in commission are going to be far higher than with most other types of trading.

Not only that but due to the high number of shares that come along with the average trade in this field, the potential for loss if a trade turns against you can be quite significant as well. In fact, statistically speaking, day trading is the most difficult type of securities trading to make a profit from in any sort of reliable fashion. In fact, a majority of new day traders experience mostly losses for at least the first month, and only about 30 percent move on from that state to be able to reliably turn a profit.

What's more, the monetary issues aren't the only barriers to entry either, and one of the biggest is the fact that the average amateur day trader is generally competing against professional organizations with a cadre of traders at their disposal and pockets that are extremely deep. As such, if you want to hope to chance of entering the market successfully then you will need to be prepared for what you are up against. Finally, many brokerages will simply not let you day trade in any way shape or form until you have already proven that you are capable of trading in a competent fashion on a more manageable scale to start.

In addition to these issues, the fact that the average day trader is self-employed means that it will simply not be the right choice for those who don't have the internal fortitude to put in the required work without having a boss standing over your shoulder ensuring that they are doing all that is needed for them to be successful. What's more, the average day trader has to fend for themselves when it comes to things like health insurance, a steady retirement plan or even a steady paycheck.

PART TWO

Introduction

Let's be completely clear about what stocks are. When you buy a "share" of stock, you are buying a share in the ownership of the company. When you do this with your brothers' small business, you might end up owning a significant fraction of it like 20%. But when you are doing this with a publicly traded company, for most people you are buying a tiny stake in the company. Nonetheless, the stock is a financial instrument that represents an ownership share in the company. Theoretically at least, it also represents a claim on the company's profits and on its assets (should the company go bankrupt). Although most people aren't aware of it, there are two types of stock:

Common Stock: This is what most people think of when you say "stock" and "stock market." A common stock gives you an ownership stake in the company, and if it pays dividends, you get dividend payments. You also get shareholder voting rights. That's for real, but it's up to you to exercise that right if they offer it.

Preferred Stock: This is a less common type of stock that offers a different set of rights. One of the main differences is that preferred stockholders get priority claim on assets of the company if it declares bankruptcy. Preferred stock can also offer a dividend payment. We won't be discussing it because most ordinary investors are not buying preferred stock.

Aligning buying choices with your goals

The first thing you should do before investing in the stock market is to sit down what your goals are when it comes to investing. Everyone has their own goals, but here are some common themes:

- Build up a nest egg for retirement.
- Build enough wealth and passive income that you can quit work early or basically do what you want (live life on passive income).
- Make midterm (3-5 year) profits off the stock market.

- Make money now. So, you're looking to buy and sell stocks to get cash this year.

The first thing that we'll note about this is that if you are looking to make money now, then that means you're looking to be a trader or speculator rather than an investor. There are multiple routes to do this, but the main ones are day trading, swing trading, and options trading. Keep in mind that there is a trade-off of risk and reward; the more you want quicker rewards from the stock market, generally speaking, the higher the risk, although the risks with options and swing trading can be mitigated.

If you are hoping to make midterm profits, then you are going to be looking at building a more aggressive portfolio. For those looking to build wealth and passive income, you may be looking at investing in stocks that pay dividends, investing in bonds, or using your stock holdings to generate income by selling options. We will discuss all of these approaches as we go on.

The last goal, building a nest egg for retirement, is a popular way that people look at stocks. In this case, you're looking for solid buys and using a "buy and hold" strategy, so that you build up a significant portfolio by the time you retire that you can slowly draw on at that time for income without having to keep working.

Aggressive vs. Conservative Investing

No matter what your strategy is outside of being a trader, you can also look at investing from another angle, which is aggressive vs. conservative approaches. And actually, there are two ways to look at this. The first is dividing your investments between stocks and bonds/money in a way that reflects whether or not you are after aggressive growth or trying to protect our capital. By money, we mean a wider array of products such as money market funds, CDs, etc. With bonds, your principal is (at least in theory) protected. The expectation is that under most circumstances, the stock market is higher risk but will grow your capital at a much higher rate than other types of investments. Of course, sometimes there are unusual circumstances, like the mid-1970s in the United States when the stock market was languishing and interest rates were sky-high. But most of the time, that isn't the situation.

So, if you are conservative, that is you don't want much risk to your capital, then you are going to put more money in proportion towards bonds, money market funds, and CDs that protect your principal, and a lower relative fraction toward the stock market. Financial advisors recommend that people do certain percentages based on their age, so the closer you get to retirement, the more conservative you should get with your investments. That way, you can protect your principal moving into your retirement years. The theory here is that if there is a significant stock market crash, your certain items in your portfolio go belly up, you would need time to recover from the losses. Younger people have time to do so, while those nearing retirement or in retirement don't have time.

The way that you distribute your investments among different types of securities for these reasons is referred to as asset allocation.

Financial advisors have a simple rule of thumb they use in order to suggest what type of asset allocation that you use. You take your age and subtract from 100, and then you put that proportion into stocks. So, if you are 45 years old, 100-45 =55, so you would invest 55% of your money in stocks and 45% in bonds and other more conservative investments.

In recent decades, they have gotten less conservative in asset allocation recommendations. Some advisors use 110, and there are others who even use 120. So, if we were using 120 and you were 45 years old, the proportion of your investment capital that should be in the stock market should be 120-45 = 75%.

The reason that financial advisors have become more relaxed about this is people are living longer and healthier lives, and many people now work past the age of 65.

Midcap, Smallcap, Largecap

Another way that you can determine the relative risk of your portfolio is by what types of companies you invest in. The first main characteristic that you can consider our market capitalization. A rule of thumb (that doesn't always apply) is that larger market capitalization means more stability and less growth, while less market capitalization means less stability but more potential for growth. Obviously, on average, smaller companies have more potential for growth, and some of them are going to grow by massive amounts and become tomorrow's blue-chip companies. Just 15 years ago, Facebook was nowhere to be seen, and Amazon and Google were much smaller in comparison to what they are today. However, you can see that this is no more than a rule of thumb, as Amazon and Google, for example, are very large corporations now and yet still capable of explosive growth. Apple also saw remarkable growth over the past decade, even though it was relatively older.

It's pretty difficult to know what companies are going to grow from small cap to blue chip if you picked Amazon 20 years ago well then you were pretty lucky. Most of us don't have a crystal ball. However, as we'll see, you can use exchange-traded funds to get a basket of stocks instead of trying to pick winners and losers.

To calculate market capitalization, you multiply the total number of shares by the price per share. Let's imagine a fictitious company. If they are trading at $100 a share and they have 2,561,780 shares, then the market capitalization is given by:

$100 x 2,561,780 = $256,178,000

So, it's easy to calculate, and even better you can probably simply look up the market capitalization of any company. What category the company falls in is defined in the following way:

- Nanocap ($50 million or less): These are small companies that could be very high-risk investments, but also with a huge amount of potential for growth. You would need to do a lot of research before investing in a company this size, and should probably limit your investment since it might go bankrupt fairly easily.

- Microcap (Above $50 million but under $250 million): Less risky than nanocap stocks, but still pretty risky. On the other hand, lots of potential for growth, and looking a little more stable.

- Smallcap (Above $250 million, but below $1 billion) these are high-growth potential stocks for growing companies that have become more stable than the microcaps. Still a lot of risks, however. You can invest in many smallcap funds so that you're not betting on one company.

- Midcap ($1 billion to $10 billion): Now we are getting into a good "mid-range" area, that gives you reduced risk that still has some growth potential. Of course, the growth potential may depend on what market the company is in. The reason the company is midcap may be its industry.

- Largecap ($10 billion to $50 billion): If you are a conservative investor, then you're going to be investing most of your funds in largecap companies. This is the old "blue-chip" category.

- Ultracap (Market capitalization greater than $50 billion): Rather than extending the largecap category, those who control such things invented an entirely new category for the Amazon's and Apples of the world.

A financial advisor will typically suggest putting more capital into midcap, largecap, and ultracap companies if you are a more conservative investor, and less capital into smallcap and the other smaller companies. It is the general perception that the largecap companies are stronger companies that can weather downturns in their industry and recessions. It's also believed that large, older companies are more stable.

However, if the 2008 financial crash taught you anything, one lesson you might take from it is that this isn't always true. Many companies got into big trouble in the 2008 financial crisis, and some of them were very well-established firms. Consider that GM, which has been a "blue chip" company for decades, had to be bailed out by the government. Bear Sterns, an investment bank, literally went under overnight despite being more than 100 years old. Its stock dropped by more than $100 a share over a short time period. Other large companies like Bank of America needed to be financially propped up.

So, while the advice given is generally true, it's not always true. If you are looking to run a self-directed investing account, you are going to have to spend a lot of time studying and decide for yourself what high risk is and what isn't.

One key strategy that can always help protect your capital is diversification. That doesn't just mean investing in more than one stock; it can also mean mixing things up among largecap, smallcap, etc. That way, you can take advantage of some of the growth potentials without risking everything in one area.

CHAPTER 1:

What Is Stock Market?

So, for those of you who are totally new to investing in the stock market, I am going to give you a basic understanding of what it is. It is basically a collection of markets that consists of shares, and there is regular issuance, buying, and selling of these shares. These shares are owned by publicly-held companies. When you buy these stocks, you basically are now the owner of a particular share of that company. The earnings of the company are what determine the price of the stocks. There are several formal exchanges through which the financial activities related to stocks take place, and they are also known as OTC or over-the-counter marketplaces. They are not allowed to perform in any way they seem fit because they are governed by a fixed set of regulations.

The basic question that every beginner has is, why do these companies sell the stocks? Now, this is because they want to grow their company and make their funds large. For example, let us say you want to start your own business, what do you do for the financing? You either use your credit card, or you apply for a personal loan, right? And then, you can also opt for loans from a bank when your company has reached a certain level. These companies are also the same. When they need money, they can first start by selling their bonds to investors they deem fit. But sooner or later, they are going to need a lot of money so that they can upgrade their business to the next level. That is when the initial public offering happens. In simpler terms, the company starts selling stocks. Now, the company is no longer the property of any single person. It has been divided into parts and every person who has bought the stocks holds some part of the company. The stock market sustains because these businesses need to raise more money for their business to grow and that is how everyone who has invested in them makes a profit.

Investing vs. Trading

Many people think that investing in stocks is the same as trading, but no, they are two completely different things. Although the ultimate aim for both these processes is to maximize your profit, they are two different entities.

If someone is trading stocks, then they are not in a particular stock for the long-term. They can jump in and out as they feel like whenever they feel they are going to make a short-term profit – it can be weeks, or it can also be minutes. They are not bothered about the prospects the company holds but rather the technical factors that are working behind the stocks. Traders are more concerned about the movement of stocks, and they try to predict these moves and also predict whether they are going to incur a profit or a loss from that move. That is how they plan their strategies.

On the contrary, investors are in the game for the long-term. No matter how much up and down the market goes through, investors usually stick through it because they are looking at the profit they are going to get in the long-term. If you are investing in the stock market and you follow the rules wisely, being a millionaire is not that much of a tough job. But yes, investors definitely need patience and enough discipline to remain in the market.

Are you confused as to what you want to be? Well, it mostly depends on how invested you want to be in the stocks market. If you want to be a trader, then you have to be prepared for spending hours in the market because you have to keep comparing graphs, check the charts, and predicting moves so that you can make a profit. But yes, no matter what you choose – be it investing or trading – you should not be investing your money in the stock market just like that without any research on a particular company.

Understand the Risk Involved

I wanted to talk about it so that you get a comprehensive idea of what the stock market is all about. Risks are always associated with any type of investment that you do. The major risk that plagues investors is an economic risk. There was a sour spell in the economy back in 2001 when there was a market bust in 2000 and the attack of 9/11. The economy definitely took years to return back to normalcy. If you are just a beginner and a young investor, I would advise you to lie low and ride out these bad phases. Also, if your domestic market is suffering, you can look to foreign stocks. But if you are nearing your retirement and suddenly the market changes its course towards the negative, then you will be in for huge losses.

You also have to deal with market value risk. It happens when there is a collapse because of more and more investors going out of the market. This is what happened recently due to the Covid-19 pandemic. But for every risk, there are measures that you can take to minimize the impact.

Participants of the Stock Market

There are different types of participants in the stock market, we are going to discuss the function of each one of them. Some of them play quite unique roles, but there are others whose roles are connected to one another. In order to allow the market to run productively, each and every one of these participants have to work in unison.

Stockbrokers

The role of buying and selling orders for different securities, including stocks, is performed by stockbrokers, and sometimes you will find them being referred to as only 'broker.' They manage the transactions of not only the institutional customers but also several retail customers, mostly through a brokerage firm. In return for the services that they are providing, the stockbrokers get their own cut known as commissions. There is no fixed rate for these commissions and the rates vary from one firm to the other. Yes, it is true that you don't have to absolutely depend on stockbrokers and you can go and buy the stocks from the company itself but in that case, you will have to take up a lot of hassle. On the other hand, buying stocks through a stockbroker makes the process so much easier to deal with.

It was not easy to approach or even afford a stockbroker mainly because they charged a hefty fee and so their use was limited only to the investors with high net-worth. But now, a lot has changed, especially because of the advances made in technology and the rapid rise of the internet. So, you now have discount brokers whose services can be availed not only much faster but also at cheaper rates compared to the scenario. So, investing in the stock market has now become more plausible because of the lesser transaction fees involved. Moreover, even if you are located overseas, you can invest in any particular stock market because of the presence of these discount brokers. The credentialing requirements, though, are not fixed and vary from one country to another.

Portfolio Managers

The next participant that we are going to talk about is the portfolio managers who are mainly responsible for maintaining the intricacies of portfolio trading, and it can be either passive or active. No matter what the type of the fund is, it is highly influenced by the portfolio manager. The returns that come from any particular fund are also highly dependent on the portfolio manager. So, in order to become a portfolio manager, you definitely have to have a strong background in relation to finance like that of a broker, trader, or an experienced investor. The selling and buying decisions of a portfolio are made by these portfolio managers, and there are several analysts who give them these recommendations.

Investment Bankers

When it comes to raising capital for different entities like the government or other corporations, then the individual responsible for that task is an investment banker. Some of the major investment banks are Morgan Stanley, Goldman Sachs, Deutsche Bank, and JPMorgan Chase. All the complicated transactions are handled by them. In order to raise the money, they help in issuing securities. By hiring an investment banker, the company saves its time because they do not have to do any research about strategies or risks involved. Everything about the present investing climate will be assessed by the investment banker, and they can also help in understanding the various regulatory requirements. When the IPO or an initial public offering of a company is held, all the shares of that company are bought by the investment bank. The bank, here, acts as the intermediary, and when the company is going public, it acts on the company's behalf. All the shares of the company will be liquidated because the investment bank will share them in the public market.

Custodian

To make sure that the customers do not face loss or theft, their securities are held by custodians for safekeeping. The securities can be held in either physical form or even electronic form. It is usually the reputable and large firms responsible for the securities and assets since it is not about a few amounts of money but sometimes even billions of dollars. But it is not only the safekeeping of assets that custodians provide, but they also offer some other services like that of transaction settlements, account administration, foreign exchange, and tax support. Based on the services that you are demanding, the fees charged will also be different. Sometimes the total value of the holdings is what determines the quarterly fees of the custodians. The custodian also has the power of limiting your account activity when the beneficiary in question is a minor.

Market Maker

The broker-dealers are known as market makers. They not only maintain an inventory of shares, but they also help in facilitating the process of trading. For any specific set of shares, the liquidity is ensured by the market makers. He/she is also responsible for the profits made in the process.

CHAPTER 2:

How to Approach Investing Trading

While everyone has different goals, the best way to invest is the same today as it's always been. You should invest with an eye toward a long-time horizon. The reality is that speculating with day trading or swing trading leads to losses for most people, probably up to 90% or more of traders. Trading options is also very risky, it's a bet on the directional move of a stock over a short time period, and guess what most people bet wrong. About 85% of options expire worthlessly. Chances are you don't have the free time necessary to stay on top of your trades anyway. Rule#1 is to buy and hold for at least a year. At the end of each year, you can evaluate your holdings and determine whether or not they are profitable and still aligned with your goals, and you might decide to replace some of them. In most cases, you will simply rebalance your portfolio, so that the overall structure of your investments helps to keep you on track for meeting your goals.

Seeking Stocks to Meet Your Goals

There is a wide range of stocks available, and it's important to have some guidelines that you can use to make your picks. Over the decades, investment experts have developed rules of thumb that can be used to decide what stocks to pick. The first factor in determining what stocks to pick is taking a look at your time horizon. Are you looking to reach your goals soon, like by the end of the year? Or are you looking at a time frame that is two years or longer? These are important questions that can be used as general guidelines. Remember that there are no absolute rules here. For example, you could buy a large/ultra-cap stock like Apple, and profit from a short-term swing in price. But Apple would also be an excellent investment for a buy and hold investor who is looking to build up a solid portfolio for retirement. But let's look at the general rules that financial advisors tend to stick by.

General investment strategies:

Conservative:

This means that you have a low tolerance for risk. The amount of money you've accumulated can be a reason for being conservative if you already have a large amount of capital; you probably aren't willing to risk losing it. Some people are conservative investors by nature. A conservative investor is going to stick to investing in large/mega cap and mid cap stocks. Depending on age, a conservative investor may also seek to protect capital by moving some of it out of the stock market and into bonds, treasuries, and money market funds. Conservative investors seek steady growth but aren't necessarily looking for large capital appreciation. The targets for a conservative strategy include a mix of more mature and established companies and some companies that are already quite established, but that may be on the smaller end and poised for some growth. If you are looking to earn income from dividends, you're also going to take a conservative investment strategy. Most conservative investors have a time frame of five years or longer.

Long-term, but high tolerance of risk:

This is a more aggressive approach to investing. You may be willing to hold your assets for 2-5 years or even longer, but you seek rapid growth and appreciation in stock price. In this case, you are going to be seeking to include smaller cap and mid cap stocks in your portfolio. You might also devote a large portion of your investments to companies that might be larger, but poised for rapid growth or market dominance. Tesla could be an example. It's a risky investment because the company can't seem to get its act together. But at the same time, they have a technology that is potentially disruptive. That means Tesla might be worth a lot more five or ten years from now. A conservative investor might not be willing to take that bet, a more aggressive investor probably is. Aggressive investors might also be interested in investing in developing markets. That carries a high risk, but also offers the possibility of greater returns.

Aggressive but short-term time horizon:

If you are looking to make profits over a time span of months to 1-2 years maximum, then you are going to be more interested in speculative moves. That means you'll take positions in stocks hoping to see asset appreciation over the lifetime of your trade. But it's a trade, not an investment. You'll be looking to exit the trade as soon as you can sell your shares to meet your financial goals. This type of investor would be a swing or position trader. You'll be seeking out low priced stocks (relatively speaking) and hoping to buy-low and sell-high if gains in the near-term are expected. The risk is higher but may help people who are cash poor generate funds that can be used for income or to put into long-term investments.

Purely speculative:

If you have a time horizon of less than a year, and seek to generate cash now, then you are a trader and not an investor. This category includes swing traders, who hold positions for a few days to months, and day traders who seek to profit off random movements in share price throughout the day. This category also includes options traders that make money on time frames of one week to a month from the price movements of stocks. Day trading is certainly not recommended. It's a very high risk. Swing trading and options trading can be incorporated into an overall investment strategy if you need to raise actual cash. Some people are also seeking a way to get rid of their day job and devote full-time to the stock market. Trading can help you generate a regular income. However, keep in mind that trading is a high risk, and doing it successfully requires studying and research. Options trading, in particular, can be quite complicated.

Investing for the Future

Remember that over the long term, the stock market always rises. There are downturns, bear markets, and recessions. Sometimes they might last a while. But the long-term trend is always in favor of increasing asset prices.

Investing is a method of securing your financial future by taking advantage of long-term gains. The primary goal is to teach you what you need to know in order to build your financial future. We want to head to a place where you achieve financial independence, and you can retire and have a good income. Building large amounts of wealth may or may not be part of your goals. The main focus should be on financial security. Therefore, long-term investing is preferred over trading and speculating. People who are speculators are looking to make a regular income each month and may be looking to "get rich quick." This is a different mindset than investing.

This doesn't mean you can't use investing to meet short-term financial goals. In fact, you can use a buy-low and sell-high strategy over any time period from a few months out to two years in order to raise capital. This can be done for any reason. Maybe you're hoping to raise money to purchase a home, or to send the kids to college. Working to meet these goals can be a part of a larger investment strategy.

Most of us fit in between these two extremes. The first question to ask yourself, once you've established your financial goals, is how much devotion you have to the stock market itself. Are you interested in being an active participant? Are you willing to devote yourself to keeping a close eye on financial news? If so, you are better suited to be an active investor. A conservative investor who wants to guard their capital is looking for proven investments. If this is your mindset, then you're looking for stable companies that practically guarantee the safety of capital and results, even if the appreciation isn't as high as you could get through other investments. While you are looking to slowly withdraw your money from investments in retirement to fund your lifestyle, you might also be strongly inclined to dividend stocks for income. Conservative investors generally want to spend less time paying close attention to the markets and are willing to hold their investments through thick and thin. They are not concerned with short-term fluctuations and see recessions as buying opportunities.

Aggressive investors are looking for breakouts. They may or may not drift into the realm of speculation. At the very least, an aggressive investor is looking for rapid and strong growth over short time periods. You're probably more interested in keeping daily tabs on the markets. You might closely follow individual stocks and hope to profit from price swings. While you may hold investments for the long term, you're looking for a rapid growth small cap or mid cap stock, or a company with disruptive technology. The innovations your favorite picks have may or may not work out, but the hope is the payoff of one or more of them will be handsome over the long-term if successful. You're willing to take a risk on a small, unknown company that might be the next.

CHAPTER 3:

What Is A Broker?

This is someone who buys and sells goods or things on behalf of someone else. They mostly are middlemen in transactions, that often they make profit out of. They only have to organize and plan for transactions to take place between a purchaser/buyer and a vendor/seller. The broker ends up getting a commission out of the deal, either from the buyer or seller. Most of the time they represent the seller.

Brokers may be individuals or firms. When it is a firm, it still acts as a go between its customer and the vendor.

Brokers exist in many different industries. An example would be real estate brokers who advertise and sell properties on behalf of the owners. We also have insurance brokers who sell insurance on behalf of firms. We have stock market brokers who work on the stock market.

Why Use A Broker?

There are a few advantages of using brokers in any kind of business. As usual, before getting into any business with a broker, always do intensive research on what you are about to get into. There are a few bad crops in the market.

They know their market well

Most brokers are people or firms who have been in the field for quite a while and always know what is best for one client to the other. They also know who to talk to if you need anything specific and always do it well knowing they will benefit.

Brokers have been on the market for a long time and have seen what goes on and know too well what to expect. They have all the information you need right from the time you enter the market to the time you leave. They are particularly important when you are entering a foreign market that you aren't familiar with. You need to take time and look for the perfect broker that will tell you what you need and how to do things the right way. However, you need to be wary of the brokers who are out to exploit you. Use referrals and other methods to try and get the right broker who understands your needs.

Wider representation

A client is able to reach more people or a wide marker when using a broker, compared to them doing it by themselves. Brokers are also quite affordable and have a network they work with; hence there is limited cost incurrence with them. Because most of them are well known, they are able to reach a wider market ratio easily.

When you decide to work with a broker, you get to cast your net wider so that you can get better business. Coming up with a network takes time, which is why it is just right that you work with a person that already has a network that you can tap in. This saves you time and effort, as well as money. Take time to work with a broker that already has a network of established clients.

Special skills and knowledge

Brokers mostly have special knowledge of the field they are in and are good at the specific brokerage area. This is because they work in detail so as to know the needs of different types of clients. Because of this, they are an asset to anyone who is looking for their services.

The skills that a broker has vary from customer relationship management to money management. They will help you to grow your empire as you sit and wait for them to do the work you want. It takes experience and a lot of patience for you to learn the skills and be able to do the things that a broker can do. So, always make use of a broker when making trading decisions.

Customer choice

Brokers always work with the customer's choice. They will always want to know what one needs they will always endeavor to ensure the customer is satisfied and has what they originally wanted, or better.

Time saving

Because they mostly know their trade well, a broker would be able to achieve more within a shorter period of time for the customer. This is because of their great networking within their field of specialization. They always know where to find what, at what time and for what amount.

The time that you save when you work with a broker can be used to handle other tasks that you have. Take time to make sure the broker knows what they are doing otherwise you will end up wasting a lot of time.

Roles Played by Brokers in Day Trading

For a long while, people have been quite skeptical about the Forex market, but this is something that has been growing rapidly in the last few years. Forex trading has become one of the leading markets in the trading world. It generally involves the process of changing one currency to another for certain reasons. Currencies trade against each other depending on the exchange rates and brokers use the growth on these rates to make profits.

Because of this, there has been a high need for Forex brokers who are the middlemen for investors who want to invest in Forex. Forex brokers are usually people or firms that provide currency traders with a platform to buy and sell their currency. They end up controlling a small portion of the large Forex market.

Their importance varies from need basis:

Link between the trader and the market

There are many investors who have a lot of funds and want to grow their wealth in Forex trading but have no idea how to go about it. This is where brokers come in, and act as their representatives in the Forex market. Brokers know all the nooks and crooks of Forex trading, and always know when to take advantage of the exchange rate changes. They are best placed to give advice on how to go about trading, as they are always doing it as a day job hence very experienced.

Brokers always know when to take advantage of the market and the different events that would lead to an increase or decrease in the exchange rate, and hence know when to make the right moves. This they do at a smaller fee, so their aim is to have as many clients as possible so they can thrive on numbers.

Help educate investors or other beginner brokers

Brokers have lots of information on trading than most people would, and it is advisable for any beginner to have one to share tips with them. They would know how to go about avoiding some basic mistakes people make when they start investing in Forex markets.

They trade and negotiate on behalf of investors

Brokers are mostly the same as sales representatives. They trade currencies online, and the skilled ones do it as a daily job hence very useful for any beginner investor.

There are very many investors who want to trade but have no time, hence use brokers who do it full time. The Forex market is a 24-hour business operation and the exchange rates tend to rise and drop every moment. This means anyone trading has to always be on standby to make a move. Brokers do this on behalf of other people who have the money to invest but have no time.

This as times is most ideal as the brokers always know the right moves that bring in profits and in case of losses, they always know the move to make to reduce the amount of losses made.

Advise traders on risks that come with Forex trading

Forex trading, just like any other trading in the stock market, is a risky affair. As it highly involves currency values, there are times that the fluctuations can affect the market and a broker should be keen enough to know the right move to make.

Every investment has pros and cons, which are risks that investors will encounter one way or the other. One might lose more than the value of their transaction, but with a skilled broker to guide you through, you might be able to salvage the situation.

Major risk factors one might encounter:

Exchange rate risk: this is the risk that comes by as a result of changes in the value of the currency. There is a constant shift in the worldwide supply and demand balance, which might end up affecting the traders' position. This mostly depends on whichever way the currencies will move based on different factors. It is in this case where a broker advises one to cut losses early enough by taking different positions. These could be the position limit or loss limit. Other risks include:

- Interest rate risk
- Credit risk
- Country risk
- Liquidity risk
- Transactional risk
- Risk of ruin

Ideas on latest trading platforms

Before you can work with a broker, you need to choose one. Choosing a broker isn't an easy task at all because you have hundreds of brokers to choose from. The best thing to do in this case is to try and make sure you work with referrals and testimonials when making a decision. Based on facts when getting the right broker.

CHAPTER 4:

How to Choose Your Broker

Tech support: It is quite normal if you are new to your broker - that you will have some questions on how to install and operate the software, a.k.a. "The trading platform." There are scores of training videos, articles, webinars, and written instructions either online / in a manual to help you learn to operate the software. It is imperative that you open a practice session (paper trading account) so you can familiarize yourself with all operating aspects of the software and to learn about the services your broker offers. Some of the brokers have 'for fee' services; my advice is that until you gain a lot of experience, you do not sign up for any of those. You will find more than enough to explore and learn without buying additional services. You should try and find answers to your questions by viewing videos and reading instructions as much as you can. When you get stuck, phone your broker and they will get you going again. As a courtesy, it is the custom that you should be as quick and specific as you can when you phone them for help. Brokers usually have a text chat help service also.

Real-Time Quotes Bid/Ask Prices: One of the first things you'll do with your new online account is to build *watch lists*. You simply put in symbols of stocks you wish to follow and the software will give you the bid/ask prices, change for the day, the ability to pull up charts for each stock, ETF, or Index, and more.

Charting-Trading Tools: When you view charts, the horizontal axis will be time/dates and the vertical will display the prices. Begin using bar charts, which display the high, low for various (selected by you) intervals of time, like 1m, 5m,15m, 30m, 1h, 4h, 1d, 1w (minute, hour, day, week.) If you wish, you may learn more about technical indicators and charting in your software. There are a hundred or more indicators, but four or five of them are used most commonly: MACD, Bollinger Bands, Resistance-Support, Momentum, and so on. Your broker will have professionally made videos you can view free – on just about any subject.

Statements and Trade Confirmations: Your daily transaction summary, statements, and confirmation notifications are listed in the program and usually you will receive daily email notifications of your transactions. When you enter an order, you will get a 'fill' the moment a transaction occurs – and usually a sounder to alert you also. The 'fill' is the same as a confirmation and gives you time/date stamp, transactions, prices, and other information. Paper statements are normally sent at the end of each month, but you can get your account status and balance, and a record of your transactions anytime online.

Entering Trades, Buying and Selling: Follow the instructions to enter trades, you will enter the quantity, price, and the type of order you prefer to use. All trading software will allow you to enter an order, and then to check it again before you SEND it; this is to avoid mistakes.

Investment Tracking: In your trading platform that will always summarize your trades, current valuation of them, and list them in an easy to interpret format.

Research Educational Material: Every online broker provides customers with many tools that include charts, news items, research material, and more to help you find the information you need. Anytime you need help, you can ask your broker to suggest videos so you can train to use the software's many valuable features. It will be time well spent. You can use your smartphone or other devices to watch this material on your own convenient schedule. Also, most brokers provide chat rooms where customers can talk among themselves, and this is a way to find ideas and help.

Money Transfers IN & OUT: When you open your account, you may mail a check if you wish. Most commonly, monies are transferred in/out of your account by wire transfers (or an equivalent) directly from your bank. You can call the account services of your broker and they can help you set this up and answer your questions. Be aware, some banks and/or brokers charge varying rates for these services. Ask your broker for suggestions, if you need help in finding the best way for your particular needs. Often, banks have ridiculous fees to make these transfers, so be sure and ask 'how much' before you authorize the transfer.

Choosing a Broker

Online brokers typically charge from $4.95 to $12.95 per transaction (regardless of the number of shares you are trading of a stock.) To be clear: Whether you buy one share or a thousand shares, each transaction will be charged this flat fee. There is one transaction for each security (stock); you can't combine stocks into one order. Often brokers will offer a number of free trades to new accounts, so ask about that when you call.

While brokers who charge $9.95 for a trade are charging almost double the $4.95 rate, it is better to use a broker that has good software, technical service, and is a good fit for you – rather than trying to save a few dollars on stock commissions. You might save $5, but wind up with software you don't particularly like; this is not advisable. *In the long run a few dollars more in commissions here and there should not be a deal-breaker if you get the broker you like.* Where you might pay $9.95 for a trade, you are still getting a good deal since full-service fees easily range from $25 and up.

Here's a partial list of some brokers you may wish to consider; go to their web sites and take a look at their trading platform (most will provide you samples or at least a video).

TD Ameritrade: Think or Swim

Fidelity
Scott Trade

Charles Schwab

ETrade
Option House

Trade King

Often brokers will have more than one version of the software. For example: a simple version for just buying and selling stocks; this version uses the simplest of screen interfaces and is very easy to use. Secondly, most experienced traders will opt for the version (still absolutely free) that has more features. This advanced version offers more flexibility and services. Most companies allow you to use them interchangeably – and you can switch back and forth effortlessly. Ask about this when you phone them.

The Importance of the Trade Simulation Mode

Sometimes, starting off with the more complicated trading software can be off-putting to beginners and they opt for the simpler version until they gain some confidence. Remember that your broker will have a trade simulation mode where you can learn to use the software without having to use real money. Your mistakes there won't cost you anything; this is a valuable service to learn to use the software, so go for it, explore and learn. This can be quite fun to trade paper money until you get the hang of things.

The experience of using a broker's software can vary widely, so you might wish to compare two or three before you decide. The brokers understand this; they help new customers every day. Ask questions, and see how user friendly your new broker will be!

The importance of learning to use the convenience and power of the trading software furnished to you by your broker cannot be overemphasized. Not too long ago, trading 'paper money' accounts, merely kept a list of trades and P/L (profit/loss). Now, you must learn to think of your trading software as your control center of trading and research. Being able to use your software is key to your success; it has powerful features and it will serve you well to spend the time to learn to use it. Your broker has free videos to make learning easy. Viewing several *short* videos works much better than watching hour-long videos – and this avoids information overload. As you are trading it is important to have confidence in your ability to find and use information. Use the trade simulation mode of your broker like a pilot would use a flight simulator. Think of it as a valuable and accurate trading tool and hone your skills with it so you can remain focused on your trading and not have half your attention diluted by not learning to use your software seamlessly. It's actually quite fun to trade in 'paper money' mode. It's a great way to test some ideas and gain confidence and experience without any of the risks.

Don't spend money you don't have...

To Buy things you don't need...

For People you don't like.

-Will Rogers

If you want to feel rich, just count the things you have that money can't buy.

Most Popular Stocks by Demographics :

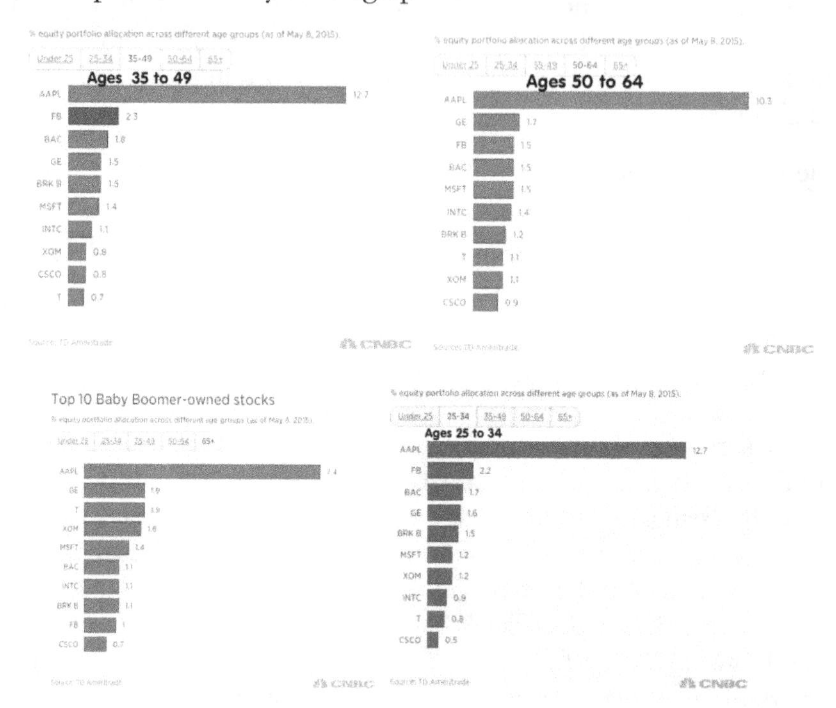

CHAPTER 5:

Choosing the Right Stocks and How Comparing Stocks

Understanding Company Value

New investors may have a gut-level understanding that Apple and Google are valuable stocks. But it's important to really understand what makes a stock valuable. Investing in hunches can produce profits sometimes, but in most cases, it will lead investors sideways or even toward losses. It's important to combine your gut-level feelings about different investments with the cold, hard facts that we can derive from doing analysis.

There are two types of analysis used by professional investors, fundamental analysis and technical analysis. Over the long-term, fundamental analysis is more important. This involves studying the company's "fundamentals" – profit margins, cash on hand, assets, liabilities, trends in revenue, products, and services the company is offering, and management. The company's plans and potential for the future also play a role in fundamental analysis. Companies that may not be profitable now may be strong investments because of the potential. For years Amazon didn't earn any profits, but investors knew it was disrupting the marketplace and was likely to become a giant. A disruptive technology might make a company well placed for future gains. An example of this is Tesla, which is currently going through some rough spots. But it may still be a good investment because over time the technologies the company is developing might turn it into tomorrow's Amazon.

The first way to assess company value is to look at its market capitalization. This is the number of outstanding shares multiplied by the current share price. So, if a company has 1,000 outstanding shares and they are trading at $20 a share, the market capitalization is $20,000. Companies with a high level of market capitalization tend to be more mature, stable, and dominant. They are poised to enjoy a solid long-term future that will bring investors good returns. Examples of companies with large market capitalization include Apple, Netflix, Walmart, and Google.

However, young companies that have lower market capitalization can be great investments as well. Smaller market capitalization is often a trade-off between risk and the possibility of substantial growth in the future. In the late 1990s, people who made that bet on Amazon when it was a relatively small and growing company have been paid handsomely for their decision. However, the risk can be high. There were many "dot com" companies around in the 1990s which seemed as appealing or more appealing than Amazon that don't even exist anymore. It's hard to know with any reasonable degree of certainty which smaller company is going to break out over time. That's one reason why diversity is important, and we'll show you ways that you can take advantage of the growth that young and smaller companies may offer without putting your investments at risk.

Investors will group companies into different categories, based on market capitalization. Values for each category are approximate.

These include:

- Mega cap (also ultra-cap): These are companies with a market capitalization that is $100 billion or more. Amazon has a market capitalization of $932 billion. Other examples include Google, Apple, Netflix, and Facebook.
- Large cap: A large cap company has a market capitalization that ranges between $10 billion and $100 billion. These are stocks that are often sought out by risk-averse investors who are looking for a relatively safe place to put their money and grow it slowly. Large cap companies can represent slow but steady growth over the long term but probably won't provide the same returns that the dominant mega cap companies provide. Examples include General Electric, Duke Energy, and IBM.
- Mid cap: Companies in this category have a market capitalization that ranges in value between $1 billion and $10 billion. These are attractive investments if you are looking for relatively safe investments that still have a lot of growth

potential. To get to this size, a company has to be relatively stable with a solid outlook. Depending on other factors, the company may have the potential to grow so that it becomes a large cap stock, which means a lot of appreciation over time.

- Small cap: These are companies with a market capitalization of less than $1 billion, but more than $250 million. Their smaller size means they have strong potential for growth, but they are also more risky investments. These companies are not large enough to be considered safe. These companies not only have the potential for growth, but they also have the potential for failure. Investors will put their money into small caps to take advantage of the growth potential, but the best way to do that is by using an index fund. Tying yourself to a small number of small cap companies could leave you in a position of losing your investment capital.
- Micro cap: Finally, we have the smallest publicly traded companies. These are companies that have a market capitalization of under $250 million. Investing in a micro-cap company carries significant risk. Of course, the higher the risk, the higher the potential reward. Micro cap stocks are going to be low priced, and if you bet right, you might realize huge profits. The problem is knowing which micro-cap company is going to be the diamond in the rough is pretty difficult, even for experienced traders. If you want to develop a solid investment plan, putting money into these types of companies is probably not something you should consider.

The best investment strategy involves a mixture of Ultra/Large cap, mid cap, and some small cap companies. The investments should be diversified, and the smaller the market capitalization, the more diversity. Your tolerance for risk, age, and investment goals will determine how much risk you should assume.

Aside: Penny Stocks

While we are on the subject of market capitalization, it's important to have a precise definition of penny stocks. The name comes from the old days when you could actually buy something for a dime, and small and risky stocks really traded for pennies. Today, the Securities and Exchange Commission defines a penny stock as any stock that is $5 a share or less. Some penny stocks actually trade on the major exchanges, others trade "over the counter" and are called pink sheets. The bottom line is that you should stay away from penny stocks. It's certainly possible that a company with stock prices this low can turn things around and experience tremendous growth, but that is a rare event. Many hucksters promote "investing" in penny stocks by peddling fake promises of riches. Don't fall for their sales pitches. Most people that try investing in penny stocks end up broke. Professional day traders might be able to make profits from penny stocks, but that is not most people and its high risk. What they do is load up on large numbers of shares and attempt to profit from very short-term price movements, or they will short the stock. Beginning and everyday investors should stay away from penny stocks. They don't provide a way to build wealth over time and trying to earn profits from short-term price movements using penny stocks is a very high-risk activity.

Company Fundamentals

The next factor to consider when picking a winning stock is to look at company fundamentals. This will include having a look at the financial statements of the company, which they are required to make available if they are a publicly traded company on a major stock exchange. These reports will help you analyze the cash flow, assets, liabilities, and revenue of the company. You'll want to use them to determine the company's profitability and outlook going forward.

Company fundamentals don't just involve financial details. You will also want to study the products and services the company offers. This means not only knowing how the company makes money now, but also how it plans to grow in the future. You'll want to know what the company's plans are for new product development and expansion into new markets.

Another aspect of company fundamentals is less tangible but equally important: management. Who is on the management team and what their backgrounds are is an important factor in determining the future potential of a company? You'll want to know their history, experience, and what role if any they played in founding the company. You'll also want to know how the team has performed in the past. Are there members of the management team that played leading roles at other successful companies? That can be a factor that increases your overall confidence in the company.

In short, there are many factors that need to be evaluated when studying company fundamentals. The complete picture is more important than one factor taken in isolation. Part of this process can be education; you can help develop your skills by reading how experienced investors like Warren Buffett evaluate fundamentals.

Price to Earnings Ratio

Price to earnings ratio compares the price of a share to the earnings per share. If a company has solid fundamentals and a high level of earnings per share, a low price to earnings ratio is a signal that the stock is available at a discount. Sometimes investors are behind the times in finding good value, and so the stock will be low priced because of lack of demand. That situation won't last forever, so if you find a stock that fits this description, it can be a good addition to your portfolio. A stock with a low price to earnings ratio is probably well-placed to appreciate in value over time.

Of course, at times the opposite can occur as well. A stock might be overvalued, and this will be indicated by an unusually high price to earnings ratio.

Aligning Stock Picks with Your Investment Goals

As we'll see, it's important to develop an investment strategy that helps you realize your financial goals. You might be late getting in on investing, and so aggressive growth through strong stock appreciation will be more important. Alternatively, you might be looking to build a safe investment income portfolio, preserving wealth and earning an income from it rather than seeking out rapid growth. No matter what your investment goals are, picking stocks that align with your goals is as important as looking at fundamentals and other characteristics like market capitalization.

Do Your Research

Doing your research is important. It will help you pick good companies that are going to help you build wealth. Doing research will also help you determine the best times to enter a position or to exit a position that isn't helping you meet your goals. A winning investor studies the companies they invest in as well as the markets. They also pay close attention to financial, economic, and political news. You need to know how the overall economy and political situation are doing as well because the overall market is often impacted by external events.

Timing Buying and Selling

Keeping an eye on short term trends can help you time you're buying and selling the right way to ensure you get the most out of your financial gains. There are different ways to do that, depending on the situation.

CHAPTER 6:

Tips and Tricks

Mastering the basics of investing is crucial for successful trading. However, there are a few more tips and tricks that beginners may try to improve their investing experience. There are several ways for investors to maximize their investments and get the greatest return possible. Investors may also consider using a 401k, 401b, or IRA to increase their returns. Investors may try a direct stock purchase plan. They may also try a dividend reinvestment plan. Finally, there are a few additional tips and tricks that may help investors to maximize their return and improve their investing experience as a whole.

Maximizing Your Investments

There are several ways that investors may maximize their investments. Of course, practicing proper trading techniques will help investors to earn greater returns on their investments. However, there are several other ways in which investors may maximize their investments and improve the returns on those investments. They may decrease investment costs, increase diversification, rebalance, and practice other techniques to improve their investments. It is important to learn about all the possible ways to maximize one's investments because you don't know what you don't know. Every bit counts. Just saving a bit here and there will quickly add up and maximize the investments.

Investors may maximize their investments by decreasing the cost of investing. There are several ways that investing may cost one money, and that money is coming directly out of the investment. Investors may switch from hiring a financial advisor to doing the investing themselves, cutting the costs of commission. Investors commonly forget about transaction costs. There is typically a flat fee for buying stock through a broker. Instead of making many small purchases, investors may save up and only buy stocks in certain increments (for example, perhaps the investor won't buy more stocks until they have saved $1000). By doing this, a much smaller percentage of the investment is being cut out and used to cover those fees. This may require more patience, but that money will add up. Lowering one's expenses will increase their return. Instead of being spent, that money may be growing and earning a return on it. Because of compound interest, this money will earn money on itself and multiply over a period of years. This is why it's crucial to save every bit possible.

Investors must also really pay attention to their portfolios. Diversification is crucial, and it can save the investor from losing all of their investment. Markets typically fall much more quickly than markets rise. This means that the investor must prepare for such occurrences. It is important to regularly rebalance one's portfolio to ensure that it is positioned correctly for the investor to make the largest possible gains.

Investors must also truly pay attention to what they want. Maximizing one's investments will depend on the person and what their goals are. Although it is wise to listen to the advice of experts and see what other ways that one may invest, it is crucial to follow the path that is best for the goals and preferences of the individual. This is why a plan is necessary and should be followed. Investors must not stop investing. This is another way to take advantage of compound interest. The investor's portfolio should never stop growing. This growth should be due to both growths in the investment and regular contributions by the investor themselves. Despite the great returns that may be experienced in a bull market, contributions are still necessary. Bear markets should also not discourage investors from continuing to invest; this can be a great time to get a good deal on a stock!

Retirement Plans

There are several savings plans that investors can get involved with. These can help to provide the investor with additional benefits that wouldn't be available to them otherwise.

One of these plans is a 401(k). This is a retirement savings plan that will be sponsored by an employer. This will allow the individual to invest their money before taxes so that they can save and invest some of their paychecks. The investor is not required to pay taxes until they withdraw this money from their account. Investors may control how to invest their money. It is common to have mutual funds that contain stocks, bonds, and money market investments. However, there are also target-date funds, which are stocks and bonds that will decrease in risk as the investor nears their retirement age. Unlike individual investing, however, this plan may not offer its users complete freedom. For instance, most employees must work for a company for a certain period of time before gaining access to their payments. Employees may even have to work for the company for a certain period of time before being able to enroll in a 401(k) at all. There are typical costs for withdrawing from these accounts before hitting retirement age as well. There are also contribution limits for each year. Investing for oneself, however, offers more freedom, and there are no limits on investing. For those working for an employer, however, this may be a good solution to investing using the paycheck given. It is a way to utilize the ability not to be taxed on one's investments from their paycheck. Employees may also enroll in Roth 401(k)s, which are not taxed for withdrawals. The better choice will depend on both the employee and the employer, as the plans are taxed differently.

403(b) plans are similar to 401(k)s, yet there are some slight differences. Both offer matching of the investments. For instance, for every dollar the employee contributes, the employer may contribute $0.50. This can prove to be greatly helpful to investors. The major differences between these are the employees that may enroll in these plans. Those in public schools, government jobs, nonprofits, and more may register for this plan. They are not for private-sector workers. Besides this, the plans are identical in their purposes. A 403(b) plan, however, may allow for faster vesting of funds and additional contributions, although the investment options may be less plentiful.

There are also IRA plans. These are plans to save for retirement. These plans have different contribution limits, tax rules, and penalties for early withdrawals. Traditional IRAs are plans that are set up to save for retirement by the individual instead of by a company. The owner of the account will make contributions to the account. To open an account, the individual must have earned income during the year and be under 70.5 years of age. Simple IRAs are set up by small business owners for their employees. Both the owner of the account and their employee will contribute. To open an account, the employee must follow any rules set by their employer. Roth IRAs do not give a tax break when contributing, yet the retirement withdrawals are typically tax-free. Those wishing to enroll in such a plan should research their options. If given the option, the individual should research the pros and cons of their options and decide which will provide them with the best way to reach their goals. Some may not have the option given to them, yet it is wise to educate oneself on where their money is going. This may help to allow the individual to see more ways to maximize their investments.

Direct Stock Purchase Plans

Direct stock purchase plans allow investors to directly purchase stock from the company without the use of a broker. These plans may be available directly to retail investors, yet some companies will use third-party administrators to handle the transactions. They will typically have lower fees and the potential for buying shares at a discounted price. This may not be an option for all companies. These plans may also come with restrictions on when the investor may purchase shares. This plan may appeal to long-term investors that lack the money for an initial investment otherwise.

The investor may choose to sign up once for this plan or they may sign up to make automatic and periodic investments through a transfer agent. This agent will maintain balances and record transactions. To keep costs low, transfer agents will typically carry out bulk transactions for the company each time period that they choose. Direct stock purchase plans are an alternative to using online brokerages, and they will typically cost less. Instead of paying higher transaction fees, the investor may pay a small purchase processing fee for each share that they purchase. These are usually quite a bit smaller than the transaction fees that investors must pay a brokerage. This means that the investor will have more money that they will be able to invest in. Instead of that money going to the brokerage, that money may be invested and generate a return for the investor. This can prove to be a wise move, especially for those wishing to buy a lesser amount of stocks. For those with greater funds for trading stocks, an online brokerage may prove more beneficial for the individual.

Direct stock purchase plans aren't for everyone. They will typically require investors to make a certain monthly commitment (i.e., $100) to investing. On the other hand, investors may buy stocks from a brokerage one time and never buy it again. Investors will also have to pay the market price for their stocks instead of being able to time it themselves. It may also be less convenient to create another account. However, once started, this will be an automatic investment and won't cost as much as it would purchase stocks through a broker.

This plan works by the investor making monthly deposits and those deposits being put towards purchasing shares of the company's stock. New shares (or portions of shares) will be purchased each month based on the amount of money available from deposits and dividends. This is a simple way to acquire shares of a company's stock slowly. This is also inexpensive, as these plans typically have either low costs or no costs at all. They also have low minimum deposits, usually ranging from about $100 to $500, although this may vary. This is a great plan for those who lack the financial power to invest otherwise. A common way that these purchase plans are carried out is by combining them with dividend reinvestment plans. These may be combined with the direct stock purchase plans to maximize the amount that the investor is investing in.

Dividend Reinvestment Plans

Dividend reinvestment plans allow investors to, as the name suggests, reinvest their dividends. These are typically free to sign up for and quite easy to get started in. Investors must simply check a box or click a few buttons to sign up, and the dividends that they earn will go towards reinvesting into shares of stocks. Perhaps the investor gets a dividend for stock x. If they have signed up for DRIP (Dividend Reinvestment Plan), that dividend will go towards shares (or portions of shares) of purchasing more of stock x. This is a great way to manage one's investments automatically. On the dividend payment date, the investor's dividend will go towards reinvesting in that stock.

There are ways to sign up for this through the brokerage that one trades through or through an investment company. Instead of taking out these dividends and spending them, they may be used for greater benefits to the investor. This money can help the investor to make more money.

CHAPTER 7:

How to Use Different Tools

The main tools you'll need for day trading are an online broker and an order execution platform. It goes without saying that you'll also need a very good internet connection and a computer on which to execute your trades on the platform. And if you're not part of a day trading community yet, you'll also need a stock scanner.

The Broker

You'll need a very good broker, who'll be your access to the securities market you plan to day trade in, e.g., the stock market. Take note that your broker can't just be good: it has to be very good. Why?

Since you can't access the stock market or other securities markets directly, you'll need to go through a broker. Even if you choose your SIPs correctly, you can still lose money in your trades if your broker's slow to execute your order at your target price or if their system suffers from frequent glitches.

It can be challenging to choose a broker because there are many of them out there. Some offer top service but are expensive while some charge very low fees but their service is crappy. Worse, some are both expensive and crappy!

Minimum Equity Requirement

The United States Securities and Exchange Commission (SEC) and the Financial Industry Regulatory Authority (FINRA) enforce rules on people who day trade. They use the term Pattern Day Trader to qualify those who can engage in day trading with stock brokerage firms operating in the United States.

The qualify pattern day traders as those who day trades, i.e., takes and closes positions within the same day, at least four times in the last five business days. The SEC and FINRA require that pattern day traders must have a minimum equity balance of $25,000 in their brokerage account before they day trade. When the equity balance falls below this amount for one reason or another, brokers are compelled to prohibit pattern day traders from executing new day trades until they're able to bring their equity back up to at least $25,000.

Many newbie day traders, especially those who only have this minimum amount, look at this rule as more of a hindrance to day trading glory rather than a protective fence against day trading tragedies. They don't realize that it's means to keep them from taking excessive day trading risks that can easily wipe out their trading capitals in a jiffy because of their brokers' commissions and fees.

While this rule is the minimum requirement under the law, many brokers and dealers may use a stricter definition of a pattern day trader for purposes of transacting with them. The best thing to do is to clarify this minimum equity requirement with your chosen broker to avoid confusion later on.

If you can't afford the $25,000 minimum equity requirement for day trading, you can opt to trade with an offshore broker instead. They're brokerage firms that operate outside the United States such as Capital Markets Elite Group Limited, which operates out of Trinidad and Tobago. Because these brokers operate outside the jurisdiction of FINRA, they're not subject to the pattern day trader rule. This means you're also not subject to the same minimum amount.

Direct-Access and Conventional Brokers

Conventional brokers normally reroute their customers' orders, including yours, to other firms through some sort of pre-agreed upon order processing scheme. Thus, executing your orders through conventional brokers involve more steps and can take significantly more time. And when it comes to day trading, speed is essential.

Conventional brokers are often referred to as full-service brokers because they tend to provide customers with other services such as market research and investment advice, among others. Because of these "extras", their commissions and fees are usually much higher than direct-access brokers. Conventional or full-service brokers are ideal for long-term investors and swing traders because they're not as particular with the speed of trade executions as day traders are.

Compared to full-service or conventional brokers, direct-access brokers focus more on the speed of trade executions than research and advisory services. And because they often skip the extra services to focus on providing fast and easy access to the stock market, they charge less commissions and fees. This has earned many of them the alias "discount brokers".

Direct-access brokers use very powerful computer programs and provide customers with online platforms through which they can directly trade the stock market, whether it's the NASDAQ or the NYSE. And while they provide the necessary trade execution speeds required in day trading, they're not perfect and they have their share of challenges.

One such challenge is the imposition of monthly trading volume quotas. If you fail to meet their minimum monthly trading volume, they'll charge you an "inactivity fee", which often serves as their minimum monthly commission from your and all their other clients' accounts. However, not all discount brokerage firms impose inactivity fees.

Another challenge particular to direct-access brokers concerns newbie day traders, i.e., familiarity with direct-access trading. With conventional brokers, all a newbie trader needs to do is tell their broker the details of their orders and the broker will be the one to take care of all things related to executing their orders in the market. With direct-access brokers, the day trader him or herself executes the orders through the broker's online platform or software.

This can be quite challenging for newbie day traders because apart from choosing their SIPs, they also need to know how to execute their orders on the platform properly. But since day trading is a more sophisticated form of stock market trading, the chances are high that newbie day traders have enough experience with direct-access trading already.

The Trading Platform

A trading platform pertains to the computer program or software that you'll use to day trade. This is different from the direct-access broker itself, but many traders make the mistake of thinking they're one and the same.

The trading platform is what you'll use to send your orders to the stock exchange, which the direct-access broker will clear on your behalf. While it's different from the direct-access brokers, it's not unusual for such brokers to develop and have their clients use their own proprietary trading platforms to trade stocks in the exchange.

The number and quality of the features of trading platforms influence the price direct-access brokers charge their clients for their services. The more features a platform has, the higher the commissions and fees may be and vice versa.

A very important feature that you should look for in a trading platform is Hotkeys. Without them, you may not be able to execute trades fast enough to make them profitable. Considering that day trading focuses on stocks with relatively high volatility, being a second or two late can spell the difference of taking and closing positions at the ideal prices and missing out on profitable day trading opportunities.

Real Time Market Data

Unlike long-term investors and swing traders who only need end-of-day price data that's available for free online, day traders need real time data as the trading day unfolds because they need to get in and out of positions within a matter of hours, minutes, or even seconds. And unfortunately, access to real time intraday price data isn't free and you'll need to pay monthly fees to your direct-access broker or the platform owner (if different from the brokerage firm) for them. Just ask your direct-access broker for details on their monthly fees for access to real time day trading data.

Two of the most basic types of data that you'll need to look at as a day trader are the bid and ask prices. The bid prices are the prices at which other traders and investors are willing to buy a particular stock. The ask prices are the prices at which other traders and investors are willing to sell a particular stock.

The bid and ask prices are arranged such that the best price is at the top. The best bid price is the highest one, i.e., the best price for sellers is the highest price at which buyers are willing to buy. It's considered the best price from the perspective of buyers. Bid and ask prices also indicate the number of shares that other traders and investors are willing to buy or sell them at specific prices.

The bid prices are usually listed on the left side while the ask prices are usually listed on the right such that the best bid and ask prices are right beside each other. If you want to execute your buy orders immediately, you "buy up" the best ask price. If you want to immediately execute your sell orders, "sell down" at the best bid price.

The Day Trading Orders

The three most important types of day trading orders are market, limit, and marketable limit orders.

Market orders refer to orders to buy or sell stocks at their current market prices for immediate execution. If you remember from earlier, these refer to buying up at the best current ask price or selling down at the best bid price.

Depending on market conditions and subsequent price movements during the day, market orders may be the worst or best prices to trade in. For example, if you send a market order to sell when the bid-ask prices are $1.00-$1.05 and the by the time your order hits the market, the bid-ask prices shift to $0.95-$1.01, your sell order will be done at $0.95. In this example, your sell proceeds get cut by a minimum of five cents multiplied by the number of shares you sold.

On the other hand, let's say you sent a buy market order when the current bid-ask prices are $1.10-$1.15. If the bid-ask prices change to $1.12-$1.17 by the time your market order reaches the market, you'll end up paying $0.02 cents more for every share of that stock.

Only market makers and professional traders with a lot of day trading expertise and experience can benefit from market orders. For retail day traders like you and me, we should avoid market orders as much as possible. Why?

Stock Pick Scanners and Watchlists

Because there are thousands of stocks that are eligible for day trading every single trading day, it's impossible to manually scan the market for SIPs fast enough to make timely day trades. That's why you'll need to use market-scanning software to short list your day trading choices.

CHAPTER 8:

Profitable Lasts Strategies

Strategy 1

Time Frame

Today many television programs, magazines, newspapers and online articles sensationalize the news. They are in the market of selling their product, not necessarily informing you of the truth. This is obvious in today's political culture; exaggerated one sided story broadcasted to create emotional anguish. This is also true of the stock market news, to lesser extent. Every small move in the market, is presented to you as doomsday! This creates panic that makes you want to tune in and worst has you go in/out of market, when you shouldn't be. The following strategy will help you rules out lots of noise and volatility that may happen every day and instead focus on larger, more significant movements of the security or the market. Of course, if you are a day trader or a very short-term trader, you probably won't want to use this method.

Some stocks have a trend but it's hard to see and when you apply an indicator it is so hard to make sense of it on the chart. The security seems to go all over the chart. It is too erratic to fit any MAVG or a good indicator. GOOG is one such example.

This is a daily chart of GOOG from June 2015-Dec. 2018 with 50-day MAVG. You can see the crossing of the MAVG frequent. If you are using MAVG as your indicator in this example, you will be going in and out unnecessarily and frequently.

Most charts are defaulted as a daily chart. You will find that you can modify chart settings to weekly, monthly or even custom days. In some cases, when you change these settings, it may seem like you are looking at brand new security. You may get a lot clearer view of the behavior of the stock. It may allow all indicators to fall in place.

This is GOOG on weekly chart with the same 50-day MAVG.

You can see this will yield a lot better predictor of a trend; it will cut out daily noise. This will prevent you from going in and out of the security unnecessary. You will also be better able to predict a larger trend and not panic on every move the stock is making.

All securities are different, but if the charts aren't making good trendy sense, try adjusting the frequency to 3-day, weekly, bi-weekly and on occasion monthly (long term 401k funds).

Some of these strategies are contradictory to other strategies. For example, RSI > 80 will tell you to sell but what if at the same time price has just crossed above MAVG then which is the strategy you should follow? That's why it's pertinent that you back-test your performance for each strategy you are implementing, to see historically how many times has the RSI>80 and MAVG crossed the price and which strategy prevailed most of the time. If this happened 50-50% of the time, none of those strategies are reliable. This is critical because some stocks exhibit certain behavior. Not all these strategies may work for you, and not all strategies work on all securities. You really do have to spend some time applying the right strategies, right settings to right security. This will take some time. You may have to tweak some of the strategies. As you get more confidant, you will start to add your own nuance to these strategies or create your own that works for you. But what if you tried several strategies and none of them fit that security? MOVE ON! There are approx. 4,000 stocks you can invest in.

As you get better and understand different indicators and what they mean, you can add multiple strategies to form one strategy. For example, you may only get into the position at crossing of 2 MAVG and RSI is just coming over 30 on a weekly chart but you may sell when RSI > 80. I can write almanac on all different scenarios; I hope this has opened your eyes to various possibilities.

Strategy 2

Stop Buy Order

In earlier strategy, if you are in a position and the market starts to go down, you enter a stop loss order, a price at which you will get out of the position. But what is a stop buy order?

In a stop buy order you are purchasing security when it hits a strike price that is higher than the current price. Once the price hits a specific price outlined on the trade, the stop buy becomes a market order. The buy-on-stop price always is set above the existing market price.

For example, stock XYZ is at $95, I place a stop buy order at $100, when the stock goes from $95 to $100, I will purchase the stock at $100! Uhm mm...why should I wait for the stock to go up to $100, when I can buy the stock at $95 (for cheaper) today? This all depends on your overall plan. We know that many stocks move in trends/consolidate/trends.

For example, this stock is at $45, rises and remains between $60-$65, then rises and remains between $75-$80 and then drops and stays between $65-$70 then rises to $95-$100. At this time, you don't know if the stock is due for a drop or rise, however based on its pattern you assume that if it breaks $100, its due for a climb up. Therefore, you only want to purchase this stock if it breaks the $100 marker!

Another reason could be, that at $100 it is going break a MAVG, and you noticed that once it breaks a MAVG it continues to climb up but if it doesn't then it drops!

Stop buy traders believe this prevents them from buying early in uncertainty, and they are ok with less profit, because they believe it gives them higher assurance.

Strategy 3

Reversal Catch

Nobody has a crystal ball; you will even find brainiest guys/gals arguing on CNBC in a language you don't even understand. Surely, they must know more than you know. They are throwing out terms that are in a foreign language. Follow them; see their picks and you will realize they are wrong half of the times. Hell, you can be right 50% of the time too. When a lot of money is on the line and your emotions are high, you will react more to stock market fluctuation than sticking to your own strategy! You will sell when you are supposed to buy and buy when you are supposed to sell. I advise you to stick to your strategy, with clear buy/sell signals before you enter the position. Let's say you are still wrong, or the volatility of the market, gets you out of the market/into the market and then takes off in the opposite direction! This has happened to me several times. I would own a security, let's say XYZ-$55 and it starts to go down on me, I had clear direction to sell, so I put a stop loss at $50, the price comes down to $49.96, I'm sold out of the position. I stop following it for a while and after 6 mos. I look at the price and it's $150! When this happened a few times, I started to develop a strategy called "Reversal Catch". In this strategy, once I get stopped out, let's say at $49.96, I continue to follow the stock more vigilantly than before!!! To make sure the execution of my trade was not just due to stock volatility but a long-term downtrend, and all my other reason to sell this stock were valid.

If the price is turning on me and headed in the opposite direction I will get back into this position! Yes, I will lose some money since most likely I will now get sold out at $49.96 and will probably buy based on certain other parameters at higher price, possibly like $55. I also won't just randomly get back into the position. One it has to be that I just got stopped out on the volatility of the market and all other conditions are the same. Secondly, I must have a clear reason to enter the position again. At times I will have reevaluate the condition before rebuying the stock, sometimes I will anticipate reversal catch buy price before even selling the stock. I may need to have reversal entry price points to be defined, for example crossing of MAVG, or breaking resistance or another indicator that I was following before I got sold out. It's hard for me to have the exact entry points here, but just know it's ok to lose some money and get back in/out of position than to have the wrong trade executed. Now, you most likely will lose money doing this trade, since you will probably have purchased/sold at the wrong time and you are buying/selling this at higher/lower price than you wanted to. This is ok, especially if this is a long-term position. Even in a semi short term position (1-6 months), this could be ok. Don't be stubborn, if the market turns on you, or you just got sold out at the bottom, don't be afraid to re-evaluate and hop back on even for some short-term loss! Don't sit on the sideline, hoping the market continues in one direction because you are in/out of the position, the market doesn't know when you bought/sold the stock, and frankly the market doesn't care!

Strategy 4

Buy on Dips!

This is a risky strategy! In this strategy, you want to be careful to own ETF or solid stocks, you plan to own. We are going to look at the same "MA" stock as we did in strategy 4. In this strategy, we are going to add to our position every time the stock dips below MAVG. We will be incorporating 40-day MAVG into this chart. Every time stock dips below 40day-MAVG will we be buying or adding to our position. In another words we will be buying on dips when the stock comes down and will accumulate much more at this price. You can see the potential return, following this strategy!

Reason this is a risky strategy, is because if you are buying on dips, what happens when a dip turns into a long-term bear market? This is the reason you want to own ETF or great companies that around for a long time, because you want to be certain that these companies are going to bounce back! Secondly, you want to purchase these great companies at a lower price is because they are a bargain! If you did valuation calculation, you would know if they are a bargain or not! Other cons to this strategy are if the market is going to dip for a while, you must have enough capital to continue to purchase on down market and be able to hold a long time!

CHAPTER 9:

What the Trend Is and How It Can Be Exploited

Traders talk about trends all the time, meaning the short-term ups and downs in stock prices. However, right now, we are going to think about trends outside the stock market. It's important to think about and examine what's going on in society at large to identify trends. The kinds of trends we are thinking about are those that will have a direct impact on the stock market. Over the past ten years, the development and rise of social media were one of those trends. Had you been paying attention; you would have been observing this trend and the rise of the new companies associated with it like Facebook and Twitter. Following that larger trend could be used as a guide for investing. As with anything, you don't want to put all of your eggs in one basket. However, recognizing the trends is an important factor in spotting coming growth opportunities. Had you realized this years ago, you would have made ground-floor investments in these companies, and you would have been able to take advantage of their rapid growth to build your wealth.

There are many types of trends to look for. Changes in demographics are an important trend. The population is becoming older and more Hispanic. Companies that provide products and services for specific demographic groups might have bright futures. In particular, pharmaceutical companies might be something you can look at with an eye to the future because as people age, they tend to need more prescription drugs to stay healthy. Another trend of late is obesity. One side effect of this is more people are becoming diabetic, so investing in companies that have or are developing new treatments for diabetes is something that might be lucrative going forward.

Research and Development

If you are looking for growth, companies that have a strong investment in research and development can be good investments. Apple is a good example – they are always spending large sums of money on developing new products and improving old ones. That ensures that they will have a leading market position, at least for the coming five years. If the company is also in a sector that would be hard for new companies to enter, that is also a plus. It would be hard for a new company to duplicate Apple's overall product line at this time. They would have to have desktop computers, laptops, tablets, and smartphones, among other things like an extensive selection of software products to compete with Apple. That is unlikely to happen, which makes Apple's position more secure than it would be otherwise.

Small caps and Emerging Markets for Aggressive Growth

It's possible to get solid and even very high returns investing in established companies. As we've seen, some exchange-traded funds that invest in major stock indexes can provide very high growth rates. However, if you are seeking the most aggressive type of growth possible, you'll be interested in small cap stocks as well as looking into emerging markets.

Let's take the latter first. If you are interested in emerging markets, it's strongly recommended that you utilize exchange-traded funds. This will save you from a lot of hassle. Doing it directly and on your own can create a lot of problems. First of all, you need to realize that in other countries you won't have the same protections that you have in the United States or a country like Great Britain. There are also other issues to worry about, such as currency exchange. You can avoid these problems by seeking out exchange-traded funds that invest in the countries you are interested in – and let the company managing the fund deal with all the headaches.

Remember that high returns usually correlate with increased risk. That said, you can find funds investing in emerging markets that have remarkable returns. For example, an iShares fund that invests in Russian companies sees 30% returns – at least for now. When an economy is still developing, it has more room to grow. But things are also less stable, and you never know when political developments could cause things to crash. Results vary. Some funds for developing markets don't even perform as well as funds investing in the S & P 500, and some even have negative returns. But if you need some rapid growth, it's something to consider.

Small caps provide the opportunity to get in early on a younger company with a lot of potential for growth. At one time, Netflix, Amazon, and Microsoft were small, unheard of companies. People who got in on these companies early were able to generate amazing amounts of wealth.

However, if you find small caps intriguing, keep in mind that the risk is high. A small proportion of small caps will grow large and be tomorrow's dominant companies. Most, however, won't do anything more than stay where they are. In fact, many of them are going to end up liquidating and going out of business. Others will do OK but never really take off.

This leaves us with two choices. We can try picking the winners ourselves, or we can invest in small cap exchange-traded funds to get some exposure to the growth without tying ourselves to an individual company. The fact is, investing in small caps is more speculative. Nobody has a crystal ball, and while it's easy to see the inevitability of a Microsoft or Apple in hindsight, at the time knowing which companies would go on to be tomorrow's giants is nothing more than making educated guesses. You also might be a little disappointed by the returns available from small cap funds, because another cold truth is that most small cap companies are not growing rapidly. If you do decide to invest yourself, be sure to carefully pick your companies, and invest in several of them so that your boat is not anchored to a single company that may turn out to be a bust. To be perfectly honest, the odds that you are going to pick a winner for tomorrows markets are pretty slim.

IPOS

People are also excited about investing in IPOs. That's a bad idea as well. You can keep an eye on companies that have IPOs, but more often than not company IPOs start on a high note and then sink. It's better to let things settle out for a year or two before deciding to invest in a company that recently went public. Remember that as a long-term investor, you are looking at five, ten, and twenty-year time horizons. So, it's not in your interest to be seeking out get rich quick opportunities.

Diversity

When it comes down to it, whether or not you are aggressive or conservative, the old rules of diversification and dollar cost averaging are the best rules for you to follow. If you stick to these rules, and invest consistently, over time, you are going to build wealth.

Rebalancing

At the end of each year, many investors engage in rebalancing. At the start of the year, you might have a portfolio with specific asset allocations to meet your goals. Say, for the sake of example, you had 65% in growth stocks, 25% in value stocks, and 10% in income securities. At the end of the year, the proportions might have changed because some stocks grew faster than expected, and some grew more slowly than expected. You might find at the end of the year you have 70% in growth stocks, 20% in value stocks, and 10% in income stocks. Maybe you will be satisfied with the change, but if you are set on keeping your portfolio within certain bounds, you will engage in rebalancing at the end of the year. This means buying and selling shares of different asset classes to maintain the percentages you seek. So, in the example that we've specified, you would sell some of your shares in growth stocks, and use the proceeds to buy more value stocks so that you kept your overall portfolio at 65% in growth stocks, 25% in value stocks, and 10% in income.

CHAPTER 10:

Set Your Budget

Sticking to a budget and living within your means – is proper money management. Look for great price bargains and avoiding bad deals when purchasing. When you start earning more money, understanding how to invest will become an essential way of reaching your goals like having down payment for a home. Understanding the importance of excellent money management will help you achieve your plans and future goals. The importance of Money Management is:

Better Financial Security

Being cautious of your expenditures and saving, you will be able to save enough for the future. Saving will give you financial security to deal with any unexpected expenses or emergencies like loss of employment, your car breaking down or even saving for a holiday. Having savings, you will not have to use a Credit card to settle crises. Saving is a crucial part of money employment as it helps you build your financial security for a secured future.

Take Advantage of Opportunities

You may encounter opportunities to invest in a business to make more money or an exciting experience like a good deal on a holiday vacation. A friend may inform you of a great investment opportunity or get a great once-in-a-lifetime dream holiday vacation. It can be frustrating not having the money to jump right to these opportunities.

Pay Lower Interest Rates

With excellent money management skills, you can determine your credit score. The highest score means you pay your bills on time and with low-level total debt. Having a higher credit score, you can save more of what you have and have a lower interest rate for car loans, mortgages, credit cards, and even car insurance. And there is the chance to brag to your friends about your high credit score at the parties.

Reduce Stress and Conflict

Paying your bills on time can have a relieving feeling. But on the other hand, being late in paying your bills cause stress and have a negative impact like shutdown in your gas and water supply. Always being broke before your next paycheck can bring conflict and, a significant amount of stress for, couple. And, as we all know, stress brings health problems, experts say, like hypertension, insomnia, and migraines. Being aware of how you can manage your finances, so you have extra cash and savings can put your mind at ease. You will enjoy a stress-free life.

Earn More Money

With your income growing, your financial planning will not only include budgeting for monthly expenses but also figuring out where to invest the extra cash that has accumulated. Knowing different kinds of investments for example stocks and mutual funds, you can earn more money from the investments than what you could have made by leaving the money in your savings account in your bank. But be aware not all investments are recognized as a good investment idea, for example, offshore casinos. One of the best benefits of having investments, you can be at work earning monthly income, and your investments, on the other hand, are making more money for you.

More saving and time

Excellent money management can assist in avoiding your finances from spiraling out of control. It is easy to be in debt if you are unaware of how all your income it's spent monthly. Effective money management means better use of your spare time. You can spend time with your family and friends, by having a clear budget; you will be able to plan for fun days out as you will have available cash to do so.

Peace of mind

Excellent money management gives you some level of calm and peace of mind. With your income and the savings, you can handle any financial demands with the confidence that you have the resources to handle any need that will arise.

Best Money Managers

When developing your investment strategy, you will find yourself seeking some assistance. A well-chosen money manager can help you achieve your financial goals. Research is vital, find the right money manager who will be the perfect fit for your financial goals. There is a lot of information you can get to be able to find a money manager. You can rely on referrals, the internet, or financial companies to get the right money manager for you. In this segment we will go through what a money manager is. How does it work? What is the difference between a money manager and a financial advisor? What is the role of a money manager? What are the pros and cons of having a money manager? And what are the fees required?

Who is a Money Manager?

A money manager, also known as investment managers or portfolio managers. It's an individual or a firm which manages investments portfolio and provide personalized financial advice to an individual or institutional investor. Money managers offer advice to clients about the steps they should take to increase their returns.

How does it work?

Money managers earn a fee for their services and not a commission. In some cases, a client will pay a percentage of the managed assets to their money manager. In this way, both the client and the money manager will work hard towards the success of the portfolio. Here is an example illustrating how money managers work:

Suppose Mary has $20,000 and she wants to invest the money. She will find a money manager to manage her new portfolio. Then she schedules a meeting with the money manager. The money manager inquiries about Mary's investment goals, the risk if the investment is a short-term or long-term, etc. Based on Mary's feedback, the money manager will choose a set of securities that will help Mary achieve her financial goals. The money manager will monitor Mary's portfolio on a monthly fee basis, the performance and the value of the portfolio.

What's the difference between a money manager and a financial advisor?

When it comes to your finances, doing it alone can be intimidating as you try to understand the game plan. You need to find the right professional to assist you in meeting your goals.

A financial advisor and a money manager have a lot in common, the two jobs are different, and they can't be handled by one person. A financial advisor is also known as wealth managers. A financial advisor understands the specifics of the client's economic life and creates a detailed investment plan, that is also known to help the client meet their financial goals. A money manager focuses on managing the strategy your portfolio is invested in.

The role of a money manager:

A good money manager focuses on successfully managing your portfolio strategies, and should be able to meet the following expectations:

√ To consistently manage investments portfolio with their stated investment objectives

√ Appropriate risk management

√ Avoid unnecessary turnover within the management team

√ Operate transparently

What are the pros and cons of having a money manager?

When you have a financial goal, you want it to be a success. One of the ways to achieve that is by getting an expert to help you achieve your goals. Do you have some savings which you are thinking of investing? Then you need a money manager for you to achieve your goals of investing. You need a trustworthy and focused money manager. Consider a lot of things before hiring one. To be able to make the right choice, here are some of the pro and cons of having a money manager:

The pros:

Your money manager knows the financial environment

Your money manager can assist you in constructing an income statement and help you understand the market competition. With a great money manager, you can get an excellent customized financial plan and gain essential insights that will help you in your journey.

Your financial manager will make sure your money financial wisely

If there was ever a time that you needed to make sure that your cash made the most significant impact, it's now. With a strained economy, there is no room for errors. Your money manager will assist you in avoiding the risks and make sure your money it's spent in a way that will bring the best returns. Wondering whether to expand? If you are also thinking of increasing your investment, a money manager makes the smartest and best-informed decisions and assists you with any questions that you might have.

A money manager will free up your time to do what's most important

Your money manager will take away the stress of financial oversight, and this allows you to focus on other vital parts of life.

Your money manager can help your business function well

If you run a business, the money manager can help you with your business. To find out why invoices taking too long without getting paid, why your business is losing cash, and you are not sure where the wastage is happening. The money manager can implement control measures that allow you to easily track your money movement.

The cons:

Your money manager could be expensive

The main reason for not hiring a money manager is the cost! Your concern is a valid one. Money managers are highly qualified and experienced and usually request higher charges. Who can afford an expensive money manager when you have come a long way without him or her up to this point? The solution here is to do your research to get an affordable money manager who will give you the best quality results as well.

Performance Not Guaranteed

Although your money is managed professionally by the money manager, there are still no guarantees. In a bad market day, even the best money manager may lose money.

Lack of Control

You might not have the time or the knowledge to wisely invest your money; it will not be 100% comforting to some people to hand over control of their money to a stranger.

CHAPTER 11:

Start to Investing Step-By-Step

Investing in the stock market is not as hard as you think. Here are a few steps that you need to follow to get started:

Step 1: Understand the Difference between Stocks and Stock Mutual Funds

Many people think that stock market investing is a complicated animal. Well, not really. You just need to understand the two investment types, namely:

Exchange Traded Funds (ETF) or Stock Mutual Funds

Stock mutual funds allow you to buy small pieces of different stocks in one transaction.

ETFs and Index Funds are stock mutual funds that allow you to track an index and replicate it. For example, the S&P's 500 fund replicates the "Standard & Poor's 500" index.

So, if you decide to invest a little bit of your money in an "S&P's 500" fund, you'll own a little piece of all the companies in it (the size of that piece depends on your investment budget). You can't choose which stock to invest in.

The upside of investing in ETFs is that it is cheaper. It's also *a great way to diversify your stock investments without spending a fortune.* However, the downside of this investment type is that it doesn't allow you to choose specific stocks to invest in. This brings us to the second investment type.

Individual Stocks

You need to invest in individual stocks if you're after a particular company. For example, if you really want a piece of Facebook, you need to buy a few FB stocks on Nasdaq.

You can also build a diversified portfolio out of several individual stocks, but you'd need to have a lot of money to do this.

Step 2: Identify Your Investing Style

You can invest in the stock market in a number of ways. You can invest in employer-sponsored accounts such as the 401(k) plan. You can directly purchase stocks or you can ask a financial advisor to manage your investments.

It's best to invest in a 401k Plan if you're on a budget and you're still working. But, if you're planning to invest a huge amount of money in the stock market, it's best to open a brokerage account or ask a professional money manager to manage your investment.

If you're not really a "hands on" investor, it's best to invest in mutual funds, index funds, or ETFs. But, if you want to choose stocks yourself, then opening a brokerage account is the best option for you.

Step 3: Set a Budget

Before you start investing money in stocks, you must set a budget. How much money are you willing to invest? Remember that the amount of money you need depends on how much the shares cost. Some stocks cost a few dollars, while some shares can cost thousands of dollars.

Step 4: Open a Stock Investment Account

You need an investment account in order to invest in stocks. You can open a 401(k) account through your employer or you could open an IRA (individual retirement account). You can also open a brokerage account if you're more of a "hands on" investor.

As mentioned earlier, you can open an investment account with your employer. But, if you decide to open a brokerage account, you should consider the following factors:

Account Minimum

A lot of brokerage firms require a minimum initial investment of $500 or more. If you plan to initially invest just a few hundred dollars on the stock market, you should choose brokers that do not require minimum investments, such as Merril Edge, TD Ameritrade, and Ally Invest.

Commissions

If you decide to invest in individual stocks, you'll have to pay for per trade commissions (usually between 4 to 7 dollars). You should choose a broker with minimal trade commission rate, especially if you're a beginner.

Trading Style

If you're new to stock market investment, you probably don't need advanced trading platforms. But you may want to choose a brokerage firm that offers educational tools like tutorials, videos, and even seminars.

High volume traders, on the other hand, need state-of-the-art trading platforms and analysis tools.

Account Fees

Most brokerage firms charge account fees such as annual fees, transfer fees, trading platform subscriptions, research fees, market data payments, and inactivity fees. It's best to choose a firm that offers free market data and research services and charges minimal account fees.

Step 5: Start Investing

Once you've opened an account, you can start investing using different strategies, such as value investing, growth investing, income investing, socially responsible investing, diversification, and more.

401(k) Plan

The 401k plan is a retirement plan that companies offer to their employees as part of the benefits package. It is one of the most common retirement savings accounts. It was created in 1978 through the 401(k) of the Internal Revenue Code. That's why it's called the 401(k) plan.

The best thing about the 401k plan is that it allows you to save on tax payments. It also allows you to take advantage of your employer's retirement contribution through the "employee matching gift" program. This program is usually offered as an incentive to prevent attrition and encourage employees to stay with the company for a long period of time.

Here's how it works. Let's say that you work in a tech company that sponsors 401k plans and you earn $150,000 a year before taxes. You agree to put 6 percent of your income, which sums up to $9000. This contribution is tax deferred. This means that you don't have to pay taxes for your contribution until you retire (you'll be in a lower tax bracket when that time comes). This means that your taxable income at the moment is $141,000 (your annual income minus your annual contribution).

As a part of the matching gift program, your employer agrees to match $0.50 for every dollar you put into your 401(k) plan. So, the company puts an extra $4500 ($9000 x 0.50 cents). This means that your total contribution is $13,500 a year. See the computation below.

Employee contribution ($9,000.00)

+

Employer contribution ($4,000.00)

Total Annual 401(k) contribution ($13,500)

What Happens to Your 401(k) Contribution?

The money invested in your 401(k) account is usually invested in stocks, bonds, and mutual funds. When you sign up for this program, you'll be provided with a list of stocks that you can invest in.

You must consider your age when choosing the right stocks to invest in. If you're still in 20s, it's okay to take a little risk. You can invest in volatile tech stocks like Netflix, Facebook, and Amazon.

But, if you're already in your late 30s, 40s, or 50s, it's best to go with more stable companies like Hormel Foods Corporation, Costco Wholesale, Cigna, and American Water works.

When you decide to quit your job, you can move your 401(k) plan to an IRA (individual retirement account). You can also rollover your existing plan to your new company's 401(k) plan. But you have to take note that not all companies accept retirement plan rollovers, so it's best to check with your new employer.

You can withdraw your 401k money even before you reach your retirement age, but the IRS (Internal Revenue Service) will have to collect a ten percent early withdrawal penalty. This may not seem much if you saved $3000. But, if you already saved a million dollars, you'll have to pay a bigger penalty.

How to Invest in 401(k) Plan

The 401(k) plan is an employee sponsored plan. This means that you have to do it through your employer.

Here's how you can invest in the 401(k) plan:

- When you get hired, choose to be part of your company's 401(k) program.
- Decide how much of your income you want to go to your 401(k) plan.
- Choose the stocks that you want to invest in.
- Check your application and then, submit it to your employer.

At this point, you don't have to do anything else. Your employer will automatically deduct your contribution from your salary. Your company also manages your investment fund, so you don't have to worry about anything.

401(k) Plan vs 403(B) Plan

Like 401(k), 403(b) is also a retirement plan set up by an employer. But the main difference is that 401(k) is offered by private and for-profit employers, while 403(b) is offered by non-profit employers, such as the government or non-profit schools.

If you work as a graphic designer in an advertising agency, you'll have the option to invest in a 401(k)-retirement plan. But, if you work for a government agency, your employer will most likely offer a 403(b)-retirement plan.

401(k) vs. 403(b)

401 (K)	403 (B)
Retirement plan offered by private for-profit companies	Retirement plan offered by non-profit organizations, such as religious groups, government organizations, and non-profit schools.
Higher administrative costs	Lower administrative costs
Has a maximum contribution limit	Has a maximum contribution limit
Has limited investment options usually selected by your employer or a financial management company	Account holders can invest in a wide variety of annuities and mutual funds

Has an employer matching program	Has an employing matching program

Pros and Cons of the 401(k) Plan

The biggest advantage of the 401(k) plan is that it comes with matching funds. So, you'll get a lot more money than you put in. Let's say, you committed to saving $7,000 a year and your company matches your contribution and also deposits $7,000 to your account each year. This means that you'll have a total annual savings/investment of $14,000. Amazing, right?

The 401(k) plan is also hassle-free. You don't have to manage your investment account. It has high contribution limits and it's protected by the ERISA or the Employee Retirement Income Security Act of 1974.

But, the downside of the 401(k) plan is that it has limited investment options. This means that you can only invest in specific stocks and bonds.

IRA

Joy is a hard worker. Although she didn't finish high school, she found a stable job. She worked as a warehouse manager for thirty long years. The pay is good, but she ended up spending all she got. When she finally retired, she only saved up $10,000, which only covers a few months of her living expenses. Her pension benefits are simply not enough.

Unfortunately, Joy's story is not unique. More and more retirees are broke. To avoid ending up like Joy, it's best to invest in an IRA.

IRA or individual retirement account is a tax-advantaged investment and a savings account that allows you to save for retirement.

There are different types of IRA, namely – traditional IRA, Roth IRA, Simple IRA, Spousal IRA, nondeductible IRA, SEP IRA, and self-directed IRA.

CHAPTER 12:

Building Your Portfolio

Benefits of Diversification

By reducing your exposure to risk, you can increase your profitability. One of the best ways to do this is by diversifying your investment portfolio. By diversifying your investment portfolio, you stand a chance to maximize the returns from your investments. Did you ever come across the saying, "Never place all your eggs in one basket?" Well, this applies to investments as well. Instead of parking all your funds in one type of investment, you must invest in different instruments. You never know the way a specific asset might perform, and uncertainty cannot be entirely removed when it comes to investing. However, there are certain things you can do to reduce this uncertainty. The basic idea of diversification is to invest in different types of financial instruments. By doing this, you are reducing your risk of losing money. There are two types of risks you must be wary of while investing. These risks are undiversifiable and diversifiable risks. Undiversifiable risks are also known as systematic risks, and it is inherent to all companies. There are different factors that cause this risk like inflation, interest rates, exchange rates, country's economic position, and even political stability. Undiversified risks cannot be entirely eliminated, but you can certainly reduce your exposure to this risk.

Diversifiable risks are unsystematic risks and are associated with specific companies, markets, or economies. The two factors that cause this type of risk are financial risks and business risks. You can tackle diversifiable risk by ensuring that you don't invest all your funds in the same kind of assets. Different assets and financial instruments react differently to different circumstances. By ensuring that you have a variety of investments, you are reducing your risk exposure. For instance, let us assume that you have an investment portfolio that comprises of airline stocks. If all the airline pilots go on a strike, then your entire portfolio will crash. You will experience a significant setback in this instance.

However, if you have a diversified portfolio, and have some railway stocks too, then the airline industry strike will not destroy your entire portfolio. An event that might have an adverse effect on one type of investment can be beneficial for another. So, by investing in different forms of investments, you are covering all your bases.

Please make sure that you not only invest in different types of companies but diversify the industry you are investing too. The way stocks react to the market conditions is quite different from the way bonds react. A combination of different types of assets will help reduce your portfolio's sensitivity toward the market. If you have a diversified portfolio, then even if one of your investment sustains a loss, the others will be fine. Diversification helps reduce your risk exposure. Even if you spend hours on end pouring overall data and statistics available, you will not be able to predict with certainty the way the market will behave. Since the forces of demand and supply control the financial markets, no one can accurately predict the market's behavior. For instance, even if all the data shows that the market will be bearish; one small change can turn the bearish market into a bullish one.

Now, you might be wondering about the number of stocks you must include in your investment portfolio. It is always better to invest in five different types of stocks than holding onto one. However, as you reach a certain point, it doesn't make any sense to keep diversifying your portfolio. There is a constant debate about the number of investments you should hold onto. When you are investing in the stock market, as a rule of thumb, don't exceed 15 to 20 types of stocks spread across different industries. Diversification will undoubtedly help to reduce the volatility as well as the risk associated with a specific instrument. It doesn't mean that you go overboard and try to include all types of assets you possibly can. Please understand that it is not just about diversification but also about portfolio management. If your portfolio is too diverse then managing it will become rather tricky. Every type of investment that you add to your portfolio must be something that you can handle. If you keep adding investments that you have no idea about or investments that you don't understand, you are increasing your exposure to risk. For instance, if you don't know how the options of the derivatives market works but you have a couple of these investments in your portfolio, then you are setting yourself up for a potential loss.

When it comes to investing, knowledge is your best friend. The more knowledge you have about specific investments and industry, the better decisions you can make. So, in your bid to diversify your portfolio, don't go overboard. You must curate your investment portfolio such that there exists a perfect balance between the risks and the returns involved. You will learn about specific rules that you must keep in mind while building an investment portfolio.

Check Your Goals

Before you can start building the perfect portfolio for your investments, it is quintessential that you understand your goals. You must consider different things like the quantum of the funds you will need along with when you need them. If you are focusing on a long-term goal like saving for your retirement, then you can consider adding certain volatile investments to the portfolio. If you are looking for short-term investments, then adding volatile instruments will only increase your risk. If you have a fixed income, then please be careful while making any investments. Different factors that you cannot control like inflation or a country's financial state can influence the profitability of your investments. If you have specific long-term financial goals, then you can hold onto long-term investments. For instance, if you're saving for your child's education, then it is a good idea to invest in zero-coupon bonds or other low-risk investments.

Your Risk Tolerance Matters

There is some risk that is involved when it comes to investing. Even with a diverse portfolio, you can't reduce the risk; however, you can balance this risk. Even certain investments that are considered to be risk-free like treasury bills or even blue-chip stocks have a certain degree of risk involved. If you cannot afford to lose money and need funds for meeting a short-term requirement, then the best investment to look at would be a savings account or a certificate of deposit. The rate of return and the risk associated with the investment are directly proportional in most cases. The riskier an investment is, the greater are the returns it offers. However, if you don't have a high-risk tolerance, then it doesn't make any sense to opt for high-risk investments. Keep in mind everything that you learned about the diversification of a portfolio while investing. According to your goals and your risk tolerance, you must develop your investment portfolio.

Different Type of Assets

There are various types of financial assets you can invest in. By now you will have realized that there is more to investing than just bonds and stocks. A great way to reduce the volatility of the portfolio is by investing in different types of assets. Adding some alternative assets like real estate or even commodities like gold can help reduce volatility. If you are willing to take on a little risk, then alternative assets are a great way to invest, especially during the times of inflation. For instance, if you have any investments in real estate and the price of real estate skyrockets during inflation, you can make a small fortune from it. If you don't like the idea of taking on such risks, then opt for investments, which are market neutral. Apart from this, please make sure that your portfolio consists of investments with varying degrees of liquidity. You might never know when you will need funds. So, having a couple of investments with high liquidity will come in handy.

While you're creating your investment portfolio, there are certain things that you must avoid at all costs. Please never invest based on fact. If you're investing based on a current trend, you might not make the right decisions. What might work for someone else might not necessarily work for you. A current trend will pass you by, and if it doesn't work out favorably, you end up losing your hard-earned money. When it comes to investing, you cannot make investments and then forget about them. You need to monitor them constantly. Yes, you can earn money passively, but if you want to be a successful investor, you need to monitor them actively. There are certain investments like treasury bills that don't need constant monitoring. However, certain other types of investments like stocks need to be constantly monitored, especially if you are involved in day trading. You must make it a point to keep updating your investment portfolio. As your needs or goals change, change the investments in your portfolio. If you notice that something doesn't work for you, get rid of it and don't let it stay for longer than necessary.

CHAPTER 13:

How to Understand and Analyzed Charts

A stock chart is a pictorial representation of information which enables a stock market trader to see at a glance how stocks are behaving. The ability to read charts is an essential skill of anybody who wants to trade at the stock market. There are various kinds of tables that you can use in the stock market. This highlight and explains some of the stock charts available in the market, the importance of charts, and how to read them.

Types of Stock Charts

There are various kinds of stock charts. These include:

1. Line charts-the line chart comprises of one line drawn from left to right. This line is used to link different closing prices. Through this chart, a stock market trader is able to see the historical and present trends in pricing.

2. Candlestick charts-the candlestick chart is a typical chart that is applied by many stock market traders. These include a pictorial presentation of data by capturing opening, peak, and closing pricing information at any specific time. The candle is composed of the body, the upper and lower tails.

3. Bar charts-these charts are also called open-high-low-close (OHLC). They resemble the candlesticks, although they don't contain any candles.

4. Point and charts-they only focus on essential price movements. Through these charts, it's simple to follow the price trends.

The Importance of Using Stock Charts

As a stock trader, it's crucial to understand how to read stock charts. There are various benefits of using this pictorial presentation of data. These include:

1. Provision of patterns-the stock charts will show patterns of how a specific stock has been behaving. These patterns are used to predict the future of that stock and an investor can make a decision whether to trade in that stock. Candlestick charts are essential as they provide information on price trends, which helps the trader to evaluate when to trade or exit the market.

2. Trading volumes and prices-the stock charts will indicate the prices and quantities of a specific stock. This information is helpful in assisting a stock trader in evaluating whether investing in that stock is beneficial or not.

3. Past and current price forecasts-before you make any investment decision, it's essential to assess the past and present prices of that particular stock. When you understand the historical and present pricing of the capital, you can easily predict its future pricing. This will, in turn, assist you in making a sound decision.

4. Time entry points-the charts can help the stock trader to understand the best timing to buy the stock. The graphs assist you to know the demand and supply aspects that will enable you to make an informed decision before you act.

How to Read Stock Charts

There are various tactics that you can utilize to read a stock chart and make sensible decisions. What you need to discover is that the charts have much information that is presented pictorially. You need to find this information by reading the chart like a pro. This gives you helpful tips on how to read charts like a pro.

1. White backgrounds and black candlesticks-these kinds of pictorial presentation offers you the simplest way of establishing patterns. According to research, traders who

apply white backgrounds accompanied by black candlesticks have around 25% higher chances of making gains.

2. Golden mean-it's vital to ensure that the candlesticks have the right height and width dimensions for simple reading.

3. Importance of historical information-as you pay attention to the current data on your candlestick, it's equally significant to pay attention to the historical data as revealed by the candlesticks. It's sad that many traders do not pay attention to historical data and end up not establishing patterns. You need to ensure that you read the historical data provided by the candlestick.

4. Apply modern charts - it's vital to desist from applying the traditional charts that are not helpful, and some have become obsolete. The current charts will show you patterns and will help you to make decisions fast.

5. The top of the chart - you will find much information at the top of each graph. For instance, you will see the highs and lows of different stocks. At the top, you'll also encounter the volume of the shares that were traded.

6. The price chart - on the stock chart; the price of the share is found in the middle of the graph. A line or small bars can represent this. You need to read this line or bars keenly as you'll get much information.

7. Price trends - it's simple to establish trends through the movement of the lines or bars. In case the line moves upward toward the right, that is an indication that the stock has an upward price trend. When the line is not showing any movement, you should realize that the stock is stagnant, and the factors of demand and supply are not pushing it.

8. Support and resistance - Support and resistance can be seen from the way the stock is moving. In this regard, you'll see a trend where the stock moves near a specific price and then bounces back many times. The rate at the lower part is called support price. The price on the upper side, on the other hand, is called resistance price. It's essential to be keen on

support and resistance aspects. This is because when the price moves beyond resistance, there is likelihood that that stock will be registering a rise in the price.

9. Volume - Volume usually is shown by a bar graph. It's is essential to read volume keen because it offers you information about the demand and supply of a particular share. For instance, when you see the volume rising, it means that the stock is sold a lot, and investors are offering the best prices. A decline in the size of the shares sold, on the other hand, implies that the demand for the stock is falling.

10. Moving average lines - the moving average offers you information on the movement of a share over a particular time. The average lines indicate the vibrancy with which a specific stock is sold.

Through stock trading, you can reap good profits within a short period. However, to benefit from this market, one must possess specific skills. This blog has highlighted and elaborated some of the necessary skills that you need to maintain to trade successfully and reap big from the market. Additionally, the blog has offered you essential tips on how to read the stock charts.

CHAPTER 14:

Risk in Stock Investing and Diversification

Risk and Volatility

Investing is wrought with risks and they can happen at any time. As an investor you need to be aware that you will be facing different types of risks at all times. In fact, the only investments thought to be without risk are fixed income assets like bonds.

Fortunately, risks can be managed. There are some risks that you can handle but there are others that are beyond your control. You can only guard against those beyond your control. However, as an investor, you need to determine your risk level and if you do this correctly, then your investment risks will remain at generally acceptable levels.

There are certain risks that we can do nothing about. These are risks that perhaps affect an entire industry and sometimes even the whole market. Such risks demand investors to take certain actions such as adjust their portfolios or simply ride out and weather the storm.

There are certain risks that are considered major by the investing community. They can be categorized into four distinct groups. Fortunately, finance experts have invented ways of managing these risks so they have minimal effect on your investments.

1. Risks Posed by the General Economy

The general economy poses a major risk to investments because it can tank at any time. Think about the terror attacks of 2001 and the market crunch of 2007. All these pose a huge risk to investments and if not properly managed could cause huge losses. When the economy falls, most indexes follow suit and it takes them months to recover. Therefore, always be wary of the general economy. When the economy is doing well, then your investments will follow suit and will thrive.

However, the reverse is also true because a falling economy will drag down the value of the stock market.

If you are a young investor, then one of the options you have is to wear out or ride out the economic downturn. Such moments are the best to buy into a solid company. Think about blue chip companies. If you are able to buy into strong companies such as major banks, telecommunication firms, multinationals, and so on, then you will be able to weather the storms and emerge even better than before.

However, some economic situations might be just too major such that there is nothing anyone can do about it. Think about the economy collapse of 2008 caused by the sub-prime mortgage market. Plenty of investors lost huge chunks of their investments. It has taken ages to recover from that economic disaster. If you are an older investor, then it is advisable to begin transferring most of your investments to fixed income securities and bonds. Fortunately such incidents are rare, few, and far between.

2. Risks Due to Inflation

We also have risks posed by inflation. Inflation can be viewed as a tax on all consumers. However, inflation is defined generally as the sustained increase in the price of goods and services within an economy. This means that costs are always going up and this affects plenty of things. As an investor, inflation might affect your investments and reduce the value. Most of the time, the government is able to keep inflation under control. However, in some instances, government borrowing and programs tend to introduce inflation.

To evade the effects of inflation, investors tend to put their money in commodities such as gold and other precious metals as well as real estate. However, stocks are thought to be the best protection against inflation. This is because companies are able to adjust prices to beat inflation.

Risk to Market Value

This kind of risk is what can happen should the market move against your investment. This usually occurs when the market changes its usual trend and pursues other interests such as the next big thing. Think about the technology bubble of the 90s. Back then, a lot of traders abandoned traditional stocks and pursued tech stocks instead. This had a huge effect on ordinary investments and investors had to make quick adjustments.

On rare occasions the market may collapse with the net effect of devaluing both bad and good stocks. While this may harm some investors, others have learnt to view it positively. They consider this as the best time to buy into strong companies.

Being too Conservative

Investors can sometimes be too conservative. While this is not necessarily a bad thing, it can have negative consequences if carried out to near extremes. Investors who never take risks and simply wish to play it safe may not achieve their financial goals. Remember the stock market is all about investing. As such, you need to take calculated albeit small risks occasionally. If you perform your analysis accurately, then you will emerge the winner most of the time. Therefore, avoid saving up large amounts of money in your savings account and put it in meaningful investments at the stock markets.

Volatility and Investments

The stock market is mostly a very volatile place. Swings tend to happen on a quarterly, annual, and daily basis for indexes such as the Dow Jones Industrial Average. Volatility left unchecked can cause serious damage to investments. However, if properly harnesses, it can grow your investments significantly and generate great value especially if you learn how to take advantage of it.

What is Volatility?

Volatility is defined as a measure of spread or dispersion across the average or mean returns of a financial asset. It can also be measured through the standard deviation. This basically indicates how close to the mean that a commodity's price is. When prices are generally closer together, then the standard deviation is smaller and widespread prices indicate a larger standard deviation.

In short, we can deduce that volatility at the stocks market is closely linked to investment risk even though it can be harnessed for profitability. To measure volatility we use standard deviation. Standard deviation is an indicator of how closely a security's price is clustered close to the moving average. It is advisable to learn some techniques of harnessing volatility in order to benefit significantly from it.

Diversification

Diversification is a very important strategy for investing. As a financial term, it means simply distributing your investments in various industries for stocks, combining different financial assets, and creating a mix of these assets that will enable you to meet your investment goals. But in the world of investing, diversification refers to a very specific strategy of investment—the careful selection of assets that would react in different ways to a particular event. So far, we have identified the events that create market volatility and make investing in the stock market a risky endeavor. A portfolio combines shares with ETFs, REITs, trust funds, bonds, and other assets, but if not done properly, it can combine assets that react the same way or in a similar manner to events in the economy.

With diversification, you put together stocks that fit together like a cogwheel so that every drop in the price of a particular asset is counterbalanced by a rise in the value of another. When the price of oil stocks goes up, you can almost be assured that airlines, which have to charge more because oil is selling at higher prices, will be doing less business. Their stocks will most probably drop. The inverse is also very true. Having a stock from each sector in your stock portfolio means that your portfolio will always be balanced out whatever happens in either industry. If the oil and airlines industries combination does not appeal to you, then you can trade out oil with railway companies. When anything happens to reduce traveler confidence in the airline industry, railroads experience a surge in travelers and vice versa.

Another fantastic combination of assets that can help you keep your portfolio balanced out is that of stocks and bonds in general terms. Stocks normally drop in price when interest rates climb, a time when the price of bonds climbs. Most investment gurus define diversification as simply ensuring that you don't keep all your eggs in a single basket. This hypothetical basket represents the geographical location, economic sector, and investment type.

Pros and Cons

The benefits of diversification have been addressed at length above. The main reason why we diversify, however, is that it allows you to secure your investments against market volatility and keep your investment stable.

Another advantage of diversification is that it allows us to cover our bases. By thinking about the risk quotient of assets before choosing to invest in them, we can identify potential hurdles before they become too problematic. For one thing, diversification forces us to think about our risk tolerance, which is the foundation for a good portfolio.

One of the biggest drawbacks to diversification comes from a very curious aspect of the diversification process—choosing your assets. With so many assets to choose from, you might get stumped, unable to choose between different assets.

Another disadvantage of diversification is that it demands that you select stocks from different, unrelated industries. Choosing between a few different good assets in the same market sector leaves the chance that the asset you forfeit is the best one of them all and you can only watch as it rises in price and you cannot take advantage. The opportunity cost of choosing one stock over another could be very demoralizing.

Another con to excessive diversification is that the balancing out of assets in your portfolio whereby a rise in one asset is met by a corresponding drop in another leads to average returns. The cost of trying too hard to ensure that your portfolio will bring you no losses is the fact that you can never make much money. The former hinders the latter.

Another drawback to diversification is that you are more likely to incur massive costs while trying to balance it out by constantly buying and selling.

So is it worthwhile diversifying? The answer is definitely! A diversified portfolio is a huge confidence booster because it assures you that your investment is secure. The only problems arise when you overly diversify or micromanage the risks associated with every asset on your portfolio. Diversification goes hand in hand with portfolio management. The more closely you monitor your portfolio, the better you can diversify. If you think the passive style of portfolio management does not pay enough attention to the assets in your portfolio, a midway point between active and passive portfolio management can allow you to hit the sweet spot between over-diversifying and not doing it thoroughly enough.

Traders must have a certain mindset when it comes to investing. Investing in stock takes a lot of self-discipline. There is a certain psychology that traders must become familiar with to be successful in their investments. There is a whole investing mindset that must be utilized to drive results. Investors must detach themselves from their emotions when investing in stock; otherwise, they risk trading out of fear and greed. Investors must also not become too attached to any stock. Although there is an art to investing, it is important that investors utilize logic to drive their actions.

CHAPTER 15:

Hard Work, Focus and Dedication

While it is advisable to invest in a wide variety of financial instruments, stocks should be at the core of your investments. Experts say that you can never go wrong with stocks. Also, all the top billionaires and wealthy individuals make most of their money at the stock market. As such, you stand to gain a lot more buying and investing in a variety of stocks.

Consider Standards and Poor's S&P 500 index. This index has, in the last 20 years, enjoyed a return of at least 7%. This is true for as far back as 1926 which is right after the market crash of the 1920s. If you are unsure about how to diversify your portfolio, then simply copy one of the popular indexes such as this or the Dow Jones. Just being in the markets is a much better option that not being in at all. Also, the compounded interest that you enjoy over the years adds up to a pretty tidy amount with time.

Maintain an Investment Journal

You need to keep an investment journal so that you have a reliable record of your investments and their performance. This is one of the best ways of learning about your style and performance. Investment tracking journals also enables you to track your trades and the actions you took during certain situations and instances. In short, an investment journal provides you with the necessary tools and information that you need to evaluate your investment activities objectively.

Also, you really should be tracking your trades throughout the day. A journal helps you to keep a record of the happenings each day as well as your reactions or actions. You plan should include a tried and tested system that suits your trading style. Make sure that you test this system and then improve your trading plans and performance.

Poor trading systems do not necessary cause failure or bad performance. Most traders lose out and incur losses simply because they do not adhere to the rules of their preferred trading system. Many lose out because they cannot keep track of their trading plan. This is where a trade journal comes in handy.

If you have serious stock market trading plan, then a journal will help you to adhere to this trading plan. By following you well laid out plan, you will have much better chances of success. It is important to keep the journal as detailed as possible. Here are some of the ways you can make your journal as thorough as possible. This is important as your journal is only as good as the information it contains.

First you need to ensure that that you are honest with the information you enter and as thorough as possible. It beats the purpose is the information provided is not accurate and honest because it will be of very little benefit to you. Also, you should learn how to enter information and data into a trading journal and how to maintain it appropriately. This way, you will become a disciplined trader.

Also, with time, you should begin reflecting on your journal entries. When you do this, you will learn a lot about yourself and you will improve your trading skills immensely. You also get to track your thoughts and trades the entire trading day.

CHAPTER 16:

Technical Analysis

This method focuses on studying the supply and demand of a market. The price will be seen to rise when the investor realizes the market is undervalued, and this leads to buying. If they think that the market is overvalued, the prices will start falling, and this is deemed the perfect time to sell.

You need to understand the movement of the various indicators to make the perfect decision. This method works on the premise that history usually repeats itself – a huge change in the prices affects the investors in any situation.

Technical analysis works on the premise of the trend. These trends come by due to the interaction of the buyer and the seller. The aggressiveness of one of the parties in the market will determine how steep the trend becomes. To make a profit, you have to take advantage of the changes in the price movement.

To understand the direction of the trend, you ought to look at the troughs and peaks and how they relate to each other.

When looking for money in options trading, you ought to trade with a trend. The trend is what determines the decision you make when faced with a situation – whether to buy or to sell. You need to know the various signs that a prevailing trend is soon ending so that you can manage the risks and exit the trades the right way.

Characteristics of Technical Analysis

This analysis makes use of models and trading rules using different price and volume changes. These include the volume, price, and other different market info.

Technical analysis is applied among financial professionals and traders and is used by many option traders.

Prices Determine Trends

Technical analysts know that the price in the market determines the trend of the market. The trend can be up, down, or move sideways.

History Usually Repeats Itself

Analysts believe that an investor repeats the behavior of the people that traded before them. The investor sentiment usually repeats itself. Due to the fact that the behavior repeats itself, traders know that using a price pattern can lead to predictions.

The investor uses the research to determine if the trend will continue or if the reversal will stop eventually and will anticipate a change when the charts show a lot of investor sentiment.

Combination with Other Analysis Methods

To make the most out of the technical analysis, you need to combine it with other charting methods on the market. You also need to use secondary data, such as sentiment analysis and indicators.

To achieve this, you need to go beyond pure technical analysis, and combine other market forecast methods in line with technical work. You can use technical analysis along with fundamental analysis to improve the performance of your portfolio.

You can also combine technical analysis with economics and quantitative analysis. For instance, you can use neural networks along with technical analysis to identify the relationships in the market. Other traders make use of technical analysis with astrology.

Other traders go for newspaper polls, sentiment indicators to come with deductions.

The major advantages of technical analysis include

Expert Trend Analysis

This is the biggest advantage of technical analysis in any market. With this method, you can predict the direction of the market at any time. You can determine whether the market will move up, down or sideways easily.

Entry and Exit Points

As a trader, you need to know when to place a trade and when to opt out. The entry point is all about knowing the right time to enter the trade for good returns. Exiting a trade is also vital because it allows you to reduce losses.

Leverage Early Signals

Every trader looks for ways to get early signals to assist them in making decisions. Technical analysis gives you signals to trigger a decision on your part. This is usually ideal when you suspect that a trend will reverse soon. Remember the time the trend reverses are when you need to make crucial decisions.

It Is Quick

In options trading, you need to go with techniques that give you fast results. Additionally, getting technical analysis data is cheaper than other techniques in fundamental analysis, with some companies offering free charting programs.

You Understand Trends

If the prices on the market were to gyrate randomly without any direction, you would find it hard to make money. While these trends run in all directions, the prices always move in trends. Directional bias allows you to leverage the benefits of making money. Technical analysis allows you to determine when a trend occurs and when it doesn't occur, or when it is in reversal.

Many of the profitable techniques that are used by the traders to make money follow trends. This means that you find the right trend and then look for opportunities that allow you to enter the market in the same direction as the trend. This helps you to capitalize on the price movement.

Trends run in various degrees. The degree of the trend determines how much money you make, whether in the short term or long-term trading. Technical analysis gives you all the tools that make it possible for you to do this.

Technical analysis uses common patterns to give you the information to trade. However, you need to understand that history will not be exact when it repeats itself, though. The current analysis will be either bigger or smaller, depending on the existing market conditions. The only thing is that it won't be a replica of the prior pattern.

This pans out easily because most human psychology doesn't change so much, and you will see that the emotions have a hand in making sure that prices rise and fall. The emotions that traders exhibit create a lot of patterns that lead to changes in prices all the time. As a trader, you need to identify these patterns and then use them for trading. Use prior history to guide you and then the current price as a trigger of the trade.

Applicable Over a Wide Time Frame

When you learn technical analysis, you get to apply it to many areas in different markets, including options. All the trading in a market is based mostly on the patters that are as a result of human behavior. These patterns can then be mapped out on a chart to be used across the markets.

While there is some difference between analyzing different securities, you will be able to use technical analysis in most of the markets.

Additionally, you can use the analysis in any timeframe, which is applicable whether you use hourly, daily, or weekly charts. These markets are usually taken to be fractal, which essentially means that patterns that appear on a small scale will also be present on a large scale as well.

Technical Indicators

Technical indicators come into play in options trading when you need to determine turning points for underlying stock and the trends that get them to this point. When used correctly, they can help to determine the optimal time to buy or sell and also predict movement cycles. In general, technical indicators are calculated based on the pricing pattern of the underlying stock. Relevant data includes highs and lows, opening price, volume and closing price. They typically take into account the data regarding a stock's price from the past few periods, based on the charts the person who is doing the analyzing prefers.

This information is then used to identify trends that show what has been happening regarding a specific stock and then using past information to determine likely results for the future. Technical indicators come in both leading and lagging varieties. Indicators that lag are based on data that already exists and make it easier to determine if a trend is in the process of forming or if the stock in question is simply trading within a range. The stronger the trend that the lagging indicator pinpoints the greater the chance it is going to continue into the future. They typically drop the ball when it comes to predicting potential pullbacks or rally points, however.

When it comes to leading indicators, they are mainly useful when you are looking to predict the point in the future where the price of a specific stock is going to crash or rally. More often than not, these are going to be momentum indicators which, as the name implies, gauge the strength of the movement the underlying stock is going to undertake.

Both types of indicators are equally useful at different times, and often in conjunction with one another as you will frequently need to know both what types of trends are forming and when they are ultimately going to peter out if you are going to want to utilize most strategies successfully. In general, you are going to want to stick to a minimum of 3 indicators at all times.

Average directional index

The average directional index can be thought of as a guidepost that confirms the signals that other technical indicators bring to light. After a trend has been identified successfully, the average directional index can then more easily determine its strength compared to the other trends that are currently taking place. The average directional index is a combination of directional indicators that are both negative and positive and thus can more easily track trends regardless of their direction. They are then unified in a way that determines the overall strength of the trend.

As an oscillating indicator, the average directional index ranges between 100 and 0. The low end indicates that the trend is essentially flat and without volatility while the high end indicates that the stock is virtually moving straight up and down very quickly. This indicator is only useful when it comes to measuring the overall strength of the trend, not which direction it is moving in or is likely to move in anytime soon.

CHAPTER 17:

Fundamental Analysis

When it comes to determining which stocks, and therefore which companies, are going to be the most likely to continue to produce dividends in the long run, one of the best ways to go about doing so is through the process of fundamental analysis. Fundamental analysis works on the economy as a whole or on specific industries, depending on where you want to start.

Fundamental analysis answers a host of differing questions including:

- Is the company being straightforward about its profits?
- Is it able to reliably pay its debts?
- Is it currently turning a profit?
- Is it strong enough to continue being profitable in the long-term?
- Is its revenue moving in the right direction?

While these can be extremely involved questions, they all essentially boil down to the decision of whether or not a company is a good investment and if they are likely to continue producing dividends in the long-term. Fundamental analysis can also be thought of as a type of toolbox that can make answering this question much easier.

Quantitative and Qualitative analysis

Fundamental analysis is all about researching the fundamentals of a given company, but that alone won't be enough to tell you what you need to know unless you know what fundamentals you are working with to start. Unfortunately, this can be more comprehensive than you might hope as the fundamentals can include practically anything that affects the economic viability of your chosen company in one way or another. Basic fundamentals include things such as profit or revenue.

Generally speaking, different fundamental factors can be classified in two ways, quantitative and qualitative. Quantitative factors are those that are purely numerical in nature, things that will be written down and during the next investors' meeting. Qualitative factors are those that focus more on the inherent qualities of the company and the things that make it great, which naturally makes them more difficult to track. Qualitative factors are generally less tangible and include things like its name recognition, the patents it holds and the quality of its board members.

Neither of these two types of factors is inherently superior to one another and they actually provide the greatest results when they are used in conjunction with one another. For example, consider the Coca-Cola Company. For quantitative factors, an analyst could look at its P/E ratio, earnings per share and, of course, its annual dividend payout rate. For qualitative factors, you would need to consider its overall brand recognition which takes it from a company that essentially sells carbonated sugar water to a company that is recognized by almost everyone on the planet.

Assumptions

Intrinsic value is the true value of a company, regardless of what its stock price might be at the moment. One of the most important assumptions when it comes to fundamental analysis is that the stock market doesn't always reflect the real value of a particular company which is why fundamental analysis is needed in the first place. As an example, let's say you come across a stock that is currently worth $20 but, after doing your homework you establish that it has a real value of $25 instead. As the intrinsic value is greater than the current stock value then you know that this is a stock worth watching.

Another crucial assumption is that the stock market will eventually reflect the intrinsic value of a company when given enough time. This realignment might happen in days, or it might take years, the only certainty is that it will happen eventually. This is at the heart of why fundamental analysis is so useful as by focusing on a particular company you will be able to suss out its intrinsic value and then find opportunities where the market has not kept up, buying into companies and receiving dividends that are only going to increase as the price of the company catches up to its true value.

There are two primary unknowns when it comes to fundamental analysis:

- It is difficult to determine if an estimated intrinsic value is correct due to the qualitative factors;
- It is difficult to determine how long it will take for the market to catch up to its intrinsic value.

Important Qualitative Factors to Consider

Business model

The first thing that you are going to want to do when you catch wind of a company that might be worth following up on is to check out its business model which is more or less a generalization of how it makes its money. You can typically find these sorts of details on the company website or in its 10-K filing.

While this can be pretty straightforward, such as the Coca-Cola Company's business model of selling carbonated sugar water to the masses, sometimes it can be more complicated than you initially anticipated which is why it is always a good idea to do your homework before making any assumptions. A good example of why this is the case can be seen in Boston Chicken Inc. which was a popular company in the early 90s. You see, despite the name, Boston Chicken Inc. didn't actually make a profit selling chicken. Instead, it sold extremely overpriced franchises to individuals and then made money on loans with exceedingly high interest and royalty fees from individuals using their name. When news of how they actually made their money got out, the company went from darling of Wall Street to delist in a matter of months.

When it comes to choosing companies to invest in, it is also important that you understand the business model of the companies you invest in. This will make it easier for you to ensure that your investments are going to continue moving in a positive direction in the long run. It will make it possible for you to understand its drivers when it comes to future growth and help to protect you from being blindsided by unexpected developments.

Competitive advantage

It is also important to consider the various competitive advantages that the company you have your eye on might have over its competition. Companies that are going to be successful in the long-term are always going to have an advantage over their competition in one of two ways. They can either have better operational effectiveness or improved strategic positioning. Operational effectiveness is the name given to doing the same things as the competition but in a more efficient and effective way. Strategic positioning occurs when a company gains an edge by doing things that nobody else is doing.

Competitive advantage comes in two types, operational effectiveness, and strategic positioning. Operational effectiveness occurs when a company is simply better at doing the things that it and its competitors do. Strategic positioning occurs when a company gets a leg up on its competition by out maneuvering its rivals by finding the same end result through different means or simply doing things its competition isn't doing. In general, a company can't maintain a competitive advantage by doing the same things just as well as its competition. There are a few different ways to generate competitive advantage, including:

- Maintaining a reliable amount of operational effectiveness
- Maintaining a strong activity system that promotes sustainability
- Continuing to perform activities that are uniquely tailored to the strategy of the company.
- Offering clear choices to its customers when compared to its competition
- Creating a unique competitive position

Leadership

The type of management that is currently leading a company is going to go a long way towards determining if it is going to be successful in the long run. After all, even the most well thought out business plan will fail without being able to rely on the right infrastructure to support it in the long run. When it comes to analyzing management, the first place you are going to want to look is the corporate information of the company's website. This won't provide you with much more than the names of the folks at the top, but if they have been around the block then names should be enough to pull up everything you need to know about their past work experiences. While this might not ultimately amount to much if there is something unfortunate in their past this should bring it to light.

Market Overview

The best time to use fundamental analysis is when you are looking to gain a broad idea of the state of the market as it stands and how that relates to the state of things in the near future when it comes time to actually trading successfully. Regardless of what market you are considering, the end goals are the same, find the most effective trade for the time period that you are targeting.

Find a baseline

When it comes to looking at the current state of the fundamentals, the first thing that you are going to want to do is come up with a baseline for the underlying asset related to the potential trade in question, otherwise you will have no reliable way of knowing what the current state of the trade actually means. For the best results, you will then want this analysis to factor in data from both the macro and the micro levels as you will need both to accurately gather all the data you will be looking for. Remember, no market operates in a vacuum and if you find the small linchpins of data on which the major moves turn then you will know where to be in order to take the fullest advantage of it possible. Fundamental analysis hinges on the belief that past market movement is a reliable indicator of future movement which means it will tell you where the next big thing is likely to hit before it does.

It doesn't matter what market you are working with; all underlying assets go through numerous different phases depending on how popular they are in the moment. If the asset is currently in a period of extreme popularity, then you will find that volatility is down while liquidity is up. Once this period can no longer be sustained the asset enters what is known as the bust period where you will notice a decrease in liquidity and an increase in volatility. There are also sub categories based on how recently the asset entered the phase in question.

Decide on the phase of the market

This step is relatively straightforward as if the market as a whole is in a boom state then liquidity will be high across the board and volatility will be low, likewise if things are currently in a bust state then volatility will be high and liquidity will be low in all corners. It is important to utilize the proper quantitative techniques when doing so that you draw your own conclusions instead of listening to what pundits or paid analysts think on the matter. While going with what the pros say will work occasionally, finding your own undervalued currency pairs will allow you to get in on the best trades ahead of the pack.

CHAPTER 18:

The Most Common Mistakes to Avoid

In the beginning, investors will make mistakes. It is all part of the learning process. As investors become more experienced, they will learn what works and what doesn't. Although learning from one's own mistakes is an excellent way to improve, it is also beneficial to learn from others' mistakes. This is why many investors talk about the mistakes they have made; it helps to prevent others from making the same mistakes.

Diversification Issues

Beginning investors must know how to diversify their portfolios properly. Investors may make the mistake of not having enough diversification, or they have too much diversification. Perhaps they are diverse in one aspect but not in another. The investor should invest in a variety of stocks in different sectors. They should also choose stocks at different price points. They must also not have a single stock make up the majority of their portfolio. Finally, it is important to have at least a couple of long-term investments among short-term investments. There are several ways to diversify one's portfolio, and it is crucial that beginners learn the proper (and improper) methods of diversification to reach their fullest potential.

There is a great balance of diversification. There is such a thing as too much diversification and too little diversification. There is no set number for how many stocks that an investor should manage at once. This is up to the investor, their goals, and their personal preferences. The investor definitely should have more than one stock. If all of their investment is in a single stock, the performance of that one stock will determine how their entire investment performs. This can be beneficial if the stock experiences great growth. However, this can also be a high-risk move if the stock does not perform well. The investor may also have too much diversification. Especially at first, there is a lot of time that must go into research and education about the stocks that the investor owns. Although there is no "perfect" number of stocks to own, it should be enough so that there is adequate diversification, yet the investor is able to keep track of all of their investments. For instance, an individual with a full-time job will not be able to handle trading hundreds of stocks at once. This requires great research and analysis. For this reason, the investor should choose a number of stocks that they can handle to keep track of.

Investors should also have stocks of different companies in different sectors. Having just a couple of stocks or having all stocks in the same sector is also a sign of a lack of diversification. There are a few ways to help this. The investor may invest in mutual funds or index funds. This will help them to have many companies in their portfolio, and they are typically diverse already. The investor may also hand-pick companies that are in a variety of sectors to allow for proper diversification and reduce the risk of all of one's investments performing badly simultaneously.

Investors should also have a good balance of prices and amounts of stocks. It is important that the investor does not have one stock making up the majority of their portfolio. Instead, they should spread their investment among several companies quite evenly. They should also diversify the price levels of the stock that they own. While penny stocks may be cheap and have a high potential for growth, it is important to have some stocks that are of well-established companies that cost a bit more. These stocks typically are more stable (plus they may pay a dividend).

Poor Speculation

The concept of speculation is that one is investing in stock in the hopes of it growing over time. There are certain stocks that are more "speculative." These are the stocks that the investor is not certain of. They may not be well-established but hold the potential for high growth. The investor will invest in these stocks with the hope that they will generate a high return for them. Investors must develop their skills in picking the right stocks. It is important that they don't risk it all on stocks that perform badly. For this reason, investors should familiarize themselves with how to speculate properly.

The definition of speculation seems to carry different meanings. It may mean choosing stocks that will perform well. It may also mean making predictions about the market as a whole. Economic speculations can cause actual economic events. For instance, when there is mass speculation that the stock market is going to drop, investors will begin selling out of fear. This fear gets in the way of making logical decisions, and this may cause an actual drop in the market to occur. Investors must know how to separate the fact from emotions. They must be able to sift through the rumors to discover the truth. There will constantly be speculations on the market; some may predict a massive dip while others predict great growth. Speculation can be good. If the investor puts great time and effort into their research, speculation can end up being highly profitable to them. Great returns may require the investor to take great risks. For this reason, speculation may be beneficial. It can help investors to choose the right times to buy and sell, and it can also help them to choose which stocks to buy and sell.

On the other hand, speculation can sometimes have negative effects. Investors expect companies to grow over time and provide returns that may not be realistic based on the economy and the company's revenue. Instead of reinvesting in themselves, the company is forced to meet expectations and pay its dividend out to the stockholders of the company, leading to its own destruction and an inevitable crash. This is caused by investor speculation. Instead of focusing so much on earnings per share, investors may choose to focus on creating the most cash flow as possible.

Speculation isn't all bad, though. A proper amount of speculation can regulate the health of the economy. Speculators may be able to point out when supply is running low, which will typically increase the demand and the price of stocks. This can prevent shortages from occurring. Speculators can predict a wide range of economic factors, such as growth, decline, and effects of the government, supply, demand, and more. Speculators will also be able to point out the facts, yet investors must know whose advice and thoughts to listen to. The best way to learn the facts is to receive a proper education and conduct thorough research that is diversified in nature.

Improper Education and Research

It is important for investors to conduct proper research and receive proper education about the stock market. They must familiarize themselves with all of the aspects of the stock market and learn how all of those elements work together to operate. This will serve as background knowledge for the topics that they will research. Investors must research the stocks that they wish to invest in. They must also research the stocks that they already have invested in to track their performance. This is crucial for one's success in investing in stocks.

It is important to have a solid background in the stock market and to become educated on it. The investor must educate themselves enough on it to understand all of the concepts necessary for trading, but it is also important to not buy into unnecessarily expensive classes on stock education. These courses will make promises on returns and dollar amounts of investors. What they typically don't explicitly state, however, is how much they cost and how much commission will be taken out. This is often in the fine print, and investors will learn this after it is too late. It is highly beneficial for investors to teach themselves how to invest. After all, experience is the best education. There are some topics that simply can't be taught; investors must learn for themselves how to invest in stocks. Each investor will also have individual goals for themselves, and one investor's "perfect" strategy may conflict with another's personal goals. Investing also depends on the market, which is constantly changing. An "ideal" stock to invest in one day may be a very unwise investment the next day. There is also a certain element of luck that is associated with the stock market. Although one can develop their skills in analyzing the market and predicting it more accurately, there will always be factors that are out of the control of the investor. Sudden changes may occur that the investor would not have been able to foresee.

There are, however, a few ways that one may educate themselves on the stock market. The first is by actually getting involved in the market and learning through experience. The investor may also read books on the topic (like this one). There are a number of articles available in both print and online. It is possible to learn from a mentor, friend, or even to hire a financial advisor. There are videos created by those who are already established in the market. Subscriptions are available for both emails and magazines. There are a number of classes, courses, seminars, and meetings for investors. It is important to diversify one's education to receive a broader knowledge of such topics. This way, the investor can learn a variety of strategies for how to invest in the stock market.

The investor must also diversify their research on stocks. They should study the company's published reports to see their net income, P/E ratio, and return on equity. Investors should look at the Form 10-K and Form 10-Q. The brokerage that the investor signed up with may also have a variety of tools for researching the market. The company's management should be researched extensively. It is important to also look at charts of the company to see how their performance has been for not only the past month or two but for the past years and even past decades. This will help to give the investor an idea of how well the company is performing currently. They can use this information to notice trends and make predictions on that company's future performance.

Inadequate Planning

Investors must plan everything out to maximize their return on their investments. Without planning, there will be no sense of direction for the investors. Investors must set goals for themselves so that they have specific achievements to work towards. It is also advisable that they plan out their schedule for trading and educating themselves to make sure that they stay on track with how much they wish to dedicate to stock. They must also find out how much they would like to save, invest, and spend to manage their budget properly. Doing these will help investors to make the best use of their money and generate the greatest return on their investments.

Investors must set goals for themselves. Trading can become discouraging for those who fail to set specific goals for themselves. Setting goals will help the investor to stay motivated and have a path to success laid out for them. Unlike a job, stock trading does not pay by the hour. It is a self-motivated task that requires the full work of the investor. Instead of dwelling on the losses, investors may have achievements to look at and celebrate.

CHAPTER 19:

Is It Worth It to Invest Stocks?

In this historical moment the search for high returns has become almost spasmodic. Unfortunately, the expansionary policy of central banks has caused the collapse of yields (now virtually 0). Anyone who wants to get a positive return must take risks.

In this context, many are deciding to invest in stocks. It certainly is worth it, but it all depends on the modality of the investment.

This is an investment that can still guarantee very high performance, provided, however, if one's to follow some guidelines.

The first tip is to use only really affordable platforms to invest in stocks. Among the best we can definitely remember Plus500 or Markets. These platforms are characterized by the fact that they are very easy to use, even for those who have never worked with the actions but, at the same time, guarantee advanced tools, suitable even for the most experienced and needs. At the time of registration, you will receive a free bonus that amounts to 7,000 euros for Plus500 and 4,000 euros for Markets. This is additional capital that can be used to operate on the stock markets but cannot be directly withdrawn. If you use the bonus and you get profits, these profits can instead be taken without any problems or constraints.

Both Plus500 and Markets are Trading Contracts for Difference (CFD) trading platforms: this is a particularly flexible and easy-to-understand derivative instrument that guarantees the possibility of obtaining high profits both when markets rise, and markets fall. This is the second condition that makes it worthwhile to invest in stocks: if you buy shares directly you earn only when the markets go up. And in today's financial conditions, it's an immense gamble. At this time, it is absolutely not convenient to buy shares, the thing that must be done is to subscribe derivatives (such as CFDs that are very simple) that have underlying actions. Plus500 and Markets are the ideal solution for investing in stocks and, incidentally, they also allow investing in forex, indices, commodities, bitcoins, etc.

If you want to invest in shares and you want to earn money, the advice is to open an account on Markets or on Plus500.

The big advantage of stock investing: leverage

Through the use of financial leverage (or simply "leverage") a person has the possibility to buy or sell financial assets for an amount higher than the capital held and, consequently, to benefit from a higher potential return than that deriving from a direct investment in the underlying and, conversely, to expose yourself to the risk of very significant losses.

Let's see how the concept of leverage works starting from a simple case. Let's assume you have $ 100 available to invest Leverage financial in a stock. Let's assume that the gain or loss expectations are equal to 30%: if things go well, we will have $ 130, otherwise, we will have $ 70. This is a simple speculation in which we bet on a particular event.

In case we decide to risk more investing, in addition to our $ 100, also another $ 900 borrowed, then the investment would take a different articulation because we use a leverage of 10 to 1 (we invest $ 1000 having a capital initial only of 100). If things go well and the stock goes up 30%, we will receive $ 1300; we return the 900 borrowed with a gain of $ 300 on an initial capital of 100. So, we get a 300% profit with a stock that gave a 30 in return. Obviously on the $ 900 borrowed we will have to pay an interest, but the general principle remains valid: the leverage allows one to increase the possible gains.

Considering the further case of the investment in derivatives; let's assume we buy a derivative that, within a month, gives the right to buy 100 grams of gold at a price set today at $ 5,000. We could physically buy the gold with an outlay of 5000 $ and keep it waiting for the price to rise and then sell it back. If we decide instead to use derivatives, we should not have $ 5,000, but only the capital needed to buy the derivative. Let's say that a bank sells for 100 $ the derivative that allows us to buy the same 100 grams of gold in a month to $ 5,000. If in a month the gold is worth 5,500, we can buy it and sell it immediately, realizing a gain of 500 $. With the 100 $ of the price of the derivative, we make a profit of $ 400, or 400%, with $ 100.

Without using derivatives and leverage, the same $500 I could have earned them only against an investment of $ 5,000, making a profit of 10%.

What are the potentials of its use?

The potential of leveraging is clear. But be careful: the leverage multiplier effect, described with the examples, works even if the investment goes wrong. For example, if we decide to invest $ 100 in our possession plus an additional sum of $ 900 borrowed, if the stock depreciated by 30%, we would remain with only $ 700 in hand; having to return the $ 900 borrowed plus interest and considering the $ 100 of our initial investment we would have a loss of over $ 300 on an initial capital of $ 100. As a percentage, the loss would therefore be 300% against a reduction in the value of the share of 30%.

Another element to keep in mind is that the different financial levers can be combined: in this way speculation operations are carried out using a "squared lever" with clear reflections on potential aptitudes.

What may appear to be an interesting tool with positive potential for the investor, on the other hand, presents risks that must therefore be taken into due consideration. In fact, if the financial system as a whole works with a very high leverage and financial institutions lend money to each other to multiply the possible profits, the loss of an individual investor can trigger a domino effect by infecting the entire financial market.

Banks are typically entities that operate with a more or less high degree of leverage: against a certain net capital, the total assets in which the resources are invested are generally much higher. For example, a bank with equity of $ 100 and leverage of 20 manages assets for $ 2,000. A loss of 1% of the assets entails the loss of 20% of the equity capital.

The development of the market for the transfer of credit risk (from financial intermediaries to the market) has meant that the traditional bank model, called "originate-and-hold" ("create and hold": the bank that provided the loan remains in the balance sheet until maturity), has been substituted for many operators from the "originated-to-distribute" ("create and distribute": the intermediary selects the debtors, but then transfers the loan to others, recovering the liquidity and the regulatory capital committed or the pure credit risk (credit derivatives), with benefits only on capital requirements), with the effect of a further increase in leverage. The spread of this second bank model is one of the factors that explain the crisis triggered on the sub-prime mortgage market.

Property price inflation has supported the issuance of securitized loans and the exponential growth of the related market, allowing banks to make huge profits and, at the same time, increase leverage. But "the money machine" could not last long and in the end many banks found themselves without sufficient capital to absorb the losses deriving from the inversion of the real estate market trend, resulting in fact as failed companies.

In the meantime, the example of the banks has spread within the financial system by spreading to all other financial institutions: leverage had prevailed, especially in the United States, generating a huge volume of risky investments that rested on a fraction infinitesimal of equity capital. We are thinking of the issue of so-called "credit default swaps" (derivative instruments used to hedge against the default risk of the debtor): some insurance companies were heavily exposed to the real estate market and when the latter collapsed and the value of mortgages fell, they began to lose without having sufficient capital to absorb the losses deriving from the issue of those instruments.

In order not to risk failing and return to sufficient levels of bank capital, capital increases can be used (not an easy task in times of crisis), the reduction of the amount of loans to businesses (granting fewer new loans and not renewal of those already issued) and the disposal of other liquid assets (mostly shares). The result of all this, in the period of the sub-prime crisis, was a credit freeze and a collapse of the stock market. These are the main channels through which the financial crisis has hit the real economy. Credit rationing affected investments and the fall in the stock market (which adds to the decline in house prices) has reduced the value of household wealth and therefore consumption.

We know that a certain level of leverage is physiological to sustain economic growth, even if we have no indication of what the optimal level is. But history teaches us how in an increasingly globalized and interdependent economic-financial system, leverage can be a trigger for speculative bubbles. And it is in these periods that the strongest disconnection between finance and the real economy is generated.

Earning potential

The stock market gives the false impression that making money on the stock market is just a matter of choosing the right securities, investing quickly, staying glued to a computer screen and spending the day obsessing over what the investment is.

But the truth about how to make money on the stock market is another and you'll find out by reading the following pages.

The secret that reveals how to earn on the Stock Exchange, buying or selling securities and shares, is well explained by the thought of an investor known throughout the world, Benjamin Graham:

"Real money is made not by buying and selling, but by owning the securities, receiving interest and dividends and taking advantage of the increase in their value in the long term".

In a simpler way, the first secret to understanding how to earn on the stock market according to Graham is to focus on long-term investments, keeping a stock for at least 5 years in your investment portfolio.

Including the first fundamental concept of investing in the stock market, we now analyse concretely how to earn by buying stocks.

Investing in the stock market, buying and selling stocks, for many people is a very attractive prospect. However, we are talking about a real investment, accompanied by risk, and it is necessary to understand that it is not easy to earn on the stock market as some may want to make you believe.

To understand how to do this, we need to be aware of what we are doing and what the factors that influence the success or failure are of our investment.

CHAPTER 20:

Understanding Types of Investment

If you already understand mutual funds, stocks, and bonds, fantastic. Five 5 of these popular investment types warrant a place in the typical investor's portfolio.

Stocks

Common stocks supply financiers with an ownership interest in a company. Shares of stock represent business equity and are called equities. Financiers can purchase and offer stocks on exchanges entities that exist mainly to produce a market for the shares. Stocks trade continuously during business hours- 9:30 a.m. to 4.00 p.m. Eastern time most weekdays with prices changing from 2nd to second.

As the value of business fluctuates, so does the cost of an investor's stock. Over the long haul, stock rates tend to rise when companies increase their earnings and sales. However, in the short-term, stocks can gyrate, moved by things like total financial patterns, news from rival companies, government action, and other aspects.

At the end of August 2013, Microsoft shares sold for $33.40, with about 8.44 billion shares outstanding. If you increase the number of shares by the per-share cost, you get $282 billion, the stock's market capitalization, frequently abbreviated to market cap. A financier who acquires 50 shares of Microsoft for approximately $1,670 would own a small portion of one of the world's largest companies. When more people wish to purchase a particular stock than to offer it, prices tend to increase. As any economics book will tell you, when items end up being scarce and the demand for them increases, prices often increase in reaction. The stock exchange will not run out of Microsoft shares must they end up being popular for any reason, however.

When purchasers outnumber sellers, the variation creates scarcity and drives the price up. The same concept applies to the disadvantage where an excess of shares and a shortage of buyers' cause falling prices.

Stock-price movements illustrate the significance of the marketplace, the value of you, the financier, because markets set stock values. The World Bank estimated the cost of all U.S. companies' stock at $18.7 trillion at the end of 2012, more than five times the worth of companies in each of the next-largest markets, China and Japan. With more than 5,000 U.S. companies trading their stock, not to mention many foreign companies with shares that sell this nation equity investor that can tap into practically any facet of the economy.

Not all stocks act the same method, which suggests they can play different parts in your portfolio. Here are some classifications all-stock investor should understand:

Development Value stocks

Financiers tend to set worth for stocks relative to their incomes (or sales, or cash flows, etc.). Value-oriented financiers gravitate toward worth stocks business that trades at a discount rate relative to their earnings or some other operating statistic.

Stocks with above-market growth of profits or sales tend to outshine their peers. These stocks tend to cost more (higher price/earnings ratios, and so on) than other commodities, as lots of financiers will pay a premium for growth.

At first blush, the concept that both high-growth stocks and value stocks can outshine noises like a contradiction within such an extensive system as the stock market, investors has found more than one way to make some earnings.

Over the long haul, value stocks tend to outperform development stocks. Growth stocks have outperformed worth stocks over the last years, yet worth shares have handled higher returns in seven of the last ten years, as displayed in Table 3.1. Whether you purchase worth stocks, growth stocks, or both, the appeal is that you can generate income, regardless of individual choice, if you choose carefully.

Year Large-company growth and worth of stocks

201215.4% 23.0%.

20114.1% -9.0%.

201015.9% 21.6%.

200927.9% 39.2%.

2008-33.7% -49.0%.

200714.1% -6.5%.

20068.9% 22.6%.

20052.8% 12.2%.

20046.5% 18.9%.

200326.3% 35.0%.

Source: (Ibbotson SBBI 2013).

Large-capitalization (large-cap) stocks. The name informs the story.

Because financiers tend to set worth's for stocks relative to earnings, companies with enormous revenues can sport massive market capitalizations. Shares of big business tend to be less unpredictable, and financiers often consider them much safer than smaller stocks.

Small-cap stocks

Stocks of smaller companies have historically provided higher returns than stocks of large companies-- once again, at the cost of higher risk. What creates a small-cap stock? This depends on who you ask, as there is no industry opinion as to where the cut-off point is between big and little. A commonly pointed out dividing line is $3 billion, with anything smaller sized classified as a small-cap.

Because of their different risk-return profiles, financiers should treat small and large-cap stocks as separate classes. You ought to own a mix of large-cap and small-cap stocks in the equity part of your portfolio. Sure, you might pack the portfolio with only large-caps or stick to simply small-caps, but you might end up with a lower rate of return (the large-cap option) or greater threat (the small-cap alternative) than you desire.

U.S. stocks

Since economic trends vary from country to country, at times, U.S. stocks will grow while the rest of the world limps along, and vice versa. As a rule, financiers consider U.S. stocks safer than foreign stocks. This belief stems a minimum from the size and liquidity of the stock market, and that U.S. accounting rules need higher disclosure of financial information than the majority of other nations.

Foreign stocks

Many investors buy foreign stocks to diversify their portfolios. Also, you can sometimes enhance returns by buying stocks of companies in emerging markets like China and India, where the economies grow far quicker than in the United States.

Pros:

Range: With the shares of more than 5,000 firms listed on U.S. markets, financiers can buy into almost any business they pick

Stocks trade all day long, which allows financiers to offer and purchase at particular levels and attempt to play short-term price relocations. Even experts make plenty of mistakes day trading, and beginners should not mess with it.).

High returns. Stocks tend to surpass bonds and other income-oriented financial investments.

Cons:

Volatility: Stock costs vary more than bond prices. Financiers need to accept that threat if they want to tap into stocks' potentially excellent returns.

Complex analysis: Stock analysis involves looking at several data, assessing trends, and approximating future development rates. It requires time and effort, which might describe, at least in part, the popularity of shared funds.

Alertness needed. Since stock costs can change so quickly, and since they frequently respond dramatically to news about the market or the company, financiers need to pay attention to them.

Bonds

As stock financiers buy equity in a business, bond financiers purchase debt. Companies and federal governments issue bonds, gathering cash-- the bond's face worth or par value-- in advance from financiers. The companies accept interest payments, usually semiannually, for a set time before paying the cashback.

The payment stays the very same for the life of the bond. For this reason, bonds and other securities that make regular payments are categorized as fixed-income. During the conversation about how to craft a portfolio, you'll check out looking for a balance between equities and fixed-income (or bonds and stocks).

Price quotes vary with regards to the size of the U.S. bond market-- which consists of the financial obligation provided by corporations, the federal government, and towns. Still, most peg the bond market at roughly two times the size of the stock exchange.

Bonds come in many ranges. Here are some of the most common:

Corporate bonds

Debt released by corporations.

Treasury bonds

The financial obligation provided by the U.S. Treasury and backed by the complete the trust and confidence of the Government of Canada. Investors in the United States and abroad usually think about Treasury bonds free of default danger.

Agency bonds

Debt issued by companies connected to the federal government. While such bonds do not technically have the support of the U.S, Treasury, a lot of investors assume they have an incredibly low risk of default.

Municipal bonds

Financial obligation released by municipalities, states, or firms connected to states or municipalities such as water systems. In a lot of cases, the interest payments from these bonds are not subject to federal income taxes.

High-yield bonds

Understood as junk bonds, any securities with a speculative-grade score fall into this group.

Convertible bonds

Businesses can issue bonds that, under particular conditions, convert into stock.

Variable-rate bonds

In many cases, bond companies make interest payments that fluctuate based upon changes in a benchmark rate of interest.

You make a bet on the credit reliability of the company when you purchase a bond. If the bond issuer is no longer able to cover the payments, the bond could default, losing the debt financiers in the lurch. The danger of default is understood as a credible threat.

Credit-rating agencies-- Standard & Poor's, Moody's, and Fitch Ratings-- examine the creditworthiness of companies and federal governments that issue bonds and appoint them ratings. Those scores show the agencies' viewpoints on the likelihood that the issuer will default. For instance, S&P's rankings range from AAA to D, with everything BBB- and greater classified as investment-grade. The agency thinks about every bond with a score of BB+ or lowers speculative- grade.

Providers pay back the bonds at the end of their term, likewise understood as maturity, bond prices tend to go back to the face worth of the bond as the maturity date nears. Assuming a financier sells a loan, receives interest payments, and then retains the face value of the debt at maturity, adjustments to the contract cost along the method do not indicate anything.

Unlike stock prices, which tend to change based upon financial and business news, bonds respond mainly Interest rates or shifts in the perceived credit risk of a business. If a business reports a strong quarter with higher-than-expected profits, the stock rate might rise while the bonds remain steady. However, if the company announces it has actually borrowed a lot of money and credit experts start to doubt its capability to please its commitments, the business's bonds might decline.

Bond prices react to modifications in interest rates because their fixed payments look more appealing when interest rates fall and less attractive when rates increase. If treasury yields climb to 4.5 percent, the attractiveness of Acme's debt decreases; financial firms need more than 0.5 percent to take up credit threat of the business bond. As a result, Acme's bonds most likely dip in the market, possibly to the point that they cost about 1.5 per cent more than Treasury bonds.

Long-lasting bonds tend to react to modifications in rates of interest more highly than do brief -term bonds. Remember, bond prices tend to go back to par value as they near maturity. A bond that grows in 3 months will not see its value change much even if interest rates move because, in three months, the company will redeem it for its stated value.

CHAPTER 21:

Ways to Make Money In Stocks

Long Term Investing

As I talk about in my free report Crush the Market, the S&P 500 has averaged 9.8% a year going back 90 years. Now obviously it's not 9.8% every year; sometimes it's less, sometimes it's more. However, over the long term, this is the average return. This means if an investor were just to buy the S&P 500, they would average 9.8% a year, not including dividends, which equate to about an extra 2% each year.

This makes long term investing in the stock market a way to not only beat inflation but also earn additional income on all the money you have invested. This is why long-term investing can be so beneficial and why so many people use the stock market as a place to put their money. If you were to put $10,000 under your mattress in 1980, it would lose a significant amount of value as years go by, being worth just $2,800 today (30 years later). And even putting your money into a savings account, which currently pays about 1.60%, would still not match the rate of inflation.

There are two main reasons the S&P 500 is able to keep up with inflation and rise past it:

• Companies raise their prices to keep up with inflation; thus, their stock prices increase

• Companies expand and grow which increase their stock prices

Knowing all this, the stock market is an excellent place to put your savings and increase your net worth over the long term. However, you obviously can't just pick any stock or ETF, as you need a plan.

Dividends

Dividends can range from less than 1% to 10% or more. Generally, you want to be wary of companies that issue dividends greater than 5%, as this high of a dividend means the company may be failing and is just trying to attract buyers. For example, in 2018, the company GameStop (GME) raised its dividend to 11% to attract more buyers to their stock. At the same time, the stock price of GME was crumbling, meaning even though investors were getting 11% annually from dividends, they were overall losing money by holding the failing stock.

There are many quality companies such as Coke (KO) and Proctor & Gamble (PG) who issue dividends, which average 2%-3% annually.

All this means is if you were to buy a company like this and leave your funds in it for the long haul, not only would you make money from the stock price appreciating, but also from all the dividend checks you would be receiving. With the power of compounding interest, this could turn into millions of dollars by the time you retire.

There's a famous true story of a janitor from the state of Vermont. He made only $13 an hour at his job and, unknown to even his children; he was worth $8 million when he died. Even with such a modest salary, he was able to become a multi-millionaire by investing in quality stocks that paid dividends.

An interesting fact is, at the time of his death, he was collecting dividend checks, which equated to $20,000 each month! He held a portfolio totaling 95 companies, which included common names such as Proctor & Gamble, Dow Chemical, and Morgan Chase.

This proves the point that dividends can be extremely powerful over the long term when used effectively. Unlike the janitor, however, you do not need to own 95 companies in your portfolio, as there are now many ETFs that make this process much easier. This is because they combine quality dividend-paying companies together into one ticker symbol. One such example is an ETF by the company Vanguard with symbol VYM, which currently pays a 3.11% yearly dividend.

Recognizing Market Cycles

Markets go through cycles, which would include bull and bear markets, terms you may have likely heard before. A bull market is characterized by increasing stock prices, while a bear market is characterized by decreasing stock prices.

On average, a bear market occurs every 8 years and is considered a 20% or more decline in stock prices from their highs. No one knows exactly how long bull or bear market markets will last, or exactly when they will occur. History has shown us however, that over the long term, stocks always do end up moving higher, eventually coming out of bear markets.

So, while no one is a psychic and can predict the exact top or bottom, traders can use clues to know when good times to be invested are, and when are good times to be more cautious. Robber markets tend to be a time where a lot of money can be made (or lost), depending on if a trader knows what is going on. For example, as one book is being published, the last bear market occurred in 2007, which was coined the "financial crisis." During this time, the S&P 500 dropped over 50% from its highs.

Had you loaded up on cash beforehand and slowly bought stock as the market was dropping, you would have come out with huge profits when the market ended up recovering a couple of years later Investors are aware that any high reward strategies such as investments promising attractive returns are almost always high-risk ventures. With time, most investments are capable of doubling the initial investment amount. However, most traders and investors prefer earning high returns within a short period. High risk with high return strategies is the preference of numerous investors despite the risks that they are exposed to.

There is no guaranteed method of doubling an investment. However, there are numerous instances where investments have more than doubled within a brief period. However, for every successful investment that doubled within a relatively short time, there are possibly hundreds of others that were not successful. This fact alone should send out warning bells to all potential investors to take caution when thinking about high risk with high return investments.

1. Investing in Stock Options

We all know options to be high risk, high reward investment vehicles. An investor who opts for this investment instrument will buy a commodity or stock equity at an indicated price that has a future date range.

These usually come in the form of a contract between the buyer and seller. Therefore, an option is a contract that contains an underlying security such as stock. The price of the contract will rely on the value of the underlying security.

2. Initial Public Offering

Another excellent investment strategy that is highly profitable is the IPO. The term IPO stands for initial public offering and refers to the listing of shares at the stock market by a company for the very first time. During an IPO, the public is invited to purchase the company's stock at a price that is considered affordable.

3. Venture Capital

Venture capitalists often provide capital to businesses, especially startups. A lot of startup businesses have excellent ideas with concepts that can be monetized. Based on these concepts, innovative ideas, and some sales, wealthy individuals, and investors with sufficient funds often make out checks to these businesses in the hope of winning big with time.

One challenge posed by startups is that their futures are always uncertain and sometimes even unstable. However, there are plenty of investors who prefer investing their money in startups.

They weight the challenges posed and believe that if they can be part of the management or board, then they can guide the enterprise to profitability.

4. Investing in the Emerging Markets

Numerous countries around the world are now referred to as emerging markets. They range from China to South Africa, Argentina, Morocco, India, Vietnam, Chile, and Hong Kong, among many others. These countries all have huge economies that are rapidly expanding as well as stable governments and political systems. Emerging economies can provide excellent investment opportunities for investors. These are growing countries that have well-established sectors and industries.

5. REITs – Real Estate Investment Trusts

Some of the most lucrative investment opportunities are found in REITs. Real estate investment funds are great because the dividends are quite high, and they benefit from government tax breaks. However, it is important to understand exactly what a REIT is.

REITs or real estate investment trusts are trust funds that invest funds in a variety of residential and commercial real estate.

As such, these trusts boast ownership to a wide variety of properties that range from hospitals and hotels to malls, office buildings, family homes, apartment blocks, and even movie theaters.

6. High Yield Bonds

We also have another exciting investment opportunity in the form of a high yield bond. Finance experts define high yield bonds as bonds that have a lower credit rating compared to municipal bonds, treasury bonds, and corporate bonds, but as a result, pay high returns.

The reason why these bonds pay high rewards is that they are high-risk investment securities. The risk is mostly due to the likelihood of default. Issuers of these high yield bonds are often capital-intensive companies and startup firms that need capital but cannot issues shares just yet.

7. Trade in Currencies

Investors can also invest in different currencies in the hope of realizing profits. However, it is traders who mostly invest in currencies. Trading can be difficult and challenging, especially in the currency markets. However, it is absolutely crucial that traders receive the necessary training in order to trade profitably in the currency market.

CHAPTER 22:

The Importance of Benchmark

We have talked several times about the benchmark and its importance. Let's try to show, in concrete terms, an example of applying the benchmark. To do this we will use a mutual fund as reference. The reader is cautioned that the choice is absolutely random and is independent of any invitation to invest in this fund. Having carried out this necessary premise, let's analyze the benchmark using a common investment mutual fund: Anima Europa class A.

The information that we will analyze is present on the AM Anima website, as well as on the fund's reference documentation (in particular, on the KIID document and on the regulation). It is possible to read the Benchmark. In this case it is composed of two indices:

- 95% MSCI Europe (reference index for the European market)

- 5% ICE BofA Euro Treasury Bill in Euro - Gross Total Return - a reference index of the money market / short-term bonds denominated in Euro

Note that the fund adopts an active investment policy: it says that the fund does not aim to "passively replicate" the indices, and uses the latter to "compare the results obtained". The investment policy is equipped with degrees of freedom, which provide the manager with the ability to graduate the riskiness of the portfolio as well as the exposure to exchange rates.

Although the portfolio tends to be exposed to 100% in shares, the degrees of freedom define, by constraint, the minimum investment in shares denominated in European currencies for at least 70%. The manager, therefore, can calibrate the composition of the portfolio, deciding to overexpose itself in shares or underexpose due to this constraint and the benchmark.

Incidentally, the possibility of being exposed to exchange rate risk (currency risk) is also expressed. This factor is also particularly important, highlighting a basically active policy of the fund with respect to the reference benchmark.

But let's go back to the benchmarks. The references for the fund in question are the two indexes \ listed. Let's see how they are composed.

The MSCI Europe index, at the end of 2019, consisted of a basket of medium and large capitalization companies in 15 developed market countries (DM) in Europe. With around 440 stocks, the index covers around 85% of the free float market capitalization in European developed markets.

It should be remembered that the MSCI indices were built by Morgan Stanley Capital International, and represent baskets of securities taken as a reference starting from a specific historical moment, built according to specific rules (so that securities can enter or leave the MSCI indices due compliance or otherwise with the aforementioned rules). The indices are used precisely as a Benchmark and as "sectoral" market references.

As an example, the cumulative and annual performances, the related risk indices, of some of the most important MSCI indices are reported:

- MSCI Europe
- MSCI World
- MSCI ACWI IMI

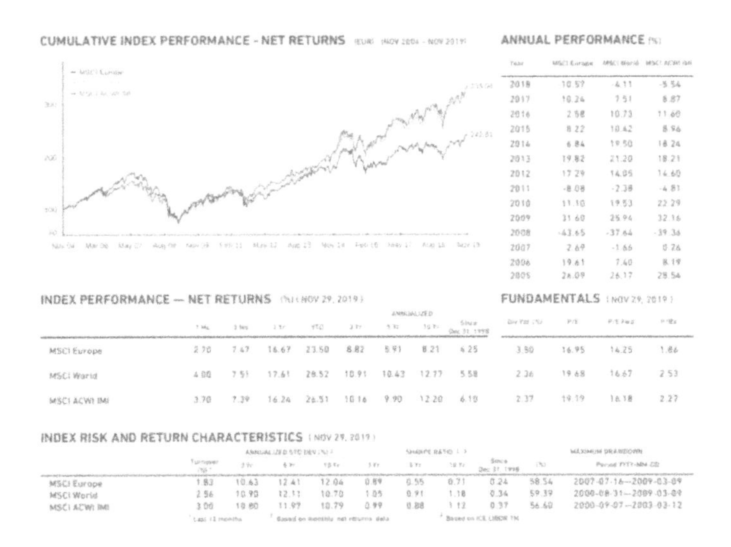

ANNUAL PERFORMANCE (%)

Year	MSCI Europe	MSCI World	MSCI ACWI IMI
2018	-10.57	-4.11	-5.54
2017	10.24	7.51	8.87
2016	2.58	10.73	11.60
2015	8.22	10.42	8.96
2014	6.84	19.50	18.24
2013	19.82	21.20	18.21
2012	17.29	14.05	14.60
2011	-8.08	-2.38	-4.81
2010	11.10	19.53	22.29
2009	31.60	25.94	32.16
2008	-43.65	-37.64	-39.36
2007	2.69	-1.66	0.76
2006	19.61	7.40	8.19
2005	26.09	26.17	28.54

INDEX PERFORMANCE — NET RETURNS (%) (NOV 29, 2019)

	1 Mo	3 Mo	1 Yr	YTD	ANNUALIZED 3 Yr	5 Yr	10 Yr	Since Dec 31, 1998
MSCI Europe	2.70	7.47	16.67	23.50	8.82	5.91	8.21	6.25
MSCI World	4.00	7.51	17.61	28.52	10.91	10.43	12.77	5.58
MSCI ACWI IMI	3.70	7.39	16.24	26.51	10.16	9.90	12.20	6.10

FUNDAMENTALS (NOV 29, 2019)

	Div Yld (%)	P/E	P/E Fwd	P/BV
MSCI Europe	3.50	16.95	14.25	1.86
MSCI World	2.36	19.68	16.67	2.53
MSCI ACWI IMI	2.37	19.19	16.18	2.27

INDEX RISK AND RETURN CHARACTERISTICS (NOV 29, 2019)

	Turnover (%)[1]	ANNUALIZED STD DEV (%)[2] 3 Yr	5 Yr	10 Yr	SHARPE RATIO[2,3] 3 Yr	5 Yr	10 Yr	Since Dec 31, 1998	MAXIMUM DRAWDOWN (%)	Period YYYY-MM-DD
MSCI Europe	1.83	10.63	12.41	12.04	0.89	0.55	0.71	0.24	58.54	2007-07-16—2009-03-09
MSCI World	2.56	10.90	12.11	10.70	1.05	0.91	1.18	0.34	59.39	2000-08-31—2009-03-09
MSCI ACWI IMI	3.00	10.80	11.97	10.79	0.99	0.88	1.12	0.37	56.60	2000-09-07—2003-03-12

[1] Last 12 months [2] Based on monthly net returns data [3] Based on ICE LIBOR 1M

Each index therefore has underlying assets. In the case of MSCI Europe, the major underlying are represented by the following:

INDEX CHARACTERISTICS

	MSCI Europe
Number of Constituents	439
	Mkt Cap (EUR Millions)
Index	8,192,253.81
Largest	280,670.30
Smallest	1,347.20
Average	18,661.17
Median	9,069.63

TOP 10 CONSTITUENTS

	Country	Float Adj Mkt Cap (EUR Billions)	Index Wt. (%)	Sector
NESTLE	CH	280.67	3.43	Cons Staples
ROCHE HOLDING GENUSS	CH	196.51	2.40	Health Care
NOVARTIS	CH	179.48	2.19	Health Care
HSBC HOLDINGS (GB)	GB	136.50	1.67	Financials
SAP	DE	121.36	1.48	Info Tech
ASTRAZENECA	GB	114.78	1.40	Health Care
BP	GB	114.76	1.40	Energy
TOTAL	FR	114.34	1.40	Energy
LVMH MOET HENNESSY	FR	113.22	1.38	Cons Discr
ROYAL DUTCH SHELL A	GB	110.98	1.35	Energy
Total		1,482.60	18.10	

As you can see, the index is made up of particularly important companies: Nestle, Roche, Novartis, etc. ..., real giants of the European economy.

In the case of the MSCI Europe index, as mentioned, the constituents are 439 shares. The diversification within the index is generally very high, the entire panorama of sectors constituting the economy of the European continent being represented.

The index is updated continuously with the daily prices of the underlying securities and with the percentage of the weight of the constituent within the index (index w.%).

The index then becomes a "reference" for many funds, ETFs, etc. ... that invest in similar instruments or similar to European equities. Beating it is a challenge for the manager and it is the rationale that should push an investor to choose a Fund (tendentially active investment policy) to an ETF (tendentially passive investment policy).

Incidentally, as it is representative of another type of financial instrument and this text is dedicated to equities.

Benchmarks are therefore fundamental tools of comparison, to guide the investor's choices and, at the same time, to guide the management policies of the fund managers. As a direct consequence, most of the finance sites and, at the same time, the same asset management companies, favor the comparison of data; in particular the following data are compared:

- fund performance vs benchmark performance
- fund risk vs benchmark risk (expressed in terms of volatility)
- risk / return of funds vs. risk / return of benchmarks

If the first two comparisons are immediately understandable, the third typology will appear rather difficult for a novice investor, therefore it deserves a minimum depth.

Over the course of time, many economists have wondered how to simultaneously "grasp" two dimensions of the same phenomenon: yield and risk.

Let's take an example to understand the problem.

An investor may be offered the choice between two equity investments. Action X, with an average yield of 5%, and action Y, with an average yield of 10%. Which title is "better" between the two? If we consider the only average yield factor, the best security is clearly the second, the Y security. But we are talking about average returns, so of returns with volatility over the time of the investment. How would the choice change if it were said that the first security, X, has a volatility (on average, therefore positive and negative) of 5% and the second security, Y, has a volatility of 50%?

From the example, it should now be understood that risk and return should be assessed together, using a photographic metaphor, captured with a single "snapshot".

Some economists have therefore built indicators that keep risk and return factors together and allow you to evaluate the "goodness", at least historical, that is based on historical series, of investments.

A very famous reference index of mutual funds, or an indicator of risk-return performance, is given by the so-called "Sharpe index". The index was created by the Nobel Prize winner for economics William Sharpe and is used to evaluate the performance of a securities portfolio.

It is therefore particularly suitable for evaluating the performance of both the portfolios contained in a mutual fund and for evaluating the performance of the portfolio underlying an index.

The Sharpe ratio is calculated as the ratio between the Return on the portfolio (net of the investment rate of risk-free securities, now close to zero) and the riskiness of the portfolio itself, measured in terms of the portfolio's standard deviation.

The higher the index, the more the portfolio is performing well. There are, however, numerous other risk-adjusted performance indicators, that is, risk-adjusted performance indicators. It is very important not to refer to a single indicator but to multiple, in order to have an effective comparison in the different results. Each index has its own peculiarities.

This text is not specifically dedicated to risk-adjusted performance metrics, so the reader is invited to carry out further research on the subject, if interested. It is anticipated that the calculation logics are often quite complex, as they are developed according to mathematical / financial theories of not simple approach.

To demonstrate the importance of the benchmark, the graph of the comparison between the benchmark and the performance of the fund is given below as an example, once again taking the Anima Europa fund as an absolutely random reference:

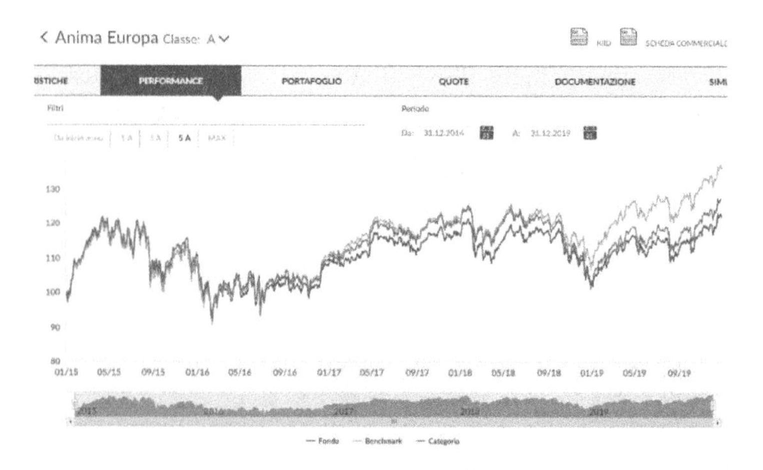

As you can see, taking as a reference a 5-year analysis period, the fund obtained performances (not adjusted for risk) that tended to be equivalent to the benchmark for the whole period from January 2015 until May 2016. It is noted that the performance graph between the Fund and the Benchmark (omit the graph of the further Category Benchmark) overlaps.

As of September 2016, the Fund appears to have performed differently than the Benchmark of reference. Movements and trends appear similar, but performance is different. It does not matter, for educational purposes, to evaluate who has performed better or worse.

As stated, for the purpose of a complete assessment, it is also necessary to introduce information regarding risk and calculations relating to "risk adjusted" performance. However, the importance of the benchmarks in the evaluation field must be evident.

CHAPTER 23:

Major Categories of Stocks

Indexing on the Rise

Passive U.S. equity funds could soon overtake their active peers

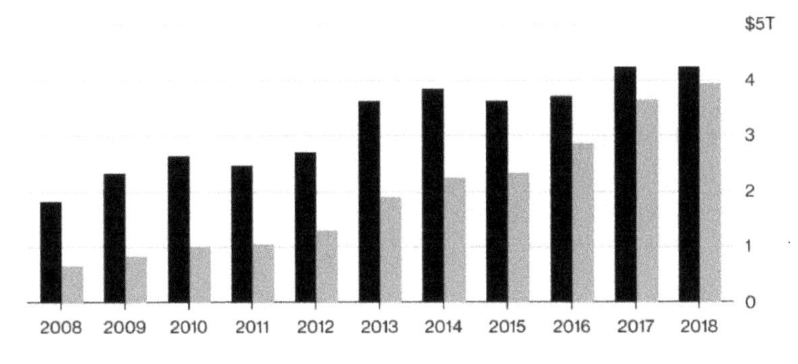

Source: Morningstar Inc.
Note: 2018 data as of Nov. 30

There are different flavors of stocks, just like there are different companies and industries. Some companies grow quickly, and other are slow and steady. Each one has its pros and cons, and each one can be valuable to your stock portfolio. Where it gets tricky is that many stocks fall into multiple categories. For example, a growth stock can also be a dividend producing stock. Putting that aside, lets first look at major categories of stocks, and reasons to invest in each.

I'll first start with a special category of stocks, the ETFs. ETF stands for Exchange Traded Fund, and is basically a stock of other stocks. Buying the SPY ETF (The SPDR S&P500 Trust ETF), for example, actually gives you exposure to all the stocks in the S&P 500. You don't actually own any of the S&P500 stocks, but the Trust does. So, this ETF tracks S&P500 performance, providing much of the diversification without the hassle of owning 500 different stocks.

At last count, there are over 5,000 ETF stocks you can buy. They cover a wide range of industries, investment styles, and also serve a wide range of purposes. The biggest benefit of ETFs is that you can benefit from diversification a lot easier than buying individual stocks.

For instance, say you want to invest in a legal marijuana company. Which should you choose? It may take a lot of research to determine which one to buy. Instead you could buy the cannabis ETF (aptly named) TOKE. This would give you exposure to the whole cannabis industry, without the risk of picking the wrong company.

Another benefit is that ETFs have pretty low management fees, especially compared to actively managed mutual funds. This sways many people to choose ETFs over mutual funds. In fact, the trend is clear. More people are investing in ETFs every year, and soon ETF investment will surpass mutual fund investment. Why pay a manager big fees for actively managing a mutual fund portfolio? Instead you could have a passive ETF with comparable performance and lower fees.

Soon ETF Investments Will Surpass Mutual Fund Investments

It should be pretty clear that ETFs can save you a lot of time and stress compared to picking individual stocks. But let's say you still want to select individual stocks. The first thing you should identify is the stock type. Stocks are generally identified in one of the following categories (but keep in mind, a stock may fit in more than one category).

Value stocks

Value stocks are generally considered "good deals." One way to think about it is buying something worth $10, but only paying $8 for it. For various reasons, investors do not value the stock as much as they should. It could have a lower price than comparable stocks in its industry, and it may have a stock price that does not reflect the company's true value.

The trick with value stocks is finding ones where the long-term prospects (ie, appreciation) are not reflected in the current price. If you get in before the market prices the stock appropriately, then you will benefit.

Dividend stocks

Some stocks return cash to investors at regular intervals. These returns are dividends, and can be a significant component of the stock's overall return. Even if the stock price remains flat, it might pay an annual dividend rate of 5%, which could make it worth holding.

There is a popular strategy called "Dogs of The Dow" where investors buy the highest yielding stocks in the Dow Jones. Each year, the portfolio is rebalanced with the 5 to 10 highest dividend yield stocks. This approach incorporates both dividend stocks and value stocks, since undervalued stocks tend to have a higher dividend.

Growth stocks

A growth stock is, just as its name implies, a stock in a corporation where revenues and earnings (profits) are rising. Many companies in this regime are young, fast growing, and higher risk. An example is first movers in a sector.

If you are a long-term investor, growth stocks should definitely be in your portfolio.

Penny stocks

Some stocks trade at a very low price. Penny stocks are the common term for them. Companies in this sector may be great, but small, companies. Or, they can be very risky, poorly run companies. Many penny stocks are sold via "pink sheets"-the stock is too small to be listed on a major exchange, so they are listed on the OTC (over the counter) market.

Penny stocks can also be manipulated by unscrupulous concerns. A common tactic is for a newsletter writer to buy a penny stock, then recommend it to his followers. The demand of the followers causes the price to rise, and the newsletter owner sells his shares to his readers at a profit. Later, when the demand for the stock dies down, the price falls back down, leaving the readers with a losing stock.

You will see many Internet ads for penny stocks; some people do very well with them. Most people, though, should avoid penny stocks.

Blue Chip Stocks

Blue chip stocks are considered the best companies to buy stock in. This does not mean they will provide the best returns, but many times they provide a more stable return to risk characteristics. Blue chips are big, established companies here for the long haul. Wal-Mart (WMT) is a good example of a blue-chip stock.

One way to think about blue chips is that they are companies you would tell your grandma to invest in. Safe and stable is the goal here.

New Stocks-Initial Public Offerings (IPOs)

In any economy, new companies are continually being born. In the beginning, company ownership includes the founders, some initial investors and possibly some venture capital firms. Eventually these groups will "cash out." They do this by offering stock to the public, via an Initial Public Offering (IPO).

For the typical retail trader, the only way to take part in an IPO is after public trading actually starts. Unfortunately, many times the stock price jumps the first day of trading, and latecomers miss out on the initial run up. If long term performance of the company is acceptable, this is not usually a problem. But some companies peak at the IPO, and their stock price never really increases after that.

Since the companies offering IPOs are generally fairly new, there is higher risk in these stocks. Some IPOs succeed, however some crash and burn. How do you know which is which? You don't, so one alternative might be to invest in an IPO ETF, which will then buy many of the IPOs offered.

Stocks by Sector/Industry

Just as you can define stocks by the type of company they are, you can also group stocks into different sectors or industries. There are important reasons why this is important. First, it is desirable to have a diversified portfolio. This means you own stocks in a number of different industries. Diversification helps limit your risk, although in bad times almost all stocks are likely to decline in value.

A second reason sector investing is important is because you can skew the portfolio balance to what you feel is best for the long term. For example, if you believe health care costs will continue to rise as the population ages, you might want to have more health care stocks. On the other hand, if you think government is going to put price caps on drugs and medical procedures, conceivably you want less exposure to this sector.

Some major sectors are listed below:

- *Energy*
- Raw Materials
- *Industrials*
- Consumer Discretionary
- Consumer Staples
- Health Care
- *Financials*
- Information Technology

When you combine the sectors with the types of stocks, you can see that the number of choices becomes overwhelming. How many Health Care growth stocks do you want? What about Financial dividend stocks? And don't forget Energy value stocks!

When you look at things this way, stock picking becomes daunting, and the myriad of choices can actually be paralyzing. It becomes so hard to decide that no decision is ever made.

My advice: don't worry about covering every sector or every stock type. Instead, focus on finding good companies, no matter the type of stock or the industry. Concurrently, check that all your eggs are in multiple baskets. Having all energy stocks, for instance, is good at times, but usually is not.

With my advice of finding good companies, that then becomes the next question: just how do you define good companies, and more importantly, how do you actually find them? And once you do, when do you enter trades?

CHAPTER 24:

Goals, Plans, and Approaches

We are going to talk about getting situated before investing in the stock market. This involves setting your investment goals, deciding whether you want to invest or be a trader, and taking stock of your current financial health.

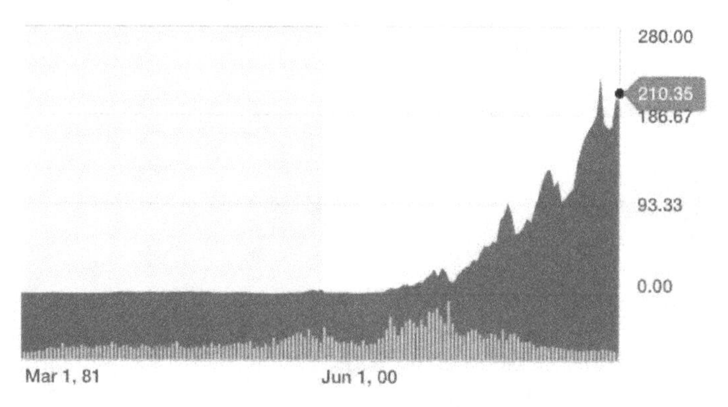

The growth of Apple stock over time shows the power of long-term investing.

Setting Up an Investing Plan

The first step when beginning your self-directed investment program is to set aside some money to use for your initial stock purchases and to sign up with the brokerage of your choice. Keep in mind that you should not try to invest every bit of cash you have at once.

Once you have gotten setup so that you can begin buying and selling stocks, you need to set up an investing plan. The first thing that does along with this is choosing a way that you plan on investing. There are many different ways that you can trade and invest, and they aren't necessarily exclusive. These can include a straightforward long-term investment plan that does not include dividend stocks. Some readers will prefer to invest strictly in dividend stocks, because they have a goal of earning income from their investments. Others are interested in trading. For now, we are going to be focused strictly on investing to build wealth – however dividend investors should also use the strategies outlined.

So, what should your investment plan include? Start by determining the end goal. Is your goal to have a million dollars at retirement? Or to be able to retire by age 55? Or maybe you are already 55 and have no retirement savings, and so you will have a different goal – aggressive investing in growth stocks to rapidly build up your assets to "catch up".

Regardless of what your goal is, you should clearly state the goal and have it clearly in your mind at all times. You need to know the end state of your investment program in order to take steps to reach it. For example, if you are 45 and want to have a million-dollar portfolio by age 70, then you need to find out exactly how much you need to invest in order to reach the goal in the time allotted, and then go from there.

As a part of developing a financial plan, you should start a journal where you can keep your goals and other information recorded. That way you can refer back to your goals and plans and update them as necessary, as well as evaluate your performance as time goes on. Keeping a written journal that you actively use in your pursuit of your goals is also a way that you can hold yourself accountable.

Keep in mind that you don't have to set permanent goals. You can change your goals as circumstances dictate, but it's recommended that you only do this once a year. You need to stick to the strict pursuit of your goal for at least 12 months to fairly and accurately evaluate your progress.

Once you have an end goal in mind, you also have to determine how often you are going to invest. At a minimum, you should be buying shares of stock at least once per month. If you can do it twice a month or even once a week that is even better, but not everyone is going to have the ability to do it more than once a month. Some people might even want to buy shares on a daily basis. Setup a time frame that works best for you.

In addition to determining how often you are going to buy shares of stock; you also have to decide how much you can invest. Of course, generally speaking people should invest as much money as they can. But you also have to balance that against the reality of your day to day expenses and other needs that will come up.

At this point we need to say a word about savings, emergency expenses, and debts. If you are carrying a large amount of debt (aside from a home mortgage), it's important to get yourself out of debt. Any debt that you are carrying in the form of personal loans, credit cards, car loans, student loans, and so forth is very bad for your financial health. Many loans may carry interest rates that will outweigh any gains you are making in the stock market, so while you are holding these debts, even if you are investing in stocks your net worth could be decreasing. You should make a plan to rid yourself of debt over a 3-5-year period for your long-term financial health. If you need to get a second job or create a small business in order to generate more income to take care of it, then you should seriously look into doing so.

Second, everyone should have some emergency cash on hand. The amount you really need varies, but you should at a minimum of $1,000 on hand to handle emergencies like car repairs, tire blowouts, roof leaks, broken hot water heaters, pet emergencies and so on. Make sure you have some kind of emergency fund on hand before you start putting all of your available cash into the stock market. Many financial advisors say you should have 3-6 months of expense covered, but of course that is a lot of money and so if you don't have any money saved up you are going to have to work on this over a period of time. For now, focus on getting a cash fund of $1,000 you only touch when you absolutely need the money. You should also avoid using credit cards to pay for emergency circumstances once you've built up a reserve.

Get a clear picture of your financial health

Before you dive into investing, make sure that you have a clear picture of your financial health. Start by listing all of the assets that you own, everything from cars, cash, retirement accounts, to computers and other items. When doing, this, only include equity in these items. So, if you owe $4,000 on a car worth $17,000, then you have $13,000 in equity.

Next, list your liabilities. You should list the total amount owed, amount needed to pay off each item, and the monthly bill. When listing your debts also include the interest rates. Also include any other debts like back taxes.

When you make a debt repayment plan, you should try to pay off debts that have the highest interest rates first. Payments on interest are money going out the window. It enriches the creditor while keeping you from devoting money toward paying off the debt.

Why have investment strategies?

The most commonly used investment strategies. Before we get to that, we need to have a clear understanding of why we would use investment strategies in the first place. The reasons include:

- Spreading risk. Remember that you should never bet your life's savings on one investment. Some investments are bound to fail, so one goal of an investment strategy is to spread the risk so that the inevitable failures don't destroy your entire investment portfolio.
- Buying at the wrong time. The last thing you want to do is be the person that is always buying at market peaks. That means you'd be buying high and then hoping the market will be rising even higher. Also, you'd be paying more for your shares than you need to pay.
- Staying focused on your goal. You want to ensure that at all times your investment portfolio is helping you maintain and reach your long-term goals.

Why Invest Long Term

Long term investing is considered the best way to be involved in the stock market according to most financial advisors. There are many reasons for this. For one, long term investing is far more likely to provide gains in wealth over time. It is the only way that you can ensure that you have wealth to draw on for living expenses during retirement. Historical data indicates that over the long term, stocks from most established companies are going to appreciate in value. And over the long term, you will have many opportunities to adjust and move your money out of losing stocks and into winning stocks.

If you also invest in dividend stocks, long term investing with dividend reinvestment will also lead to the benefits you get from compound interest, which means that you will have your money working for you to grow even more money. Short term traders don't benefit from compound interest in any way.

Another advantage of long-term investing is that it's low-key and low stress, not to mention something that isn't complicated. With long term investing you simply pick out a set of solid companies (and possibly some index funds) and buy shares at regular intervals. A long-term investor should not be concerned with the short-term fluctuations of the stock market, even recessions – because over the long term the fluctuations and volatility average out, and recessions are overtaken by future economic growth. While traders are sweating bullets over short term fluctuations in the stock market, long term investing doesn't require you to get stressed out over daily or weekly ups and downs – the kind that always occur.

While commissions can cut into the profits of traders who are buying and selling on a frequent basis, often making small per share profits, commissions are not that important to long term investors. You aren't going to be making multiple trades in a day and most long-term traders won't be making multiple trades over the course of a week, so you will be far less impacted by commissions on your bottom line. Also, over the long term, if you pay a $5-10 fee for a trade now, that small amount isn't going to matter compared to the appreciation the stock is likely to see over 5, 10, or more years.

A long-term investment strategy also removes the trader way of trying to get in and out of the market at the exact right moment in order to profit. This reduces stress, and it also significantly lowers risk. When you are trying to exactly time buying and selling of stocks, chances are you are going to have a lot of errors and so you're going to lose money – or put another way it's a much higher risk.

Everyone has their own preferences and level of risk they are willing to accept, and some people even find the pressure cooker of day trading, swing trading, and options trading exciting. Others prefer the comfort, stability, and likelihood for success that long term investing provides. So, this is something you will need to evaluate for yourself, and you will need to be sure to go into your investing or trading with open eyes, so that you know exactly what you are getting into.

CHAPTER 25:

Behavioral Finance

Almost every branch of study or practice can either be classified as arts or science. Only a selected few amongst them hold the characteristics of both. Share market investment assumes undeniable position in this distinctive group. Science that is made up of numbers, formulae, graphs and statistics is inseparably blended with the art of psychology which deals with emotions and expectations of investor community.

Human being possessed the sixth sense for many hundred thousand years now. However, history repeatedly reminds us that man has exhibited irrationality, inconsistency and incompetence (despite his rational sixth sense) when surrounded with uncertainty, fear and insecurity.

We are able to see this irrationality in stock market more than anywhere else in this universe. Emotionally driven mistakes are not only everlasting, but also predictable. Given this realistic background, can't we foresee and avoid them? If possible, we can also have it work in our favor.

Success in stock investment is not purely dependent on your ability in systematically analyzing companies with a set of selected methods. Neither is it based on IQ levels of individuals. If so, a person who scored a centum in tenth standard mathematics paper can make more money than another person who scored 60 marks.

It is very evident that the stock market is a combination of economics and psychology. Systematic economic factors are disregarded and overruled by emotional behavior of investors and traders alike. A relatively new branch of study with a name 'Behavioral finance' tries to answer the causes and effects of this overruling.

Overconfidence

The word is self-explanatory. It comes with an unshakable confidence that whatever analysis or decision we make would be correct. The sheer belief that we can beat other investors and the whole market is an explicit outcome of this confidence. Seeds of this overconfidence are inside all of us.

This is one of primary reasons why many self-employed businesses end up being unsuccessful. When they start the business, they give more than deserved weight to the positive factors while heeding no attention to negative factors. Many researches have exposed this folly. I recall one of them in which I read this. Almost all the new entrepreneurs anticipated a 70 per cent chance of their business becoming a hit. At the same time, they predicted other ventures with similar size had only 39 per cent chance of existence.

There is an inbuilt superiority complex with all of us. Whether we recognize it or not is a different thing. But that complex erupts in the form overconfidence in almost everything we do.

A survey was conducted in a popular American university, which revealed similarly interesting facts in different format and degree. Eighty per cent of the students believed that they would make in the first half (fifty per cent).

Probably I should not have wasted much space in this category with these citations. You can recognize it yourself. Try to find a group of ten women of any age group and ask them individually to rank her relative beauty in the group. If you find anyone rating herself below 7, please send me an email. I would like to know.

This attitude extends into and in fact flourishes in the stock market as well. Almost 80 per cent of the active market participants believe that they can comfortably beat the index. At the end only 20 per cent of them – not necessarily the subset from that 80 per cent – are able to produce that outcome.

Street Dog Principle

Street dogs are very astute. They reveal enough facts or behaviors worth many PhDs. If an unfamiliar street dog crosses the border and enters into different territory, resident dogs of that territory furiously bark and chase that poor guy away - back to his street again. Interestingly, these brave soldiers turn submissive if they happen to visit areas outside their border. As a whole, street dogs precisely know their circle of control.

Majority of the stock investors don't possess this obvious quality from dogs. Investors should try to assess their strengths in terms of cognizance about a particular industry or companies, and more important they should be able to tell the areas they are not aware of. For example, you might understand the business dynamics of steel industry. But pharmaceutical companies operate under different environment where you cannot deploy same approach. As a whole, we should define an imaginary 'circle of competence' and precisely know its boundaries. Under no circumstance, you should dare to cross the periphery of this circle and get bitten by strange dogs. If you really need to explore new horizons outside your circle, you should work very hard in acquiring necessary knowledge and courage to expand this border. But for that, I repeat, you should work very hard.

Don't be a Roman in Rome

Wrapping a piece of cloth around your hip in *nudeville* makes you a ridiculous person. For the fear of getting ridiculed, we comply with the majority both in opinion and action notwithstanding its illogical stance. This happens at home, school, peer groups, workplace, Facebook and where not? When everyone in group talk rubbish, we tend not to disagree with them – we rather prefer to keep quiet. Even though our opinion might be right, we don't take the pain of challenging popular opinion.

We would have studiously analyzed the stocks of a company. Based on the estimate resulting from our analysis, we might have assessed current market price overvalued and given up the idea of buying that stock. But the price is continually surging. Then we slowly begin to compromise by saying, "there might be something else that I missed out. Price discovery carried out by millions of investors in this well-structural system should be correct only" and buy the same stocks that we decided to give it a miss. But when the inevitable happens… we'll have to weep more than the rest of all.

So, if the share market happens to be Rome, you don't necessarily have to be a Roman.

It's me

If our investment turns out to be good, we tend to conclude that our decision was right. We might also attribute success to our abilities. Similarly, if the stock price goes down after our investment, we distrust our analyzing skills and investing abilities. There is an equal chance for these beliefs to be true or be a mere coincidence. The habits of confusing luck with talent and talent with luck are so hard in Dalal Street to be unlearnt so easily. A conscious effort is to be made to distinguish luck and talent, and to advance further.

Loss Aversion

Sadness caused by ten-rupee loss is much bigger than the happiness produced by twenty-rupee profit. A Rs 100 loss during my MBA time was much painful than the job resulted from one lakhs rupee gain in the later years. (100 and one lakh are relative numbers) That is the reason why many people lean towards fixed deposits despite the paltry return produced by them. Some other brand of people identifies outstanding investments, but sells them immediately after a tiny rise thanks to their apprehension that they might miss a profit booking opportunity. Is it like divorcing a beautiful wife with the fear that she might run away with someone else? In effect they miss out a great long-time investment opportunity.

Sizable numbers of otherwise wise people who also theoretically realize that stock investment is prone to fluctuation are not able to absorb even a small percentage of loss. Only logically explainable answer for this behavior is 'pain of loss' or 'loss aversion' theory. This is coupled with excessive self-esteem. Accepting that our investment decision is wrong and selling under loss is a big blow to that esteem. This causes lot of chaos in handling loss making investments, however tiny it may be. We refuse to accept our failure, if not mistake. (being right and being successful are not the same) Selling at profits elates us, but at the same time realizing even a tiny loss makes us highly uncomfortable. This attitude is deep rooted in human minds and becomes dangerous most of the times.

You don't want to book loss and therefore wait until that particular investment comes back to your original purchase price. You pay your back for getting out – notwithstanding months/years of redundancy –

without any loss at the end. On the other hand, if you had sold that share long time back (even in loss) and shifted to another good company, you would have probably accomplished better gains.

Getting Attached with the Investment – Emotionally

We have seen or at least heard about some movie stars claiming that they became inseparable with the character they played. Very true!

If we become interested in something, we really identify ourselves too much emotionally with those things, entirely defying reality and nature. I had a habit during my college days. We used to bet when watching cricket games. I had strongly believed that India would win – even after losing eight wicket and needing 80 runs in ten overs – if I had put money on India's favor. Surveys among gamblers also confirm the same human attitude. Their belief about the winning ability of a horse goes up many times after they bet on any particular horse.

What is the reason behind this folly? Due to some of our actions – either knowingly or unknowingly - we begin to emotionally engross ourselves with anything related to those actions. An obligation to be loyal to them arises inside us. The desire to justify out decision always rules so high that its shuts down other thinking organs.

Sadly, this attitude misleads us in the process of information gathering as well. We want to accept only such information that conforms to our mind set and preconceived expectation.

The same mistake is obviously visible in the stock market in various forms. Once we buy a company, we look around for good and supporting news justifying our purchase. And, we not only neglect to read or gather disapproving facts, but also disregard them even if we come across them. Due to this, we lose our sixth 'rational thinking' sense and substantial amount of hard-earned money.

CHAPTER 26:

Types and Purposes of Investing

Investing is all about making money. There are various ways you can make money when you consider trading financial products on a stock exchange. The purpose of investing is always going to be about money. How much money can you make off the type of investment you decide to put your money into? How you make the money is also a factor.

You can invest in stocks for income, discount value, and growth. Growth investments are the most typical types of investing conducted. You also have day trading for profit, but not in too much detail.

Growth and Stocks

Google is always a great example for growth and stocks. In 2004, when it was launched, Google seemed like another search engine company. Yahoo was the forerunner in all things search engine, with Microsoft working hard to get their cut. Little search engine companies' start popping up in the form of browsers like Crazy Browser, Mozilla Firefox and others. Now fast forward 12 years, and the world of search engines looks completely different. Google holds the market share for most growth and consistent customer base, not only for the number of people around the world that use Google Chrome and Google for searches, but also the number of products they have like Google Chromecast, Google Analytics, and AdWords.

Google is a powerhouse that seemed to grow overnight. Anyone who bought in during the IPO has made a great deal of profit on their stock, including through dividends. To make the money on a stock like this, you would have had to believe it was more than a regular search engine. You had to believe it would become the company it has become today. It takes research. Aside from the research required, you also have to determine what others say about the company and if the projected future growth is going to happen.

When you invest in stocks for growth, you have a firm knowledge of the company's industry sector, what the CEOs and top management are capable of, and what the company is looking to do in terms of growth. Google started as a search engine. It has expanded to offering computers, internet TV options, books, and much more.

A company that shows they have their funding through the IPO and projected products that will sell, is a company you can buy shares of and expect to make a profit over the long term.

Let's look at oil as an example. Oil is a commodity that you can buy. Oil reserves are notoriously low in supply because we have been using oil for decades and current drilling locations are drying up. Due to the low supply, and the high demand, oil stocks continually increase. When there is an announcement that oil held in reserve will be released, dropping the price of oil products like gas at the pump, oil prices decrease. There is a supposition that oil will someday run out completely and there will be no place to drill anywhere on earth. There are also suppositions that oil can be found in places that are too tough to drill or require equipment that is currently in development.

It is a give and take that keeps prices bouncing, where profits can be made over years, as long as you can believe oil will continue to be found under the earth or ocean's surface.

Let's take a look at the tablets as another example of stocks for growth. Tablets and iPads are the newest technology to hit stores. They are small, easy to carry devices and perfect for replacing bulky laptops. When tablets hit the market, you had to find out which company would have the best technology and the potential to carry the demand for the products, thus the continued growth of the tech company.

In the same line of thought, a few years ago 3D televisions were considered the next big things. Tablets took off, 3D televisions are back in the 80s for most people. Now, we have curved TVs that are supposed to be better, but again the majority of people are happy with their thin, flat TVs, and don't see the point in upgrading to something with a curve. Would investing in a company switching completely to their curved TV line be smart? Probably not. Go to a store, and you will see the flat, non-curved TVs in the carts of 80% of the buyers.

When you invest based on company growth, in terms of the stock price continuing to increase, due to the stability of the company and its R&D ideas, you have to know the industry. You also have to be willing to invest for the long term to see the rewards of a newly launched project based on stock price increases.

The question then comes to be as to whether you stay in your stock, take the entire profit and capital, or just take the profit. Taking just the profit ensures you own shares in the company as they work on new developments, while not jeopardizing your profits from the last increase in stock price. Stock prices can become overvalued, to a point that they naturally decrease after a little time. This is often based on the day traders overvaluing the stock to earn income for the day and getting out after a couple of hours or eight hours.

Investing for Income

Income investments are about choosing a growing stock that will be stable and have profits each year. You are investing in the stock to use the dividends to live off of. The idea in this option is that you will always hold stock in that company and you will transfer the stocks to the next generation, so they may also live off of the dividends. Dividends are usually paid out on a monthly or quarterly basis. A company that offers high dividends is the one you want to invest in, or you need multiple companies that pay a fair number of dividends. For those who are successful in scouting for stocks with high dividends, there is a potential that you can take a vacation, pay for your mortgage, or even live a modest life off of those dividends. It is not for everyone. Investing for income using dividends requires you to know various industries, choose stable companies that will not get rid of dividends during restructuring, and keep the dividends fairly high. Some companies have paid out dividends that were high, reduced the amount based on a restructuring of the company, and eventually lost the profit to pay out dividends to small stock holders. It is possible that you can start to make money this way. It will take work and the right choices. It is not for everyone because it does take your time to be able to research and find proper dividend paying stocks.

Investing for Discount Value

Obviously, all investments are made for value, but there is a difference between regular value and discount value. Discount value is where a stock is undervalued for some reason. This reason has to be valid, such as day traders, who got into the stock, pulled out and made the stock devaluate. There are times a stock is undervalued because the company made bad decisions and there is no hope for repair of that value. You have to be able to tell the difference for why a stock has become less than its true value. When you do find these stocks, you can buy in low and then when the stock rises to its true value you can sell out and take your profit.

This is another type of investing style that will take time. You will need careful research and understanding of why the stock is undervalued. If you can learn the market by studying it, successfully, then you will know what to choose and what is not going to increase in the future. For example, some stocks have an undervalue because there is a stock split. The stock is about to split and investors are deciding to get out and take their profit. Others remain in, accept the split and start making money in two stocks. It is all in how you understand the stock market, stock splits, and what may happen if a new CEO is elected.

CEOs or new managers can impact a stock's value based on shareholder sentiment. If a shareholder does not have faith in the new leaders of the company, they may sell their stock. If enough pull out from a stock, then the company's shares can begin to suffer from the loss of demand.

CHAPTER 27:

Investor Psychology

The Importance of Having an Investment Strategy

There are several benefits to having an investment strategy. Especially a concise, workable strategy.

It Helps Minimize the Risk of Losses

For the entrepreneur/investor, the threat of losses always hangs over his head. At every turn, he is always assailed by the news of others who had invested the same way he did and incurred losses. It is for this reason that investors are always interested in any means to undercut losses and maximize their profit.

Of course, losses are inevitable, no matter how hard the investor tries to forestall it. But there are ways of minimizing the losses an investor may encounter. One of such is through employing an investment strategy.

An investment strategy takes into consideration the uncertain nature of the investment clime. It provides the investor with options, and alternative routes to employ in the event that he faces a loss. It also provides fail-safes, hacks and other such information with which the employer can make smarter decisions.

Furthermore, a strategy helps you focus on the reason you started investing in the first place. It helps narrow down your vision to avoid distractions. This is particularly important because a lot of investors run into losses when they lose focus. An investment strategy keeps you on a defined path, drastically reducing the chances of failure.

Thus, when you eventually develop an investment strategy, ensure that it fits with your overall aim for investing. The primary reason for investing for most folks is to make profits. But then, what do you intend doing with the profits as they roll in.

It Helps Provide Clarity on Your Long-Term Goals

For a lot of investors, investing is not a side hustle. They do not engage in investing in stocks, bonds, and securities for the immediate benefit. For many such individuals, they are in it for the long run. They are usually not into investing just for the immediate gratification they could derive from the investment. In that regard, having a strategy can prove to be helpful.

It is during the process of developing a strategy that you decide on how far your long-term goals are. You also make the decision of where you want to see your business, say in the next ten years. How much the stocks you invested in should have been worth by then, etc.

Thus, when you develop a business strategy, you gain the benefit of clarifying your own long-term goals. This knowledge will then help you plan several other areas of your business as well.

Opens You Up To the Possibility Of New Opportunities For Your Business

Developing a strategy helps open you up to the idea of different other possibilities that could exist for your business. This is because, during this process, your creative juices get flowing. It does not mean that these opportunities would not have existed before that point. It does not also mean that they suddenly get created in that instant. What happens rather is that your eyes just get open to their possibilities.

Also, through the process of your strategy, new ideas get developed. Developing an investment strategy involves trying out different possibilities and discarding some. When you do that often, you will become aware of the opportunities you had not even bothered exploring up to that point.

As earlier stated, the process grants you clarity. This helps you see the entire investment process in a newer, fresher light.

It Helps In the Efficient Allocation of Time and Resources

Developing an investment strategy helps bring to your notice what has been working and what hasn't. You are made aware of the time and resources that aren't used effectively, giving you the opportunity to re-assign them. The result would be a more efficient investment process.

Furthermore, it equips you to resist resistance as they spring up. In this instance, you are not just reacting to situations as they come up. You are prepared as you already have anticipated them and are prepared for them.

As an investor, you need to understand that there is no overemphasizing the importance of a business strategy. A sure recipe for disaster is beginning your investments without having a direction. Or worse still, just swinging it as they come along. You are sure to lose, and to lose a lot even.

A strategy has the advantage of providing you with a clear concise plan on a course of action. Perhaps then the question is not that you do not have an investment strategy. It could be that you do not have an efficient one, the next subheading would take care of that.

Criteria for Developing a Good Investment Strategy

It is not just enough to have a strategy. In fact, having a terrible strategy is almost as bad as not having any strategy at all. The question then becomes: what strategy should an investor employ to ensure that his investment plan is top notch?

Make Sure Your Strategy Fits with the Overall Direction of the Investments

Before you decide on what strategy you would employ in the pursuit of your goal, you need to ask yourself some questions. First on the list is whether the strategy fits with the direction you have in mind concerning your investments. You should be sure why really you want to invest. You should also be sure of how you want to invest.

Always bear in mind that what works for one person may not work for you. Also, the area you want to invest – bonds, stocks, etc. – would definitely influence what strategy you eventually employ.

The company or companies you invest in and the rate at which you invest are all subsumed in your strategy. Also, the amount you intend investing with would also determine the investment strategy you will employ. And to a large extent, all of those would be impacted by what strategy you eventually choose.

Be Sure Your Strategy Matches the Resources You Have At the Moment

A good strategy takes into account the resources you have at your disposal at that moment. You should always choose a strategy that makes use of the resources you have while maximizing returns.

Resources to be taken into account include the finances you have, both in liquid and fixed assets. It also takes into consideration other intangible assets such as willingness and cooperation of friends and family. When all of these are taken into consideration, it will give an accurate depiction of your current state. Thus, it would then reveal the most feasible path to achieving your goals.

Conclusion

I encourage you all to rethink the way you value your time. A lot of us live like we are immortal, like we have all the time in the world to pursue our goals and dreams. We give our time to others like it means nothing. All we can do is manage our time more effectively and spend our precious time on the things that matter. We all want to achieve our goals.

To manage your time effectively, start thinking about what will start producing results today. Do not get caught up crossing items off your "to do" list. Stop doing activities that do not immediately help you accomplish your goals.

Trading takes many forms, and it is dynamic as well. Times change and with the change, markets and operational methods also change. With the advent of computers, it was logical that trading would become better and faster. This came to pass, and traders now have the capacity to trade on the go and use programs that make trading easier.

One of the best methods to use to run trades with more confidence is Algorithmic trading. This makes use of mathematical calculations to help you predict trading actions. When you do this, you eliminate various errors including the emotional aspect of trading that tends to affect the outcome of trades. Success is all about knowing when to place a trade, how much you need to invest and the right platform to use for trading.

While you can come up with your own system, it takes time and the best way can be going for a ready-made system that gives you the capability you are looking for. We have tackled the various systems that you can use and the advantages of each system. Most of the systems give you a trial period that you can explore before you make the decision to take it up or not.

Finally, we looked at back testing. Back testing is an ideal way to use historical data to come up with assumptions about the future. Since you are using facts to determine the future, you stand to reduce many errors in future trades.

There is an underlying principle when it comes to technical analysis. This principle dictates that the stock market price of a security represents all essential information that can have a significant effect in the market. Because of the availability of essential information, technical analysts see no need for fundamental or economic analysis. The opinion of technical analysts is that stock prices tend to follow trends.

They also believe that history has a tendency to repeat itself especially on matters of market psychology. There are two primary indicators that are popularly used by technical analysts. These indicators are technical indicators and chart patterns. Chart patterns are needed to identify areas of resistance and support. On the other hand, we have technical indicators which are basically a form of technical analysis. These technical indicators include moving averages which are among the most popular.

Before you start, take a moment, and think about the idea that prompted you to opt for the particular stream, or option that you did. Is money the only reason that motivates you? The ability to generate passive income mainly depends on the audience. If the audience detects that it is all about making money for you and not serving their needs, then they won't be too kind to your business idea. Whenever you do something solely for money, you won't succeed. Your intentions need to go beyond acquiring the right bank balance if you want to achieve success. Unless you have a reason that provides you the drive to excel, you will not shine. Money is a byproduct of the desire that keeps you going. So, take some time and think about the reason and motivation for you to do so.

When it comes to putting your money back into your dividend portfolio, do not do it too soon, and let your dividends build up. This is where the power of compounding interest comes into play, where you are gaining more money in a shorter time. Not everyone uses that strategy and will most likely hold their money for safer reinvestments and keep them with the steady growths.

As with almost everything in this world, the earlier you begin, the more options and knowledge you tend to have. Similarly, when it comes to your retirement funds, the longer that you have had them invested, the higher your return on investment, and your options will become better

Now, all that you need to do is get started. There is no time like the best to start.

The idea of starting a new business on your own might seem slightly daunting. All it takes is the first step to obtain the necessary momentum to keep going. So, don't be afraid and take the first step. If you put in the necessary hard work, dedicate sufficient time, and be patient, you will become a successful business owner.

An unfortunate fact is, most businesses fail in their first year, and only a few succeed. If you want to be a part of the successful minority, then you need the necessary motivation, strength, and determination to succeed. Failure must be considered as a stepping-stone to success. If you fail or run into obstacles, just pick yourself up, dust yourself off, and get back in the game. It is not easy, but when you succeed, there is nothing that can replace the high that success gives.

Take everything in your stride and think of it as a learning experience. You can start your passive income journey today, and with the right mindset, it can be easy. The only thing that withholds you is your mindset. Remember that it is never too late to start, and you can always achieve something better for yourself. Don't give up on this feeling and keep it alive throughout your life

Data states that the average investor makes just 2% a year, but you don't have to fall into this category. Ultimately long-term investing is the best way to make money in the stock market, and should be what you focus on in your portfolio. There are a lot of promises on the internet related to becoming a millionaire in the stock market. Claims such as "trader had $400 in his bank account and is now a millionaire" litter the internet, and I'd say 99.9% of any promises you hear like this are complete BS. Many "educators" on the internet do not actually trade stocks, but instead make all their money from selling dreams. Anyone can claim they are a millionaire, but flashy marketing and rented sports cars do not mean they are telling the truth.

A lot of business ideas fail because people try to develop a product or build a business that caters to the needs of everyone. When you try to serve everyone around you, you cannot help anyone. You have to select a specialty and then build a niche or search for an existing one. Find a market that suits you or choose a market that you want to cater to. While you select a niche, your target audience takes into consideration your education and your interests as well. Your earnings are proportional to the audience base you serve.

If you think that you can find an income stream that is 100% passive, then you are sadly mistaken. Let go of the thought that once you create a product, you can just bask in the sun and sip margaritas. Even with real estate rentals, you have to manage the property, or with the stock market, you have to continually keep an eye on the portfolio and handle it as well. Even with an online business, there isn't any such thing as 100% passive income. Passive income rests on the concept of the creation of business automation. However, if you want to keep yourself or your business automated, then keep the business going, then you need to put in a lot of time and effort. You cannot earn money without any effort

cannot expect to become a millionaire overnight. You have to put in all the necessary efforts and dedicate the time required to get there. Do you know that Angry Birds was the 52nd game that Rovio designed? So, even when something might seem like an overnight success, it probably isn't. It takes a while for the business to kick off. However, don't expect results if you don't want to put in the necessary efforts.

If you need more time to save, no problem at all. In the meantime, you can still start by studying more about the market. For instance, you can start collecting information about the companies you are interested in. You may also start studying entire industries so that you will be ready to make your investing decisions when you are ready with your capital.

Start by performing paper trades. You can practice the skills of fundamental and technical analysis using the charts and graphs.

Also, start reading the financial reports from the companies you want to invest in. They are usually provided on the corporate website of the companies. They are business documents so you could expect them to be a bit boring. However, reading them will give you insights on the performance and the strength of the company you wish to invest in

When it comes to saving, a good rule of thumb is to save at least 10% of your income. If you can save more, that is better, but if you cannot afford to save anything else, save at least 10%. Saving money will build your confidence, and when you see that money begin to accrue, you will feel more motivated to save and you will spend more efficiently as you do not want to diminish what you have.

Remember, procrastination is your biggest enemy: do not start tomorrow, start today.

Spending is a subject that will continue to be of much importance all your life. The largest purchase any individual may make is his home. It is advisable to purchase a home rather than renting. There are multiple benefits to be a homeowner, and by paying rent you are only helping your landlord get richer. When it comes to other investments, I also recommend that you never take advice from someone who, frankly, has no idea what they are talking about.

Do not take investment advice from your gardener; you want to consult professionals who know what they are talking about. Remember, above all, do not confuse want and need. We all want nice things. I would love to have the newest model of the latest car, but it is not worth putting myself in a risky financial situation. Frugality is essential to success, especially to beginning investors.

Always keep learning about the stock market, and as you gain knowledge and experience, you will become a better trader